Cover
Cape Kidnappers,
the world's only mainland gannet colony.
(Courtesy Air New Zealand)

First published 1985 by Pacific Tourism Promotions Ltd, 105 Federal Street, Auckland, New Zealand. (PO Box 6190, Wellesley St. Auckland 1, New Zealand)

Distributed in New Zealand by Hodder & Stoughton Ltd, 44-46 View Rd, Glenfield, Auckland. (PO Box 3858, Auckland)

ISBN 0 9597733 0 4

Typeset by Auckland TypoGraphic Services Ltd, Auckland.
Printed by Kingswood Printing Co. Ltd, Auckland

While editorial material covers all the possibilities, the commercial listings are of companies pre-selected by us, to ensure that their service was of a high standard. These companies were required to participate upon a strictly factual basis and a charge was made to cover the cost of preparing the material. This has subsidised the cost of the book to you.

All care has been taken to ensure that all information is correct, but we can accept no responsibility for omissions or changes.

The exclusion of any company does not mean that its service is in any way inferior to those listed.

EDITORS:

Gary Hannam and Lesley McIntosh

Dedication

*To Lynne and Hunter,
Denise, Eliza and Philip*

Acknowledgements

To those who believed in a new concept and whose enthusiasm carried us over the difficult times . . . in particular: Ian John, Matt Ramsden, Chris Smith, David Elworthy, Richard Brookes, Russell Topliss and Graeme Cowely. And to those whose work made it a reality: Stephen Barnett, Christine Brown, Geraldine Oliver, Ron Monton, Susan Gibbs, Liz Greenslade, Sandra Coney, Kate Liggett, Carol Sellens, Fiona MacDonald, Carolyn Grant, Jane Connor, Barbara Neilson, Ruth Hamilton, Chris Anderson, Anne Burton, Anna Rogers, Chris O'Brien and Pam Brown.

Mts Ruapehu and Ngaruahoe, Volcanic Plateau.
(Courtesy Turangi Scenic Flights)

CONTENTS

Introduction

Take three deep breaths of fresh, clean air and start to relax. New Zealand is a reminder of an unspoiled quality of life that many parts of the world will never again know. It offers something to everyone.

Isolated for aeons at the southern end of the vast Pacific Ocean, it is now as accessible as any other part of our ever-diminishing world, and with its small population, offers a rich diversity of sporting, scenic, and cultural experiences.

This book will introduce you to the great range of activities you can enjoy while travelling through New Zealand, whether an overseas visitor or a New Zealander. It has been designed primarily for those travellers who want to make up their own minds about what to do and see – those prepared to allow time out to sample the experiences packed into this small country. There are some major resort areas developed for travellers, but the country also lends itself to exploration off the beaten track. It would be hard to find another country on earth so small that it offers holiday-makers who enjoy cultural diversity and action so great a choice. From a beachcomber's paradise of deserted coast, you can be experiencing the thrill of snow skiing with only two hours' travelling time.

New Zealand is an extraordinary amalgam of physical characteristics that often seem reminiscent of somewhere else, yet remain decidedly and uniquely New Zealand's own – the long, lonely beaches of Northland, the kauri forests where trees take hundreds of years to reach maturity in a complex, sensitive ecological system, the coastal river valleys drowned by the rising seas as glaciers melted creating great bays filled with islands.

The southernmost point in the Pacific's 'ring of fire' turns northward again through New Zealand, on the edge of the Pacific plate, giving rise to a region of intense volcanic and thermal activity in the centre of the North Island. Here a cataclysmic blast 1800 years ago was one of the most violent in human history.

The alps of the South Island are one of the world's great mountain ranges, their valleys carved out by massive glaciers. Some of these glaciers ignored climatic changes and survive as the largest in any temperate zone in the world. In this land of contrasts there are mountains two million years old and mountains 200 million years old, but surely the most outstanding feature of New Zealand's topography is its sheer diversity, concentrated into a relatively small country.

On clean, clear waters – on isolated mountain lakes or in coastal bays dotted with islands – enjoy a huge variety of boating activities: take off on some of the world's wildest rivers in raft or canoe; go boating in a row boat, jet boat, launch, sail boat, or luxury keeler; try windsurfing or para-sailing.

Experience alpine New Zealand – this is a land of superb skiing, especially glacier and heli-skiing, and truly challenging climbing on mountains that produce world-class alpinists.

One of the major appeals of this country is the vast expanses of land, often empty of people. Trails through forests, hills and valleys, across plains, rivers and mountains, alongside isolated lakes and beaches make this a hiker's paradise.

Fishing is a national pastime enjoyed by anyone with a line and the time. In lakes and rivers trout and salmon grow to a great size. There is superb game fishing, especially for striped marlin, on the northeast coast; excellent line fishing from boats and surfcasting from rocks or long empty beaches. Some of the world's finest deep-sea diving provides exciting variety in the rugged bays and islands.

There's no closed season on hunting several varieties of deer, wild pigs, chamois, thar and goats. If your perfect holiday includes a round or two, or much more, of golf, you'll be delighted to learn that New Zealand has more golf courses per head of population than any country in the world; and visitors are warmly welcomed on the country's courses.

For the individual traveller there is still a great deal more to see and do. One traveller may become absorbed in the Polynesian culture of the Maori, whose origins are to be found hundreds of years ago far across the Pacific Ocean. For some visitors the lingering impression is of a volatile place, where the earth's crust is perilously thin; to others it may be the wildlife, particularly the rich unique assortment of birds, or the native flora. All travellers will be amazed at the predominance of bright green pastures dotted with sheep. These animals outnumber the human population many times over and will be one of the first sights you see as your aircraft swoops in towards Auckland or Christchurch International Airport.

Because it developed in isolation from other land masses, New Zealand has a unique plant and bird life.

The closest relatives of New Zealand forest plants are found in other parts of the Pacific and in South America. Seventy-five per cent of flowering native plants are found only in New Zealand, including such beautiful oddities as the white mountain flower known as the Mount Cook lily, which is, in fact, the world's largest buttercup. Strange also is the occurrence of rich, evergreen rainforest, a jungle-like covering rarely found in temperate regions.

The birds of New Zeland evolved in isolation, in a land without predators, so losing the need for strong wings. Best known is the national symbol, the nocturnal flightless kiwi.

Other endemic birds include the impertinent, flightless weka, which will cheerfully raid campsites; the kea, a bold mountain parrot living in the South Island high country; the kaka, a shy bush parrot that lives in the deepest forest and the tui, a bush songbird that lives on nectar, common in forests and gardens throughout the country.

Other bird treats include the yellow-eyed penguin, which can be seen at Taiaroa Head on the Otago Peninsula, the only known mainland Royal Albatross colony in the world (also at Taiaroa Head) and the only readily accessible gannet colony in the world (at Cape Kidnappers).

In this land of contrast even the weather is predictably unpredictable – the country is surrounded by seas and therefore susceptible to sudden changes. Where the sea is close by on both coasts, as in Auckland, there may be clear, cloudless skies one day and torrential rain the next.

In the South Island contrasting weather patterns are accentuated by the Southern Alps. Prevailing winds drop rain on the west coast, creating rainforest thick with ferns, mosses and vines. East of the alps the landscape can sometimes resemble a semi-desert with not a tree in sight.

Travellers in New Zeland should expect such variations as warm, humid, semi-tropical weather or hot, dry weather with little humidity; sudden heavy downpours of rain or drifting mists, and cold, crisp winters. In the simplest terms, pack a sunhat and raincoat because you will need them both.

There is a great diversity in the cities, towns and villages – some with quaint, pitch-roof wooden or stone cottages built over a hundred years ago; some, like Napier, that went through intense development after an earthquake, when art deco was the style of the day; and some such as Twizel that are so new that fifteen years ago the town site was wilderness.

The country's largest city, Auckland, sprawls across a narrow isthmus with dozens of extinct and dormant volcanic cones creating vantage points. The houses and buildings of Wellington, the capital, perch on steep hills spreading up from the closely contained city centre on the harbour edge.

Christchurch, the South Island's largest city, has the gentle, leisured pace of an English country town, enhanced by Gothic-style stone buildings. Dunedin, the fourth major city, has a distinctly Scottish heritage and elaborate, grandiose Victorian architecture.

Other smaller cities include Whangarei, where the forest spills down hills to city perimeters, Hamilton with its prosperity based on the Waikato dairy industries and the Waikato river flowing through its heart, Rotorua with its emphasis on the extraordinary thermal activity and surrounding beautiful lakes, and Nelson, caught between the exquisite, indented coast of the Marlborough Sounds and the sweeping beaches of Tasman Bay.

In travelling around the country, it can often seem at first that there is little for the visitor to do – New Zealanders outside the main tourist centres tend not to proclaim or promote the attractions of their towns, villages and surrounding countryside. But pause awhile and ask. If there's no local information centre, ask in the motel or hotel, at the desk or in shops, restaurants, coffee shops or tearooms. New Zealanders are immensely friendly and justly proud of their country, and you will find them delighted to advise you.

It's not uncommon for New Zealanders to take a visitor under their wing, show them around and invite them home after a chance meeting. But bear in mind also that New Zealanders tend to be reticent people, careful not to intrude – it's up to you to chat to them if you wish.

This same reticence affects the service you will find in hotels and restaurants. What may seem like reluctant or indifferent service is often simply 'different'. If you want something, ask for it pleasantly, don't wait for it to be offered or expect your needs to be anticipated.

Although the people of this country are isolated, New Zealanders have achieved fame in many fields of endeavour – from Sir Edmund Hillary's successful ascent of Mount Everest to Sir Ernest Rutherford's splitting of the atom.

An independence of spirit and natural inventiveness are hallmarks of the New Zelander character.

Settlement

The first Maori settlers arrived in New Zealand about 1,000 years ago from a homeland known as 'Hawaiki', believed to be somewhere in east Polynesia. Maori society is based on a hierarchical system with chiefs, elders and tohunga (priests) heading tribes and sub-tribes. The central marae or meeting place in the communal villages was the forum for elaborate, formal debate – in a system with no written language oratory became a finely polished skill.

By the 1820s the first Europeans began to arrive; traders in flax and timber, sealers, whalers and missionaries. By the 1840s the flow of Europeans was increasing and the pressure on the Maori population was beginning to show. Their culture was increasingly undermined, their land bought for inadequate payment and the people decimated by European diseases such as measles or the common cold.

By the 1860s conflict was unavoidable, in spite of an agreement, the Treaty of Waitaingi, signed in 1840, which ceded New Zealand to the British Crown and guaranteed certain rights to the Maoris. To this day the treaty and its intentions remain a subject of controversy.

Twenty years of bitter fighting between Maori tribes and British troops finally drew to a close in the early 1880s, and the country set about developing itself into a nation.

The Maori people took a long time to recover from the effects of a colonisation that demoralised them, alienated them for their land and undermined their culture. But a resurgence of interest and pride in a unique culture and language has gained momentum in recent years, and those interested in Maoritanga (culture) will find a vital, lively Polynesian culture in New Zealand. It is expressed in song and dance, in weaving and carving.

Maori and European intermarried to an extent that was exceptional in British colonies, and today many New Zealanders have a racial background that is both Maori and pakeha (European).

Although the first European settlers were predominantly British in origin, there were other nationalities who settled various areas. Among the first sealers and whalers, some of whom stayed on, were Americans. Many of the first immigrants were Scots, particularly in Otago and Southland, areas that retain a strong Celtic flavour, but also in Auckland. Waipu Cove in Northland was settled by a group of Scots, not from Scotland but from Nova Scotia.

In the Franklin County area, just southwest of Auckland, the first organised immigration brought many British and Irish settlers from South Africa. The Taranaki centre of New Plymouth was founded by settlers from Devon and Cornwall, the city of Christchurch was a carefully planned Church of England community, and the South Island's west coast attracted the Irish.

Settlers also came from other European countries – the small towns of Norsewood and Dannevirke owe their origins to forest workers from Scandinavia. The tiny village of Puhoi, north of Auckland, retains pride in its origins as a settlement of immigrants from Bohemia, now part of Czechoslovakia. (The Puhoi pub is well worth a detour.) Several villages in the Motueka valley in the Nelson region were founded by German Lutherans.

Yugoslavs from Dalmatia arrived near the turn of the century to dig out kauri gum in the peatlands of the north. Most stayed on, importing brides from their homeland, and their descendants today play a significant part in communities such as Kaitaia, Dargaville and Henderson (west Auckland).

Chinese arrived first as goldminers – traces of their camps are still to be seen in Otago – but most returned to China. Later immigration has boosted the number of Chinese in the community and Indians, from India or by way of Fiji, are yet another significant minority group.

After World War II there was large-scale immigration from Britain, but also a considerable number of Dutch from the Netherlands or from former colonies in South-east Asia.

In the 1960s people from neighbouring Pacific islands, such as the Cook Islands, the Tokelau Islands and Western Samoa, began settling in New Zealand in increasing numbers. It is a continuing story. The people of New Zealand are almost as varied as the country they live in.

How to Use this Book

1.

We set out to make a different type of guide-book with a format suited to New Zealand. A holiday here is based on doing things as well as seeing the sights – even if some may require more energy than others – or just relaxing. Our holiday guide presents activities available, a selection from the very active to some ideas for a more relaxing holiday, and a regional touring guide. A number of writers prepared the introductions and, quite separately, the commercial listings were compiled to give factual information and a good selection of facilities, not an overwhelming plethora of detail.

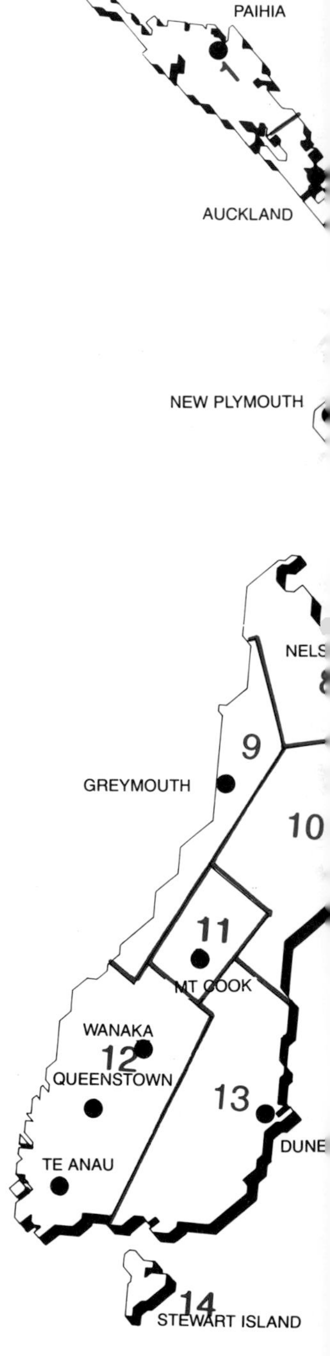

2. THE ACTIVITIES (Pages 12-113)

Each activity is introduced with an editorial review of what is available and a map shows the regional location of each facility. The commercial listings follow, giving details as to when you can do the activity, what to bring and approximate cost. To assist the planning of a tour through New Zealand or to various parts of the country, each commercial listing in the activities sections is cross-referenced to the regional touring Section.

For example:
Fiordland travel (Yachting and Cruising), is cross-referenced to Region 13 – The Southern Lakes – where more regional listings apply.

Cross-references are also used for commercial listings included in more than one activity or region. Listings from the regional section cross-reference back to the activities sections. To access the cross-references, follow the 'See Also:' notes at the end of each section. The first words apply to either the activity or regional section in which the cross-reference is first mentioned.

3. TOURING IN NEW ZEALAND (Pages 114-131)

For a national transport, accommodation and food guide, refer to this section. Also included are specialist holidays such as rafting trips, adventure holidays and special interest tours. (Accommodation is also presented in the regional guide.)

4. THE REGIONAL TOURING GUIDE (Pages 132-263)

Firstly, you are given an introduction to travelling around both the North and the South Islands, then each region is explored in detail. We have created our own definitions of the regions to best serve the holiday-maker. Our main objective is to help you to organise your time. For each region, a regional centre has been selected which becomes the focal point for what to do within one half, one, two and three hours driving time (except for the West Coast, Mount Cook, and Stewart Island). (Detailed road maps required for executing your journey may be obtained from most book shops, vehicle service stations or the Automobile Association in New Zealand.)

The format is similar to the activities sections. An introduction is given to the region, then the regional centre. Listings with details on local sights are provided and activities are cross-referenced to each place so that you can plan your time.

How to Use this Book

Each region has a map showing the activities available within the time zones from the regional centre. For convenience, map symbols are explained alongside each map together with a quick reference map showing driving times to other regional centres. The maps show the places mentioned in the text rather than all place names, and include the major activities of the area as noted in the listings.

Driving time is calculated at 80 kilometres per hour (50 mph), with a rest break every few hours and consideration taken of the terrain.

Editorial also introduces the main areas outside the regional centre which offer points of interest. Each region has an entertainment, accommodation, food and a travelling around review and guide.

Note:
It is impossible to include all relevant information in one publication, so references for additional information are provided. Additionally, the Public Relations Office or Information Centre is noted for each town. Most have excellent local information.

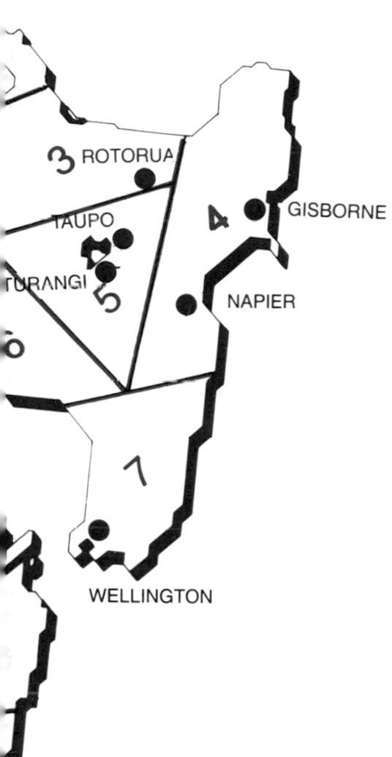

PLANNING AND BOOKING

1. Many activities require pre-booking of up to three months ahead. Every activity can be booked directly or through a travel agent. Plan what you want to do and check ahead to avoid disappointment.
2. Take note of the seasons for various activities (e.g. except in some parts of the North Island most white-water rafting closes from April until November). See the Sports Calendar for details of hunting and fishing.
3. Each time you use one of the facilities mentioned in this travellers' guide, let the proprietor know, and if there is something we have missed out or something you are dissatisfied with, please write to us.
4. The prices indicated are a guide only, accurate at time of compilation.
5. For overseas visitors: Mid-December and January, Easter and the first three weeks of May are times when New Zealanders take holidays. For skiing, the August school holidays (usually last three weeks of August) means some ski areas are relatively crowded.

TOURING REGIONS:
1 Northland
2 Auckland
3 Waikato–Bay of Plenty
4 East Cape–Hawkes Bay
5 Volcanic Plateau
6 Taranaki
7 Wellington
8 Nelson–Marlborough
9 Westland
10 Canterbury
11 Mt Cook
12 Southern Lakes
13 Otago–Southland
14 Stewart Island
REGIONAL CENTRES ●

A BONUS: A BOOK AND FILM

For the first time a book is complemented with an entertaining, high-quality film available in any video format.

If the book provides the detail, the 25-minute film captures the spirit of travelling in New Zealand and shows some of the many ways to enjoy this challenging destination.

Send it to a friend or take one home.

Write to: Pacific Tourism Promotions Ltd.
PO Box 6190, Wellesley Street
Auckland. New Zealand
Phone: (09) 733-631, Telex: NZ 60127

If you are in Auckland, call us. We would be delighted to hear from you and of any suggestions you may have regarding this book.

Hikers rest above the Tara Lakes on the slopes of Mount Ngauruhoe, an active volcano in the North Island chain of fire. *(Mal Clarbrough – Dept of Lands & Survey)*

The national and maritime Parks of New Zealand are unique in the world. Nowhere on earth is there such a variety of landforms and experiences within such a small geographical area.

The visitor with a month to spend could go from tropical coastline and islands to volcanic peaks, to snow-covered alps, to southerly fiords in one continuous trip of only 1,000 easy kilometres (620 miles).

The incredible variety of landforms in the parks arises from the country's position at the junction of two of the crustal 'plates' of the earth's surface, which we now know to be constantly moving. The volcanic activity of the North Island parks rises through the crust where one plate is diving under the other, melting as it goes. The result is several active volcanoes and extensive geothermal areas of hot pools of mud or water. The magnificent South Island alps sit astride the collision zone between the two plates, where neither will yield and fold under the other. The collision has pushed the land upwards to a height as great as Mt Cook's 3,764 metres (12,349 feet). Great glaciers still grind the alpine valleys. One of the world's longest glaciers outside polar regions is the 29-kilometre (18-mile) Tasman. Ancient glacial valleys now drowned by the sea created a convoluted fiordland, surrounded by one of the world's great rain forests.

There are ten national parks and three maritime parks. The national parks occupy about eight per cent of the nation's land area. New Zealand was the fourth nation of the world (after the USA, Australia and Canada), to establish a national park system in 1887. The first park, the volcanic Tongariro mountains, was a gift from a visionary chieftain of the first New Zealanders, the Maori. Te Heuheu Tukino IV gave the young European settlement, Tongariro, seat of his ancestral hearth fires, to preserve the land from development. Maori identity is inextricably linked to ancestral land, and the park preserved this for all time.

The national parks will celebrate the centennial of Te Heu Heu's gift in 1987, with many special activities taking place at Tongariro in September. A Centennial Commission has been formed to promote and oversee the event. There will be many other special activities in the months prior to 1987. The symbol at left identifies Centennial activities.

These parks exist to preserve and protect unique natural features and New Zealand's heritage of native plants, animals and landforms. They also provide for the physical and spiritual recreation of people. Their scenery alone is awe inspiring and breathtaking. Parks are natural areas with a variety of activities available for visitors. Active outdoor holidays of tramping (hiking), climbing, skiing, canoeing, fishing or hunting (in limited areas by permit) can be balanced by relaxed motor touring or resting at facilities provided. Nature study is as near as the doorstep of accommodation, or as far as the feet wish to go. Visitor services vary from park to park. Public transportation is generally readily available.

Mt Cook Lily

Though the climate varies considerably through the seasons, the parks are all open year round. They offer different experiences according to season: tramping, camping, boating and fishing are less possible in winter of course, but are replaced by skiing and other winter pursuits. The North Island maritime parks and the thermal areas in and around Tongariro National Park also offer pleasant winter activities of a more temperate nature. Except for the far south or high country, New Zealand's winter is fairly mild by northern-hemisphere standards. Touring and vacationing in winter are definitely reasonable. However, summer is the season for the wide variety of planned and conducted activities.

National Parks

The National Parks division of the Department of Lands and Survey administers many resources other than the parks. There are hundreds of scenic, nature, recreational or scientific reserves throughout the country, most open to the public. The nation is criss-crossed by a system of over 100 developed walkways of varying character, in addition to the tracks in national parks. It is possible to walk almost the entire length of the country without setting foot on a paved surface. There is also a system of farm parks throughout the country. These combine New Zealand's unique agriculture – a worthwhile tourist attraction in itself – with nature conservation and recreation. The farming areas are open to public view and include many interesting stock operations, such as sheep herding with dogs, and shearing.

From the coasts to the mountain tops, from top to bottom, New Zealand's great natural bounty preserved for tomorrow's enjoyment beckons the traveller. Uncluttered, sun-kissed, relaxed and friendly times and places await visitors to New Zealand's national and maritime parks, reserves and walkways..

NP MP

The walkways and nature reserves

The highest mountain in Australasia, Mount Cook, rises 3764 metres (12,348 ft) above the Southern Alps of Mt Cook National Park. *(Brian Ahern – Dept of Lands & Survey)*

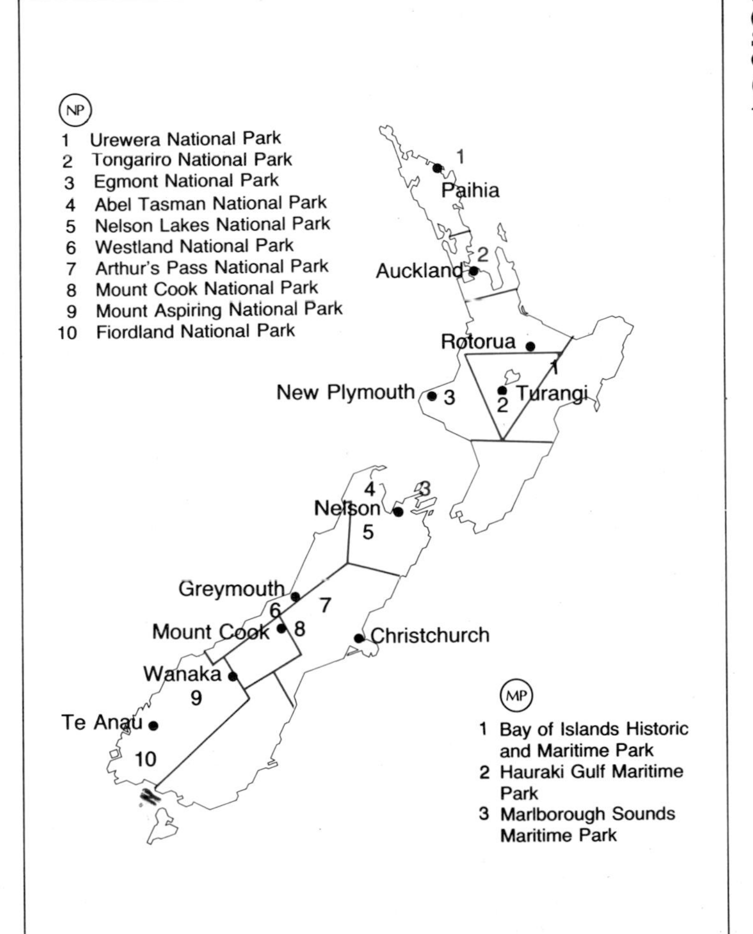

Bay of Islands

There are many Maori pa sites, and famous battles were fought in the Bay of Islands. Waitangi, Russell and Kerikeri also have reserves of historical interest. The Bay of Islands has superb recreational opportunities, warm, dry summers, and unparalleled scenic attractions.

Activities: swimming, picnicking, camping, boating, walking, tramping, fishing, scenic drives, viewing historical features, skin diving, charter-boat trips.

Hauraki Gulf

Public use of the islands varies considerably. Some are so remote and difficult to reach that they cannot be used for recreation. However, their very isolation makes them ideal for the study of New Zealand wildlife in its natural state. Many islands are the home of insects, birds, animals and plants no longer found on the mainland.

Activities: boating, sea fishing, swimming, tramping, camping, nature walks, scenic flights.

A tidal pool on the sandstone beach of Motuihe Island reflects the serenity of the Hauraki Gulf Maritime Park. ***(Tony Lilleby – Dept of Lands & Survey)***

Aerial view of the Coromandel Peninsula. ***(Courtesy Michael Kopp Dept of Lands & Survey)***

National Parks

Tongariro

Three volcanic peaks, Ruapehu (2,797 metres, 9,177 feet) Ngauruhoe (2,291 metres, 7,516 feet) and Tongariro (1,968 metres, 6,457 feet) dominate this park, which is within a day's easy driving from almost anywhere in the North Island. Mt Ruapehu is the North Island's highest mountain and major ski resort. Ngauruhoe and Ruapehu are active volcanoes, and Tongariro, although regarded as dormant, has hot springs gushing out of its upper slopes in the Ketetahi area. Area: 76,198 hectares (188,200 acres).

Activities: skiing, tramping, hunting (red deer, pigs), climbing, sign-posted walks, guided trips, illustrated talks and audio-visual programme in headquarters building, nature programmes in summer.

Children play at the base of a waterfall in Mt Egmont National Park. ***(Herb Spannagl – Dept of Lands & Survey)***

Urewera

Urewera National Park has magnificent native forests, lakes and waterfalls. It is rich in bird life. Much of its beauty can be seen from the Rotorua-Wairoa State Highway, which winds through approximately 80 kilometres (50 miles) of bush and lake scenery. Of all New Zealand's national parks, Urewera preserves most strongly the influence of the traditional culture of the early Maoris. Area: 211,777 hectares (523,000 acres).

Activities: tramping, hunting (red deer, pigs), trout fishing, boating, easy sign-posted walks.

Egmont

The almost perfect cone of Mt Egmont (2,518 metres, 8,261 feet) dominates the Taranaki Province. The volcano and the native forest that surrounds it make up Egmont National Park, readily accessible from neighbouring centres and ideal for all mountain activities. Area: 33,532 hectares (82,820 acres).

Activities: skiing, tramping, climbing, easy sign-posted walks, nature programmes in summer, hunting (goats).

Information about the national park system, walkways and scenic reserves is available from many travel agents or New Zealand Government representatives abroad. It is also available directly by mail from the Department of Lands and Survey, Private Bag, Wellington. Telephone: Wellington (04) 735-022.

A tramping party crosses one of innumerable streams in Mt Egmont National Park. The rocks take on rainbow colours from the various minerals spewed out of the volcano. ***(Herb Spannagl – Dept of Lands & Survey)***

Marlborough Sounds

A tramper says good morning to New Zealand's native parrot, the kea. ***(David Gregorie Dept of Lands & Survey)***

Rich in history, some of the reserves in the park show evidence of pre-European occupation and others of early European explorers from Captain James Cook to Dumont D'Urville and the early whalers.

The unique blend of a myriad of bays and coves in sheltered warm tidal waters, set against a backdrop of attractive native bush, interspersed with private holiday residences and farm land, makes the park a popular playground for the holiday-maker and tourist.

Activities: fishing (blue cod, tarakihi, snapper), pleasure boating, water skiing, swimming, picnicking, camping, tramping, nature walks, hunting (wild pigs, goats and deer), scenic drives, mail and charter-launch trips, and viewing of historical features – Maori pa and pits.

Abel Tasman

Abel Tasman National Park has numerous tidal inlets and beaches of golden sand. The coastline is rich in history, having been visited by the Dutch explorer Abel Tasman in 1642 and thoroughly explored by the Frenchman Dumont D'Urville in 1827. The granite hills of the park support a wide variety of vegetation from warm-temperate beech forest to shrubland and reverting farmland. Area: 22,370 hectares (55,250 acres).

Activities: tramping, boating, good sea fishing, hunting (pigs, goats, opossums, a few red deer), swimming, walks.

Nelson Lakes

The two beautiful lakes, Rotoiti and Rotoroa, both fringed to the water's edge with beech forest, form the focal point of Nelson Lakes National Park. The surrounding country is rugged, forest clad, and mountainous, rising to over 2,100 metres (6,890 feet). It offers scenery and sport hard to better in New Zealand. Area: 57,450 hectares (142,000 acres).

Activities: tramping, hunting (deer, chamois, opossum), climbing, skiing, swimming, boating, fishing (brown and rainbow trout), sign-posted walks.

Arthur's Pass

A striking contrast between the mountain beech forests and wide river beds of Canterbury, and the mixed rain forests and swift-flowing rivers of Westland, the park is a popular family playground and also attracts naturalists, mountaineers, trampers and casual visitors. Area: 98,408 hectares (243,000 acres).

Activities: tramping, climbing, skiing, hunting (red deer, chamois), guided walks, nature programmes in the school holidays. Evening programmes of slides, films and talks held in visitor centre during school and public holidays.

Totaranui Beach, Abel Tasman National Park, Nelson. ***(Andris Apse Ltd)***

National Parks

(NP) (MP)

Westland

Westland National Park rises from just above sea level to more than 3,300 metres (10,827 feet). Its attractions are as varied as its altitudes, ranging from numerous glaciers including the Franz Josef and Fox Glaciers, hot springs, placid lakes, and mountain and lowland bush. Area: 88,753 hectares (220,000 acres).

Activities: tramping, climbing, hunting (red deer, chamois and thar), fishing (quinnat salmon and trout), heli-hiking (helicopter flights onto glaciers for hikers), scenic flights that land on glaciers, easy sign-posted walks, guided trips, nature trips in summer and illustrated talks.

The Hollyford Track winds its way up the distant floor of the old glacial valley of the Hollyford River in Fiordland National Park. ***(Mal Clarbrough – Dept of Lands & Survey)***

Mount Cook

Mt Cook (3,764 metres, 12,349 feet) is New Zealand's highest mountain. More than one third of the park is in permanent snow and glacier ice. One of the longest glaciers in the world, the Tasman is 29 kilometres (18 miles) long and up to 3 kilometres (1.8 miles) wide. The ice at one point is estimated to be 600 metres (1,969 feet) thick. Area: 69,957 hectares (173,000 acres).

Activities: tramping, climbing, alpine skiing, hunting (chamois, Himalayan thar), scenic flights, easy sign-posted walks, guided trips, nature programmes in summer.

Mount Aspiring

The focal point of the park is Mt Aspiring (3,027 metres, 9,931 feet), the country's highest peak outside Mount Cook National Park. The Haast Pass highway passes through the northeast corner of the park, and from the road you can see mountains, river valleys, and forest typical of this remote area. Area: 287,254 hectares (709,500 acres).

Activities: tramping, climbing, hunting, (red deer, chamois and goats), trout fishing, guided trips on Routeburn Track, scenic flights, scenic drives.

Fiordland

One of the world's largest national parks, Fiordland is renowned for its rugged grandeur. The sheer mountainsides, the many beautiful lakes and the fiords make a lasting impression on the visitor. A rare bird, the takahe, previously thought to be extinct, was rediscovered in the park in 1948. The park is also one of the habitats of an even rarer bird, the kakapo. Area: 1,232,000 hectares (3,043,304 acres).

Activities: tramping, climbing, hunting (red deer, wapiti, pig, chamois), fishing (brown and rainbow trout, Atlantic salmon), sea fishing in sounds, scenic flights, launch trips, nature walks, guided trips (Milford, Lower Hollyford and Routeburn Tracks). Permit required to traverse Milford Track unless on guided tour.

Horace Walker Glacier, Westland National Park. *(Andris Apse Ltd)*

Skiing the Tasman Glacier, Mt Cook.
(Andris Apse Ltd)

Take a New Zealand skiing holiday and discover some of the best skiing in the world. From June to October each year there is no better skiing anywhere than in the New Zealand mountains, and for those who delight in spring skiing, the season can stretch into November.

During the northern summer top European ski teams come south to New Zealand for the hard mid-winter racing snow – teams from Canada, the USA, Austria, Italy, France and Norway as well as from Britain and Japan. What draws these top skiers are the same conditions that attract any skier – plenty of good snow, good weather, challenging runs and reasonable costs.

But skiing is far more than a mere escape from high-altitude slush in the northern hemisphere. There is something for everyone, every kind of skiing and all kinds of snow conditions, wrapped up in a country that's smaller than California. As a bonus, there are some features that are unique. It is a new skiing experience.

Just as much snow falls on New Zealand's mountains as on the European alps, and that's a lot of snow, enough to ensure skiable slopes somewhere, even in the mildest winter.

You can ski conventional ski fields (ski areas, as they are also known), or indulge in special alpine thrills such as heli-skiing, glacier skiing (with ski-plane transport), ski-mountaineering or ski-touring. You can ski above mountain lakes, in sight of the Pacific Ocean, on the snow-covered mountain pastures of a high-country sheep station or on the slopes of a live volcano. And all the slopes you ski will be absolutely treeless – just wide open spaces of snow and more snow.

Skiing in the North and the South Island has its own distinct characteristics. On the cluster of volcanoes in the centre of the North Island, skiers can trek to the edge of a steaming crater lake at the summit of Ruapehu (2,797 metres, 9,177 feet) before making a run of several kilometres down a glacier and back to the services of the ski field at Turoa, which offers about 4 kilometres (2½ miles) of continuous skiing from its top lift down to the bottom. Whakapapa, on the northern slopes of Ruapehu, is New Zealand's largest ski field.

In the South Island the chain of the Southern Alps runs for almost 800 kilometres (497 miles), creating an area crammed with peaks, 17 of them over 3,000 metres (9,843 feet), hundreds over 2,000 metres (6,562 feet). With their sharp, steep upper slopes fanning out into wide, gentle valleys, these are classic alps. But unlike the European alps, the mountains rise abruptly from near sea level, giving extraordinary length and angle in proportion to their height.

Most ski fields in these mountains, such as those at Mount Hutt or Porter Heights, are formed in basins, with terrain to suit all grades of skiers – sharp, challenging runs from top ridges drop to an area of moguls to provide exhilarating advanced skiing. Long, more leisurely routes bring intermediates back to base and the wide, undulating slopes of the valley floors are splendid for learners. For a family or group with mixed skiing ability, there is plenty of skiing for all.

If stunning mountain scenery appeals as much as the prospect of good snow, you won't be disappointed – the alpine views are magnificent and varied. In the Mount Cook region, ski in deep powder snow looking down on one of the world's largest glaciers; at Coronet Peak enjoy sophisticated facilities and views of lake and massive mountains stretching to the

horizon; at Treble Cone, Cardrona and the Harris mountains near Wanaka, the views are matched only by the diversity of isolated slopes and long runs; at Mount Hutt stand on top of a 2,000-metre (6,562-feet) peak, above a skiing vertical of 650 metres (2,133 feet), and look out across coastal plains to the blue Pacific Ocean – a survey at Mount Hutt has shown the scenery rates highly with skiers, who return again and again.

Overseas skiers revel in the uncrowded ski slopes on New Zealand fields. Crowds – and queues – are the exception, not the rule, so that time and money isn't wasted in long periods of waiting. Skiing is mainly a weekend sport and, as a result, there are crowd-free slopes for mid-week skiers, except during the school holidays in late August.

Even then, weekend and holiday crowds can be compared favourably to weekday crowds on many overseas fields. Most of your time skiing is spent actually skiing.

All the major fields have excellent ski schools, with instructors from Europe, Japan, Canada and the USA as well as New Zealand, so the latest methods from Kitzbeuhl or Colorado are taught on New Zealand slopes.

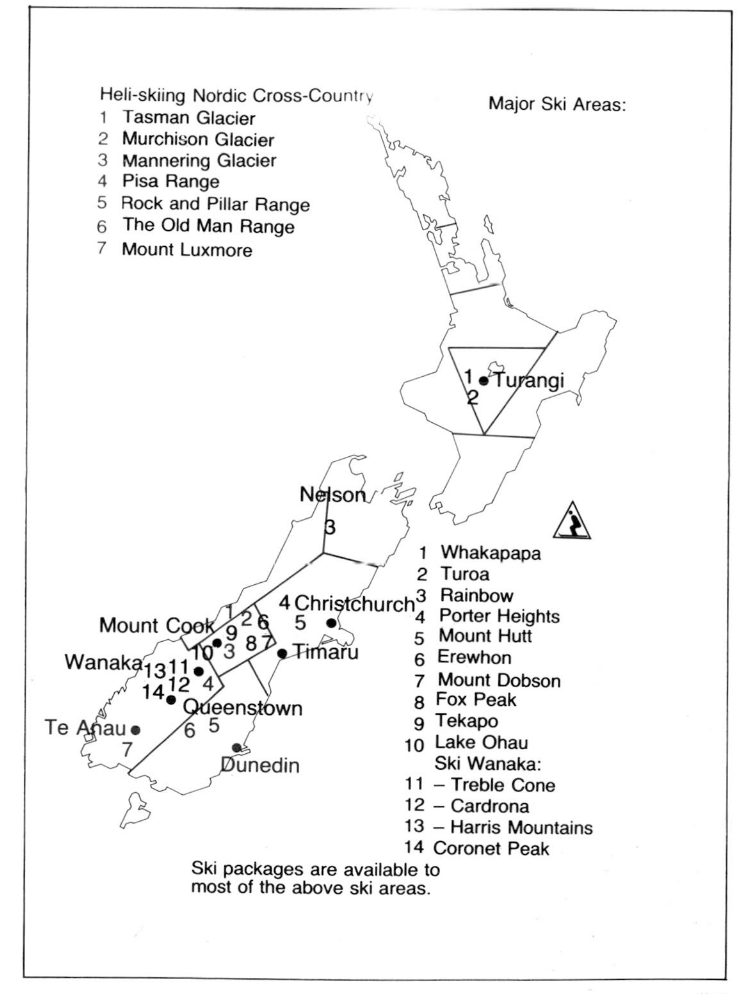

For those who want more than the thrills of downhill skiing from the chairlift, there is fresh powder snow and fresh excitement skiing on glaciers or heli-skiing.

To find glaciers comparable with the 29-kilometre (18-mile) Tasman Glacier, you would need to take an expedition into the Himalayas or Antarctica. The Tasman, however, is minutes away from civilisation, by ski plane that lands skiers and guides on the longest single run in the Southern Hemisphere – 13 kilometres (8 miles) of untrammelled powder snow. Walled in by some of the highest mountains in the country, the fall of the Tasman is mild, through a series of glacial bowls, making it an exhilarating run for intermediate and advanced skiers.

There are steeper, more daring glaciers, such as the Murchison or Mannering, also reached by ski plane or helicopter, and glaciers that extend down to unusually low altitudes where dense rain forest fringes the edges.

Heli-skiing also takes skiers and guides into the enormous, untracked terrain of otherwise inaccessible mountain valleys – so great is the choice that it is possible that you will have the chosen mountain all to yourselves. Ski the Harris mountains near Wanaka (a choice of 30 mountains) and you need never ski the same ground twice.

For those whose skills and ambitions include mountaineering, there is the adventure of ski-mountaineering tours. These take you into the alps for days, with expert guides to minimise the risks and maximise the adventure, climbing and downhill skiing from mountain hut to mountain hut through terrain where Sir Edmund Hillary, the first conqueror of Everest, learned his mountain craft.

Or try the pleasures of traditional Nordic-style cross-country tours, travelling above mountain lakes and into the alps for several days or more.

Heli-skiing in the Ben Ohau Range, Mt Cook Ski Region. ***(Andris Apse Ltd)***

Skiing

Heli-skiing in the famous Harris Mountains (Wanaka) can be enjoyed by strong intermediate and advanced skiers, not just experts! This company pioneered and now regularly skis over 60 different runs on 35 mountains, varying between 2,000 and 4,000 vertical feet (600 and 1,200 vertical metres) on treeless, sheltered basins, mountain flanks and glaciers, all reached by jet-turbine helicopter. Ski in small groups (of your skiing level) with a professional guide, on runs suited to your ability. Snow conditions offer fine powder or beautiful spring corn, depending on month. Season runs July to October. Weather conditions variable, allow extra time to ensure satisfaction. All safety aspects ensured. Bring warm clothing and accessories. Excellent equipment available for hire in Wanaka. Cost: half-day from $126, full-day (lunch, 4 runs and guide) from $175. Ski weeks, packages and special runs available, plus summer mountain guiding program on request.

Ski Guides (NZ) Ltd
PO Box 177
Wanaka
Telephone: Wanaka 7930 or 7804
Telex: NZ 5636
Owner and Chief Guide: Paul Scaife

Ski during winter within easy reach of Dunedin in acres of snow – free of lift lines or crowded slopes. Nordic skiing (the fastest growing winter activity) is the ideal sport for these ranges. With names reflecting their gold-mining heritage – 'The Old Man Range', 'Rock and Pillars' and 'Pisa' – these extensive high plateaus are now home (during the summer) for thousands of sheep. You will live as the back country sheep musterers do – in rustic mountain huts, basic but comfortable, surrounded by a vast winter wonderland of untracked snow. Wilderness Shop organises all your requirements for this unique skiing experience: four-wheel-drive access, food, equipment and a professional guide, as well as instruction, weekend trips or week-long ski tours. From $45 to $250 depending upon your requirements.

Nordic and Cross-country Skiing
Wilderness Shop
101 Stuart Street
Dunedin
PO Box 5175
Telephone: (024) 773-679
Owners: Chris and Wendy Knol

Spring skiing, from late September into November, often brings weather mild enough for T-shirts. The slopes are even less crowded as local skiers abandon skiing to prepare for summer sports. Most likely venues for great spring skiing are Mount Hutt, Mount Cook, Turoa and Whakapapa.

The weather? It is as contrary as anywhere else in the world. As the country is long and narrow, surrounded by ocean, sudden weather changes are a feature of alpine life.

But such is the effect of micro-climates in the mountains that the chances are that when the weather closes in on one field, another field, not too far away, will be open and enjoying good weather.

A skiing holiday needn't be all skiing – you won't find yourself trapped in a mountain resort with nothing else but skiing or snow sports. There are plenty of other activities at hand. Take a break from the snow fields at Turoa or Whakapapa and try bathing in the natural hot pools, horse riding, trout fishing, bush walks or golf. Go spring skiing in the South Island and coincide with the trout and salmon fishing season. At any time, take jet-boat rides on rivers and lakes, play golf, go horse riding – there is always plenty to do.

Because skiers live off the slopes, it is simple to vary a skiing holiday with all the other activities – fish one day, ski the next. The family with diverse interests can go their separate ways on the same holiday, up the mountain or onto the lake as the whim takes them.

Accommodation in hotels, tourist lodges, cabins, self-catering motel units or youth hostels is usually in a village about 30 minutes away from the skiing, with regular skiers' transport provided. On-field accommodation is minimal or non-existent, part of a policy aimed at protecting the mountain environment. Building on the ski fields is limited to essential services such as cafeterias and ski hire.

Those who like to rest their weary ski boots in style after a hard day's skiing will find the most sophisticated comfort near large, well-developed ski fields. Yet even at the smartest hotels the emphasis is on open-fire comfort and friendly bonhomie. The atmosphere is relaxed and welcoming, not haughty and exclusive.

Après-ski is based on the same friendliness, not jet-set high style. Even Queenstown, with a wide selection of hotels and plenty of après-ski diversions such as discos, bars and restaurants, remains a lively small town with the accent on super fun rather than super chic.

Skiing in New Zealand is low on pressure, high on relaxation and friendliness and pleasantly kind to the pocket. On-field skiing costs are about half those of Europe, so your skiing dollar provides twice the action.

Value can be even greater – some heli-skiing rides offer twice the skiing vertical for half the price at popular European venues, and that is a lot of untracked snow. For Australians, a skiing holiday in New Zealand, including airfares and accommodation, can prove cheaper than skiing in Australia.

Whether you settle for one ski field, spread your skiing holiday over several fields or attempt to sample the lot, you will discover that some of the cheapest skiing in the world can also be some of the best.

SEE ALSO:

Climbing: Alpine Guides (Mt Cook), Mountain Guides (NZ) Ltd (Twizel).
Lodges: Milcroft (Timaru), Alpine (St Arnaud).
Regional: Otago: Wilderness Shop (Dunedin).
Many motels and hotels near skiing areas offer ski services.

Skiing

Whakapapa
Ruapehu Alpine Lifts Ltd
PO Box 11-049
Wellington

Whakapapa is New Zealand's largest developed ski area. It has three double chairlifts, one single chairlift, six T-Bars and several beginners' platter lifts and rope tows, giving it an uphill capacity of over 13,000 skiers per hour. Within these 250 hectares (617 acres) is some of the best skiing you will find anywhere. Gentle beginners' slopes, undulating bowls and steep chutes offer excellent skiing for all. There's an international school with over 50 qualified instructors and a very up to date ski rental operation. The 590 vertical metres (1,936 feet) of lift-serviced slopes are groomed throughout the day but the upper slopes are left for the adventurous. Above the lifts is another 500 vertical metres (1,640 feet) of exciting skiing. A hike to the top is rewarded with breathtaking views, from Mount Egmont in Taranaki to Lake Taupo – not to mention the ski down. Whakapapa is renowned for its spring skiing. In September – October thousands of skiers enjoy long, hot days and excellent 'corn snow'.

Within the vicinity is a range of accommodation to suit all tastes and budgets, from the opulent T.H.C. Chateau to the motels and club huts, and you'll find the atmosphere relaxed and friendly. As a break from skiing, go trout fishing at Lake Taupo, white-water rafting, jet boating, flight-seeing or soak in hot pools. There's lots to do and see. The North Island's other international ski area, Turoa, is only forty-five minutes drive by car. From $10 (mid-week day passes), $8.50 (ski lessons), $10.50 (rental equipment). For further information, write direct.

Mount Hutt International
Methven
Alpine Tourist Company Ltd
PO Box 446
Christchurch
Snow reports, Telephone: (03) 792-720
Telex: NZ 4308

This ski area has become the choice of champions, offering superb skiing, facilities and spectacular scenery.

Promising more than five months per year of consistent skiing, this field is the only one in the Southern Hemisphere to offer a 'Money Back Snow Guarantee'. No fewer than ten various lifts cater for all grades of skier and offer 674 metres (2,210 feet) of vertical skiing, over some 283 hectares (700 acres). Facilities include a large day lodge, which offers child minding, cafeteria, sun balconies, extensive equipment hire (beginners to top-flight) and storage for luggage and equipment. A full range of instruction is offered including a recreational race department staffed by five race instructors. Heli-skiing is available. Major credit cards accepted. Accommodation and night life offered at foot of the mountain at Methven or Ashburton.

'Fox Peak'
(22 kilometres, 13½ miles, from Fairlie)
Tasman Ski Club
PO Box 368
Timaru
Field telephone: (0505) 8539

With 2,100 vertical feet of ski lifts, five high-grade tow ropes, ten ski trails, heli-skiing and no road toll, this club-owned field is a delight for skiers (beginners to advanced) who enjoy uncrowded slopes in a friendly atmosphere. Facilities are limited (ski hire available in Fairlie only), but include canteen. Closest accommodation is Fairlie. No public transport. Operates winter only. Cost: lift fee $10 (adults), $5 (children). Enquiries to P.R. Office.

Treble Cone (Wanaka) Ski Area
PO Box 206
Wanaka
Telephone: Wanaka 7443
Contact: Ski Centre
Ardmore Street
Wanaka

Twenty-nine kilometres (18 miles) from Wanaka, this major skiing destination provides stunningly beautiful scenery and exciting sport for all. It is equipped with up-to-the minute Doppelmayer double-chair lift, two T-bars plus three fixed-grip learner lifts, and offers groomed slopes, great powder snow, minimal waits in queues! Services: NZIA Ski School, heli-skiing, professional ski patrol/medical services, ski hire, carpark, cafeteria and two well-appointed day lodges. Major credit cards accepted. Access by private/public transport/heli-taxi from Wanaka township, from nearby ski fields and from Queenstown.

Tekapo Ski Field
PO Box 7
Lake Tekapo
Telephone: (05056) 852
Owner: Karl Burtscher

Overlooking beautiful Lake Tekapo and snow-covered Godley Peaks (July through September), this field is ideal for families, children, beginners/intermediate skiers. Well equipped with twin-seat Doppelmayer chair and platter lifts, ski-instruction programmes (both group and private), excellent hire equipment, canteen and shop, day room, car park, air strip and ski patrol. Closest accommodation is Lake Tekapo. Access by private car, daily bus or Air Safaris ski plane.

Mount Dobson Ski Field Ltd
PO Box 45
Fairlie
Telephone: (0505) 8039
Owners: Peter and Shirley Foote

Mount Dobson, a newer and privately owned ski field, lies between Fairlie and Tekapo. With easy road access, it is already known for its powder snow conditions, long sunshine hours, friendly staff and spectacular views. A new Doppelmayr T-bar to 2,010 metres (6,600 feet), the longest platter in New Zealand (serving a massive learner area), access and fixed grip tows plus an upper tow for advanced skiers, allow an hourly lift capacity of 2,300 persons. Main runs groomed and lifts operational from 9.30 a.m. – 4.00 p.m., through winter. Amenities: well-stocked canteen, heated day hut, restrooms and private first-aid room. Closest accommodation is Fairlie and Burkes Pass. Equipment for hire and qualified tuition at all levels. From $13 (adult day, all lifts) to $18 (private lessons) Special youth rates. Packages include transport, accommodation, lift passes and food – from $145 for three days. Write for brochure and package bookings.

A sample of some of the ski fields available

Ski services

Live-Life New Zealand Ltd
Action Tours and Activities
CPO Box 4517
Auckland
Telephone: (09) 768-936

Go snow skiing for 2-day adventures or longer: at Turoa, North Island (from Auckland return), Mount Hutt, South Island (from Auckland return), or in the Southern Alps (adventurous intermediate to advanced skiers), glacier and heli-skiing. Flexible options available. Main meals, accommodation (any standard required),transport and hire equipment arranged. Skiing is fun and exciting and you will see the real New Zealand while doing it! For brochure/further information, contact direct.

Newman's Skihomes
PO Box 22-413
Otahuhu
Auckland

These 'winterised' motor caravans offer an economical and convenient way to make the most of your skiing holiday. Great for small groups of families (sleep four). Forget accommodation problems and enjoy your holiday being warm, comfortable and self-contained. The location of our ski areas makes Newman's Skihomes the ideal accommodation/transport to see and ski more in the time available. From $40 per day.

Educational Tours Unlimited
PO Box 51
Ohakune
Telephone: (0658) 58-799 or 58-733 (after hours)
Hosts: Don & Sue Allomes

Enjoy the thrill of skiing for the first time in your life, or improve your skills with expert, personal tuition from qualified ski instructors. Courses are flexible, either weekly or weekend. Everything is arranged for you, from prior advice on fitness training, accommodation, meals and transport to ski hire. Training locations are Turoa and Whakapapa. Weekend courses from $150. Week courses from $220.

Foothills of the Southern Alps, mid-Canterbury.
(Bob Girvan)

Go climbing in the Southern Alps of the South Island and you are in one of the world's great mountaineering areas, where famous mountaineers practise skills that take them to the top of the world in the Himalayas.

For the experts New Zealand is well known. But, it's also a place for the less experienced to learn alpine skills. Alpine guides in main climbing areas provide expert assistance for those unfamiliar with the conditions and terrain or for those who have never tried a climb in their lives. You need only be fit and agile, have a head for heights, a taste for adventure and the desire to test yourself against the tough mountains.

Few places in the world, outside Europe, can offer such a range of climbing so close to civilisation – climbing in New Zealand is an experience, not a major expedition. Even out-of-the-way mountain country can be reached with ease, by jet boat up fast, shallow rivers, by ski plane or helicopter onto snowfields, or by light aircraft onto high-country airstrips, built originally to serve sheep stations or deer cullers. Of course, those who prefer to acclimatise themselves slowly to new terrain and conditions can still take the long way in on foot.

The best-known climbing centre is Mt Cook, an alpine resort village surrounded by the massive mountains of the Mt Cook National Park, including the country's highest mountain Mt Cook 3,763 metres (12,342 feet) and another 140 peaks over 2,000 metres (6,560 feet). Climbing here began in the 1880s, but Mt Cook itself was not conquered until 1894 and has claimed more than 140 lives, so it is not an easy stroll.

The Mt Cook region is an area of spectacular mountain scenery, great glaciers (only the Himalayas and Antarctica have comparable glaciers), deep glacial valleys, sheer mountain faces, sharp ridges, ice, snow and rock – one third of the national park is covered in permanent snow and ice. And there are climbs and high-altitude treks suited to all ability levels.

Sharing a mountainous border with the Mt Cook Park is the Westland National Park, with mountains rising to 3,498 metres (11,473 feet), virtually from sealevel, glaciers and dense, lush rain forests on lower slopes, evidence of the heavy annual rainfall.

Another major centre is Arthur's Pass National Park, on the route across the alps from east to west and right in the middle of climbing country. This is 92,422 hectares (228,282 acres) of snow-covered peaks, forests, rushing rivers and waterfalls. Further south is another area popular with climbers, the 287,319-hectare (709,677-acre) Mt Aspiring National Park. with demanding mountain peaks and gentle valleys. And then there is the immense Fiordland National Park.

North Island mountaineering concentrates on the Tongariro National Park, with short, sharp climbs offering variety on snow, ice and volcanic rock.

But for those serious about a climbing holiday, the South Island provides infinite possibilities, inside and outside the national parks.

The southern mountains are sharp and steep and, because they rise almost from sealevel rather than from high plateaus, they provide a lot more alpine country than their official heights might suggest. Even quite small peaks can often present a major climb.

Perhaps because the mountains are so accessible, the inexperienced sometimes underestimate them. New Zealand mountain conditions can be as tough as anywhere in the world – no one unfamiliar with them should head up into the mountains without a guide or, at least, good local advice, which will be given readily and free. Mountain-safety experts maintain that one of the main causes of accidents involving

visiting climbers has been lack of knowledge about terrain, weather and conditions peculiar to New Zealand.

The rock in these mountains is generally less stable than that encountered in other countries, a fact sometimes not appreciated until too late. And for anyone used to weather conditions on large continental land masses, the changeability of New Zealand mountain-top weather can be an unwelcome surprise. The mountains have their own micro-climate, in which cloud, mist or blizzard can sweep in with speed, while the lower slopes bask in sunshine.

Don't take the mountains lightly and, unless very experienced, take a guide. Says one keen climber: 'When you are cold, tired and scared you want someone there to make the right decision.' He climbs every summer, with a guide.

Fortunately for the newcomer, national park rangers will tell you all you want to know about conditions, equipment, routes and guides. All climbing equipment can be bought or hired in main cities or alpine resorts, and guides are based in all the best climbing areas. They will teach correct climbing techniques on rock, snow and ice, awareness of snow and ice conditions, crevasse and avalanche precautions, route finding, an understanding of the weather, and will take you on the climbs best suited to your level of ability.

For those who prefer to clamber underground, New Zealand limestone country hides the kind of caves that cavers dream about.

Expert speleologists have the prospect of exploring the complex system at Mt Arthur, near Nelson, which includes the largest cave in the Southern Hemisphere. Not only has the system yet to be fully explored, it is suggested that at least another 30 years of exploration will be required before the maze is fully charted.

Another region of important caves and unexplored systems lies in the dramatic limestone country at Punakaiki on the South Island's West Coast – territory for the true enthusiast and definitely not for the inexperienced.

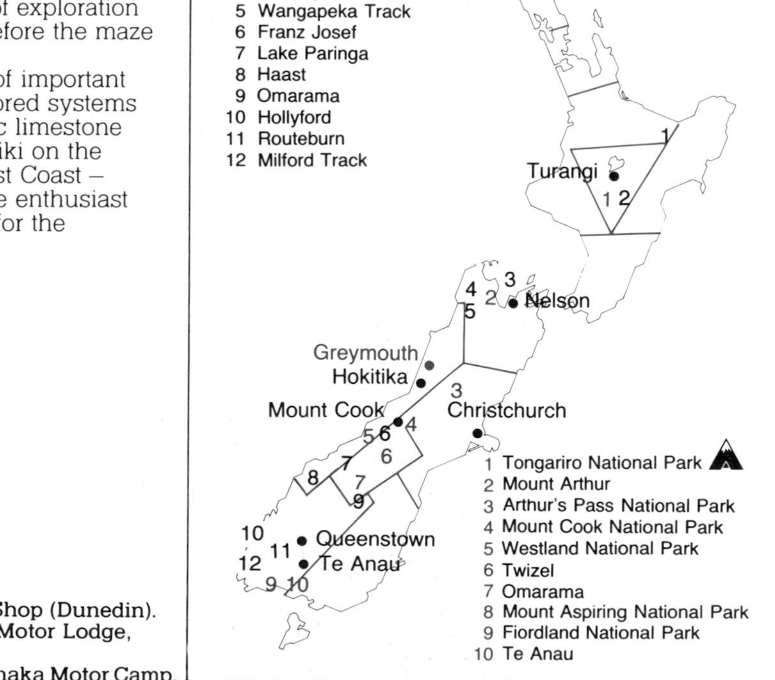

SEE ALSO:

Regional:
Otago: Wilderness Shop (Dunedin).
Mt Cook: Omarama Motor Lodge, Lake Ohau Lodge.
Southern Lakes: Wanaka Motor Camp.

Mountain Guides New Zealand
PO Box 93
Twizel
Telephone: (05620) 737
Owners: Nick Banks, Gary Ball, Russell Brice

This group of internationally known and qualified mountain guides offer a complete New Zealand and world-wide guiding, instructional and skiing programme. A combined wealth of experience ensures the highest standards of tuition and guidance, specialising in rock- and ice-climbing courses and ski mountaineering. Full programmes are held within New Zealand in addition to Himalayan and Antarctic guiding, training, safety planning and consultative work. Operating from Twizel, the service is centrally located adjacent to the high Southern Alps. New Zealand: eight and 14-day intensive courses, aimed at leaving participants self-sufficient at their own climbing standard. Instructor:student ratios are low and high mobility ensures climbing each day. Two- and three-day climbs also conducted for climbers with some experience. From $150 per day (one climber), to $1,250 for a 14-day course. Other costs as per requirements.

Alpine Guides (Mount Cook) Ltd
PO Box 20
Mount Cook National Park
Telephone: (05621) 834
Telex: NZ4308

Within the awesomely beautiful Mount Cook National Park this company is the sole concessionaire, offering a complete year-round guiding service to all visitors. With 21 peaks over 3,000 metres (9,843 feet) and great glaciers, the region has an international reputation for mountaineering and unique ski adventures. During winter (June through October), take advantage of some of the finest skiing in the world, on glaciers and spectacular alpine runs. Go heli-skiing, Nordic Skiing, ski touring – day trips or multi-day packages. Rental equipment supplied as necessary. During summer, Alpine Guides runs a climbing school programme and private guiding service. All guides are exceptional mountaineers/skiers, and most are internationally qualified (U.I.A.G.M.). Courses from 7-14 days (introductory to advanced tuition). A short coach excursion trip to the Tasman Glacier is run in summer. Note: Weather is variable. Costs on application. Enquiries direct. Advance booking essential.

Mt Sebastapol, Mt Cook National Park. *(Andris Apse Ltd)*

Start of the Milford Track, Fiordland.
(Courtesy Tourist Hotel Corporation)

An early morning start.
(Courtesy Air New Zealand)

hether you are an experienced hiker who likes to head for the solitude of the hills for weeks on end, or a tenderfoot in search of a soul-restoring interlude, there is a walk to suit you within easy distance of any New Zealand town.

Hiking, rambling, backpacking and trekking are all known as 'tramping' in New Zealand, and heading for the hills is a national pastime. Yet despite this delight in tramping, those tracks and trails are remarkable for their isolation. The reason is simple – there are so few people in New Zealand, and there is so much wilderness.

There are millions of hectares of national parks, forest parks and scenic reserves and only 3 million people. The largest of the 10 national parks, Fiordland, is larger than Yellowstone Park in the USA and so wild parts have yet to be explored.

Trekkers in New Zealand can concentrate on the beauty of the world around them without tripping over hordes of people. Nor do they need to watch for poisonous creatures or dangerous wild animals – there are none. The only precaution to take against wildlife is a good insect repellent – and insects carry no nasty diseases, they are merely a nuisance, not a danger. The birdlife is fascinating, with many species found only in New Zealand (for example: kiwi, paradise duck, weka, blue duck, kaka, morepork, tui, native wood pigeon, kea, rifleman, grey warbler, bush robin).

Walks range from the easy terrain of the national 'walkways' to rigorous trails where mountaineering experience is needed. But for every grade there are guided treks providing a problem-free way to discover the meaning of getting away from it all.

In the North Island these treks might lead across rugged hills with forests of giant kauri trees and flowering rata, through great pine plantations or beside mountain streams where rockhounds may gather gemstones.

They may travel through remote regions of rain, mists and myths, beautiful lakes and wild rivers where rare birds and wild deer live in the dense forest; or to the rim of live volcanoes, amid old lava flows, hot springs, volcanic sands, mountain daisies and buttercups, glaciers and waterfalls.

In the South Island there are limitless opportunities, with seven national parks. Trails lead along deserted golden beaches and high into mountain beech forests and tussock grasslands, along wild, rocky shorelines or into the mountains of the Southern Alps. You can follow packhorse trails to the old goldfields (and try panning for gold) or clamber along ridges surrounded by deep fiords, glaciers, great mountains, bush-fringed lakes and waterfalls that cascade and thunder from the mountain heights.

Here is the famous Milford Track, a three-day walk often described as 'the finest walk in the world' and with good reason. This leads high into the towering mountains, above lakes and by the Sutherland Falls, third highest in the world at 530 metres (1,738 feet). Lesser known, but exciting, are the nearby Hollyford and Routeburn walks.

Guided treks in both islands range from a few hours to two weeks and often combine exciting trails with other activities – rafting, canoeing, jet-boat rides, hunting, trout fishing, bird watching, ski-plane and helicopter rides.

Such trips use organised camps and huts, provide sleeping bags and cooked meals – all you need is clothes and stout walking boots. Everything else is taken care of – some even provide waterproof parkas (you can't have rain forest without some rain).

For novice trampers and families who want to do it alone, the national walkway system is a network of well-maintained, easy paths, where the scenery can be superb. Some walkways cross private land and farms, many are close to cities, most lead through areas of special charm or beauty – through wild meadowlands by a river, along barren cliffs where the Pacific crashes on the rocks below, across hills and valleys thick with tree ferns, among waterfalls, high-country farmland and mountains.

More experienced hikers who want to take to the wilderness burdened with their own heavy backpacks, but free from the organisation of a guided trek, may do so with ease. The New Zealand back country is at the doorstep of every town, often a short bus ride away.

Go tramping and trekking with these New Zealand Forest Service-approved guides through the beautiful Kaimanawa Forest Park and see flora, fauna, volcanoes and lakes. Facility operates through summer months, winter walks by prior arrangement only. Geared to your time and fitness, all you need is sturdy footwear and suitable clothing. Transport from Turangi provided if necessary. From $12.50 to $80 per person.

Central Safaris Ltd
PO Box 146
Turangi
Telephone: (0746) 8370
Hosts: Vince and Shane Dennis

A combination of launch trip and guided walk, hosted by the Wilsons, makes this 4-day adventure very special. Relax, swim or fish on the voyage. The skipper gives a personal commentary of historical/geographical interest. Walking track begins at Tonga Bay, through unspoiled native forest, following the coastline of gently curved golden sand beaches, separated by rocky granite headlands. Three nights are spent in 'The Lodge' (cottage comforts) at Torrent Bay – fishing, diving, yachting and boating available (no additional charge). This is an enchanted coast with delightful waterfalls spilling into tranquil lagoons, many native birds, plus dolphins, seals and penguins. Packs carried and meals prepared. Year-through operation. Bring good walking shoes, warm gear and rain wear. Average fitness required. Suitable for all over 10 years of age. Departs Monday and Friday. From $265 adults, $245 children.

Abel Tasman National Park Enterprises
Green Tree Road, RD3
Motueka
Nelson
Telephone: (0524) 87-801
Hosts: The Wilson Family

A venture offering outdoor experiences for women of all ages and fitness levels, from introductory walks for those uncertain of their abilities to full tramping. A personal service of small, friendly groups, with many stops to enjoy and learn about local history, botany, ornithology and geology, in addition to skills from map reading and river crossing to massage. Day and weekend trips outside Christchurch, to Banks Peninsula and into the Southern Alps. Camping trips of longer duration through the South Island and Stewart Island. All transport and food is provided (gourmet and vegetarian a speciality). You need sturdy footwear and clothing (packs and waterproof parkas are available for hire). Some walks are seasonal. All require five persons booked. Men and family groups by arrangement only. From $16 (day trips), $45 (weekends), $85 to $300 (camping holidays).

Women Walk
21 Toledo Place
Christchurch 8
Telephone: (03) 841-921
Guides: Pauline and Alison

Hollyford Valley Walk
Hollyford Valley Tourist and Travel Company Ltd
PO Box 216
Invercargill
Telephone: (021) 4300
Telex: NZ5737

The remote Hollyford Valley, Fiordland National Park region, offers varied scenery of unspoiled beauty and real appeal to all. Throughout is prolific native flora, varying from luxuriant fern growth to giant rimu and matai trees. Wildlife includes seal colonies, penguins, glow worms and the occasional dolphin or rare white heron. Here is your opportunity to see the isolated beauty of this area, through organised and novel adventures. With an experienced guide, tours cover the Hollyford River through to Martins Bay at the West Coast, and return. More than just a walk, this experience includes jet boating and flying. Options: a four-day, walk in-fly out tour, or a five-day walk in-walk out tour. This means of travel is geared towards making your experience even more memorable.

Walk through bush, by snow-capped mountains and thundering waterfalls, see historic sites of remote pioneer's homesteads and towns, with leisure time for beach combing, swimming and fishing. Thrill to jet-boat rides through river and lake. (The fly-out tour gives an aerial view of the region, second to none.) Accommodation while enroute is in well-appointed lodges, complete with all facilities. Regularly scheduled tours leave from the Hollyford Road end car park, with courtesy transport from Marian Corner. Transport: to Marian Corner from Queenstown, Te Anau and Milford, by NZR Road Services or by rental car. Closest accommodation is Te Anau, 86 kilometres (53 miles) away. Season runs October through April. Special group tours May/June by arrangement only. Suitable for ages 7 to 70. A reasonable standard of walking fitness required. Tour costs are all inclusive: Adults: $390, children: $260.

Milford Track
(Head of Lake Te Anau – Milford Sound)
Fiordland National Park
Tourist Hotel Corporation
Telephone:
Auckland (09) 773-689
Wellington (04) 729-179
Christchurch (03) 790-718
Telex: NZ 3488

The Milford Track is accepted by people everywhere as 'the finest walk in the world'. Thousands take up this 55-kilometre (34-mile) challenge yearly, braving the sometimes torrential rain, conquering a mountain pass, crossing rivers – thoroughly captivated by the magic of this desolate, awe-inspiring region. See splendid scenery, including towering rock walls, the thundering Sutherland Falls and beautiful bird-filled native bush. The only way to experience this wonder is to walk. Accommodation is provided in rustic but comfortable lodges (with hot showers and delicious farm-style cooking), and walkers are accompanied by experienced, knowledgeable guides on each stage of the trek. This service and track itself are administered and well maintained by the THC. You will require suitable clothing, personal equipment (including camera and film), and adequate fitness levels. Track is open November through March. From $450 adults, $300 children.

SEE ALSO:

Outback Safaris: Te Rehuwai Safaris (Ruatahuna), Danes Back Country (Queenstown).
Cruising: Fiordland Cruises (Te Anau).
Regional:
Northland: Smiths Holiday Camp (Paihia).
Westland: Punga Lodge (Franz Josef), Haast Motor Camp, Lakeside Motels (Lake Paringa), Riverside Motel (Haast).
Otago: Wilderness Shop (Dunedin).
Mt Cook: Omarama Motor Lodge, Omarama Caravan Park, Lake Ohau Lodge.
Southern Lakes: Wanaka Motor Camp.

Solitaire Lodge, Lake Tarawera, Rotorua.
(Courtesy Solitaire Lodge)

A rare combination of luxury, sophistication, seclusion and relaxed informality surrounds guests at exclusive lodges and grand country houses. They cater for the individual wish and whim, organise the activities that interest you and pamper you with superb comfort, food and wines.

Find this leisured holiday style in perfect settings: on a lake shore where bellbirds and tuis sing in the trees by your room; amid acres of smooth lawns and English-style gardens overflowing with flowers; under spreading trees by a swirling river edged with wild broom; on a private island where lawns and trees run down to the lagoon – the 12 metre (40-foot) yacht anchored in the bay is for your exclusive use; in a sprawling sheep station homestead with beach in front and rugged hills behind; in a Victorian mansion set by a remote lake and surrounded by snow-capped mountains.

Log fires blaze in great stone fireplaces on crisp winter evenings; in summer there may be poolside barbecues under shady trees.

Dine on the very best New Zealand fare – sweet fat oysters, baked rainbow trout, smoked marlin, smoked eel, pheasant, wild duck, venison steaks, ribs of sweet baby lamb, rabbit pie, freshly caught crayfish, scallops, blackberry pie, strawberries and thick cream, excellent cheeses.

Enjoy the best New Zealand wines, or those imported from Australia, France and Germany.

Many lodges are furnished with splendid antiques but also provide the important modern comforts. Sleep at night between crisp linen sheets on an antique brass bed – with modern mattress.

Every lodge offers an almost bewildering choice of activities, arranged exclusively for you. One may provide water skiing, windsurfing, line fishing, game fishing, sailing, surfcasting, tramping; another can arrange sailing, trout fishing, tramping, horse riding, golf, tennis, hunting; and yet another might offer hunting, flight-seeing, trout fishing, jet boating, rafting, canoeing, tramping, skiing, climbing and cross-country safaris. Some can offer almost every possible outdoor activity organised just to suit your wishes.

And if you would prefer to do absolutely nothing at all, not even cast a line into the lake or river by your door, there could be no more ideal place to relax in style and tranquility

Some of these are places that international celebrities, visiting royalty and heads of state, film and music stars, choose when they want a holiday away from the public gaze.

Most take very few guests at a time, hence the individual attention, and for those who like or need their privacy protected, this can often be guaranteed.

You can holiday like a prince but not always pay princely prices for this perfection and cossetting.

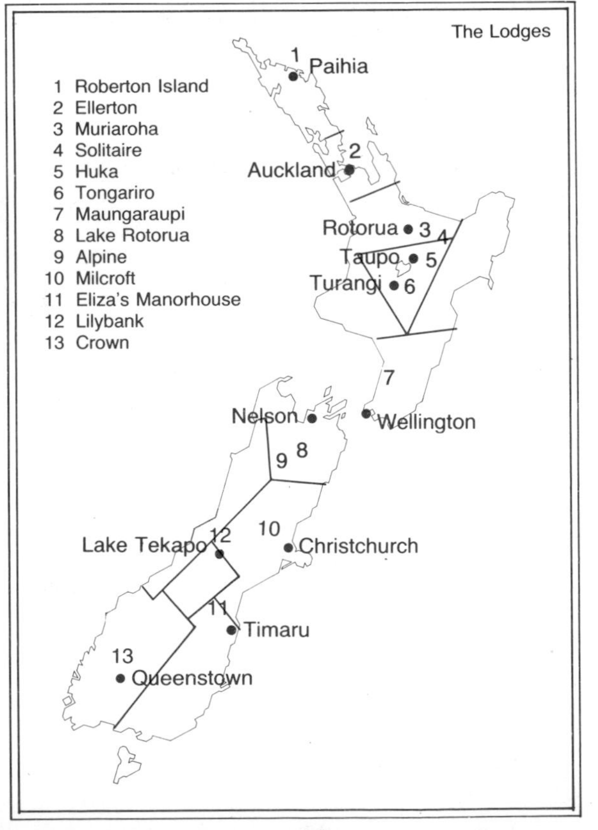

Lodges

Solitude is a sun-drenched, subtropical isle in the Bay of Islands. Have at your disposal a delightful and comfortable house situated between twin lagoons, your own 12-metre (36 foot) sailboat and a motorboat to go fishing in or visit historic Russell just across the Bay. A chef is provided on request. From $115 per night (two days provisions included).

Roberton Island
Bay of Islands
R.H.C. Reservations:
Telephone: (03) 799-126/7
(USA: 800-874-7207)
Telex: NZ 4051 RHCHOT
(USA: 8874486)

Ellerton offers the private luxury of a colonial home. From Devonport, Ellerton looks across the lovely Waitemata Harbour to bustling Auckland – minutes away by ferry. Each suite has an individual balcony overlooking the harbour, large swimming pool, spa pool and barbecue area. The facility caters for small numbers of exclusive house guests who are cared for by your host, John Hoskins. Price Range: From $92 (including cooked breakfast).

Ellerton
Devonport,
Auckland
R.H.C. Reservations:
Telephone: (03) 799-126/7
(USA: 800-874-7207)
Telex: NZ 4051 RHCHOT
(USA: 8874486)

This dream of a house is elegant yet informal. Amenities include hot mineral pools and a steam-heated lake pool and waterfall, bordered with ferns and flowers. The cuisine is New Zealand at its best, including wines. A speciality is the hangi – a traditional Maori feast cooked in an underground oven. Rosalie Ellis, your hostess, is renowned for her hospitality. From $180 (Drinks and meals included).

Muriaroha
Rotorua
R.H.C Reservations:
Telephone: (03) 799-126/7
(USA: 800-874-7207)
Telex: NZ 4051 RHCHOT
(USA: 8874486)

Situated on a half-island overlooking tranquil Lake Tarawera, 'Solitaire' offers recreation at its best. Enjoy delicious meals, go hunting, fishing or just laze around in glorious surrounds. Forests full of birdlife provide great walks. Reg Turner, your entertaining host, arranges all the hunting or trout fishing you want. Do as you please, in your own time – Reg ensures this. From $180 per night (including drinks, meals and fishing equipment).

Solitaire Lodge
Lake Tarawera
Rotorua
R.H.C. Reservations:
Telephone: (03) 799-126/7
(USA: 800-874-7207)
Telex: NZ 4051 RHCHOT
(USA: 8874486)

Huka Lodge is inimitably 'Kiwi'. Exceptional comfort, scenic beauty, outdoor living – as easy or as rugged as you wish. Hunting, fishing, horse riding, tennis, golf, do-as-you-please, go-where-you-will. It also offers fascinating company and great conversations, stimulated by Harland Harland-Baker, a most accomplished host. From $145 per night (including dinner and cooked breakfast).

Huka Lodge
Taupo
R.H.C. Reservations:
Telephone: (03) 799-126/7
(USA: 800-874-7207)
Telex: NZ 4051 RHCHOT
(USA: 8874486)

This retreat is a unique combination of first-class cuisine, relaxing comfort and the widest possible range of activities – not forgetting the Tongariro River, the best fishing water in the country, some say in the world. Tony Hayes and Margaret Coutts are delightful hosts and Tony is a renowned fishing guide. Relax in the evenings around the open fire in the lounge. The bar is first class. From $95 per person, per night, including dinner and cooked breakfast.

Tongariro Lodge
Turangi
R.H.C. Reservations:
Telephone: (03) 799-126/7
(USA: 800-874-7207)
Telex: NZ 4051 RHCHOT
(USA: 8874486)

Stay in this gracious country home on an old farming estate. In the grounds guests may enjoy beautiful bush walks, croquet, tennis, and see farm life. Nearby enjoy trout fishing, deer stalking, white-water rafting, jet boating and golf. After dining on farm-fresh foods, see a filmed history of Maungaraupi or soak in the turret spa pool. Designed by a famous architect, Tilleard Nartusch, the 836 square-metre (9,000 square-feet) home, built from native timbers, offers magnificent suites, each with a different view of the estate. Only limited numbers may enjoy this farming family's hospitality. Fly to Palmerston North where Jim will meet you. From $125 per day. Book direct or through R.H.C. Reservations, telephone (03) 799-127; Telex NZ 4105.

Maungaraupi Historical Country Estate
Leedstown Road
RD1 Marton
Telephone: (0652) 6735
Host: James Anson

Lake Rotoroa Lodge
Nelson Lakes
R.H.C. Reservations:
Telephone: (03) 799-126/7
(USA: 800-874-7207)
Telex: NZ 4051 RHCHOT
(USA: 8874486)

Situated in this unique lakeside setting, Rotoroa Lodge is a nineteenth century fishing and hunting villa, but with all the comforts of the 1980s. Spend days hunting deer, wild boar, chamois, quail; year-round trout fishing in the lake or river. Each day ends pleasantly – the splendidly appointed bar, an excellent game-food dinner and lastly, the supreme comfort of an old-fashioned bedroom. From $98 per night (including dinner and cooked breakfast).

Alpine Lodge
C/- Post Office
St Arnaud
Nelson Lakes
Telephone: (05436) 869
Host: Mr Bill Mitchell

This luxurious new Lodge is unique in the area and is situated in St Arnaud Village on the shores of Lake Rotoiti. Alpine Lodge offers you the New Zealand outback in style and comfort – 20 fully serviced units, conference facilities for 40, a large bar with open fire and superb views of the National Park and a licensed restaurant complete with Australian chef. Bill will organise skiing, trout fishing, hunting, white-water rafting, tramping, mountaineering and farm visits in this beautiful area. Hamper meals supplied on request for day trips. Access is easy – only 35 minutes direct flight from Wellington by Air Albatross charter to an airstrip,eight minutes away; or an hour's drive from Nelson or Blenheim. From $42 single, $52 double. Major credit cards accepted.

'Milcroft'
Temuka
R.H.C. Reservations
Telephone: (03) 799-126/7
(USA: 800-874-7207)
Telex: NZ 4051 RHCHOT
(USA: 8874486)

Relax in this beautiful home with landscaped grounds, spa and swimming pool. Hosts Ken and Elaine, offer privacy and personal attention, first-class cuisine, chauffered transport, de luxe twin/double rooms, child-minding and children's facilities. Enjoy a friendly and comfortable atmosphere – go fishing, skiing, play tennis or golf, view farms, visit the Temuka Pottery or the site where Richard Pearse pioneered powered flight in 1903. From $85 per night (includes everything except travel).

Eliza's Manor House
Christchurch
R.H.C. Reservations
Telephone: (03) 799-126/7
(USA: 800-874-7207)
Telex: NZ4051 RHCHOT
(USA: 887-4486)

A superb stay is assured at this early Christchurch mansion, where Roz and John Smith will look after all your needs. Rooms are appointed for relaxing comfort and include eight bedrooms (mostly ensuite), combining Victorian charm of brass beds with modern comforts. English cooked breakfasts are provided, weekend stays offer Saturday evening dine and dances in sumptuous banquet rooms. Magnificent architecture. From $75 per night,per person(breakfast,dinner,drinks inclusive).

Crown Lodge
Arrowtown
R.H.C. Reservations
Telephone: (03) 799-126/7
(USA: 800-874-7207)
Telex: NZ4051 RHCHOT
(USA: 887-4486)

This romantic lodge nestles amongst forested mountain farmland, overlooking Queenstown valley, and is handy to major ski areas – Coronet Peak, Cardrona (30 minutes) and Treble Cone (90 minutes). Built in 1890, this retreat's original furniture and open fireplaces create an atmosphere both comfortable and intimate. Communal meals feature imaginative regional cooking. Attentive hosts Ean and Frederick organise a variety of activities for you. From $68 per day (bed/breakfast), $100 per day (all inclusive).

Muriaroha Lodge at night, Rotorua. *(Courtesy Kerry Grant Photography)*

Horse-trekking on Mt Cardrona, Wanaka.
(Courtesy Gin & Raspberry Stables)

n outback safari is a multi-adventure holiday, available in many guises, but all safaris have one thing in common – they get you far 'off the beaten track' in a way that no ordinary sightseeing trip can ever do.

You can take outback safaris by the day – and return at night to a soft bed, plenty of hot water and a well-stocked bar in the nearest town.

Or you can spend days on the move through high-country tussock, stony river valleys and thick forest, with nights around the campfire.

There is even a kind of stay-at-home safari tour – you are taken into the wilderness to settle down in luxury lodge, cabin or tent and take advantage of whatever adventure appeals most: tramping, four-wheel-drive excursions, horse treks, deer hunting (with rifle or camera), trout fishing, swimming, rafting or canoeing.

Day-trip safaris are as varied as the country's geography: travel in four-wheel-drive vehicles across giant sand dunes to windswept gumlands where turn-of-the-century settlers eked out a living digging precious kauri gum, see the wrecks of sailing ships half-buried in sand on wild surf beaches, and try surfcasting for snapper.

Cross rugged farmland to idyllic bays or travel over treacherous sands where unusual seabirds congregate.

Take hair-raising rides up mountainsides, even through the desolate ash and debris of a volcano that last exploded only 100 years ago.

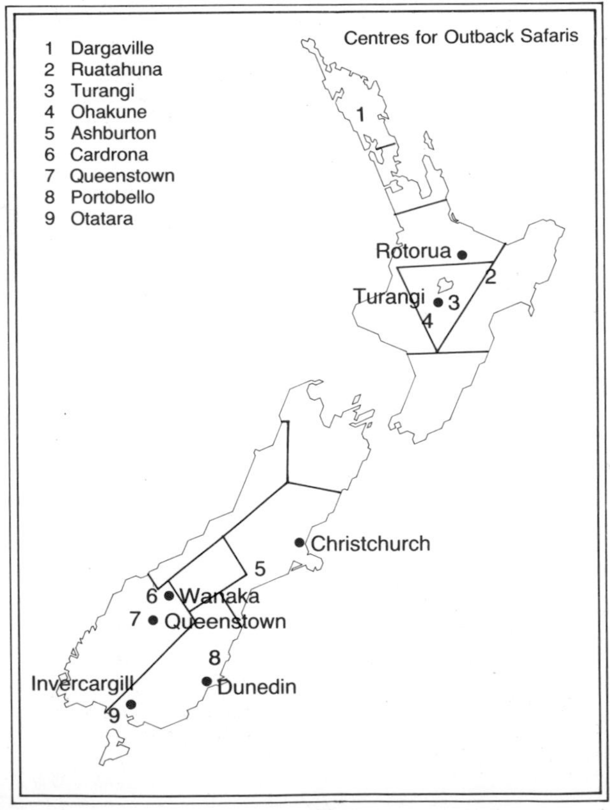

Drive through pine forests, giant kauri forests, dense moss – and fern-filled rain forests or high-country beech forests.

Follow old mining and logging trails into country once accessible only on foot or horseback.

You can do all of these on day safaris or you can extend the excitement into true adventures and spend days in the hills, mountains and forests with time out for hiking, trout fishing, deer hunting, rafting, canoeing or leisurely panning for gold.

For those who don't relish a bumpy journey or sleeping under the stars (even in a tent), there are comparatively sedate outback four-wheel-drive tours, such as a journey through several high-country sheep stations with stops for easy walks and overnight accommodation in hotel comfort.

Set out on a week-long outback safari as the highlight of a New Zealand holiday, or include a safari tour as only one component of an adventure-filled holiday.

Outback safaris

Offers two unique tours: 'South Adventure' – 6-hour four-wheel-drive, coastal tour to historical Pouto Lighthouse, set on wild wasteland. Go swimming, exploring sand dunes. 'North Adventure' – includes Trounson Park, famous Waipoua Kauri Forest, beautiful Kai Iwi Lakes (surrounded by white sand) and 32 kilometres (20 miles) of wild west-coast beach. Champagne and chicken lunch served. Bring swimwear, jacket, walking shoes. From $150 (four persons inclusive).

Kauri Coaster Tours
PO Box 254
Dargaville
Telephone: (0884) 8339
Hosts: Arthur and Shona Keoghan

With members of the Tuhoe tribe as guides, explore the dense subtropical rain forests of the Urewera National Park, a park noted for its variety of native flora and fauna, including kiwi whose calls can be heard at night. These remote mountains have also endured as a historical focus of ancient Maori culture and traditions. The Tuhoe people will show you their forests, their ancestral homes and their way of life. Three-, five- and seven-day safaris offered, from November to Easter. All food, equipment and accommodation provided. You will need warm clothes, water-proof gear and sturdy footwear. A good general level of fitness is required. Public transport to Ruatahuna. From $203, $295, $400 per person for three-, five-, and seven-day treks. Book direct by mail or telephone, through G.T.B. or travel agent.

Te Rehuwai Safaris Ltd
Ruatahuna
Private Bag
Rotorua
Telephone: (073) 65-131
Host: Mrs Biddle

'It is the safest, least expensive, adrenalin-surging natural "high" that you have ever experienced.' Thus Iain describes the service his company offers, specialising in half-day, one-, two-, four- and ten-day horse riding and rafting trips. Take your choice of a selection of graded rides on North Island rivers, from the exhilaration of grade 5 to more sedate and leisurely scenic adventures. Most trips encompass New Zealand wilderness in its pristine state, rivalling the most beautiful elsewhere in the world, and often uninhabited. For additional adventure, both hunting and fishing safaris are offered. Hunting safaris are designed for the serious trophy hunter, with a trophy animal guaranteed from among any of these species: red, fallow, sika and rusa deer, goats, Persian sheep and wild boar.

Fishing safaris are combined with rafting trips, getting the fisherman to otherwise inaccessible stretches of river – full of rainbow trout. You will be in expert hands – all company personnel are trained to New Zealand Rafting Association standards, hold first aid certificates and are superb bushmen. Tours leave from Rotorua. Safety equipment and all other equipment is supplied – all you'll need is a change of clothes, sand shoes, a sleeping bag and your camera. The season runs from September through May. Age restriction is a minimum of 13 years of age and a reasonable standard of fitness is essential. Cost: Rafting and wilderness adventures – $40 to $1,000, depending on your requirements; hunting and fishing trips by contract with the company. Advance bookings are essential. Make enquiries and bookings direct by telephone, mail or telegraph or contact the Government Tourist Bureau. Member of the New Zealand Professional Rafting Association.

Rough Rider Rafting Company
PO Box 2392
Rotorua
Telephone: 80-233
Telegraphs: ROUGHIT
Director: Iain Batchelar

A personalised service where the emphasis is on having fun. Trained horses suit novice and rider alike. Experience exhilarating rides through bush, or quiet river trails. Day rides with barbecues and summer moonlit-night adventures. A gig ensures that everyone can join in. You need only shoes and sturdy jeans – all else is provided. From $12 to $50 per person. Transport provided.

Turangi Trail Rides
28 Raukura Street
Turangi
Telephone: (0746) 8321
Hosts: Margaret and Lawrence McArthur

Ruapehu Outback Adventures
PO Box 51
Ohakune
Telephone: (0658) 58-799 or 58-733 (after hours)
Hosts: Don & Sue Allomes

An action-packed introduction to outback New Zealand, for all ages. From Ohakune, discover this wonderful wilderness and all the excitement it has to offer, on half or one-day tours. Take a breath-taking four-wheel-drive safari among the three famous volcanoes, Ngauruhoe, Tongariro and Ruapehu, the National Park, through scenery so spectacular it has been the filming location for several New Zealand feature films, and enjoy 'billy' tea and a barbecue. For further adventure, ride a jet boat, transfer to a helicopter into the far reaches of the Wanganui River, and then raft down! (Suitable for ages 11 to 100). Other adventures include white-water rafting on wild mountain rivers, horse trekking, flight-seeing and canoeing. Accommodation at the Ruapehu Homestead and all equipment provided. Warm clothing essential in winter. From $20 to $200.

Four Seasons Scenic Tours
PO Box 333
Ashburton
Telephone: (053) 4497 or 5404
Hosts: Dave and Grant Bisset

These enthusiasts specialise in showing you the variety of terrain and activities within the central South Island with emphasis on your personal interests. Whether it be rock or spider collecting, bird watching, gliding or fishing, day tours are designed for your enjoyment. Interested in farming techniques? There's a huge variety from intensive dairying to back country. Or go shooting Canada Geese and Paradise Ducks. See remote and splendid scenery (access pre-arranged with property owners) in well-equipped, heavy-duty vehicles, picnic lunches provided. Many activities are seasonal or weather related and cannot always be assured. Get ready to discover this magnificent region. Bring warm clothes, sturdy footwear and your camera. Costs: between $200 and $300 (for four), depending on requirements. Enquiries and bookings direct, or to Bryant Motor Lodge, telephone: (053) 89-595.

Outback safaris

Danes Back Country
PO Box 230
Queenstown
Telephone: 1144/789
Telex: NZ5678
Owners: Messrs Dale Gardiner and John McCormack

Since 1970 this company has been sharing the back country experience with travellers. Based around the beautiful rivers and valleys of the Southern Lakes region, these qualified professionals offer a variety of adventure trips. Experience with them this unspoiled wilderness by hiking, graded rafting, flying and four-wheel-drive, with time built in for relaxing, gold panning, fishing and exploring. Thrill to the matchless excitement of white-water rafting on the historic Shotover, an 80-kilometre (50-mile) long river fed by snow and ice melt, which drops over 152 metres (500 feet) through the country's largest canyon. Once home to thousands of gold miners, the river is now rated as the second richest gold-producing river in the world. The Lower Skippers Canyon is an exhilarating grade 5 trip of five hours, the Upper Canyon (grade 3), some 8 hours long, after flying in to the upper reaches.

Other trips include two-, three- and five-day extravaganzas on the Shotover, Landsborough and other rivers, reached only by plane and helicopter and camping out under the stars. Schools in rafting and kayaking available. For a land adventure, take a half-day trip through the famous Skippers Canyon. Gold prospectors arrived here in 1862 and the canyon road follows the old miners' wagon track along the river, through sheer drops and stunning scenery. Take time to pan for gold and have your camera ready! Rafting season – October to April, sightseeing – all year. Trips accompanied by professional guides. All safety equipment supplied. Other, such as tents, etc., available for hire. You will require warm clothing and sand shoes. From $30 to $350.

Getting away from it all: camping on a rugged shore, West Coast, South Island. *(Andris Apse Ltd)*

Gin and Raspberry Stables
(Highway 89)
Cardrona RD1
Wanaka
Telephone: Wanaka 8152
Hosts: Martin and Kay Curtis

Half-day horse treks on Mount Cardrona or treks of one to four nights on pack trails through open tussock country of Pisa Range; staying in musterers' huts (elevation 1,500 metres)! Enjoy gold panning, swimming, spectacular alpine scenery. Suitable for confident beginners, minimum age 10 years. Wear sturdy trousers/footwear (bring sleeping bag and overnight gear). Only half-day treks operate Christmas through January. Courtesy transport from Wanaka. From $16 (half-day), $55 per day (overnights).

Moonlight Stables
PO Box 144
Queenstown
Telephone: Queenstown 818M/838R
Hosts: Mr and Mrs McLeod

Enjoy the rugged grandeur of the Wakatipu region from horseback, riding along old gold miners' trails high above the Shotover Gorge. Service operates half-day and full-day tours, departing 6 kilometres (4 miles) from Queenstown (courtesy transport from Queenstown provided). Everything is supplied. Wear sturdy trousers and footwear, bring a warm jacket and camera. Closed June and July. Previous riding experience unnecessary, minimum age 10 years. From $20 (half-day) and $45 (full day).

Hillandale Rides
RD1
Dalefield
Queenstown
Telephone: Queenstown 823M
Host: Glenys Young

This service operates for experienced horse riders over 12 years old. Escorted three-hour rides through lovely countryside with spectacular mountain views. Groups are small and friendly, with opportunities to trot and canter. Horses matched to rider's ability where possible. Courtesy transport provided from Queenstown. You require sturdy jeans and footwear; hard hats are available. Cost: $25 inclusive. Book at Mount Cook Travel (telephone: Queenstown 592), or direct. May be closed July to August, so check first.

Hereweka Pony Treks
674 Highcliff Road
Portobello
Dunedin
Telephone: (024) 780-884
Hosts: Sandra and Victor Carlson

People of all ages have experienced the thrill of pony trekking around the deserted harbour inlets and bays of the beautiful Otago Peninsula. Seabirds, penguins, sea lions and seals can often be sighted along the sands of the ocean surf beach. Historic Maori sites and settlements are visited, and the rides provide a close look at life on a New Zealand sheep farm. Horses available to suit every rider and well-trained staff take the greatest care of the beginner, while offering as much excitement as the experienced rider desires. No experience necessary and everything supplied (wear sturdy jeans and flat shoes). Service is closed June and July. Public transport operates from Dunedin to Portobello, Monday to Saturday. Costs: 1 hour, $10 per mount; half-day $20; full day (6 hours and lunch), $35. Note: full-day ride requires minimum of four persons.

Otatara Riding Centre
Oreti Road
Otatara, Invercargill
Telephone: (021) 33-127 or 57-305
Owner: Mr Irwin Black

Just minutes from Invercargill, experience the beauty of this area with trail rides beside rivers, through ocean surf, farmlands and bush. Horse and pony hire available, as is tuition. Previous experience is unnecessary as beginners are supervised. Operates all year round with evening riding offered from November through February. You will require jeans or trousers and footwear. From $8 (adults) per hour, $7 (children). Tuition additional.

SEE ALSO:

Water Adv: Silverpeaks Tours (Dunedin).
Regional: Otago: Wilderness Shop (Dunedin).

Whitewater rafting.
(Courtesy Ruapehu
Outback Adventures)

Sports calendar

OCTOBER

Spring weather throughout New Zealand. Opening of fishing season in most lakes, streams and rivers. The last runs of fresh spawning fish in the Tongariro River. Harling beginning on Lake Taupo, particularly early morning and evening. Deer are dropping their antlers.

NOVEMBER

The start of summer weather, but often windy. Some good dry-fly hatches, particularly in the South Island waters. Smelting starting in all lakes. Excellent wet-fly fishing and harling on Lake Taupo.

DECEMBER

One of the least crowded months to fish New Zealand waters up until Christmas day. Very good fishing throughout the day on all lakes, streams and rivers. Excellent dry-fly and nymph fishing throughout the country, particularly in mountain streams accessible only by aircraft.

JANUARY

The busiest month of the year with most of the country on holiday. Stream fishing limited to nymphs in many instances, however some good wet-fly fishing beginning at stream mouths. Excellent harling both morning and evening on Lake Taupo, but often deep trolling during the day. Start of the big-game fishing season.

FEBRUARY

Usually the hottest month of the year. Weather very settled for fishing in mountain streams. Fly fishing around the stream mouths is very good, both during the day and at night. Still very good harling on Lake Taupo. Start of the salmon runs in South Island rivers. Deer coming out of velvet.

MARCH

Weather still warm and settled. The last month of good fishing in mountain streams. Good salmon fishing and dry-fly fishing in the South Island. Excellent wet-fly fishing around stream mouths at Lake Taupo, however the good harling is almost over. One of the best months for big-game fishing. The start of the deer-hunting season.

APRIL

Leaves beginning to show signs of autumn. Last month of fishing season in some districts, the first runs of fresh spawning trout in the Tongariro River. The best time for wet-fly fishing around mouths of streams flowing into Lake Taupo. The deer are mating and so the best time for hunting.

MAY

This is the time for catching trophy trout, particularly at Lake Tarawera. Big runs of spawning fish in Taupo rivers. Good stream-mouth fishing in both northern and southern lakes, although deep trolling is now required for boat fishing. The last month to catch that marlin or shoot a deer. The opening of duck season and upland game.

JUNE

The real start of winter. Last month of fishing season in most districts. Excellent fly fishing on the Tongariro River and deep trolling on Lake Taupo.

JULY

For the hardy angler, the Tongariro River offers some of the best fly fishing of the year. Deep trolling on Lake Taupo still very good. Start of the snow-skiing season on most fields.

AUGUST

Often the quietest month of the year for fishing, but most days are cold and clear. Tongariro River fishing well but deep trolling on Taupo is inconsistent. Best month for snow skiing in both islands.

SEPTEMBER

First signs of spring with New Zealand at its greenest. Lots of new lambs and calves. Taupo fishing improving again and opening of fishing season in south Westland and Fiordland for sea-run trout.

It can be done

A remarkable aspect of fishing and hunting in New Zealand is that in the period of just a few hours it is possible to catch a big-game fish, catch a trout and shoot a deer. Patience, persistence and precise planning paid off for Johnnie Boyle on 13 January 1979. After hooking a striped marlin at 10.10 a.m., he landed the 120-kilogram (262-pound) big-game fish at 10.30 a.m. Arriving at Lake Taupo by float-plane alongside Simon Dickie's vessel *Awatea* at 12.30 p.m., it took less than five minutes to hook a trout and by 12.40 p.m. Johnnie was away by helicopter for the third trophy of the 'Big 3'. The deer was shot at 1.25 p.m., giving a total time of 3 hours 15 minutes for all three trophies – a new world record.

(Courtesy Simon Dickie and Miles Johnson, South Pacific Sporting Adventures – see FISHING section.)

Bull thar.
(Gordon Roberts)

Red deer in forest interior, Henry River, North Canterbury. *(Gordon Roberts)*

Unlike many countries, New Zealand offers continuous access to game animals – no closed seasons and no limit on numbers.

here can be many reasons for hunting: the desire to challenge a wild animal in its natural habitat, the delight of walking the hills and forests, the escape from crowds and pollution, the collection of a top trophy, the relaxation and the excitement. Hunting can represent many things. All of them can be found in the New Zealand hills.

Because wild deer, chamois, thar, wild goats and wild pigs are classed officially as vermin, rather than revered species, they are yours for the hunting.

If the aim and object of your hunting is to gather a top trophy, you can decide on a guaranteed hunt. Large areas of forest and mountain country have been fenced in as special game areas and stocked with first-class animals for overseas hunters determined to collect a world-class trophy. Accommodation is often provided in luxury lodges in these hunting areas, which are true wilderness although enclosed. A 'guaranteed hunt' means just that, you get what you want. If you want an absolutely first-rate chamois, that is what you will get.

Alternatively, take the pioneering route and rough it in forest huts.

But for the hunter who enjoys the recreation as much as the kill, there are still enough red deer left in the wilds. You just can't be certain that you will emerge from the bush with a magnificent seven-point stag.

Red deer are the most prolific, most widely hunted game animal in either island, having adapted more than happily to the range of climates and vegetation. It was the damage done to young forest plants by browsing deer that led to their blacklisting as pests – the New Zealand native forests did not evolve to cope with foraging creatures and concern for the environment led to the official classification of deer as pests.

Of the other species, fallow deer is the most common. Sambur, sika and rusa are concentrated in the central North Island, wapiti in the South Island and Virginian in Otago and Stewart Island.

Chamois, from the European alps, and thar, from the Himalayas, are both highly prized hunting animals in their native lands and both adapted readily to a new environment in New Zealand. Released in the Mt Cook region early this century to provide game sport, they increased in numbers and did enough high-country damage to join the list of pests.

Chamois are now found throughout the alpine country in the South Island, and thar generally between Arthur's Pass and Lake Wanaka. Hunting either of these mountain-roaming creatures requires more than a good eye with a gun – an ability just short of mountaineering helps.

Wild goats and wild pigs are, strictly speaking, feral animals. Both were first released into the New Zealand bush by Captain Cook in 1773, with their numbers subsequently boosted by the escape of domestic animals brought by pioneer settlers. As game animals goats are not held in great esteem – they are, perhaps, too easily hunted. But the wild pig is another story. Although descended from domestic pigs, the New Zealand feral pig has more in common – in size, temperament, appearance and taste – with the true wild boar than it has with any farm-bred porker.

Wild pigs are found throughout North Island high country with the Coromandel, Urewera and Tararua ranges favourite hunting areas.

Local information centres and forest park rangers can advise

visitors on the best game hunting in their areas and in restricted places such as recreational reserves. Although hunting licences are not needed, permits are often required for particular areas and all guns must be licensed. Permission should always be sought for hunting on private land.

Hunting guides take care of the necessary formalities and provide equipment, accommodation, food and transport, most commonly four-wheel-drive vehicles but also helicopter, light plane, jet boat, horseback, raft or canoe. A hunting holiday needn't be all hunting – a combination of 'huntin' and fishin', whether trout, salmon or sea fishing, can easily be organised for an all-round holiday.

Feathered game is hunted under a different set of rules – the seasons for shooting waterfowl and upland game birds vary with different districts but are usually around late autumn and early winter, April to June. Limit bags and licences apply. (Licenses are available from sporting shops for a few dollars.)

In the marshy wetlands, rivers and lakes there are wild ducks, mainly mallards, black swan, Canadian geese (protected in the North Island) and pukeko (a blue swamp bird). Away from the water are pheasant and Californian quail and, in the South Island high country, chuckor (Indian partridge).

Hunting and shooting New Zealand style are not exclusive pastimes of the rich – here the weekend hunter is as likely to be a bus driver as a businessman – and the sports can be as expensive and as organised or as casual as you wish. You can relax at the end of the day in the comforts of hotel or lodge, or return to the simple, spartan base of a Forest Service hut, free of charge.

Bull thar, Murchison Valley, Fiordland. ***(Gordon Roberts)***

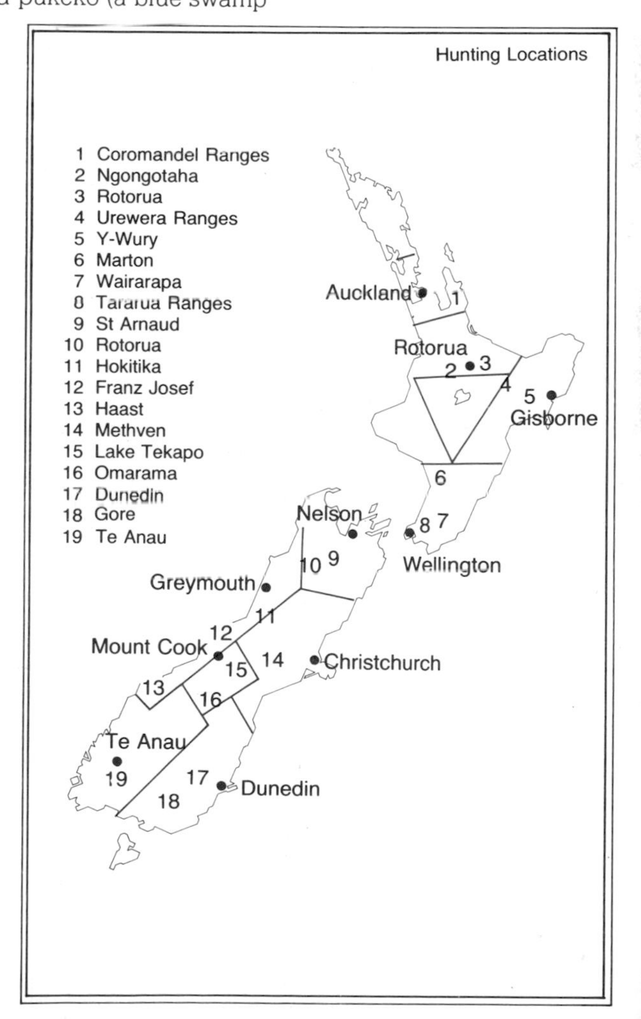

SEE ALSO:

Outback Safaris: Rough Rider Rafting Co. (Rotorua).
Lodges: Alpine (St Arnaud), Lake Rotorua, Huka (Taupo), Maungaraupi (Marton), Solitaire (Rotorua).
Live with NZ: Y-Wury (Gisborne), Wharekauhau (Wellington).
Water Adv: Silverpeaks Tours (Dunedin).
Cruising: Fiordland Cruises (Te Anau).
Regional:
Westland: Punga Lodge (Franz Josef), Erewhon Motel (Haast). Mt Cook: Stage Coach Inn (Omarama).

Tarawera Deerland
RD 2, Ngongotaha
Rotorua
Telephone: (07323) 457
Hosts: Harry and Colleen Bimler

For the serious trophy-hunting deerstalker, this experience is not to be missed. Personally guided day hunts cover 240 hectares (600 acres) of natural wilderness high in the Mamaku Ranges. A head is guaranteed. Varieties include sika, fallow, rusa and red stags, big-horned feral goats and Persian rams. All equipment is supplied if necessary, but your own rifle is preferred. Trophy season is February to August. Harry is considered to be an authority on deer and hunting in New Zealand and offers a first-rate service – a specialised adventure that will return wonderful memories, photographs, venison and antlers/horns. Deposit of 25% confirms booking. Trophy deer heads: $2,000 each, other animals: $500 each. Closest town and accommodation is Rotorua, ten miles (16 kilometres) away. Harry will collect you from town or airport or you can drive by rental car.

Mount Hutt Country Club
Hunting Safaris
PO Box 55
Methven
Telephone: (053) 28-271
Telex: NZ 4997
Host: Stephen Cohen

Outstanding big-game hunting for red stag, Himalayan thar, chamois, wapiti, fallow deer, whitetail and sika deer is all within an easy drive of your accommodation base at the luxurious country club. Success is guaranteed. You require outdoor clothing and footwear, all other requirements provided, including guide. Non-hunting companions welcome. From $510 per day, depending on requirements.

Westland Guiding Service
PO Box 261
Hokitika
Telephone: Hokitika 1557M
Host: Stan Peterson

Go big-game hunting and fishing through beautiful and remote Westland, a sportsman's paradise. Hunt chamois, thar and red stag; special arrangements made to include sika, white tail, fallow and rusa deer. Freshwater fishing for brown and rainbow trout,salmon and perch.Saltwater fishing on request. Big game hunting safaris from $1,600. Fishing $120 (half-day).

Lilybank Safari Lodge
PO Box 60
Lake Tekapo
Telephone: (05056) 522
Owner: Susan and Gary Joll

This is New Zealand's only government-licensed hunting lodge, with a service equal to the best of international standards, world-renowned for consistently producing superb trophies (no trophy, no pay). Gary provides a personal service that is uniquely New Zealand, with 20 years experience in conducting guided hunts for thar, chamois, red stag and fallow buck. Hunts are on foot and horseback, returning to the lodge each evening. Accommodation features private guest rooms, each with own bathroom, central heating and facilities, plus beautiful dining room and restful trophy lounge. Ideal for non-hunting wives. Susan serves delicious New Zealand fare, featuring game, local wines and cheeses. Close to Mount Cook, in the central Southern Alps. Cost: Per trophy only.

New Zealand Trophy Safaris
12 Kerwood Place
Gore
Telephone: (020) 5033
Hosts: Stuart Rees and Alan Stewart

Within this wilderness preserve, are an abundance of quality red deer trophy stags, and trophy success is guaranteed. Season: March through August, April being favoured. While hunting, stay in your guide's home, wilderness cabin or tent camp. Fair-chase hunts are offered for red and fallow deer, whitetail, wapiti and goats, if arranged in advance (no guarantee of success). Non-hunting companions welcome, and a video of your safari will be provided, if desired. Duck shooting available during May, and trout fishing on the famous Mataura River, October through April. Courtesy transport available from Invercargill or Dunedin Airports, point of outfitting or pre-arranged location. Accommodation, food and transport from point of outfitting is provided. Additional charges: liquor, hotel accommodation, crating/handling of trophies or further mileage at a client's request.
From $300 per day plus trophy fees.

Fishing

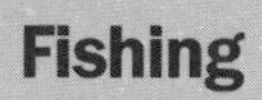

Fly-fishing near Ashburton, Canterbury. *(Bob Girvan)*

Fishing in New Zealand can be many different things – sitting in the sun on a rock, wading into an icy glacier-fed river, cruising through an ocean swell surrounded by diving gannets – and each of them will be first rate.

or over 50 years fishing enthusiasts 'in the know' have been travelling to New Zealand for the single purpose of catching fish. They know that New Zealand is the world's finest fishing mecca, and they would be hard pressed to find another place to compare with it.

All types of fishing – deep-sea angling, line fishing, surf casting, trout fishing – are superb, easily accessible, comparatively inexpensive and found amid scenery that ranges from enchanting to awesome.

The visiting enthusiast is never at a loss for local advice – he may find it given free across the counter of a local sports shop or over a beer in a country pub, or he may choose to pay for it in the form of an experienced guide. But he or she will never have difficulty finding out all about tackle, times and fishing spots.

The big-game fish of the Bay of Islands and the rainbow trout of Taupo are well known world-wide. But the excitement of hauling in a 300-kilogram (660-pound) blue marlin in the Bay of Islands or a 4-kilogram (9-pound) rainbow trout at Taupo is only part of the New Zealand fishing story, albeit an important part. What is less well known is that you can fish your way from one end of the country to the other, one way or another.

There is a Sydney businessman who recounts with delight the best, most relaxing fishing holiday he has ever enjoyed – line fishing from a small boat. It went like this: by air from Sydney to Auckland, taxi to the harbour, sea plane to an island bay. Just over four hours out from Sydney and he and his friends had the beach and its cottage to themselves. For a week they lolled about fishing for snapper and then repeated the simple journey in reverse, back to Sydney.

There is an American angler from Maryland who visits New Zealand every year, staying up to two months at a time. He makes his base at Wanaka, a South Island lake heavily stocked with brown trout, but also offering the chance of rainbow trout and land-locked quinnat salmon. Unlike many visitors, he knows about the excellent South Island fishing – 47 lakes all stocked with trout, most of them easily reached and fished by any visitor, and all the adjacent rivers and streams as well.

167kg (367lb) striped marlin caught in the Duke of Marlborough billfish tournament, Bay of Islands, by Neil Campbell. ***(Courtesy Fast Photos, Paihia)***

Big-game fishing

For thrill-of-a-lifetime fishing that needs no prior expertise, take to the sea with big-game fishing – even if you've never caught so much as a sprat, you've got every chance of landing a monster marlin. Game fleet skippers in the Bay of Islands, the acknowledged centre of deep-sea fishing, estimate that 80 per cent of people setting out in their boats have never been fishing before.

You can charter a game-fishing boat by the day, half-day, overnight or longer. If a boat all to yourself is too expensive – although economical by world standards – a share charter system spreads the cost among several people. This brings a day's fishing within the reach of anyone, with time in the game chairs organised by the skipper so that everyone gets the chance of a big strike.

The game fish most likely to take the bait are striped marlin, blue marlin and black marlin, as well as several varieties of shark, broadbill swordfish, blue-fin and yellow-fin tuna and yellowtail kingfish.

The North Island's east coast is studded with game-fishing ports. Paihia and Russell are the best-known departure points,

opening the way to the Bay of Islands, considered by experts to be the best striped-marlin fishing ground in the world. The Bay of Islands boasts an impressive number of records for several species of big-game fish – 18 world records and 48 national records at last count.

But there are many other places. Among them are: Whangaroa, a village on one of the world's deepest natural harbours that must also be one of the most beautiful and unspoilt; Tutukaka with excellent rock fishing, line fishing and diving as well as deep-sea fishing; Whitianga on the rugged Coromandel Peninsula; Tauranga and Mount Maunganui for the waters around Mayor Island; Whakatane for White Island.

Game fishing in the South Island centres on the deeply indented Marlborough Sounds, with boats leaving from Picton.

Join the local game-fishing club for a nominal visitor's fee of a few dollars and enjoy the facilities that will certainly include a convivial bar as well as practical assistance with your weighty catch.

Whether you want to have your large fish smoked for eating, mounted or follow the increasing trend to have it tagged and returned to the deep is your choice. Whatever you actually do with the fish, the heady success of landing a big-game fish will remain an incomparable memory.

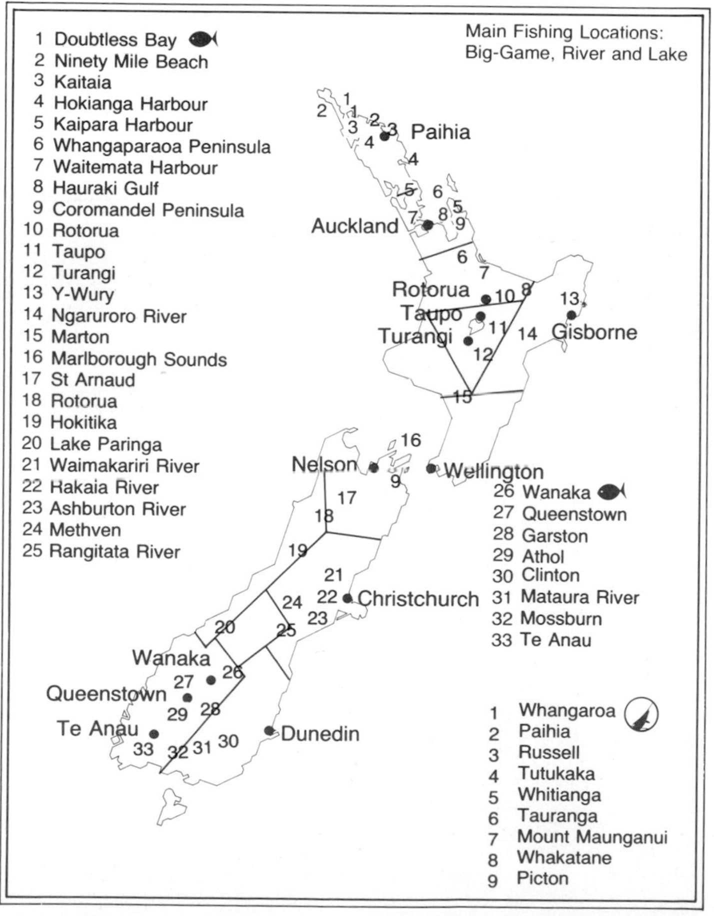

Trout and salmon fishing

Trout fishing, Lake Rotorua. ***(Courtesy Brian Colman)***

The clear lakes and fast-flowing rivers of New Zealand proved a perfect environment for the brown trout and rainbow trout introduced at the end of the nineteenth century from Britain and California. Here they grow to a size and condition uncommon elsewhere, with little competition for food and vast, unpolluted waters in which to roam.

There are no private fishing waters in New Zealand and so no exclusion from the best stretches of stream or river, nor payment of expensive fishing rights.

The country is divided into 26 fishing districts, each with its own regulations and seasons. Taupo and Rotorua offer year-round fishing, but most other districts open from the beginning of October to the end of April, with local variations. In the Southern Lakes district, for example, river fishing runs to the end of May, fishing in Lakes Wanaka and Hawea until the end of July.

Licences are cheap, a few dollars, and there are special licences for overseas visitors on a fishing tour – you don't need a new licence for each new fishing district.

Trout fishing in either island can be as gentle or as exciting as you wish, although it is always exciting at that moment when the fish strikes.

You can seek out trout by trolling, spinning, dry- or wet-fly fishing. Whether you have spent a lifetime angling or have never seen a trout, guides will organise the best fishing for your abilities – they provide expert local knowledge, tackle, gear and transport.

You can base yourself in a luxury fishing lodge with all the attendant comforts, or more economically in a country hotel or motel.

Fishing for brown trout, Waikaia River, near Gore, Southland. ***(Arthur Bremford)***

Fishing

Enjoy the rural charm of fishing the nearest lake, river or meandering stream, day after day; or take off on a trout- and salmon-fishing excursion through the country (in the South Island, one holiday provides campervan and suggested itinerary). En route, delight in a variety of waters and the full range of New Zealand scenery from mountains to meadowlands, tussock moors, beech forest and subtropical rainforest. You could make trout fishing a casual interlude, a leisurely afternoon's break in a busy schedule.

The pleasure of trout fishing in tranquil surroundings can be combined with the thrills of high adventure: take off by air in helicopter or sea plane to remote back-country areas, skim up-river by jet boat or down-river by raft or canoe, or set off on horseback.

If time is tight and you plan to catch a rainbow trout, shoot a deer and land a marlin with only a couple of days to spare, there are sophisticated operations that will see that you do it all.

Those interested in salmon fishing must concentrate on the South Island, where land-locked salmon are found in lakes and streams, and sea-run salmon converge on river mouths such as the Waimakariri, Rakaia and Rangitata in Canterbury during the November to April season.

Diseases in New Zealand's fisheries and water fowl are relatively unknown. All trout fly-tying material – loose feathers and feathers attached to skin – and used fishing tackle – rods, lines, reels, nets, waders – **must be fumigated by Ministry of Agriculture & Fisheries' inspectors at the port of entry.** Please help keep New Zealand disease free.

Boat, line and surf fishing

Boat fishing needn't be deep sea, of course. The relaxing pastime of line fishing from boats happens wherever a boat can be launched, and there are plenty of places that qualify. Even the treacherous, wild, west coast has long, wide harbours with excellent small-boat fishing – top spots for such fishing on this coast are off the usual tourist routes, places where time seems to stand still in tiny harbour-side settlements such as those on the immense Kaipara Harbour, with its 3,000-kilometre (1,800-mile) coastline, or the long Hokianga Harbour fringed with mangroves.

Line fish from boats in sheltered bays and harbours, particularly in Doubtless Bay (also excellent deep-sea fishing), the Bay of Islands, Whangaroa Harbour, around the Whangaparaoa Peninsula, on the Waitemata Harbour, around the islands of the Hauraki Gulf, both sides of the Coromandel Peninsula, the Marlborough Sounds.

Expect to catch fish such as snapper, yellowtail kingfish, kahawai (Australian sea trout), trevally, hapuku (groper), tarakahi (Australian morwong), blue cod, gurnard, barracouta.

Visit sweeping open beaches on either coast at any time of the year and you will find surf casters in action. Using strong rods and fishing from rocky promontories or wading deep into the surf to cast long lines, surf casters seek the excitement of hooking a fighting fish such as yellowtail kingfish, snapper or kahawai.

You will find surf casters from one end of the country to the other – local sports shops in popular surf-casting areas can supply equipment and many have a rental service.

For surf casters, the Ninety-Mile Beach Surf casting Snapper Competition offers five days of fishing and the promise of prizes – $1,000 for the heaviest fish caught each day and $15,000 to the overall winner (26 February to 2 March 1985 and annually) information from PO Box 71, Kaitaia).

SEE ALSO:

Lodges: Tongariro (Turangi), Huka (Taupo), Alpine (St Arnaud), Maungaraupi (Marton), Solitaire (Rotorua), Lake Rotorua.
Live with NZ: Riverview (Athol), Birch Hill (Garston), Y-Wury Station (Gisborne), Kai Iwi Lakes Farm Stays.
Hunting: Westland Guiding Service (Hokitika).
Outback Safaris: Danes Back Country (Queenstown), Rough Rider Rafting Co (Rotorua).
Diving: Paihia Dive Hire & Charter.
Water Adv: Marine Enterprises (Queenstown), Silverpeaks Tour (Dunedin).
Cruising: Fiordland Cruises (Te Anau).
Regional:
Otago: Southern Air (Invercargill).
Westland: Punga Lodge (Franz Josef).

Further Reading:
New Zealand Trout Fishermans Guide: *Rivers and Lakes of the South Island, Rivers and Lakes of the North Island.* George Ferris, Heinemann (NZ) Ltd.
For an introduction to fishing, especially sea fishing, *How to Catch Fish and Where.* Bill Hohepa, Rugby Press. Excellent maps and description of fish.

Bryan Colman Trout Fishing
32 Kiwi Street
Rotorua
Telephone: 87-766
Host: Bryan Colman

A professional fishing guide, Bryan offers trolling and fly-fishing in lakes and rivers, year around. Fish from Bryan's boats in all weather or order a helicopter for remote stream fishing. Everything is supplied – from polaroid photographs, licences and refreshments to selected trout, canned for export. Tackle and transport is provided free of charge. Costs range from $44.00 to $1,100.00 dependant on requirements.

Fishing

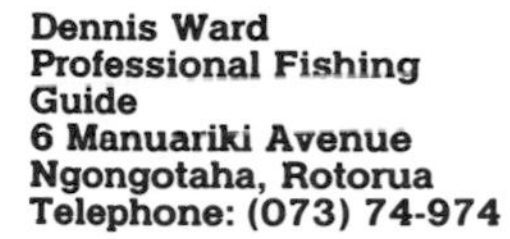

Picture yourself beside a clear and beautiful river – relaxing in peace over a delicious lunch and a bottle of good wine, having just fought and caught the biggest trout you have ever seen, laughing with new friends over old fish stories. A member of the NZ Professional Fishing Guides Association, Dennis specialises in dry-fly, nymph and wet-fly fishing, offering tuition to 'first-timers'. Within one hour's drive you can be at any of a wide range of streams or rivers – all providing excellent fishing the whole year round. Whether you require helicopters for a full safari, or simply to experience the thrill of catching trout during a few spare hours, you will thoroughly enjoy this friendly, personal service. Everything is provided. From $30 to $50 per hour depending on requirements.

Dennis Ward
Professional Fishing Guide
6 Manuariki Avenue
Ngongotaha, Rotorua
Telephone: (073) 74-974

This company is a safari-organising agency controlled and operated by sportsmen, offering a unique travel experience for those who are interested in fishing and hunting tours within New Zealand. This is the largest trout-fishing outfitting and guiding organisation in the region, with a justified reputation for excellence of service. The facilities and services have been developed with a distinctive style, suited not only to the experienced sportsman, but to individuals and groups who just want to get away from it all in one of the world's most enviable holiday environments. Each of the guides is a professional, offering fly- and spin-fishing tours throughout the Taupo region. All your requirements are catered for – from hiring small row boats for a few hours to chartering cruisers for several days, living aboard in comfort, with luxuries such as a full-sized bath and small indoor fireplace. From brief fly-fishing trips on local waters to spectacular helicopter safaris for trophy trout. Everything is provided – latest tackle, complete food and beverage service (including liquor), all hunting and fishing licences. From $20 an hour depending on requirements.

(See SPORTING CALENDAR and BIG THREE record.)

South Pacific Sporting Adventures Ltd
PO Box 682, Taupo
Telephone: (074) 89-680
Hosts: Simon Dickie and Miles Johnston

This first-class guided trout and salmon fishing service will delight novice and experienced fishermen alike. Using jet boats, fish the best spots on the Rakaia River or nearby lakes and streams. Stay at the luxurious Mount Hutt Country Club, enjoy your catch for dinner, or have it smoked, frozen or mounted. Hire car service provided from Christchurch airport. From $75 half-day, depending upon requirements.

Mount Hutt Country Club
Salmon and Trout Safaris
PO Box 55
Methven
Telephone: (053) 28-721
Telex: NZ4997
Host: Stephen Cohen

Guided salmon- and trout-fishing trips – using four-wheel-drive vehicles and jet boats to reach superb fishing spots, often unknown and usually inaccessible by car. Every need is catered for – from waders to wine, licences to photographs. Ian will organise night trips, special short trips to suit tight schedules, part-day trips, etc. Visit remote mountain lakes for brown, rainbow and brook trout, jet the many quinnat salmon rivers, some of which flow 100 kilometres (60-70 miles) from the alps to the sea. Enjoy your catch served for dinner or mounted by a leading taxidermist and sent home. Nearest accommodation is Ashburton. Service operates 1 October through 31 May. Suitable for all ages. Book by writing, telephone, travel agent or Government Tourist Bureau. From $200 per day, per person, depending upon requirements. 50% discount for groups of four or more, credit cards accepted.

'Fair Play' Fishing Safaris
256 Moore Street
Ashburton
Telephone: (053) 5478/ 83-181
Host: Ian Wills

Paul Miller Trout Fishing Guide
Wanaka Lake Services (Lakefront)
PO Box 20
Wanaka
Telephone: Wanaka 7495

Experience superb trout fishing in the Wanaka region – a delight for fly fishermen, spinners and trollers. Paul is Wanaka's longest-established, full-time, professional guide, offering sound experience and personalised service, including boat-in, fly-in (fixed wing/helicopter) and beach barbecues. A well-equipped, comfortable launch is provided for fishing pleasure. Season may be closed August and September, so check first. From $30 per hour, $200 per day, per boat.

Queenstown Trout Safaris
8 Argyle Place
Arrowtown
Telephone: Arrowtown 467
Host: Arthur Frew

Fish clear mountain rivers and streams of the scenic Southern Lakes district for rainbow and brown trout from 1.36 to 4.5 kilograms (3 to 10 pounds), or try lake trolling. Jet boat across Lake Wakatipu to river mouths inaccessible by road, or discover remote regions by helicopter or fixed-wing aircraft. Beginners welcome and everything supplied. Season October to July. From $60 (two hour), $110 (half day), $200 (full-day). Overnight camp-outs on request. Book direct or through Mount Cook Travel, Rees Street, Queenstown.

Southern Lakes Guide Service
PO Box 84
Te Anau
Telephone: (0229) 7565
Hosts: Murray and Lloyd Knowles

Enjoy guided fishing trips, by four-wheel-drive vehicle, launch and jet boat through the beautiful lakes and rivers of Fiordland. Specialising in fly fishing, spinning and trolling, Murray and Lloyd cater for lone fishermen or parties of up to six, providing meals, transport and equipment by arrangement. Warm clothing recommended. Season: October through April. From $100 to $250. Members NZ Professional Fishing Guides Association.

Te Anau Lake Services
97 McKinnon Loop
Te Anau
Telephone: (0229) 7883
Host: Mr Frank McPeake

Go fishing for brown, rainbow and salmon trout on this beautiful lake, chartering an all-weather cabin launch, or hiring a cabin runabout for private use. Frank personally caters for one to twelve people on an hourly basis, or one- to three-day, fully catered safaris. Equipment supplied. Season: October through July. From $40 per hour, reduced day-charter rates.

Seven Rivers Lodge
PO Box 85
Mossburn
Telephone: Mossburn 24-S
Hosts: Jos and Phil Rossell

The visiting angler's major problem is where to start, in a bewildering variety of location and climate. The lodge was established to assist the discerning fly fisherman achieve a memorable trip, providing top guides, location transportation and accommodation. This lodge lies in the heart of some of the world's finest fishing country, in a backdrop of unmatched scenery, and offers fly fishermen all that they could wish for: fish, fellowship, warmth, comfort and fine food in a relaxing, small and rustic setting. Seven fine rivers and several small lakes, within an hour's drive, contain brown and rainbow trout and in lower reaches, huge sea-run trout. There is real variety – fast runs for the upstream nymph, backwaters and slow reaches for the dry fly. Season: October through April. From $50 plus fishing.

Fishing Paradise Safaris
101 Main Road
Clinton
Telephone: Clinton 153
Hosts: Dennis and Dawn Holden

South and west Otago have a reputation for fine fishing, particularly the famous Mataura River, with its wily brown trout. With 20 years experience, Dennis organises dry-fly, nymph, spin and bait fishing, providing everything you require to make your safari a memorable one. Itineraries drawn up to suit your programme, transport provided from Dunedin Airport if required. Season: October to April inclusive. Cost: from $150 per day (maximum four persons). Accurate quotes given.

Jet boating. *(Andris Apse Ltd)*

In a land where rivers rush down from the mountains in a steep, wild run to the sea, white-water rafting, canoeing and jet boating are great adventure sports.

uperb rafting rivers throughout the wilderness in both the North and the South Island include some of the world's best. Wild water and rugged scenery combine for the perfect rafting adventure – when Coca-Cola wanted to film an international rafting commercial they chose a New Zealand river, the Rangitaiki.

Canoeists also have plenty of rivers to choose from, calm or wild, with the New Zealand Canoeing Association listing some 1,500 rivers for enthusiasts.

Less strenuous perhaps, but no less exhilarating, are jet-boat rides with passengers carried at high speed through twisting gorges. The jet boat is a New Zealand invention, designed to operate in as little as 10 centimetres (4 inches) of water and incredibly manoeuvrable. Under the control of skilled drivers, jet boats make almost instantaneous changes of direction at high speed, taking river travellers close by rocks and over shallow water in safety. Try the thrills of driving a jet boat yourself in the calmer waters of a lake by hiring a self-drive jet boat.

In comparison with rivers such as the Colorado in the USA, the fall from mountain to sea on New Zealand rivers is sharp. Yet many rivers are surprisingly long, taking tortuous routes to the ocean or lakes.

The Landsborough, one of the top ten rafting rivers in the world, gives 70 kilometres (43 miles) of wild water travelling through remote mountain scenery and falling over 300 metres in the first 25 kilometres (985 feet in 15½ miles). The less turbulent Clarence winds 200 kilometres (124 miles), cutting its way through a wide, high-mountain gorge on a spectacular route to the Pacific Ocean.

Rafting rivers are graded on a scale from one to five, so you know what you are attempting from the start. A grade five is heart-stopping excitement, the most difficult water rafted by commercial operators. Experts suggest a day trip on a grade two or three river for a first-time rafter – rivers such as the glacier-fed Rakaia or the bush-fringed Waimakariri. Then if you want to graduate to more exciting water, look for grade four or five.

Each New Zealand river has its own character, thrills and charm – no one river is quite like another.

Ride the North Island's Wairoa, for example, on a brief breathtaking grade-five rafting run where there is little time to admire the scenery – this is a two-hour hair-raising run with turbulent rapids living up to names such as 'Rollercoaster'. Or try the Motu River, which draws rafting enthusiasts as much by its wild, untouched beauty as by its grade three and four water. Trips on the Motu range from two to six days, camping out in the bush-covered gorge.

Then there's the South Island's Shotover, one of the best-known rafting and jet-boating rivers, with a variety of water as the river swoops and twists down through steep, stone canyons.

Travel the Shotover by raft or jet boat, surrounded by the stark, overwhelming scenery, and discover reminders of gold-rush days, 120 years ago, when the Shotover was described as 'the richest river in the world'. The claim may sound boastful but this was the river where two men went in search of a dog and returned instead with 12 kilograms (26 pounds) of gold scooped from the rocky crevices of the riverbank.

Rafting trips on wild rivers range from a few hours to seven

days, with the best companies providing highly skilled boatmen and first-rate equipment. Standards of safety and comfort can be as variable as the rivers, so prospective rafters need to make full enquiries with any operator – rafting companies that belong to the New Zealand Professional Rafting Association must meet certain standards.

The rivers were the first great highways in New Zealand. Since the invention of jet boats and tough, inflatable rafts, the rivers are reverting to routes of adventure, opening up the rugged interior for all groups – from children to grannies, as well as the adventurer. There is something suitable for everyone to enjoy at their own level.

Combine River rafting, jet boating, tramping – plus spectacular Fiordland scenery, unusual vegetation, penguin & seals at the Hollyford valley! These are many combinations.

Raft rivers such as the Landsborough, Hunter, Matukituki, Waiaoto and Kawarau and take time to trek in the surrounding forests and mountains. On the West Coast's Waiho, rafting trips can include a helicopter ride or gold-panning. On some rivers, such as the Mohaka, which flows through beech forest and grasslands, rafts are used for transport on hunting and fishing holidays.

Take off down the rivers of New Zealand by raft, canoe or jet-boat and combine your river adventure with other outdoor activities. On the bush-fringed Wanganui, imbued with Maori and European history, take a canoeing holiday and take time out for swimming, bushwalks, sunbathing and sightseeing or combine a jet-boat holiday with a holiday on a sheep station.

Silverpeaks Tours
Dukes Road
RD2
Mosgiel
Host: Mr Alan McKay

Experience river rafting at its best here on the magnificent beauty of the Taieri River. Less than three-quarters of an hour from Dunedin City, the Taieri is proudly acclaimed as one of New Zealand's most exciting rafting rivers. Its scenery is unequalled and the native bush grows right down to water level. Enjoy great southern hospitality combined with the fun of rafting. There is a selection of trips suitable for everyone, ranging from two hour (suitable for all ages) to the ultimate challenge of about five hours (suitable for advanced rafters). The service is available all year around and all equipment and safety gear is provided. All you will need is your sand shoes and camera. Silverpeaks Tours also provides a host of other exciting tours. Write direct for information/bookings, or telephone Chris Knol (024) 773-679.

Smiths Jet Cruises
PO Box 41
Paihia
Telephone: Paihia 27-678

Owned and operated by the Smith family, this is the only jet-boat service in the Bay of Islands. Experience the exhilaration of this sport, the scenic beauty and historic features of the upper reaches of this magnificent harbour. The jet boat *Kiwa* provides sightseeing trips, all water sports, plus 24-hour water-taxi service. Scenic trips depart hourly from Paihia wharf, year through. All safety equipment provided. From $10 per person per hour.

Whitewater rafting.
(Andris Apse Ltd)

River Adventures

Take time out to explore this lovely bay. Hire a canoe and paddle leisurely through clear waters to a bush-covered island, climbing to its summit for a wonderful view of the whole bay; or paddle under the Waitangi River bridge and up the peaceful river to the magnificent Haururu Falls. In addition to being Paihia's sole canoe operator, Bay Beach Hire offers a wide range of paddle-boats (family fun on a half-hourly or hourly basis), windsurfing boards, catamarans, and a 4-metre (14-foot) Wild Cat for the proficient sailor. All offer guaranteed enjoyment. Try something new with confidence – free and full tuition is offered, plus all equipment and life jackets! Look for the blue, yellow and red-striped sails on the beachfront at Paihia. Service operates October to 15 May. From $3 per hour, depending on equipment.

Bay Beach Hire
PO Box 158
Paihia
Telephone: Paihia 27-147

Go rafting from Auckland (or anywhere, by special arrangement), transport provided, sightseeing en route.

OPTION ONE: The gentle Waikato River, suitable any age or state of fitness. Wine/hot scones served.

OPTION TWO: The Wairoa River, Tauranga or Rangitaiki River, Rotorua. Wild Water day trip. Minimum age is 13, reasonable fitness level required.

OPTION THREE: Wild Water with camping expedition. Motu River, Opotiki. Age and fitness as for option two. Two- and three-day duration, fly in by helicopter.

Rafting is fun and exciting and you will see the real New Zealand while doing it! For brochure/further information, contact direct.

Live-Life New Zealand Ltd
Action Tours and Activities
CPO Box 4517
Auckland
Telephone: (09) 768-936

Woodrow Rafting Expeditions
PO Box 770
Tauranga
Telephone: (075) 62-628
Hosts: Mark and Kathy Row

From the adrenalin rush of the mighty 'rollercoaster' to fishing in the peace of 'the forgotten river', rafting provides enjoyment of our beautiful outdoors as well as the excitement of shooting wild rapids. Mark is an experienced Grade A boatsman, recognised by the NZ Professional Rafting Association, and provides a variety of one-day excursions and multi-day camping trips, plus a choice of graded rafting on many North Island rivers to delight novice and experienced alike. All safety and camping equipment and food provided, with wetsuits for hire. You need sand shoes and warm clothing. Minimum age – 13 years. A reasonable fitness level preferred. Rafting subject to water levels, best months during spring/autumn. Book in advance by mail or telephone or call Stars Travel, Telephone: Tauranga 80-009.

Turangi River Rafting
Taupehi Road, Turangi
Telephone: (0746) 8856
Hosts: Peter and Anna Dawson

Experience white-water rafting on the beautiful Tongariro River, with great scenery and secret grottoes that only Peter knows about! He can even take you to fishing spots accessible only by raft. This service specialises in small groups of adventure enthusiasts. Everything supplied from wet suits to safety equipment, bring your sand shoes. Operates all year. Rides graded to age groups. From $10 to $200.

Pipiriki Jet Boat Tours
RD6
Wanganui
Telephone: (0658) 54-633
Owners: Ken and Raewyn Haworth

This company operates daily jet boat tours from Pipiriki on the magnificent Wanganui River, all year round. All tours include the world-renowned 'Drop Scene' area, where the river suddenly disappears in front of you! These middle reaches are acknowledged by travellers as the most spectacular and beautiful of the entire Wanganui River (once the North Island's 'main route' and travelled by river boats). Jet boating is suitable for all ages and is great fun. Trips range from half an hour to half a day. Closest accommodation is Raetihi, Ohakune or Wanganui. A mini-coach departs from Wanganui Monday to Friday, not weekends or statutory holidays. Wet-weather gear and safety equipment are provided. Bring your own refreshments and camera. From $10 to $30; half-price for children. Note: minimum of three adult passengers required for any trip.

Wanaka Riverjet and Riveraft
C/- Wanaka Information Centre
Wanaka
Telephone: Wanaka 7277

Go scenic riverboating on the mighty Clutha River with a choice of a fast ride in a famous Hamilton Jet, or a tranquil drift by raft through superb scenery. Rafting suitable for ages five and over. A barbecue is provided, as is safety equipment. Trips run daily and often during summer months only. Courtesy transport provided from, and all bookings taken at, Information Centre. Cost: $17 adults, $9 children.

Silverpeaks Tours
Dukes Road
RD2
Mosgiel
Telephone: Mosgiel 6167
Host: Mr Alan McKay

New Zealand is the home of the famous Hamilton jet boat, now used world over. For sheer exhilaration, jet boating is unmatched as a sport, and is suitable for all ages. This experience takes you skimming up 25 kilometres (15½ miles) of the beautiful Taieri River, through gorges, amongst unique native bush, sightseeing from a steel-hulled jet boat. The trips depart from a point about thirty minutes drive from Dunedin, and transport is provided from Dunedin by comfortable safari wagon. Trips range from one to two-and-a-half hours in length, or you can combine this experience with a rafting trip. Safety equipment is provided – all you need is jacket and your camera. From $12.50; combined rafting from $40. A wide range of other exciting tours are available from Silverpeaks Tours. Write direct for information or bookings, or telephone Chris Knol (024) 773-679.

River Adventures

Marine Enterprises Ltd
PO Box 97
Queenstown
Telephone: Queenstown 647 (after hours 747)
Owner: Richard Rout

Jet the Shotover with us. Our company offers real raw water adventure and variety, including the unparalleled 'Shotover canyons'. Courtesy coach departs from our Queenstown jetty (near steamer *Earnslaw* wharf). You can drive your own Hamilton jet – we are New Zealand's only operators offering jets for public hire – for half an hour or longer. Full instruction on safety and operation given.

Explore the unspoilt beauty of Lake Wakatipu, or take advantage of Queenstown's golf – travel by jet water taxi to the international Kelvin Heights Golf Course (our lake charter operates a 'set down - pick up' service to any part of Lake Wakatipu).

For the trout fisherman, we provide full trolling safaris and shore casting. Gear supplied. Licences available at jetty. Our services operate all year round. All prices and enquiries at our office/jetty or all leading booking agencies.

Twin Rivers Jet (1981) Ltd
PO Box 55
Queenstown
Owners: Geoffrey Stevens and David Black

Experience the excitement and thrills of superb jet boating in the shallows of the Shotover River and the unsurpassed scenery of the Kawarau River – both offering jet boating at its best! The trip takes about one hour, and is believed to be the longest river jet boat ride available. Courtesy transport from Queenstown to the jetty site and return. Light spray jackets and safety equipment provided. You need warm clothing and your camera. Note: Occasional flooding of the Shotover River may mean a cancellation or the excursion limited to Kawarau River. Suitable for ages 5 to 75 years, this sport is fun for all and is at its best in this unique country where the Hamilton Jet was invented. Book through local travel agents. Cost: Adults $25, children $16. Group discounts available for nine or more.

Value Tours Queenstown Ltd
PO Box 53
Queenstown
Telephone: Queenstown 1340

This is the South Island's largest rafting company specialising in river-running tours from half-day to four days duration. A variety of rivers include the world-rated Landsborough (a four-day Wilderness Expedition); the spectacular Shotover River and the high-volume Kawarau River. The company's experienced guides are all New Zealanders and are registered, professional boatmen. Tours depart from central Queenstown, transport provided. Wet suits and safety equipment supplied. You will require warm clothing and sand shoes. Service operates October through April. During this time, trips on the Shotover and Kawarau run daily and are suitable for ages 13 and over; the Landsborough Wilderness Expedition runs each Friday and is suitable for ages 15 and over. Book through G.T.B., travel agent or direct by telephone or mail. From $39 to $385, depending on trip.

SEE ALSO:

Outback Safaris: Danes Back Country (Queenstown), Rough Rider Rafting Co. (Rotorua), Ruapehu Outback Adventures (Ohakune).
Tramping: Hollyford Valley Walk (Te Anau).
Flightseeing: Heli Jet Adventures (Queenstown).
Lodges: Alpine (St Arnaud), Maungaraupi (Marton).
Live with NZ: Riverview (Athol).
Regional:
Bay of Plenty: Blue Lake Holiday Park (Rotorua).
Volc. Plat: Discovery (National Park), Judges Pool Motel (Turangi), Courtney Motel (Taupo).
Marlborough: Gem Resort (Marlborough Sounds).
Westland: Haast Motor Camp, Lakeside Motels (Lake Paringa).
Mt Cook: Omarama Motor Lodge, Stage Coach Inn (Omarama).
Otago: Wilderness Shop (Dunedin).
Southern Lakes: Wanaka Motor Camp, Airborne Hovercraft (Queenstown).

Waitemata Harbour, Auckland. *(Courtesy Air New Zealand)*

Yachting and cruising

With thousands of kilometres of coastline indented with bays, coves and harbours, and dotted with islands, taking to the sea is second nature for New Zealanders.

It has been estimated that there is one boat for every 15 people in the country and some 'boaties' consider that estimate to be very conservative.

For visitors this national obsession means there will be plenty of opportunities to get off dry land and experience the country from the sea. Make friends with a local (that's not difficult) and the chances are you will be invited out in his boat. New Zealanders love the sea and love to introduce others to the delights of their coastline.

Charter boating began in a small way around 1975, long after charter cruising was well established in centres such as the Greek Islands and the Caribbean. It is still low key, remaining a personal, friendly operation. The people in the charter-boat business are there because they love sailing – they have turned their passion for the sea into their livelihood.

Operators find overseas visitors like to be treated as guests rather than tourists. Get away on a luxury keeler and it will probably be crewed by the owner and his regular crew, not owned and operated by a large, impersonal company. Even the largest bare-boating company has a fleet of about 20 boats, compared with 150 or so in Mediterranean operations.

For sail-yourself holidays, otherwise known as bare-boating, you and your friends or family are the skipper and crew but everything else, right down to the can opener, is supplied.

Yachts larger than 12 metres (40 feet) are usually available only with skipper and crew – understandably owners are reluctant to commit a $250,000 luxury yacht for bare-boat cruising. But the skipper will certainly be an experienced blue-water sailor who will know how to make the very most of your cruise.

Smaller yachts can also be hired with a crew – splendid for those who lack the experience to take the helm themselves. It is also possible to have a skipper aboard to teach the necessary skills until you feel ready to take over yourself.

Flotilla sailing is another variation, a compromise that allows bare-boats to sail themselves under the guidance of a lead ship and so explore far from the home port, cruising around isolated offshore islands..

Cruising New Zealand is not coconut palms and tropical heat. The summer temperatures are similar to the northern Mediterranean, with pleasantly hot days and warm evenings. New Zealand's east-coast sailing grounds reveal mile after mile of fine golden sand, unspoiled wooded islands and thousands of nautical square miles of unpolluted cruising water.

Sail away in the Bay of Islands, the best known area for bare-boating, and you can wend your way around 522 kilometres (365 miles) of coastline and 144 islands in the broad, sheltered bay, relax on tree-shaded sandy beaches with not a soul in sight and feast on the fish you have caught. And all for around the same price as a hotel room.

Other charter centres include Auckland's Hauraki Gulf with 1,200 nautical square miles of cruising and 100 islands, Lake Taupo where you can sail off to a deserted bay and fish for rainbow trout, and the Marlborough Sounds, deep bush-fringed sheltered waters at the northern end of the South Island.

Charter sailing is only one of many cruising opportunities – there are boating variations to suit anyone's taste, time and pocket.

Day cruises and sundowner cruises on board large skippered yachts give a taste of the sea for those on a tight time schedule.

Yachting and cruising

There are holidays afloat on less conventional craft such as an old kauri schooner that takes passengers island hopping in the Hauraki Gulf. The comforts are not up-market but the cruise is great fun. At the other end of the sophistication scale are luxury motor-launch holidays that pamper guests while they sightsee, sunbathe or try deep-sea fishing.

Sightseeing launch trips operate from almost every town with wharf access to sea or lake. Some offer chicken and champagne lunches aboard or picnic barbecues on beaches.

The best-known sightseeing cruise is probably the Bay of Islands' Cream Trip, delivering mail and supplies to outlying islands and following a route once taken by launches collecting cream from island dairy farms.

The many others include: harbour launch cruises and casual ferry-boat rides from Auckland to nearby islands; regular summer launch trips from Tauranga to Mayor Island, place best known for the adjacent deep-sea fishing, but also an unspoilt, bush-covered island that hides two volcanic lakes and masses of native birds; and excursions through the deep, almost roadless sounds that form the coast at the northern end of the South Island.

Take a launch trip along the coast of Abel Tasman National Park, with granite cliffs, sandy bays and bush-covered islands. Or combine a launch trip there with a guided trek along the shore.

Down in the deep south the lakes abound with boat trips. There's a one-day excursion on Lake Wakatipu aboard an old-time lake steamer that calls in at an isolated sheep station. At Lake Te Anau you glide through glow-worm caves in a small boat. At Lake Manapouri, a deep, dark lake of brooding beauty, a launch trip down the lake links with another down a spectacular fiord.

Spend several days at Doubtful Sound, living on board a cruising launch, amid the majesty of the remote fiords, and discover the history of Cook's visit and the tragic lives of later settlers.

No matter where you are in New Zealand the sea or lakes are not far away, whether you want to spend an hour or two or a week or two afloat.

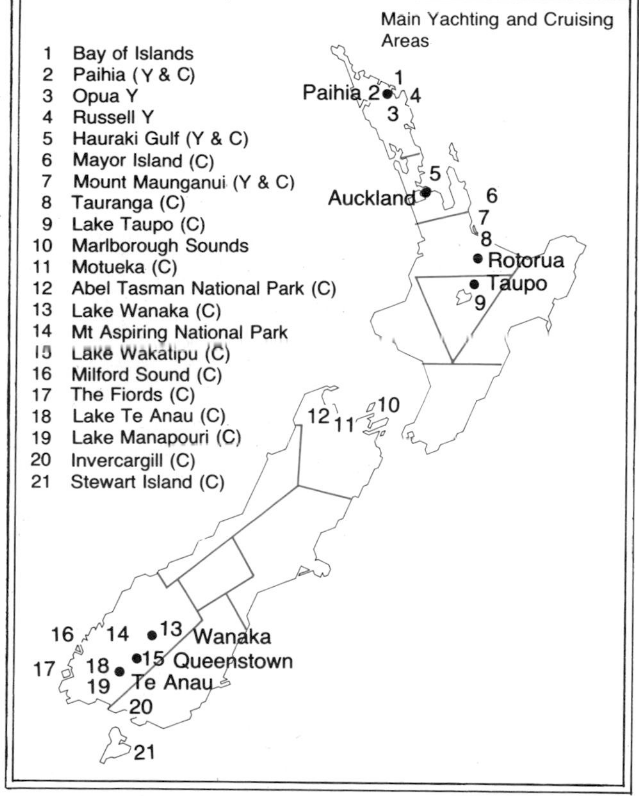

Seclusion in the Bay of Islands. *(Courtesy Rainbow Yacht Charters)*

Rainbow Yacht Charters
C/- Post Office
Opua
Bay of Islands
Telephone: Paihia 27821
or Auckland (09) 790-457
Hosts: Evelyn and Roger Miles

With a splendid cruising area from the Bay of Islands to Whangaroa, some 900 kilometres (560 miles) of secluded bays, islands and inlets are yours to explore. 'Rainbow' offers the largest fleet of yachts and motor cruisers in the country. Your alternatives:

INDEPENDENT BARE-BOATING: yachts from 6 to 12 metres (20 to 40 feet), and 11-metre (36-foot) motor cruisers; accommodating four-six persons. Some boating experience required by at least one person. Boats are fully equipped for overnight cruising. From $65 per day (6-metre sail), $225 per day (11-metre cruiser).

CREWED AND SKIPPERED CHARTER: *Shalimar*, 14-metre (46-foot) centre-cockpit cutter, offers luxury – two private double or twin cabins accommodating up to six guests (crew quarters are separate). A fast and beautiful, ocean-going yacht. From $90 per person, per day. All food, wine, skipper and crew supplied.

Freedom Yacht Charters Ltd
Matauwhi Road
PO Box 34
Russell
Telephone: Russell 37-781
Telex: NZ 2583

Sail yourself or retain a skipper and cruise the famous Bay Of Islands, living and sailing on a modern, fully equipped cruising yacht. Enjoy the freedom, the fishing, beaches and clear water of the bay, for as little as $80 per person per week! Adventure holiday or sedate family sail – the choice is yours. Everything supplied except food. From $400 per week (off-season rate) for five-berth Bonito 22.

Katena Sailboat Charters
1242B New North Road
Avondale
Auckland 7
Telephone: (09) 883-225
Hosts: Anne and John Poland

You can afford this dream of a holiday on your own skippered, luxury yacht, in the fabulous Hauraki Gulf, with its myriad of islands and bays – sailing, sightseeing, shore adventures, sports fishing, swimming, diving and relaxing. Anne and John know this gulf intimately. From $230 (3-day weekend) and $600 (7 days) per person (includes meals and wine. Bring only personal effects. Major credit cards accepted).

Totaranui Beach, Abel Tasman National Park, Nelson. *(Andris Apse Ltd)*

Yachting and cruising

This service provides a boating experience not to be forgotten among the beautiful islands and bays of the magnificent Hauraki Gulf Maritime Park (over 1,100 square nautical miles). Vessels are government approved, ranging from 6 to 14 metre (20 to 46 feet). Your requirements are met through a variety of options. Sail your dreams aboard larger skippered vessels with everything provided, or 'bare-boat' sail under your own command. Go cruising with a group of friends in the privacy of your 'own' yacht or experience a 'Learn To Sail and Cruise' vacation, learning to sail before you venture off. Captain Whiteman will assist you with a package holiday – flights, accommodation and rental cars – in conjunction with your boating experience. Best sailing December to April. Costs: $20 to $100 per person per day, depending on requirements.

South Seas Yacht Charter Ltd
PO Box 38-366
Howick,
Auckland.
Telephone: (09) 534-2001
Cables: MARCONSULT – NZ
Hosts: Brian and Vivienne Whiteman

Enjoy three hours of fun on Lake Wakatipu, at Frankton Arm – water skiing, windsurfing and sailing on Hobie catamarans, with a continuous barbecue available. Novices welcome as full tuition is given. All you need is a towel, everything else (even a drink) is supplied. Service operates November through March. Transport provided from Queenstown. Cost: $25 per person. Book direct.

Queenstown Waterski and Sail
36 Cedar Drive
Kelvin Heights
Queenstown
Telephone: Queenstown 1085R
Host: John Corboy

SEE ALSO: (Yachting)
Tramping: Abel Tasman Enterprises (Motueka).
Regional:
Bay of Plenty: Windscene Windsurf Shop (Mt Maunganui).
Otago: Southern Air (Invercargill/Stewart Island).
Southern Lakes: Fiordland Travel (Te Anau).
SEE ALSO: (Cruising)
Water Adv: Bay Beach Hire (Paihia).
Lodges: Roberton Island (Bay of Islands).
Regional: Northland: Centabay Lodge (Paihia).

Wanaka Hovercraft
PO Box 77
Wanaka
Telephone: 7024
Owners: Mr and Mrs E. McCammon

During this 45-minute trip, experience the beauty of Lake Wanaka and the grandeur of the Mount Aspiring National Park. Glide over lake, river flats, farm and swampland on a cushion of air, in a warm and comfortable craft. Operates from 8 a.m. daily, all year through. Departs from the lake foreshore. Restricted by adverse weather. From $12 to $20, pre-schoolers free of charge.

Wanaka Lake Services (Lakefront)
PO Box 20
Wanaka
Telephone: Wanaka 7495

Enjoy launch trips (from hour to half-day), to view this beautiful lake, (full commentary provided). Half-day afternoon trip visits Pigeon Island, allowing time to walk, fish, swim, relax and enjoy billy tea. Comfortable launches seat 6 to 50 passengers. Special charters available by arrangement to all parts of the lake (camping, tramping, fishing, etc.). Bookings advisable. Service operates daily. From $8 (hour trip), $20 (afternoon), plus charter/children's rates.

Red Boats
THC Milford Sound Cruises
Tourist Hotel Corporation
Telephone:
Auckland (09) 773-689
Wellington (04) 729-179
Christchurch (03) 790-718
Telex: NZ 3488

Take a long or short cruise on Milford Sound, enjoying the delights of this beautiful waterway in style and comfort. Licensed bar, refreshment service and commentary provided. Departing daily at 10.30 a.m. and 1.00 p.m., a Red Boat offers a full scenic tour to the Tasman Sea and back. En route viewing includes magnificent mountains such as Mitre Peak (carved out by ice millennia ago), mighty waterfalls, seals and dolphins. Round off the trip with a delicious crayfish and champagne lunch (by arrangement), moored at the foot of a glacier! Short cruises depart the jetty daily at 11.30 a.m. and 1.30 p.m. (times may change, check daily), giving superb opportunities to see and photograph highlights. NZR coaches provide connecting transport from Queenstown and Te Anau. Book through THC offices, THC Hotels, travel agents. From $12 (long), $10.50 (short); lunch from $6.50 each. Operates year through, subject to weather.

Hydrofoil Cruises Ltd
PO Box 58
Queenstown
Owner: Wayne Perkins

"Meteor III" is New Zealand's only operating hydrofoil, offering the fastest, most exciting ride you can take – three feet above the surface of Lake Wakatipu. This beautiful lake abounds in scenic and historic attractions that are yours to enjoy on either of two great cruises operating from the Queenstown wharf. The Snowline Cruise is fifty minutes long – a fascinating 39 kilometre (24 mile) cruise, that explores the lake's alpine beauty and pure water, and offers views of the massive high-country farms that border the lake, and the wild mountain goats and deer browsing along the shoreline. The mini-cruise is of twenty minutes duration, viewing Queenstown from the lake and following 16 kilometres (10 miles) of shoreline. From $7 (adult for mini-cruise) to $15 (adult for Snowline Cruise). Snowline departs 10.30 a.m., 2.00 p.m. and 3.00 p.m., daily; mini-cruise departs 11.30 a.m. and 1.15 p.m. Note: Cruises operate for minimum of six passengers only.

Te Anau Lake Services
97 McKinnon Loop
Te Anau
Telephone: (0229) 7883
Host: Mr Frank McPeake

This extensive boat-hire service allows you to explore the lake's remote beauty by cabin runabout, motorised dinghy, canoe or catamaran. Or for more luxury, take a scenic day or evening launch cruise, enjoying a picnic or barbecue across the lake. A water-taxi service operates for tramping and hunting parties. Closed June and July. From $4 per head to $40 per hour.

Yachting and cruising

Fiordland Travel Ltd
PO Box 1
Te Anau
Telephone: (229) 7416
Telex: NZ 4583

The Doubtful Sound Triple Trip takes you into the heart of legendary Fiordland, legacy of a collision of the Indian and Pacific coastal plates millions of years ago, since carved by glaciers into this fiord system of lush subtropical forest, towering peaks, deep lakes and fiords of pure sparkling water. The day trip takes you the length of Lake Manapouri by launch, past caves and islands once inhabited by ancient Maori tribes, into the depths of the giant hydro-electric power station by coach and then over the spectacular Wilmott Pass to Deep Cove. Here you will board M.V. *Friendship*, enjoying a hot drink as you cruise this beautiful shoreline of Doubtful Sound. Packed lunches may be pre-ordered with booking. During season a cruise departs from Manapouri at 10 a.m. Check other departure times and book through travel agents, G.T.B. or any Fiordland Travel Office. Cost: $61, with children's rates.

Fiordland Travel Ltd
PO Box 1
Te Anau
Telephone: (0229) 7416
Telex: NZ 4583

See the awesome majesty of Milford Sound from aboard M.V. *Milford Haven*. Three spacious viewing decks enhance scenery described by Rudyard Kipling as the eighth wonder of the world. In warmth and comfort, see breathtaking glacier-carved walls rising to sheer thousands of feet, Mitre Peak, 'the Queen of the Sound', the thundering Stirling Falls and lush native forests – as dophins and seals playfully greet you from the clear depths of this famous waterway. A licensed bar, smorgasbord meals and snacks are available on board. Bring your raincoat, camera and insect repellent. Recommended for all ages. Cruise departs all year round from Milford at 1 p.m. Additional times during season: 11 a.m. and 3 p.m. Access transport by NZR coach or car. Book through travel agents, G.T.B. or with any Fiordland Travel Office. Cost: $13, with children's rates.

Fiordland Cruises Ltd
C/- Post Office
Manapouri
Telephone. (02296) 609
Owners: Cliff and Irene Barnes

Until recently, only the fit or fanatical could penetrate Fiordland's rugged bush, deep glacial fiords, towering snow-capped mountains and spectacular waterfalls. Now you can explore this awesome beauty and isolation on three- and six-day cruises – learning early history in fiords where Captain Cook anchored, seeing natural wonders and animal life. Cliff knows the area thoroughly. Or simply relax or go tramping, deerstalking, fishing and beachcombing. Enjoy the comfort and camaraderie of a motel afloat, with four two-berth cabins, dining/living area, even a flush toilet. Big-game fishing and special charters taken by arrangement. Everything is provided, even rifle permits. All you require is warm and comfortable clothing, waterproof coat/footwear and camera. Service operates selected months only. From $280 to $620 plus special rates.

Airborne Hovercraft Services
PO Box 186
Alexandra
Telephone: Queenstown 976

This company offers amazing journeys along Queenstown's most scenic waterways. Marvel at the unique feeling of traversing water and land from the security of highly sophisticated hovercraft. Hour-long adventures include complimentary mini-bus transport from Queenstown to Frankton Hoverport (return) plus journey on Frankton Arm, Kawarau River and lower Shotover flats. Service operates year round, whatever the weather. From $20 adults, $10 children.

Air Safari's flightseeing the Grand Traverse in the Southern Alps. *(Andris Apse Ltd)*

AIR SAFARIS

Take to the air and the contrasting landscapes of New Zealand can be seen at their very best – snow-covered mountains, grassy plains, arid semi-desert, thick rain forest, steaming volcanoes or tranquil lakes. Some flights can encompass all of that in less than two hours.

here is flight-seeing from airports, large and small, all over the country. From lakes and bays you may take a novel flight-seeing trip in an amphibian, taking off and landing in a flurry of water.

Fly over islands in the Bay of Islands and the Hauraki Gulf or over the active, steaming volcano, White Island. Fly to deserted bays on small islands, into long sheltered harbours, onto the dark, deep waters of fiords far away from roads. Fly over forests and mountains to land on high, remote lakes.

Or fly direct to lake or beach resort and land almost at the doorstep of your hotel – amphibians land on floats and then trundle up the beach on wheels.

In South Island mountain country small planes take off from airfields to land, with outsize skis, on snowfields and glaciers – a unique style of transport for sightseers and skiers. You don't simply fly over the mountains, you fly among them, at times breathtakingly close. Remind yourself ski planes have been making these mountain tours for more than 25 years.

From the North Island town of Rotorua, fly over the moonscape colours of the steaming thermal areas, over lakes and forests, the Tongariro mountains and the barren dark Rangipo Desert, on an excursion that takes only 90 minutes.

Use small aircraft, float planes, ski planes and helicopters not just for spectacular sight-seeing but as a fast way in to an adventure holiday – hunting, fishing, trekking, rafting, jet boating and skiing.

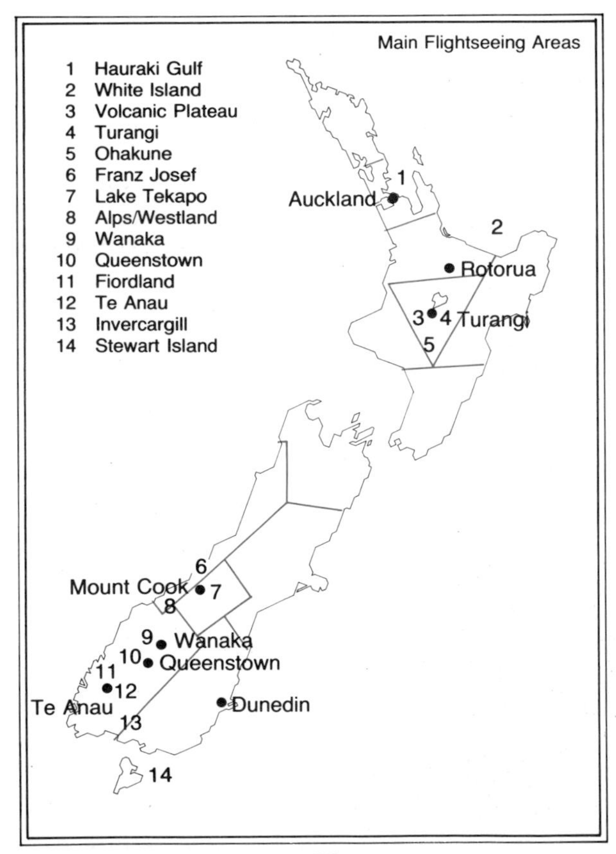

For flights that take you exactly where you want to go, when you want to go, charter your own plane and pilot, whether on a short trip to a fishing spot or a country-long tour from Kerikeri to Queenstown.

It's possible to charter an aircraft even in out-of-the-way places, as small towns often have an airstrip and aero club. Club members are hobby pilots, but many clubs also run charter services with licensed commercial pilots and have planes for hire for those qualified to fly themselves.

Naturally, each club has regulations governing the use of its hired aircraft, which limit the scope of private pilots wishing to fly over unknown territory – the club wants its planes back in one piece. But for those who meet the New Zealand requirements, fly-yourself excursions are a great possibility.

Flying schools are often attached to aero clubs. Take a cheap trial lesson and find out if flying is the hobby skill for you.

Gliding clubs also operate from club fields, for example, the excellent facilities at the Matamata field, and Omarama in the Mount Cook Ski Region.

Flightseeing

If you want to take to the air in the simplest fashion, floating on the winds with a hang-glider, New Zealand is an ideal place to try. With its open countryside, cliffs, hills and mountains and sea-borne breezes, it is not difficult to discover the perfect hang-gliding conditions.

Flight historians now believe that a New Zealander, Richard Pearse, was probably the first man to fly, taking to the air on his back-country farm several months before the Wright brothers. (See a replica of his machine in Auckland's Museum of Transport and Technology.)

This service offers a variety of scenic flights through the wonders of the Volcanic Plateau, starting from a ten minute joyride around the southern shores of Lake Taupo, the world-famous Tongariro River and Turangi township, through to two fifty minute flights – one taking in the many colourful volcanic lakes, National Parks, extinct craters, the continuously active Mts Tongariro, Ngaruahoe and Ruapehu – and more. The second flight covers Lake Taupo, Taupo township, the Waikato River (longest river in New Zealand), beautiful Huka Falls, the steaming Wairakei Thermal Region. Flights are also available into the beautiful Kaimanawa Forest Park (for hunters, fishermen and trampers). Operates year through. Courtesy transport from Turangi township available. From $10 to $120 per hour. Book direct or through Government Tourist Bureau.

Turangi Scenic Flights
PO Box 260
Turangi
Telephones: (0746) 7870
Hosts: Cam and Kris Shepherd

Hover over the craters of Mount Tarawera, which erupted less than one hundred years ago, the sparkling Blue and Green Lakes, the incredible Waimangu Thermal Region, and many more highlights of this spectacular area from the armchair comfort of a Bell Jet Ranger helicopter. Full in-flight commentary is given through complimentary headsets. Charters, photographic and special-interest flights arranged by request. From $20 per seat.

The Helicopter Line
PO Box 631
Rotorua
Telephone: (073) 59-477 or 479-810

Combine the thrill of taking off from water with the amazing beauty of this volcanic region. See the full panorama of beautiful lakes, mountains and craters – from active White Island to sites of past eruptions – steaming valleys and huge, man-made forests. Scheduled or customised flights available. Transfers arranged to airports, lodges and lakes by float or twin-engined, all-weather aircraft. From $40 to $114 (adults).

Floatplane Air Services Ltd
PO Box 640
Rotorua
Telephone: (073) 84-069 (after hours 59-120)
Telex: NZ 60736
Owner: Captain John Burns

The 'Grand Traverse' scenic flight around the Mount Cook and Westland National Parks from Lake Tekapo is fifty minutes of breath-taking flying through 200 kilometres (124 miles) of New Zealand's most spectacular alpine scenery, and over eleven major glaciers, including the Franz Josef, Fox, the Tasman and Murchison Glaciers. Regular departures daily from Lake Tekapo (and Glentanner Park), subject to good weather, in seven fifteen-seater aircraft. From $48 (adult), $34 (child).

Air Safaris and Services (NZ) Ltd
PO Box 21
Lake Tekapo
Telephone: (05056) 880

Aspiring Air (1981) Ltd
PO Box 68
Wanaka
Telephone: Wanaka 7943

This company offers the greatest New Zealand flight-seeing experience, through superb mountain and glacier regions. Save hours of driving time and fly direct to Milford. Flight times vary according to both your requirements and the weather, which can change rapidly. A variety of alpine scenic flights is offered all year round, including Mount Cook and Mount Aspiring. From $50 (adults), $35 (children). Book direct – after hours (8054) – or through the Wanaka Information Centre (7277).

Heli Jet Adventures Ltd
PO Box 338
Queenstown
Telephone: Queenstown 1216
Owner: Ross Marett

Ready for real river excitement? This company has it all. Go jet boating in a Hamilton Jet down the scenic Kawarau River, or combine the excitement of vertical helicopter flight in a famous Bell Jet ranger with the thrill of jet boating. Board the 'chopper' at Frankton, whisk past the beautiful 'Remarkables' and skim the surface of the Kawarau River, landing on the riverbank. From here you meet the river at high speed, head off in the jet boat, and still have a return flight to look forward to. Now if that isn't enough, take the Triple Trip: heli-jetting, and then into wet suits for a white-water rafting thrill. Courtesy coach provided from Queenstown. Protective wet-weather/safety gear provided, but bring a change of warm clothing. Operates year through. All ages enjoy heli-jetting, but Triple Trip not suitable for under 15 year olds. From $36 to $60, depending on trip.

Fiordland Flights
90 Te Anau Terrace
Te Anau
Telephone: (0229) 7799
Telex: NZ4583GXI
Owners: Tony and Gay Gibson

Fly by helicopter through the Fiordland National Park. This service offers scenic flights (specialising in the Mount Luxmore/South Fiord areas) and seasonal charters. Get to ski fields quickly, or try heli-skiing in winter; and in summer, fly to beautiful Mount Luxmore and enjoy the walk out, take a fishing charter (October to July) or fly/dine at a well-known restaurant/game park. From $16 to $180.

Waterwings Airways (Te Anau Ltd)
PO Box 222
Te Anau
Telephone: (0229) 7405
Senior Pilot: Mr Chris Willett

A wonderful way to see the beauty of Fiordland – experience the real thrill of taking off from and landing on water, viewing the world-famous Milford Track and the awesome, thundering magnitude of the Sutherland Falls; snowy peaks towering over fiords (with water so pure it is to be exported), and remote natural forests. The only operators of float planes in the far south, this company offers scenic flights and charter services for hunting, fishing and tramping trips. Although specialising in this area, they will fly charters to any part of New Zealand. Flights depart from the lake front outside the Te Anau Hotel. Scenic flights are restricted in adverse weather. From $15 to $500 depending on requirements. Shared costs negotiated and special rates for children.

Flightseeing, White Island, Bay of Plenty. (Courtesy The Helicopter Line)

SEE ALSO:

Airlines: Auckland Aero Club, Air Albatross (Wellington), Southern Air (Invercargill).
Outback Safaris: Danes Back Country (Queenstown), Ruapehu Outback Adventures (Ohakune).
River Adv: Silverpeaks Tours (Dunedin).
Tramping: Hollyford Valley Walk (Te Anau).
Regional:
Mt Cook: Omarama Motor Lodge (Gliding), Lake Ohau Lodge, Stage Coach Inn (Omarama).
Volc. Plat: Judges Pool Motel (Turangi).
Westland: Punga Lodge (Franz Josef).
Otago: Southern Air (Invercargill).

Diving at the Poor Knights, Northland.
(Courtesy Sportsways Aqualung Centre)

New Zealand is surrounded by sea, has an irregular, indented coastline and many islands. Put it all together and you have one of the longest coastlines of any country in the world.

he country stretches through latitudes from subtropical to subantarctic, offering a range of diving experiences that includes discovering huge sponges and lacy corals in the surreal underwater world of the Poor Knights in the north and cavorting with seals in the south.

Visiting divers enthuse about the clarity of the unpolluted waters and the variety and abundance of marine life.

Diving in New Zealand can be separated into game diving for lobsters, clams and fish, which takes place all around the country, and adventure diving, of interest to overseas divers in search of excitement.

Top of any list is the Bay of Islands and Poor Knights, a marine reserve with over 50 diving spots and served by a large fleet of dive boats. The water here is sharply clear and alive with subtropical and tropical fish such as groper, parrotfish, red pigfish, yellowbanded perch, Sandager's wrasse, stingrays, sunfish, conger eels, dolphins and all kinds of sharks. Less mobile sights include black coral trees, brightly coloured sponges and gorgonian fans. An added novelty is fish so friendly they hang around to be handfed by divers.

The diving opportunities at the Poor Knights are both strange and spectacular. You can see a mix of tropical and subtropical fish, kelp and coral side by side, rocky cliffs that continue below the surface, underwater tunnels, pinnacles and archways of giant proportions.

The Poor Knights are special and spectacular, but there are many other diving excitements. There's the magnificent Whangaroa Harbour where giant crayfish are common and sharks rare; the Cavalli Islands where subtropical species include bluefish, goldribbon groper, bonito and flying fish; Cape Brett with rugged, varied terrain – reefs, guts, canyons – and sea life ranging from tiny reef fish to marlin and bronze whaler sharks.

From Tutukaka, a whole coast of diving opens up. Boats leave from here for the Poor Knights, but the long mainland coast also offers excellent diving. For a diving fanatic, Tutukaka makes a good base.

Within easy distance of Auckland by car is the village of Leigh, the take-off point for dive boats heading to the Mokohinau Islands, where the flora is similar to that of the Poor Knights, and monster crayfish, kingfish and groper can be found.

Right by Leigh is a marine reserve and research area around Goat Island. Marine life here is fully protected but recreational divers are allowed ready access and the result is a remarkable experience – crowds of fish that show no fear and flock after divers to be hand fed. Blue cod, maomao, leatherjacket, kelpfish and snapper all cluster around.

Preparing to dive, Bay of Islands. ***(Courtesy Paihia Dive Hire and Charter)***

The rocky headlands, deep inlets and islands of the east coast of Northland, and the warmer waters (20 – 22°C), make the area a main attraction for adventure divers. As one goes south the water temperature drops – by almost 15°C – and the emphasis is more on game diving.

Boats from Whitianga and Tairua on the Coromandel Peninsula give access to the peninsula's east coast and many islands. The wild terrain that waits under water – steep cliffs, sharp pinnacles, reefs and caves – echoes the wild terrain of the land above. The species of fish and flora are just as varied, from scallops to marlin, black coral and sunfish.

The Bay of Plenty lives up to its name for divers with boats leaving from Tauranga, Mount Maunganui and Whakatane.

The main destination from the first two ports is Mayor Island, long known for deep-sea fishing. As the tip of a dormant volcano, Mayor Island provides an undersea world of rugged, unpredictable terrain that attracts plenty of marine life. As well as common fish such as snapper, yellowtail kingfish and John Dory, there are demoiselles, bonito, sponges and corals.

Kapiti Island, within easy reach of Wellington is washed by warm currents and is an attraction for divers. The island's underwater reefs, rocks and caves attract an extraordinary range of fish from the ubiquitous snapper through to skipjack tuna, albacore, dolphins, orca and sharks.

In the South Island the deeply indented Marlborough Sounds produce over 100 kilometres (60 miles) of coastline, most of it inaccessible except by sea and most of it attracting a marvellous variety of sea life – shipwrecks and scallops are specialities.

The Otago Peninsula is one of the best areas for diving in colder waters, with common southern fish such as butterfish, red cod, blue cod and moki. Here too are kelp forests and the chance to watch seals underwater. It is also an area frequented by white pointer sharks, an advantage or disadvantage depending on how you care to view a chance encounter.

Compared with some popular diving spots in other countries, sharks are a minor danger. Says one keen diver: 'Shark attack is about as likely as being hit by lightning down there. It is the least of our worries.'

Diving in New Zealand is a year-round sport, although summer is the most popular time. Wet suits are essential for winter diving and are usually worn at all times of the year. Bring your own gear for a diving holiday or hire equipment from well-stocked local suppliers. You will find excellent dive shops in all main cities and on popular diving coasts, and also plenty of air-filling stations.

The best diving season is January through to May; from October to December a heavy plankton bloom turns the water a milky green.

With marine life that includes tropical, subtropical, temperate and subantarctic species, there is a lot of diving waiting in New Zealand waters.

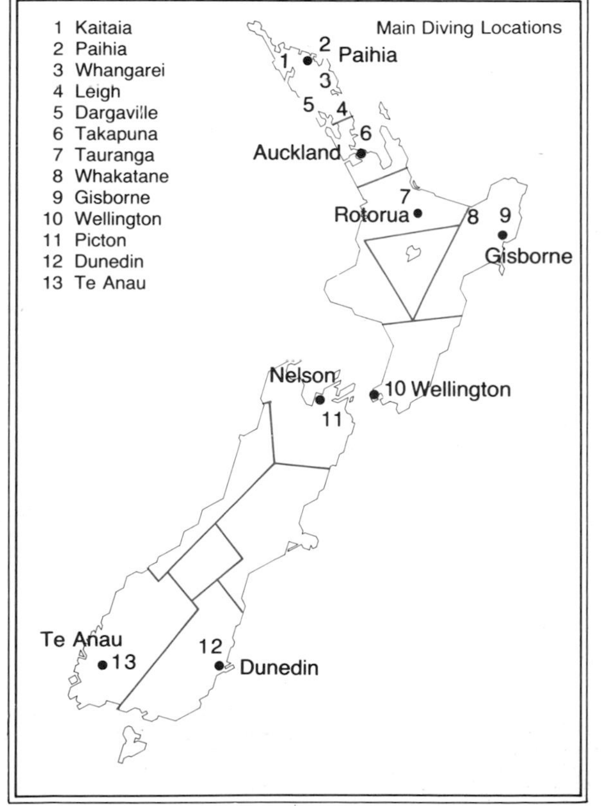

SEE ALSO:

Cruising: Fiordland Cruises (Te Anau).
Regional: Marlborough: Gem Resort (Picton).

Paihia Dive Hire and Charter Ltd
PO Box 210
Paihia
Telephone: Paihia 27-551
Telex: C/- NZ 21616
Owners: Garth Craig and Anne Corbett

Established 1978, these professionals are based in the world-famous subtropical diving and fishing area, the Bay of Islands. Dive all year, with the best months January to May, when water temperatures average 18° Celsius. These unpolluted waters teem with schools of fish (which you can hand feed), brilliant sponges and anemones. Especially famous with divers are the Poor Knights Islands, situated 40 kilometres (25 miles) from Bay of Islands. This company offers total diving exhilaration – take a dive/resort course with qualified PADI instructors; hire first-class scuba/snorkelling equipment; enjoy one-day diving/fishing charters; service, sales and air fills provided at the pro-dive shop. Boats available for longer charters. Note: Combined Poor Knights/Bay of Islands, multi-day dive charters recommended. From $35 diving (per person), $50 fishing. Book direct or through travel agents (USA bookings: Rainbow Adventure Holidays, telephone (213) 702-0011, (800) 227-5317).

Sportsways Aqua-Lung Centre
234 Orakei Road
Remuera
Auckland
Telephone: (09)542-117/(09)546-268

Many of New Zealand's most popular dive locations are found in the upper part of the North Island, east and north of Auckland. The best locations are accessible only by boat and are open-water dives. Whilst a variety of charter boats are available, the most hassle-free way for individuals or small groups to dive these great locations – at short notice – is to contact Sportsways' Trips and Travel Department upon arrival at Auckland International Airport. This company offers excellent boats, going to excellent locations, at excellent prices. A full day's diving can cost as little as $30.00! New Zealand's water temperatures are sub-tropical and a 5-mm wetsuit is required. The density of the marine life is renowned, large fish and 'drop-offs' being the main feature. Sportsways are a P.A.D.I. International training facility and a complete professional dive store at their Orakei Road operation.

Fish schooling, Poor Knights, Northland. *(Courtesy Sportsways Aqualung Centre)*

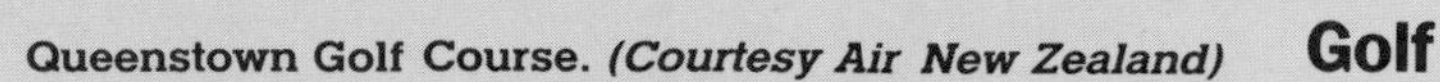

Queenstown Golf Course. *(Courtesy Air New Zealand)*

Wherever you are, in city, town or village, there is a golf course nearby. New Zealand has over 400 golf courses – more per head of population than any other country in the world.

Auckland has 17 courses within easy reach of the city, Christchurch has 12.

And the courses, like the rest of the country, are seldom crowded. Only at peak times are popular courses under pressure and golf, in New Zealand's equable climate, is a year-round sport.

The courses are as varied as the country and the top courses are superb. There's Titirangi, in Auckland, designed 50 years ago by the famous Scot, Dr Alister McKenzie. Set amid large trees, Titirangi is a beautiful course that makes the most of the gently sloping countryside.

Wairakei is a course that Arnold Palmer said everyone should play and Peter Thomson described as the best in New Zealand. It is certainly exciting, and cleverly designed as a testing course for both advanced and average golfers. And it is a public course, with no club membership, open all the year round.

If you are planning an action-packed holiday, the Wairakei course is in the centre of the North Island, close to trout fishing, boating, trekking, rafting, hunting and the Ruapehu ski fields.

Other top courses include two near Wellington – Paraparaumu, an excellent championship course in the Scottish links tradition, and Heretaunga, an elegant course set in a parkland of streams and trees.

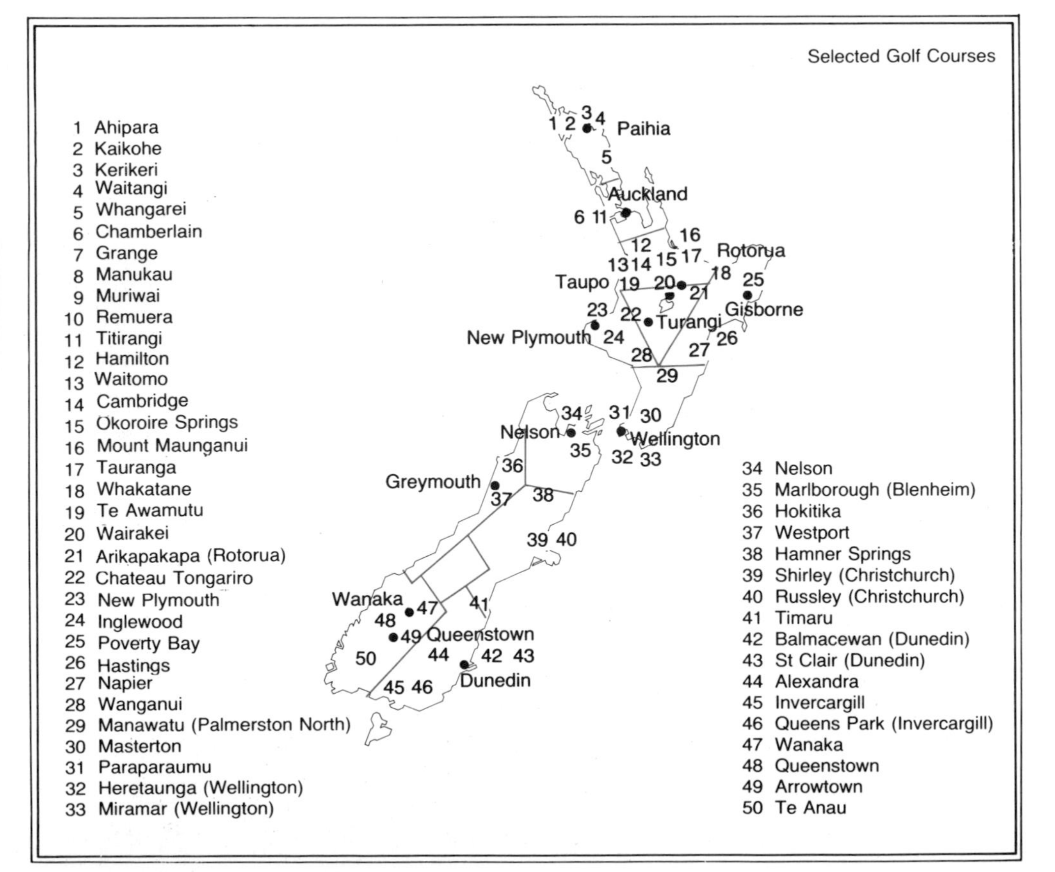

Golf

Dunedin, a city settled by Scots, naturally has excellent golf courses – Balmacewn, founded by the Otago Golf Club in 1871, is a championship course with many fine holes; St Clair is a course set spectacularly amid pine woods on the coast.

Some good courses are renowned for their setting as much as for the golf they offer. At Waitangi play on a beautifully kept course in a historic area, looking out over the blue waters of the Bay of Islands. At Queenstown the setting is a knock-out, with a backdrop of spectacular mountains – jet-boat transport on the lake from town to course gives quick and novel access.

That's only nine golf courses – there are about 390 more, such as those at Ahipara or Muriwai on reclaimed sand dunes alongside pounding surf beaches, the pleasant course and rural charm at Kerikeri, the excellent Arikikapakapa course at Rotorua, with a background of thermal steam and geysers, the splendid Shirley course at Christchurch, the Miramar course right in the centre of Wellington.

Some courses are public, owned and maintained by the local town council, government tourist department or similar authority, with unrestricted access for anyone; others are club courses with private membership but these all have access for non-member golfers – the conditions vary with each club. Almost all welcome visitors. Some may limit visiting players to weekday golf, others simply charge non-members a higher green fee.

But wherever you play in New Zealand you will find green fees amazingly cheap by world standards — no more than a few dollars. A $5 fee might even include hire of a trundler (motorised carts are not used on New Zealand courses).

SEE ALSO:

Auckland: Chamberlain Golf Course.
Bay of Plenty: Wairakei International Golf Course.

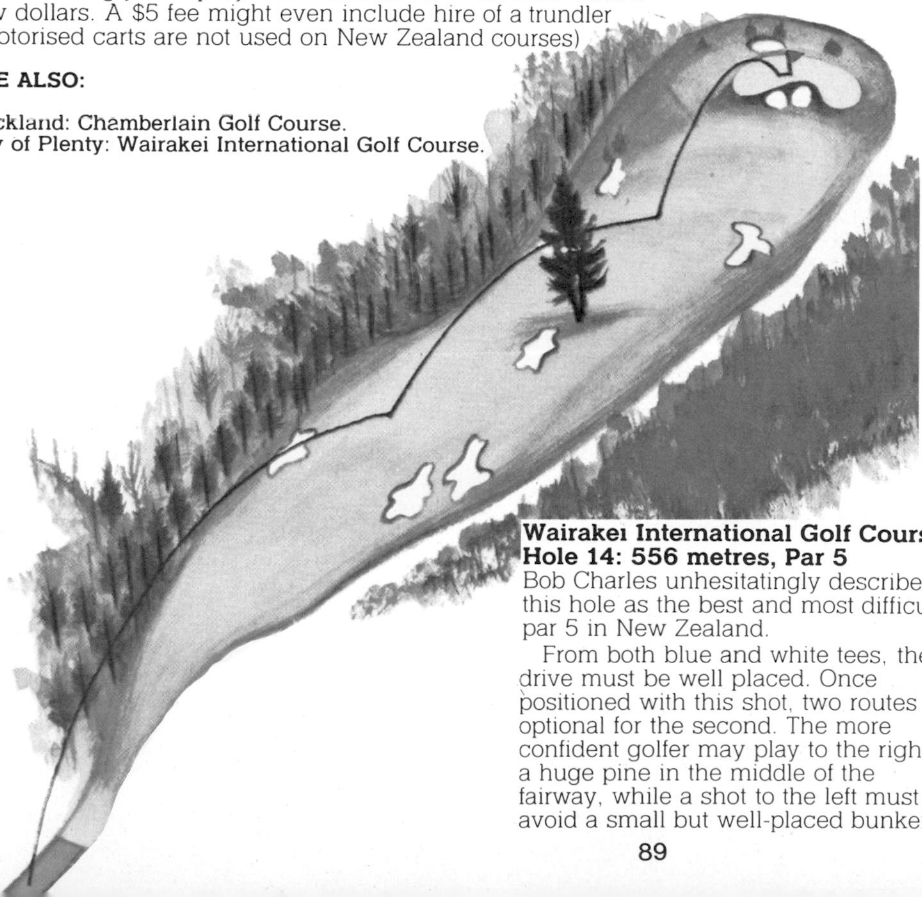

Wairakei International Golf Course
Hole 14: 556 metres, Par 5

Bob Charles unhesitatingly described this hole as the best and most difficult par 5 in New Zealand.

From both blue and white tees, the drive must be well placed. Once positioned with this shot, two routes are optional for the second. The more confident golfer may play to the right of a huge pine in the middle of the fairway, while a shot to the left must avoid a small but well-placed bunker.

In Touch with History

History is recorded not only in the dry stuff of manuscripts and books. It lives on in towns and in the countryside, and in New Zealand carved even in the hills. By looking around we can see the past and explore it. From the marks that have been made on the land, we can find out which people at various times in past centuries have come to New Zealand, from where they came, and when.

One Tree Hill, Auckland. (Courtesy Air New Zealand)

History of the Maori

ost New Zealanders have grown up believing in the Maori myth of Kupe, the Polynesian discoverer of Aotearoa, and of a great fleet, that followed 400 years later in 1350 A.D.

Modern scholarship has shown that early historians erred by uncritically unifying Maori tribal traditions into a national one. Each tribe has its own distinct whakapapa (genealogy) tracing their traditions back through the generations to a founding canoe. In the Taranaki Museum may be seen the traditional anchor stone of Tokomaru, the canoe of Te Atiawa people, as well as the greenstone adze, Potamawhiria, with which the canoe is believed to have been carved. Separate tribes tell separate Kupe legends. The National Museum in Wellington displays the large pierced stone said to be the anchor of Motahorua, Kupe's canoe. Only 30 years ago the Maori people of Hokianga placed a sacred white obelisk in the shadow of Whiria Mountain Pa beside the road near Opononi to mark Kupe's embarkation point for his return to Hawaiki. Auckland Museum's new Maori court will show a prized pearl-shell lure, evidence that the earliest voyagers came from an eastern Polynesian homeland. Also on display is a unique carved door lintel from Kaitaia clearly showing Eastern Polynesian influence.

Twentieth-century archaeology has traced New Zealand's earliest settlement back to at last least 1000 A.D., when the Maori camped in bays and river mouths, hunting inland for the huge flightless bird, the moa (see a reconstructed moa at the National Museum). In rock shelters they scattered bones of rats, fish and birds, some of which, like the moa, are now extinct, and drew with black charcoal and red ochre on the rock walls. (Visit the Timpendean Rock Shelter at Weka Pass in Canterbury to see a famed early rock-art site).

Canterbury Museum has a display of finds from the ovens and rubbish dumps of the important Wairau Bar moa-hunter settlement in Marlborough, which was occupied perhaps 800 years ago. From the summit of Auckland's Mt Eden, a later pa site, you may look out at distant Motutapu where an early Polynesian settlement was buried by the ash from the firey birth of the nearby triple-peaked Rangitoto in the fourteenth century.

By 1350 the big bird was becoming rare and the South Island Maoris increased their forgaging for fern roots and smaller birds. Kumara and taro, brought from eastern Polynesia, flourished in the North Island's warmer valleys, encouraging a more settled lifestyle, which gave dominance to the northern tribes. Visit Rewa's kainga (unfortified village) at Kerikeri and you will see simple whare puni (sleeping houses) made of the reed raupo, and pataka (food storehouses) typical of the eighteenth-century Classic period of Maori culture. From the reconstructed village look out across the now peaceful inlet to Kororipo Pa, from which the chief Hongi launched musket raids on the almost defenceless southern tribes. Near to the pa may be seen the historic Stone Store, together with New Zealand's oldest mission-period building, Kemp House.

The more permanent lifestyle resulted in an increase in inter-tribal fighting and the development of fortified hilltop villages or pa, to which the people retreated in times of danger. The carved war canoes joined the whare runanga (meeting house) as one of a tribe's most treasured possessions. See Te Mata o Hotoroa in Wanganui Museum, and the huge canoe Te Toki a Tapiri at Auckland Museum, saved from being burned following the wars of the 1860s.

In Touch with History

The Auckland isthmus with its steep headlands, islands and volcanic cones was especially densely populated, with probably 3,000 to 4,000 inhabitants in pre-European times. The flanks of mountains like Mt Eden, Mt Wellington and One Tree Hill, though now bare of their wooden palisades, are carved with broad terraces and steep scarps, signs of their former occupation. At Turuturumokai Pa near Hawera in Taranaki the deep trenches and underground passages made it a formidable stronghold. Ruapekapeka in Northland was so strongly fortified against the British that it took 20 men to uproot a single post after its capture. Its largely underground refuges served as a model for trench warfare in World War I.

At Auckland's west coast beach, Piha, climb the 100 metre (330-foot) Lion Rock, once an island pa but now accessible at all tides, and look south across the bay to Taitomo (Camel Rock), protected on three sides by sheer cliffs. Both were used as refuges during the intertribal conflicts of the eighteenth and early nineteenth centuries.

The first European explorers and missionaries brought potatoes, iron implements and axes, helping Maori farming to expand, but they also brought guns. The early 1800s saw much bloodshed and changing of tribal boundaries as well as skirmishes with visiting Europeans who came to loot for kauri spars, seals and whales and to 'save souls'.

It was this period too that saw the development of elaborate meeting houses beside the marae, the open space where tribal matters were discussed. Te Hau ki Turanga in the National Museum was built in Poverty Bay in the 1840s and is considered the finest example of a carved meeting house. Hotunui at Auckland Museum was carved in 1868. Also at Auckland is Hotunui Pukeroa, the gateway figure from a Rotorua pa. Stripped of the ubiquitous rust-red paint used in the late 1800s, it reveals its true colours – white, red, black and green.

The Waitangi Meeting House beside the Treaty House in the Bay of Islands has no name. It belongs to the Maori people as a whole, its carved figures representing heroes and ancestors of all the main tribes.

The Bay of Islands represents a turning point in New Zealand history, for it was here that the missionaries set up headquarters and here that the first town, Kororareka, now Russell, began as an untidy village of shanties, stores and pubs. Across the Bay from here in 1840, the British Government and Maori chiefs signed the still-controversial Treaty of Waitangi at the Georgian-styled Treaty House. Above the present town of Russell (formerly Kororareka) looms the flagstaff that Hone Heke, one of the first Maori signatories to the treaty, cut down repeatedly in frustration when he saw the promises of the document not being honoured.

SEE ALSO:

Outback Safaris: Te Rehuwai Safaris (Rotorua).
Regional:
Bay of Plenty: Ohaki Maori Village (Te Kuiti), Ruihana Wood Carvings (Rotorua).
Wellington: Wanganui Regional Museum.

Historic Places

Travellers in New Zealand can visit historic places owned or administered by the New Zealand Historic Places Trust from Kerikeri in the far north to Waikouaiti in Otago.

Beside the Stone Store in the Kerikeri basin stands New Zealand's oldest wooden building, Kemp House, built in 1822 for the Anglican Mission established there by Samuel Marsden. Constructed with hand-made nails and a kauri shingle roof, the house was home from 1832 to the blacksmith-missionary James Kemp, and generations of Kemps lived there till it was handed to the nation in 1974. The Kemps also ran the Stone Store as a shop. It still operates today.

Inland from the Bay of Islands, at Waimate North, is New Zealand's second oldest surviving house, once part of a thriving Selwyn-founded mission farm. Built in 1831-32 by Maori workers, it stood in the centre of a large Maori population and it was the place where the great Ngapuhi chief, Hongi Hika, had his cultivations. In its heyday the mission was a busy village with a mill, English crops, pigs and poultry. But the farm was uneconomic and during the war in the north in the 1840s all the buildings, fences and gardens suffered badly while British troops were stationed there. The mission house escaped serious damage and has been returned to its original condition. Even the green walls one missionary wife called 'dismal' have been repainted to the original colour.

The Catholics founded missions too, and Pompallier House, named after New Zealand's first Catholic bishop, still looks out over the bustling Russell Harbour. The 1841 house is a substantial pisé-de-terre (rammed earth) structure with two-foot-thick walls and light, airy verandahs. For eight years Pompallier House served as the mission printery and published religious books in the Maori language. The original Gaveaux press was later used by the Maori King Movement in the Waikato, but was returned by the Maori Queen as prize exhibit for the present museum in the house.

Hurworth, near New Plymouth in Taranaki, is the plain timber house of Harry Atkinson. He arrived in 1853, took up 80 hectares (200 acres) of bush land and sawed his own timber for the modest house he built. From this beginning he went on to become Sir Harry, and premier of New Zealand four times.

From early in the nineteenth century European whalers tracked their prey in New Zealand waters. In 1842 a Scot, Robert Fyffe, established a shore-based whaling station and whaled on the Kaikoura Peninsula in Marlborough. His brother George built the home that is all that remains of the enterprise. Fyffe House is in many respects a typical early weatherboard

Waimate Mission House, Waimate North. ***(Courtesy Historic Places Trust)***

Hurworth, New Plymouth. ***(Courtesy Historic Places Trust)***

Pompallier House, Russell. ***(Courtesy Historic Places Trust)***

Alberton, Auckland. ***(Courtesy Historic Places Trust)***

cottage, but the whaling background is built into the house. The piles of one wing, still visible at the back of seats under the verandah, are large whale vertebrae, and the house's pink hue comes from a paint mixture of whale oil and red and white lead.

In Auckland the history of Ewelme cottage shows how extensively Auckland has sprawled in 120 years. Built in 1864 on the open fields of Parnell, Ewelme was city home for Vicesimus Lush, vicar of coastal Howick. The journey is now made through unbroken suburban housing. The land wars of the 1860s did not reach Auckland so the cottage was a refuge for the Lush family from the more vulnerable Howick. The house remained in the family for over 100 years and was altered little in that time. The family preserved an extraordinary amount of the ordinary paraphernalia of a Victorian household; even early carpets and wallpapers survive to be admired.

Much grander Auckland houses are Alberton in Mt Albert and Highwic in Newmarket, both dating from the same period as Ewelme. Highwic, with its expansive view and sweeping lawns, was built in early English style for a prosperous stock and station agent, Alfred Buckland. Successive extensions accommodated his 21 children. Behind the grand ballroom and lavish dining room, a clutter of kitchens comprise the work area.

Timeball station, Lyttelton. ***(Courtesy Historic Places Trust)***

Another successful settler was Allan Kerr-Taylor, who invested profit from his 220-hectare (550-acre) farm in forestry and gold mining. As his fortunes grew so did his house, from a simple gabled farmhouse to an ornate mansion featuring towers and balconies that reflected Kerr-Taylor's Indian birthplace. Alberton was a great social centre, host to dances, archery parties and hunts. A team of servants, living more austerely in spartan attic rooms, serviced the family's luxurious lifestyle.

Industry too had its place in Victorian New Zealand. The Trust has cleared the scrub and gorse hiding the Brunner Industrial Site in the Grey Valley on the west coast of the South Island. Here coal was mined and coke, fire-bricks and other products were manufactured from the 1860s to the 1940s.

Ewelme, Auckland. ***(Courtesy Historic Places Trust)***

At Totara Estate near Oamaru you can visit the birthplace of New Zealand's export meat industry. This is where the stock for the first shipment of frozen meat was killed and dressed; the carcasses were then taken to Port Chalmers where the refrigerated sailing ship *Dunedin* waited to take her historic cargo to Britain.

The Lyttelton Time-ball Station, erected in 1876, enabled sea captains to check the accuracy of their chronometers. Stations like this existed in ports all round the world, but few survive in working order, as Lyttelton's does.

Further south at Oturehua in Otago the Trust operates a rural engineering works. In 1895 Ernest Hayes manufactured pollard cutters (pollard was a bran mixture used for poisoning rabbits), while his wife Hannah cycled the countryside, returning with farmers' orders that turned this into a flourishing farm-equipment business. The smithy is still operational.

Antrim House in Wellington's Boulcott Street is home for the Historic Places Trust. Appropriately it's a historic house itself.

Hayes Engineering Works, Oturehua. ***(Courtesy Historic Places Trust)***

SEE ALSO:

Regional: Wellington: Kawana Mill (Wanganui), Old St Pauls (Wellington).

Historic Places

Bulldozers and cranes are the tools of the demolition trade, ripping into central Auckland's Victorian remnants and earthquake-prone Wellington's shakey core. But the new plate-glass and steel structures still jostle buildings that have escaped the wrecker's hammer. Take a look above the verandahs in any New Zealand city and you'll find the stone or wood pediments and cornices of the older city. Some are preserved, like Auckland's Custom House and Wellington's old Government Buildings, the largest wooden building in this hemisphere. But observant visitors will discover many for themselves.

From Antrim House in Wellington, get written guides for walks that will take you through historic Thorndon, the wharves and Aro Valley.

In Auckland the City Council operates free guided tours that show you the old Custom House, old Government House, and Auckland's original shoreline. Take yourself up Victoria Street West and see the pillars and verandahs of an earlier town.

Follow on to Victoria Park Market on the site of the old city incinerator and you'll be standing on the reclaimed shore of Freemans Bay, the wharves distant behind motorway fly-overs and cricket pitches. A little further on Renall Street preserves a narrow slice of nineteenth-century Auckland, artisans cottages stacked against each other down a hill.

Dunedin's Public Relations Office has a city walk that shows you the grand facades of historic buildings, the railway station and the police station. Dunedin's Pacific Street in Roslyn is worth a visit to see some historic houses, as are London Street, Maori Hill and upper High Street.

Increasing industrialisation brought people to the cities and jobs, and each family wants its quarter acre. The suburbs of Auckland's Massey and Wellington's Porirua contain acres of low-cost housing. Distinctive blocks of identical homes, the older ones with tiled roofs and high windows, are part of the state housing schemes first instituted by the Labour government after the depression of the 1930s to house New Zealand families. Orakei has older state houses; Mangere has modern developments.

Urban drift has brought what is called the 'new Maori migration' as Maoris leave depressed rural areas for city jobs. A Maori Affairs crash housing programme in the 1960s created the South Auckland suburb of Otara. In Rotorua tours can include an overnight stay at a marae. South of Matamata (on the Tauranga road) stop for fresh pikelets and tea at Te Omeka Marae, a rural marae that functions as a community centre for local people. Notice the symbols of the Ratana Church on the front of the building. Arepa and Omeka were the prophet Ratana's two sons, named after the Greek letters, alpha and omega, the beginning and the end.

Away from the larger cities, many small towns reflect the history or hint at the future. Walk down the enormously long main street in the old gold-mining town of Thames and note the many splendid Victorian pubs in fine condition; or Oamaru's Thames Street with its distinctive white limestone commercial buildings, the courthouse, gaol, stable, banks, and the Brydone Hotel.

To bring you into the 1980s, visit Kawerau, east of Rotorua. Kawerau was carved out of the bush and bracken to service the huge Tasman Pulp and Paper mill started in 1953. In 30 years the population has grown to over 8,000 people, but the mill downwind to the east still dominates the town with its mountain of logs and chips.

In Touch with History

Between the cities and the towns, wander off the main highways; the landscape is much the same as it was 50 or 100 years ago, except that the farm bike has replaced the horse.

Travel on to country roads with untidy verges thick with rank grass, gorse and wild flowers. Occasional bursts of rambling roses are legacies of colonial settlements. Drive past farmyards cluttered with oil drums and farm machinery, both functioning and dead. Corrugated iron characterises the New Zealand landscape, invariably rusty or bearing the faint markings of long-ago paint. Corrugated iron is used in New Zealand for everything from house roofs to water tanks to warehouses and houses. See one of the largest corrugated-iron buildings in the South Island at Dunedin – John McGregor's Engineering and Boilermaking firm.

Note also the miles upon miles of barbed wire, taut and gleaming, or sagging and dotted with white tufts of sheep wool.

SEE ALSO:

Regional:
Northland: **Kerikeri Stone Store.**
Wellington: **Alexander Turnbull Library.**
Westland: **Mitchells Gully Gold Mine, Shantytown.**
Otago: **Olveston, Olivers Courtyard and Restaurant.**
(NOTE: **Museums are listed under the For a More Relaxing Holiday section.)**

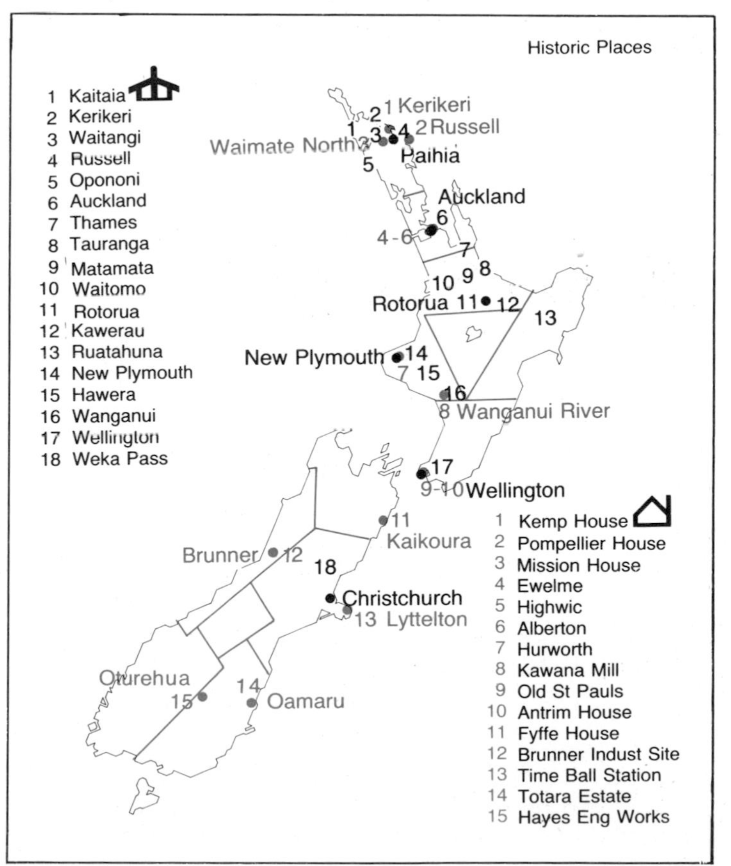

Down on the farm. *(National Publicity Studios)*

New Zealand supports around 3 million people, 10 million cattle and 60 million sheep. Ask any visitors for their lingering impressions of the country and the answer will inevitably include 'sheep', along with 'mountains, lakes, rivers and friendly people'.

Sheep are everywhere, even in city parks, and cows, responsible for the famous rich butter, graze wherever there is lowland pasture. You can't miss noticing either.

But visitors who want more than a passing glimpse of life 'down on the farm in New Zealand' can gain a close-up view by visiting a farm or taking a farm holiday.

You can discover why this land is one of the best, most efficient, agricultural producers in the world by making day visits to farms. Tour a dairy farm with its highly mechanised milking system – cows are milked by machines that deliver the milk to holding tanks, from where it is syphoned into large tankers for transport to factories.

You can visit a high-country sheep station where a shearer can remove the wool from 300 sheep in a day. Tour a deer farm where deer are bred for velvet and venison. Learn that the ubiquitous kiwifruit is the product of carefully tended vines growing in rich soil in a subtropical climate. Tour vineyards, large and small, and take the opportunity to sample the products. See some of the world's largest man-made forests where *Pinus radiata* romps to maturity in 25 years. Take a look at stud farms with prize cattle, sheep or racehorses.

Visitors with a special involvement in a particular aspect of agriculture can arrange to visit a government research station. In the midst of the Waikato dairying country, the largest such research centre has five dairy farms and concentrates on soil fertility, weed control, irrigation and animal health. Nearby is the world's largest milk-processing plant, which can cope with 1,688,000 litres (375,000 gallons) a day.

To see the latest in farm equipment and expertise, join the 75,000 visitors to the annual three-day National Field Day at Mystery Creek, near Hamilton, in June. The innovations range from earth-moving machinery to electric fencing, the stock from prize bulls to prize rabbits. It is one huge farming market that attracts farmers from as far afield as Europe, North America, South America, the Middle East and Asia. Even if you're not shopping for the latest tractor, Mystery Creek is worth a visit.

In a farming country there is always something going on somewhere. There are special tourist displays such as Rotorua's Agrodome or Queenstown's Cattledrome, but you can also find the real rural New Zealand at a show day, an agricultural exhibition, sheepdog trials, shearing contest or sale day. Catch the rumbustious atmosphere of sale day in country towns such as Feilding, where animals are herded into the stockyards to be sold at auction.

Get a taste of rural life at an Agricultural and Pastoral Society Show – every farming community has an annual A & P Show. In small towns the show is a festival of rural living, an annual fair where the best local breeds and produce are on display, children parade their pet lambs and calves, riders and horses compete for prizes in the show ring and farmers' wives compete for prizes with cream-laden cakes and jars of preserves.

The biggest A & P Show is a city show, the annual Easter Show in Auckland. For an excellent large country fair, the Hastings A & P Show in October is hard to beat.

In the hill country and mountains, sheep such as hardy Merino are bred for their wool. On lowland farms, Corriedale, Romney and cross-breeds are fattened for meat, which will find its way onto tables throughout the world.

Down on the farm

Dairy farms are found from Northland to Southland, but the main dairying areas are the Waikato and Taranaki in the North Island. Beef cattle too are found everywhere but are most common on the hills of the North Island, run together with sheep.

Less traditional farms include angora goat farms, deer farms, rabbit farms and fitch farms. Forest farms combine grazing stock with commercial pine forest. Farm parks are working farms, often on the coast, giving free access to the public, such as the Cape Colville Farm Park on Coromandel Peninsula. This farm concentrates on breeding Hereford cattle, is fringed with sandy bays and beaches and allows some camping.

With an excess of fresh clean air, water and soil, all kinds of crops thrive in a variety of climates – from avocados to cherries, asparagus or apricots.

There are subtropical orchards concentrated around Kerikeri in Northland and Te Puke in the Bay of Plenty, growing sweet oranges, mandarins, kiwifruit, tamarillos, avocados, persimmons and babacos. Stone and pip fruit such as apples, peaches and plums are grown everywhere, but the main commercial orchards are found around Auckland, Hawkes Bay, Nelson and Central Otago. Almost every area has its specialist crop – asparagus in Hawkes Bay, garlic and grapes around Blenheim, oranges in the north, blackcurrants and apricots in the south. If you are driving around and see P.Y.O. signs, they mean 'pick your own'. Either buy produce fresh at the orchard gate or even cheaper and lots of fun, pick your own.

Bay of Islands Scenic Farm Safari Tours
PO Box 36
Paihia
Telephone: (0885) 27-379
Owner: Dorothy and Roger Bayly

A personally conducted overland tour of 2½ hours duration, in a modern Land Rover, will take you through historic "Wairoa" station, first settled in 1837, now one of the most picturesque sheep and cattle stations in New Zealand.

The station, consisting of 890 hectares (2,200 acres), winters 6,000 Romney sheep and 1,200 predominantly Angus cattle, all high-quality stock. This tour offers modern farming techniques together with fabulous coastal scenery. See where the first horses landed in New Zealand in 1839 from Valparaiso in Chile; see also seasonal occupations such as shearing, silage making, lambing, docking, etc. Also to be seen are many free-ranging peacocks, turkeys, geese, guinea fowl and ducks.

Morning and afternoon teas are served in a private home during the tour. There is ample time for photos and questions. Adults, $12; children under 12 years, $7; children under 5 years, free. Prices include morning and afternoon tea.

Longlands Farm
Burwood Road
Matamata
Telephone: (0818) 6588
Hosts: Kerry and Silvia Simpson

Whether you have a special interest in dairy farming or would simply like to see this highly mechanised, low labour industry in operation, visit the lush green pastures of Longlands Dairy Farm and watch a milking demonstration. After viewing and listening to commentary on the day-to-day running of the farm, join Kerry and Silvia for lunch, overlooking the pool in the beautiful garden. Specialities include barbecued lamb, a great array of fresh salads and New Zealand cheeses, complemented with New Zealand beer, wine and fruit juices. Kerry and Silvia cater for both large and small groups and the farm can also be visited through the Farm Highlights Tour operating from Matamata. Brochures available in four languages, including German and Japanese. Book through your tour operator or direct by telephone or mail. Cost: $14 and well worth it! Geared for group tours.

The Agrodome
Riverdale Park
Ngongotaha
PO Box 634
Rotorua
Telephone: (073) 74-350

Not to be missed, the Agrodome is a large building set in lush green pastureland, a permanent exhibition built from prime timbers. Browse around the Sheepskin Shop (full of quality woollen products) and take a coffee break in the Farmhouse Tearooms. Then take your seats for the stage show – a wonderful 60-minute entertainment (rated the best of its kind in the world), starring the top nineteen ram breeds in New Zealand, sheep dogs and one human master of ceremonies. A unique multiple-language sound system is provided for the benefit of all. You will learn about wool, see a sheep-shearing demonstration and an exhibition of New Zealand sheep dogs working the stock. Three shows are held daily, at 9.15 a.m., 11.00 a.m. and 2.30 p.m., seven days a week. A bus service operates from Rotorua. Don't forget your camera, you'll need it. Bookings unnecessary unless a very large group. From $3.50 adults, $1 children. Family concessions, group rates.

Expo Cattledrome
Skippers Park
RD1
Queenstown
Telephone: Queenstown 882M

The only show of its kind in the world – an amazing live stage show offering wonderful family entertainment. Stars are selected cattle that represent New Zealand's beef and dairy industry. Touch these animals and experience the thrill of hand-milking a cow! Two shows held daily, 9.30 a.m. and 2.15 p.m. (check times June through August, usually one show daily). H&H coach departs 9.00 a.m. and 2.15 p.m. daily (Arrowtown optional). Bring your camera. Bookings not essential, unless large tour party. From $3.50 adults, $1 children. Discounts for large groups on application.

SEE ALSO:

Lodges: Maungaraupi (Marton).
Regional:
Bay of Plenty: Farm Highlights Tours (Matamata), Matamata Racing Club, McLoughlins Orchards (Te Puke).
Southern Lakes: Cecil Peak Station (Queenstown).

Drovers and cattle.
(Andris Aspe Ltd)

Living with New Zealanders

ecide on a farm holiday and you won't find yourself on a 'dude' farm but on a real, working farm. Paying guests stay in farmhouses that offer high standards of comfort; houses vary from rambling, colonial charm to modern, sophisticated design. You live with the family, get to try your hand at farmwork if you wish and enjoy typical hearty farm fare – cooked breakfasts, rich roasts of lamb, mutton or beef, and between-meal sustenance of scones and sandwiches. It is a great way to experience New Zealand life, and for those with particular farming interests it offers the chance to gain some first-hand knowledge.

The farms may also offer contact with history – an old goldmine, magnificent old machinery, small country settlement or an old pub. And there are different types of farms all over the country: beef, sheep, dairy, horticultural; farms in the lowland, the high country, near towns or in the outback.

'Homestays' is the term given to urban accommodation with New Zealand families. Host families from many walks of life invite you to their homes, which range from some of the great historic houses of New Zealand to modern suburban houses.

Living with New Zealanders is an excellent way to learn about local social and political issues, sports and the arts, or, if you have a special interest, to meet others so inclined. Most home host organisations can arrange for special interests if given sufficient time. Out of this contact come friendships that sometimes last many years, and a real insight into the lives of some New Zealanders.

One of the best ways of getting to know the country is to stay with the people. Not only do you meet one family, but they may also introduce you to their friends and different ways of life.

'Aspley House' Farm Stay
Atkinson Road
Ohaeawai RD
Bay of Islands
Telephone: Ohaeawai 424
Hosts: Frank and Joy Atkinson

Five minutes from State Highway 10 at Puketona Junction, find this stately and attractive old colonial styled home, a landmark seen from the road, in its rural setting of gently rolling hills. The 304 hectare (750 acre) farm carries Romney sheep and Hereford cattle. The house is surrounded by spacious lawns and gardens, with a magnificent kidney-shaped pool for summer swimming. The views are superb and accommodation comfortable, in twin-bedded rooms with private facilities. Enjoy delicious gourmet meals, go duck and pheasant shooting May/June, or join in farm activities if you would like to. Experience the many attractions of this historic and beautiful area, all only short driving distances away. Frank and Joy will be happy to assist with sightseeing arrangements. From $40 per day, meals included.

Kai Iwi Lakes Farm Stays
Lakes Road, Omamari
RD 3 Dargaville
Telephone: Mamaranui 564
Hosts: Nancy and Basil Finlayson

Situated 34 kilometres (21 miles) north of Dargaville in green farmland, this 202-hectare (500-acre) mixed farm offers a wonderful holiday. Named after the famous nearby Kai Iwi Lakes with their white sandy beaches and pure waters. These lakes are wonderful for swimming, yachting, water skiing, picnicking and fishing, and contain an abundance of rainbow trout; Basil (an experienced fisherman) will be pleased to organise a sortie. Stay in a fully self-contained unit (sleeping four) with its own kitchen facilities. You are invited to dine with your hosts if you choose. Walk across the farm to a lovely and endless sandy ocean beach; go horse-riding, or take part in farm activities and see working dog trials. The farm offers real solitude from the city crowds, and traditional Northern hospitality. Courtesy transport available from Dargaville. From $50 per unit. Meals additional, from $15 (including wine).

New Zealand Home Hospitality Ltd
PO Box 309
Nelson
Telephone: (054) 82-424
Telex: NZ 3914
Owners: Dulcie and Allan Carson

One of the real attractions of our country is the friendliness of its people. Staying with New Zealanders in their homes as you travel around must be one of the loveliest ways to make the most of your visit – learning how we live and making life long friends while enjoying personal comfort. This is a reservation service for home-hosted accommodation with private families throughout New Zealand. Each host family – whether farm, city or country dwellers – provides quality accommodation and delicious home-cooked meals within the warm and friendly atmosphere of their homes. Hosts live in all the major tourism centres, main entry and departure cities, on farms with traditional or new farming and horticultural activities, in historic homes, on high-country sheep stations, by lake and seashore. Wherever you wish to visit, this company is sure to have a host. A minimum stay of two nights is recommended. The service is flexible to suit your travel plans, with three options: one or more reservations to stay with hosts in the location of your choice, bed and breakfast (New Zealand style, booking as you go) or complete holidays – the first night in a hotel, rental car and either free-wheeling or reserved home-hosted bed and breakfast. Note: Free-wheeling packages may not be available during winter months. Individuals, couples and family groups are all catered for. Children accommodated without their parents are charged at full adult rates. From $40 to $60 per night, depending on requirements.

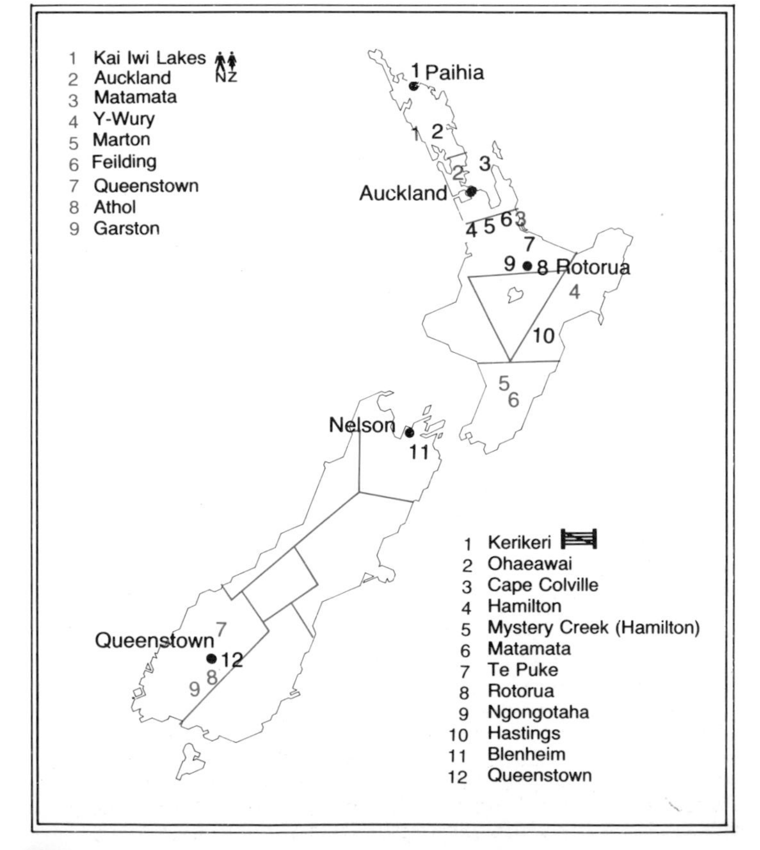

Living with New Zealanders

Growse House
13 Allender Drive
Torbay
Auckland
Telephone: (09) 404-6603
Hosts: Kathleen and Jeremy Rees-Webbe

Enjoy home-style accommodation in a friendly atmosphere. Situated in the lovely East Coast Bays of Auckland's North Shore, handy to beaches and the many attractions of the city. Growse House accommodates small numbers of guests in well-appointed, private facilities. Delicious New Zealand home-cooked meals and congenial company (Kathleen speaks German and French). Picnic lunches prepared as required. Courtesy transport is provided from the airport. From $40 per night.

'The Homestead'
Morgan Road
RD2
Matamata
Telephone: (0818) 8426
Hosts: Shirley and Rex Stead

In the heart of the Waikato (rich farming and horse-breeding country) enjoy country hospitality as a part of this family, staying on their 61-hectare (25-acre) property, set in a tranquil valley 10 kilometres (6 miles) from Matamata. Shirley and Rex cater to your requirements (even providing 24-hour service when required) with delicious home-cooked meals, your favourite drinks, sporting equipment (from squash to golf and fishing), personally escorted trips to thermal Rotorua, Waitomo Caves, the beaches of Mount Maunganui (short trips from your base), and farm/stud and dairy farm visits. They will meet you at Auckland International Airport on arrival, if desired. You nominate your activity, the Steads oblige, aiming to make your stay with them as relaxed and pleasurable as possible. Accommodation is in tastefully furnished twin bedroom with private lounge, bathroom and toilet facilities. From $100 per day (depending on requirements).

Y-Wury Station
Private Bag
Gisborne
Telephone: (079) 37-176
Hosts: Tim and Bronwyn Gaddum

Experience everyday life on a high-country sheep station, staying at Y-Wury – spectacularly located 600 metres (1,696 feet) above sea level, looking out over hills and ocean) 'off the beaten track', with a superb climate. The modern homestead offers accommodation for four guests, with private double bedrooms and bathroom facilities, or a cottage sleeping six where you provide what you need. Go farming – mustering and shearing sheep, horseback riding, lambing (spring) and four-wheel-drive excursions. Or take it easy going for walks in the country air, playing tennis and relaxing in the spa pool. Less than one hour's travelling to safe swimming beaches and Gisborne, 'Y-Wury' is handy to excellent fishing and hunting grounds. Enjoy convivial country hospitality, farm-fresh food and relaxing evenings around an open fire. From $10 to $210 according to requirements.

Riverview
PO Box 19
Athol, Southland
Telephone: Garston 866
Hosts: Liz and Winston Soper

On the main route between Queenstown and Te Anau-Milford Sound, is 'Riverview', a 350-hectare (865-acre) sheep station situated in the heart of the scenic Southern Lakes. Participate in the busy farm schedule, mustering, shearing, working sheep dogs, and outdoor activities or relax and enjoy the peace. The homestead overlooks the Mataura River, with gardens, swimming pool, children's play area and trampoline. Comfortable accommodation for two couples or one couple and three children, plus large living area complete with billiard room. Liz prepares superb meals, with specialities like fresh trout, wild duck and venison, garden fresh vegetables and fruit – barbecues and picnics during summer. For outdoor enthusiasts, go tramping, walking, horse riding, trout fishing, gold panning, and kayaking. Access by N.Z.R. Road Services, the Kingston Flyer or flight from Queenstown; or rental car. From $70 per night. Special rates for children.

Wharekauhau Lodge
Wairarapa
R.H.C. Reservations:
Telephone: (03) 799-127
(USA: 800-874-7207)
Telex: NZ 4051 RHCHOT
(USA: 8874486)

This genuine New Zealand sheep station has the second-oldest Romney stud in the country – running 10,000 Romney sheep and 500 head of prime Hereford cattle, managed from a comfortable and well-appointed colonial homestead. It is situated on the coast, looking out across Cook Strait to the distant mountains of the South Island. In high, forested ranges, go pig and stag hunting with an experienced guide. Bill and Annette, your hosts, are a typical New Zealand family, with a flair for making guests feel at home. The station, with all this, is a mere 90-minute drive from Wellington,or short flight by helicopter. From $115 (all drinks and meals included).

Birch Hill
Garston
R.H.C. Reservations
Telephone: (03) 799-126/7
(USA: 800-874-7207)
Telex: NZ4051
(USA: 8874486)

Set in the Southern Lakes district, one hour's drive from Queenstown, this lovely homestead offers friendly country living on a sheep farm. Experience farming activities, go tramping, fishing and angling, or simply relax. Comfortable accommodation in two twin rooms with private facilities. Dine in a family atmosphere enjoying delicious country cooking. Hosts are happy to arrange special tours or sightseeing trips. From $95 per person, per night (meals, drinks, transport from Garston inclusive).

SEE ALSO:
Regional: Southern Lakes: Cecil Peak Station (Queenstown).

Apsley House, Ohaeawai, Bay of Islands. *(Courtesy Apsley House)*

For a more relaxing holiday

Whale Bay, Whangarei. *(Courtesy Ron Monton)*

If you want to holiday at a more sedate pace, or you need a restful breathing space, New Zealand offers many choices. In these small islands interesting sights and experiences are never far away.

For tired limbs, soak in a hot mineral pool. You can often hire a private pool and loll in the steamy water with friends. There are well-known pools in Rotorua, and at Waiwera and Parakai north of Auckland. But try Hauraki Hot Springs on the flat plains farmland at Miranda; Morere, south of Gisborne, where you can also picnic in a pleasant bush reserve; Te Puia on the East Coast Road; Okoroire under its sheltering plane trees in the Waikato. You'll need a spade at Hot Water Beach on Coromandel Peninsula. Dig your own bathing hole in the sand at low tide; adjust the temperature by digging deeper.

In the South Island, Hanmer Springs in North Canterbury was once a fashionable spa, the thermal pools reputed to ease arthritis and skin diseases. At Maruia Hot Springs on the Lewis Pass Road, you can take the waters while admiring a spectacular setting of bush and snow-covered hills.

In warmer weather the beaches beckon. In Wellington and Auckland there are splendid clean beaches right in the city; try especially tree-fringed Thorne's Bay on Auckland's North Shore, good for swimming at all tides. But a little further afield New Zealand has hundreds of beaches from well-populated resorts to untouched gems fringed with scarlet-flowered pohutukawa and plume-headed toitoi. East coast beaches have golden sand and even surf. On the west coast the iron sand is black or the beaches are pebbly, and the sea surges in across the Tasman in rolling breakers. Most of the popular beaches are patrolled by surf clubs.

Visit the fishing village of Makara, west of Wellington, or take an impromptu lunch of french bread and smoked fish roe to Auckland's dramatic west coast beaches from Karekare to Muriwai. On a good day take towel, togs (bathing suit) and a book and idle the day away.

Literature

Reading fiction will open to you the world of New Zealanders. All towns of any size will have a library and bookshops. In fact, New Zealanders buy more books per head of population than any other nation. Browse through them and look for New Zealand authors.

Katherine Mansfield was part of the same literary set as Virginia Woolf and Vita Sackville-West. Read her short stories 'At the Bay' and 'The Garden Party' for memorable scenes of middle-class colonial life.

The traumas of growing up in the early years of this century are the subject matter of two autobiographical novels: Robin Hyde's *The Godwits Fly* and Labour politician John A. Lee's *Children of the Poor*. Ronald Hugh Morrieson's novels of small-town New Zealand, *Pallet on the Floor* and *The Scarecrow*, have been made into films and have made him into a cult figure for a younger generation. And Maurice Gee creates heroes of 'ordinary' New Zealanders in *Plumb* and *Meg*. Read Barry Crump's on-the-road type novels, especially *A Good Keen Man*. Try Maurice Shadbolt's collection of short stories *The New Zealanders*. In *Smith's Dream*, C. K. Stead takes us into a near future where riot police and US soldiers battle ordinary citizens, turned guerillas.

Two New Zealand authors are currently enjoying international recognition. Janet Frame's novels explore the inner world – *State of Seige* and *Living in the Maniototo* – and experiences in mental institutions – *Faces in the Water*. The first volume of her autobiography – *To the Is-Land* – has been much praised. Sylvia Ashton-Warner is internationally acclaimed as an educationalist and a writer. Her novel *Spinster* tells of a young woman teacher in a small New Zealand school; it was filmed starring Shirley MacLaine.

Younger writers who are making a mark include Sue

McCauley, whose *Other Halves* examines the pleasures and pain of a love relationship between a European woman and a younger Maori man; and Maori writer Keri Hulme, creator of the epic novel *The Bone People*.

Other Maori writers specialise in short stories, especially Wiiti Ihimaera, who in *Whanau* and *The New Net Goes Fishing* looks at rural Maori life and the effect of the shift to industrial cities. In *The Dream Sleepers* Patricia Grace paints evocative pictures of Maori family life and the clash of traditional Maori and modern European values. Ihimaera and D. S. Long have co-edited an anthology of Maori writing; called *Into the World of Light*, it represents a range of Maori writers.

Small children will delight in two recent picture books: Patricia Grace and Robyn Kahukiwa's *The Kuia and the Spider* and Miriam Smith and David Armitage's *Kim and the Watermelon*.

Films, Music and Theatre

If you like seeing rather than reading, look in daily paper's entertainment pages for recent New Zealand movies that may be playing. There's a small but active industry here; an exhibit at the Film Archive in Wellington traces the industry's development.

In the entertainment pages look too for gigs featuring local musicians. At concerts, open-air soundshells (in the summer) and in pubs you'll hear everything from rock to country and western. Maori music might be heard on the hit parade, or featured at Maori or Polynesian festivals and cultural events.

At live theatre you could see a local production of overseas work by anyone from Shakespeare to Caryl Churchill, or catch a New Zealand play. In Auckland visit Theatre Corporate or the Mercury; in Wellington, Downstage and Circa; in Christchurch, the Court; in Dunedin, the Fortune; and in Hamilton, the Founders Theatre.

The Fine Arts

At the Founders also admire the Ralph Hotere mural. You'll notice murals also in other places you visit. At Auckland Airport waiting in queues is brightened by huge 40-metre (120-foot) long murals. The Beehive in Wellington is dominated by John Drawbridge's mural, and enormous woven wall hangings. Auckland University's School of Architecture, the new Arts/Commerce block and the Medical School all feature stunning wall art. Artist Robin White painted the Otago Peninsula and healing words on her mural at Otago Medical School; Pat Hanly uses the spectrum of colours on a festive theme to adorn the new Christchurch Town Hall. In Auckland see bright street murals commissioned under a Labour Department Artworks scheme employing young artists.

If you want to see something smaller, visit public art galleries in all the centres. Most have collections that include colonial artists like John Kinder and John Gully, important twentieth-century artists like Frances Hodgkins and Rita Angus and contemporary artists like Toss Woollaston, Colin McCahon, Selwyn Muru, Gretchen Albrecht and Tony Fomison. Look out for the Lindauer Maori portraits at Auckland, Len Lye's kinetic sculptures at the Govett Brewster in New Plymouth, the Edith Colliers at the Sargeant in Wanganui, Colin McCahon's Northland panels and the Rita

Maori carver at work, Maori Art's and Craft's Institute, Whakarewarewa, Rotorua. ***(National Publicity Studios)***

Angus collection in Wellington, early New Zealand water colours at the Bishop Suter in Nelson and famous Goldie Maori portraits in Dunedin.

Private dealer galleries exhibit the latest paintings and prints of contemporary New Zealand artists. A print showing landscapes or social life by Stanley Palmer, Marilynn Webb, Nigel Brown or Fassett Burnett can be bought at a reasonable price and will hold special memories of the country. In Auckland visit Denis Cohn, RKS and New Vision; in Hamilton, Centre Gallery; in Wellington, Janne Land, Gallery Legard, Peter McLeavey and next door, Louise Beale; in Christchurch, Brooke Gifford; and Dunedin, Red Metro and the Bosshard. Have lunch or supper at the City Limits Cafe in Wellington or The Last and First in Auckland and you'll see the latest work of young artists.

The Art of the Maori

Public museums show examples of Maori art from incised domestic gourds and ancient heirloom greenstone hei tiki, to soaring carved meeting houses and canoes to seat a hundred warriors.

Spears, adzes, even fish hooks of stone, bone, wood and jade were brilliantly finished, polished and carved with spiral and other symbolic patterns. The whare runanga (meeting houses) have carefully chiselled support and facing posts, painted rafter patterns and tukutuku weaving on the walls. All designs have special meaning to the tribe who created them, celebrating ancestors and spiritual roots, and each whare runanga is named. Pataka, or elevated store houses, are also elaborately decorated.

Maori weaving created treasured ceremonial cloaks of dog skin, gleaming kiwi and kaka parrot feathers, and korowai (cloaks) decorated with black-dyed tags. At Ohaki Maori village near the Waitomo caves, visit a weaving centre built by the family of Rangimarie Hetet and her daughter, Digger Te Kanawa, to show their skill at weaving flax korowai. Visitors

Lake Hayes, near Arrowtown, Southern Lakes. ***(Andris Apse Ltd)***

can see all parts of the weaving process and feel the flax in their hands.

Crafts

In craft shops watch out for beautiful traditional woven kits made from harakeke (flax).

Rotorua is the home of the Maori Arts and Crafts Institute at Whakarewarewa, where you can see a Maori carver working. Also see a carver at work at Rotorua's Ohinemutu village on the lakeside, next to Tama-te-kapua, an outstanding whare runanga containing carvings of passengers on the ancestral Arawa canoe.

Moko or facial tattoos were very beautiful, but most old people bearing them have died – see them in photographer Marti Friedlander's book *Moko*. If you want to know about Maori mythology, look for *Wahine Toa*, in which writer Patricia Grace and artist Robyn Kahukiwa reinterpret Maori myths, emphasising strong women mythological figures and explaining Maori symbolism.

See superb examples of traditional Pacific art at Auckland and Dunedin's museums.

New Zealand is renowned for its pottery, which ranges from delicate translucent porcelain to chunky earthy stoneware. For something special visit the Hereford Fine China Studio in Hamilton, where figurines and miniature animals are made by skilled craftspeople.

The Dowse Art Gallery in Lower Hutt has a permanent collection of pots giving an overview of New Zealand pottery. Craft shops in cities and suburbs sell pots, but look also in country and seaside settlements for potteries set up by escapees from the city. Northland, Coromandel and Nelson have attracted many such alternative lifestylers.

Fine china at the Hereford Fine China Studio, Hamilton. (Courtesy Hereford Fine China)

Museums

Inside still, visit museums, large and small, public and private, to learn about New Zealand's Maori and colonial past and its natural history. All over New Zealand are pioneer villages, recreations of Victorian shops and streets, restored houses and specialist museums. You'll find museums specialising in the army (Waiouru), clocks (Whangarei), kauri timber milling (Otamatea at Matatoke, Northland), steam engines (Tokomaru), gold mining (Shantytown, Greymouth; Coaltown, Westport), native plants (Otari at Wellington), agriculture (Brayshaw, Blenheim), shipwrecks (Waitangi), cars (Queenstown), and the only major gallery of rugby memoribilia going back to the 1870s (Palmerston North).

Scenic Drives and Picnics

Ask at the local Automobile Association for scenic routes that will present spectacular views of coast, countryside and cities. Auckland's Scenic Drive takes you high above the city through native bush. From Christchurch drive round the five Signs of the Takahe or over the Cashmere Hills to Lyttelton via Taylors Mistake and other beautiful beaches. Drive round Wellington's sombre hill-locked harbour to the bays, where you'll see a plaque marking Katherine Mansfield's house. Go to the top of Bluff Hill and look beyond the aluminium smelter at Tiwae Point to Awarua Lagoon and Foveaux Strait beyond. From Tauranga's The Minden, you can see from East Cape to Coromandel in the west.

Combine a picnic with a drive. Most towns and cities have domains or botanic gardens where you can spread a rug and bring out the thermos and sandwiches. Very beautiful are Ashburton Domain with its massive trees and Christchurch's Botanic Gardens. On the Avon feed the ducks with lunch scraps then slide along the river in a hired punt.

Further out of town, bush reserves and beaches offer auspicious spots for an idyllic outing. Sit on the sun-baked rocks at McLaren Falls near Tauranga. Out of New Plymouth see the spectacular sight of conical Mt Egmont mirrored in the water at Lake Mangamahoe. Near Blenheim picnic on the Wairau Bar opposite an ancient moa-hunter site. The Otago Peninsula has many fine picnic places with the added attractions of an aquarium, pa sites, lighthouses, soaring cliffs, an albatross colony and a castle to be seen on the way. For something quite different, try the world's first timber maze at Wanaka.

Also visit the graveyard at Otakou Maori Church, the last resting place of three great South Island chiefs. Churchyards often have much to tell of New Zealand's past from historic events to domestic tragedies – small children died of influenza, young men drowned while whaling. At Christ Church in Russell, see the graves of the Ngapuhi chief Tamati Waka Nene, members of the family of the first honorary US consul, Clendon, and *Hazard* crew members killed in a clash with Hone Heke's men in 1845. At Waimate North see the graves of early missionaries and settlers as well as carved wooden Maori headboards seen only in Northland. At Queenstown cemetery see a plaque commemorating Chinese goldminers and at Otemataha Military Cemetery in Tauranga, sited on an old pa, read inscriptions the graves of Maori and Pakeha dead from the Gate Pa and Te Ranga Battles.

For a more relaxing holiday

To experience mainstream New Zealand social life, lean on the bar at the local pub or tavern with a handle of beer. You could try the carpeted, revamped lounge bar of one of the trendier hotels, then cross the road to where it's linoleum and formica tables for 'serious' drinking. There could be a game of darts or billiards in progress, or the radio or television giving the latest sports scores or racing results.

New Zealanders watch sports as much as they play. You can join the local crowds and maybe see some of the best sportsmen and women in the world – runners like Allison Roe and John Walker or world-famous All Black rugby players – and the sleekest, fastest horses. Enter Auckland's Ellerslie raceway through an avenue of towering phoenix palms. Further south visit Te Rapa at Hamilton, or Riccarton at Christchurch. Trotting is the specialty at the Alexandra Park Raceway in Auckland and Trentham in Wellington.

In the winter wrap up warmly and go to a rugby game – the major parks are Eden Park in Auckland, Athletic Park in Wellington, Lancaster Park in Christchurch, Carisbrook in Dunedin. In the summer watch a sparkling game of one-day cricket. All year round, watch wet-suited surf-board riders waiting like seagulls for the right wave at Piha near Auckland, Raglan west of Hamilton, and the golden Mt Maunganui.

Then there's polo at Clevedon and annual events like Auckland's yachting regatta and Round-the-Bays run. In the most out-of-the-way spots you might be entertained by a sports-loving New Zealander – a hang-glider circling over a deserted beach or a wind surfer in a remote bay.

New Zealand is a water-bound land, with cities and towns clinging to the shores of glistening bays and harbours studded with islands. To see Auckland's harbour take a ferry to the historic marine suburb of Devonport, to lovely Waiheke Island or the more distant Great Barrier Island. In remote areas join a rural mail and stores run. Nose into silent coves and nudge up against weathered jetties on the famed Bay of Islands Cream Trip or the Queen Charlotte Sound Mail Run in Marlborough.

SEE ALSO:

Museums:
Northland: Far Northern Regional (Kaitaia), Otamatea (Matakohe).
Bay of Plenty: Clydesdale, Waikato Art and History (Hamilton), Firth Tower (Matamata), Waikino Pioneer.
Wellington: Wanganui Regional.
Westland: West Coast Historical (Hokitika).
Southern Lakes: Sound and Light (Queenstown).
Historic Parks and Vintage Engine Museums:
Wellington: Tokomaru Steam Engine.
Canterbury: Yaldhurst Transport, Ferrymead (Christchurch), Plains Vintage Car (Ashburton), Pleasant Point Railway (Timaru).
Southern Lakes: Queenstown Motor, Matuku Engine (Te Anau).
Arts and Crafts:
Auckland: Auckland City Art Gallery, Clevedon Woolshed.
Bay of Plenty: Hereford Fine China International, Van der Sluis Pottery (Hamilton).
Canterbury: Ferrymead Bridge Gallery (Christchurch).
Mt Cook: Country Crafts (Omarama).
Westland: Hokitika Free Form Glass Factory.
Southern Lakes: Central Art Galleries (Queenstown), Jade Shop, Lake Country Press/Exclusive Crafts (Arrowtown).
And Different:
Auckland: Waiwera Hot Pools Resort (Auckland).
Southern Lakes: The Wanaka Maze – the original.

For a country that stretches 1,600 kilometres (1,000 miles) from north to south, with only 3 million people, the transport system is surprisingly well developed. While the cost sometimes may be higher than the heavily patronised routes of Europe or North America, the traveller has a good choice of alternatives.

In organising travel, remember that it takes longer to drive distances in New Zealand than might be expected. For example, the 657 kilometres (394 miles) between Auckland and Wellington takes 11 hours to drive (at legal speed limits with meal stops allowed), compared to 8½ hours for the 725 kilometres (435 miles) between San Francisco and Los Angeles.

Roads, however give access to the remote corners of the country, by car, campervan or scheduled bus service. When you run out of road try a horse or helicopter, or walk.

More limited in scope is the passenger rail service between Auckland and Wellington. A daylight journey on the main trunk line (13 hours) is very picturesque. Part of the track, known as the Raurimu Spiral, at the edge of the Waimarino Plateau, is an engineering feat of international note. Here the land rises 215 metres (700 feet) in 5.5 kilometres (3½ miles). To overcome the steep gradient, an ascending spiral in the form of a circle, three horseshoes and two short tunnels was constructed, increasing the distance to 11.5 kilometres (7 miles) – and thus reducing the gradient.

Branch lines operate from Wellington to New Plymouth, and Wellington to Gisborne. The New Zealand Railways (NZR) also run a car and passenger ferry service across Cook Strait and an intermittent passenger ferry service across Foveaux Strait.

The South Island main trunk runs from Picton to Christchurch and Dunedin. A branch line runs from Christchurch to Greymouth. NZR also runs an extensive scheduled bus service.

Scheduled bus services and regional touring services offer a comfortable and relaxed way of seeing some of the scenic areas of New Zealand. Large companies like Newmans, Guthreys, Mount Cook Lines, Fourways Pacific and H & H operate nationally, with many regional tours, for example Newtons (Dunedin), Pacific Tourways (Christchurch). Local tours, for example, out of Queenstown, can provide relief from driving in the high country.

Air travel connects most cities and towns in New Zealand and makes it possible to move quickly around the country.

In four to five hours, given changes of planes, it is possible to fly from remote Fiordland to Auckland by scheduled service. Three tiers of service exist: a national carrier (Air New Zealand), a sub-national carrier and tour operation (Mount Cook Line), plus a variety of small regional airlines that often operate charter aircraft and flight-seeing services.

Given the geological and scenic diversity in the country, air travel, especially by small plane, should not be missed. And there is a wonderful variety of aircraft as well: Boeing 737, Fokker F-27 Friendship, Hawker-Siddeley 748, Nomad, Islander, Cessnas 180/185s (ski planes), Banderantes, Piper Navaho, Metroliners, Cessna 402/Titan, Grummon Widgeons.

Touring in New Zealand

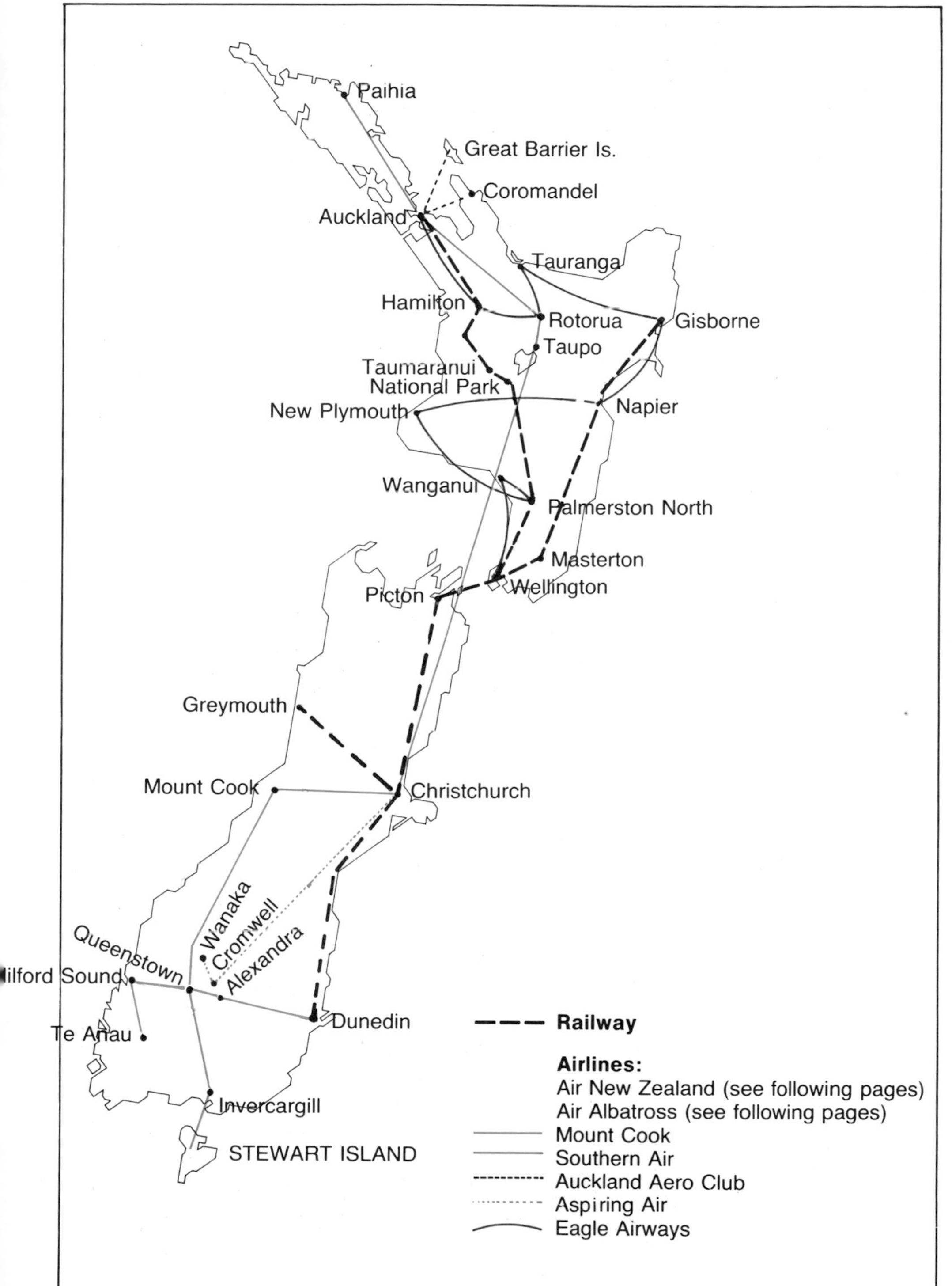

Getting about with air new zealand

Your time in New Zealand can be structured and organised (especially good if your stay is short) or casual and spur-of-the-moment so you can touch all places at leisure. Air New Zealand operates to 24 cities and towns from the far north to the deep south, and you can connect with rental cars (fly/drive), chauffeur cars, mini-buses, intercity buses and air-conditioned super coaches for regional guided tours. Roll-on, roll-off vehicle and passenger ferry boats operate between the North and South Islands.

Air New Zealand treats its guests to everything they are accustomed to receive anywhere else in the world and more. The welcome as you step aboard your Air New Zealand aircraft reflects not just great pride in the presentation of a commercial service, but a real happiness that you have chosen to discover and share our South Pacific paradise.

Any day of the week, Air New Zealand makes at least 220 flights between the 42 airports and 15 countries in its network. Twenty-three of these airports are in New Zealand and the others are spread between Australia, Fiji, Western Samoa, New Caledonia, Norfolk Island, the Cook Islands, Tahiti, North America, Tonga, Papua New Guinea, Singapore, Hong Kong, Japan and Britain. Air New Zealand has offices in each of these countries and in other major cities throughout the world.

Boeing 737s operate on the main routes within New Zealand as well as some South Pacific island destinations. Fokker Friendships link provincial centres with the main cities. The long-haul international sectors are flown by Boeing 747s, as are most of the South Pacific destinations.

The Koru

This symbol used in Maori art is shown on the tail of all Air New Zealand aircraft. The design symbolises the uncurling of native fern fronds, and also signifies continual growth and rebirth. It was first seen on the prows of early Maori canoes that navigated the vast reaches of the Pacific Ocean centuries ago. It is fitting that an airliner which spans the globe, bears the symbol high above those same seas.

Air New Zealand First Class

Fly first class on Air New Zealand and you'll be a very special passenger. First-class comfort, first-class service, first-class surroundings are made totally enjoyable by crew dedicated to ensuring your journey is pleasant and relaxed. And there is a first-class menu of gourmet dishes and connoisseur's wines. On these Boeing 747s a sheepskin-covered Recaro sleeper seat (which is really something to talk about) awaits you.There are just four rows of Recaro sleeper seats, with each row staggered to give a feeling of privacy. First-class passengers also enjoy easy check-in facilities and access to Air New Zealand V.I.P. lounges, available at most airports. Your baggage will be tagged 'first off' for quick retrieval at your destination.

Air New Zealand Pacific Class

For a little more than the normal economy fare, appreciate the extra space, relaxed atmosphere and special service of Air New Zealand's unique Pacific class on Boeing 747 aircraft. Pacific class is located on the upper deck, reached by an easy-access stairway. There are 16 wider-than-normal sheepskin-clad seats with special in-flight service to match. Pacific class travellers also enjoy special check-in facilities and access to Air New Zealand V.I.P. lounges at most airports and baggage is tagged 'first off' for quick retrieval at your destination.

Touring in New Zealand

Air New Zealand Economy Class

Quite often economy class can be a label for second class. Not with Air New Zealand. Every passenger is somebody special. To make your flight thoroughly enjoyable, there's Air New Zealand's renowned in-flight service, carefully prepared and presented meals plus a wide selection of wines. As with first class and Pacific class fares, normal economy class fares allow you maximum flexibility. You can book at any time right up to departure and change your booking at any time without penalty. There is no minimum stay requirement. Your ticket is valid for one year from commencement of your journey and if you decide to amend your travel plans, any portion of travel unused is fully refundable.

Children

Children under 12 years pay only two-thirds of the adult fare, while infants under two years not occupying a seat pay only 10% of the adult fare (limited to one infant with each accompanying adult).

Accommodation

Organise your travel and accommodation together with one telephone call! Refer Hotpac Listing in this section.

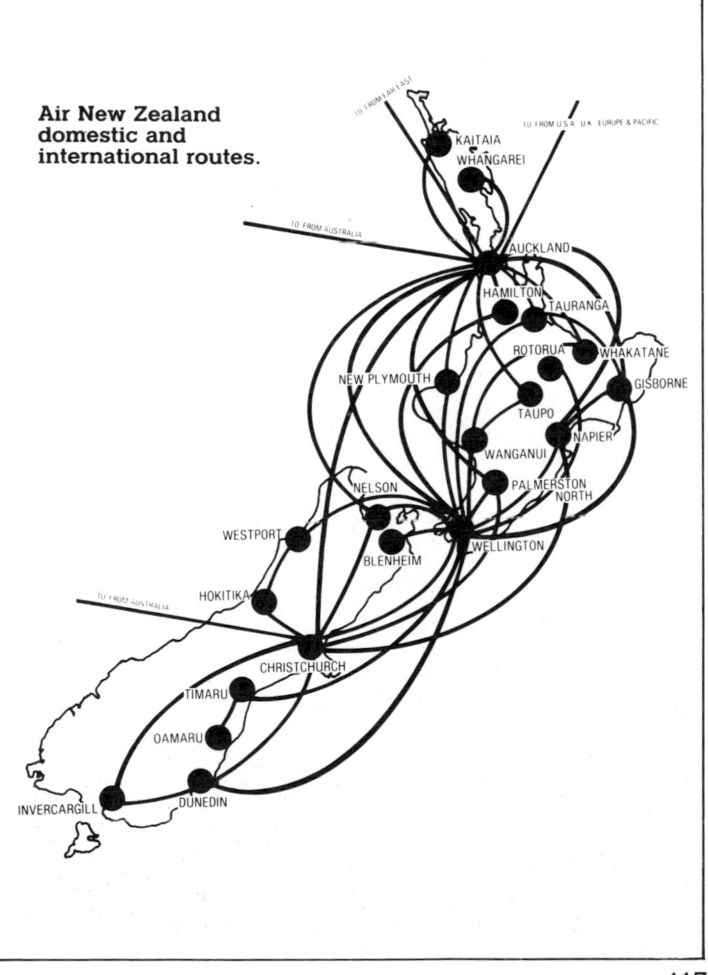

Air New Zealand domestic and international routes.

Auckland Aero Club Inc.
C/- Ardmore Airfield Post Office
Papakura RD
Auckland
Telephone: (09) 299-8590

The Auckland Aero Club Inc. was founded in 1928 and has over fifty years of flying and charter experience. Scheduled services to Great Barrier Island operate daily, and to Coromandel, four days per week (Monday, Wednesday, Saturday and Sunday). The club provides a charter flight service to any licensed public airfield in New Zealand, all year round. The fleet includes 21 well-maintained charter and training aircraft, single- and twin-engined aircraft and 10 full-time instructor and charter pilot staff. Closest accommodation – Auckland, Papakura or Takanini. Access from Auckland by bus or train to Papakura, and then taxi, or rental car to the Ardmore Airfield. Suitable for all ages (if disabled, please advise). Hire costs for aircraft vary according to requirements. Quotes for all services, fares, etc., on application.

Aspiring Air (1981) Ltd
PO Box 68
Wanaka
Telephone: Wanaka 7943

Aspiring Air operates daily services between Wanaka – Cromwell – Christchurch, all year through. An ideal service for skiers, businessmen and holiday makers with limited time. Flights depart from Wanaka township, on Highway 6 9 kilometres (5½ miles) at 8.30 a.m., from Cromwell at 8.45 a.m., arriving Christchurch at 10.30 a.m. From Christchurch, departure is at 3.30 p.m., arriving Wanaka at 5.15 p.m. Cost: from $138 one way. Bookings essential: either direct, through Wanaka Information Centre (7277), Wanaka Travel (7415) or Newmans Travel, Christchurch.

Southern Air Limited
(Invercargill Airport)
PO Box 860
Invercargill
Telephone: (021) 82-168/ 89-120
or Half Moon Bay 69
Manager: Max Paulin

Links Otago and Southland with beautiful Stewart Island. Less than 20 minutes away from Invercargill by air, Stewart Island is a historic fishing community, set in an environment offering wonderful flora and fauna. Amid breathtaking scenery, tramp, fish, hunt, scuba dive, swim and sightsee. Three return flights daily to Stewart Island from Invercargill. From $37, adult; $18.50, child (Invercargill-Stewart Island).

Mts Ruapehu and Ngaruahoe, Volcanic Plateau.
(Courtesy Turangi Scenic Flights)

Touring in New Zealand

Air Albatross, New Zealand's fastest-growing airline has become a firm favourite on the routes it operates. Passengers who choose to fly with the Wellington-based 'no frills' airline are inevitably won over by the friendly, efficient service and keep coming back for more. Air Albatross' popularity on the Wellington-Blenheim-Nelson route is such that it has become known affectionately as the 'Cook Strait Commuter'. The airline is committed to opening up the undiscovered Nelson Lakes District and beautiful Marlborough Sounds to international travellers. Fly direct to Nelson from Auckland or Wellington and have more time to spend discovering the beauty of the Northern South Island and Westland, before continuing on to resorts such as Queenstown and Te Anau.

Airfields have been established at Speargrass in the heart of the Nelson Lakes National Park, and at Collingwood near the Abel Tasman National Park. Travellers can maximise their time and fly directly from Auckland or Wellington to these beautiful areas, before continuing on their journey through Westland to the rest of the South Island. The airline has a fleet of 16-seater turbo-prop Metroliners and 9-seater Cessnas, aircraft ideally suited to New Zealand's flying conditions. There are excellent views of some of the country's best scenery as flight paths generally take you below cloud level. Other airlines fly above the clouds. Charter flights are also available. Reservations can be made for flights with Air Albatross from any major travel agency in the world. Within New Zealand the airline has offices in Auckland, Nelson and Blenheim with the head office located in Wellington. Fly Air Albatross and see more of New Zealand, get more value for your money. Book through your nearest travel agent or contact Air Albatross direct in Wellington, Auckland (telephone (09) 735-825 or 275-9389), Blenheim (telephone (057) 84-708), and Nelson (telephone (054) 80-853 or 80-131).

Air Albatross
PO Box 21-007
Wellington Airport
Telephone: (04) 887-132
Telex: NZ 31136

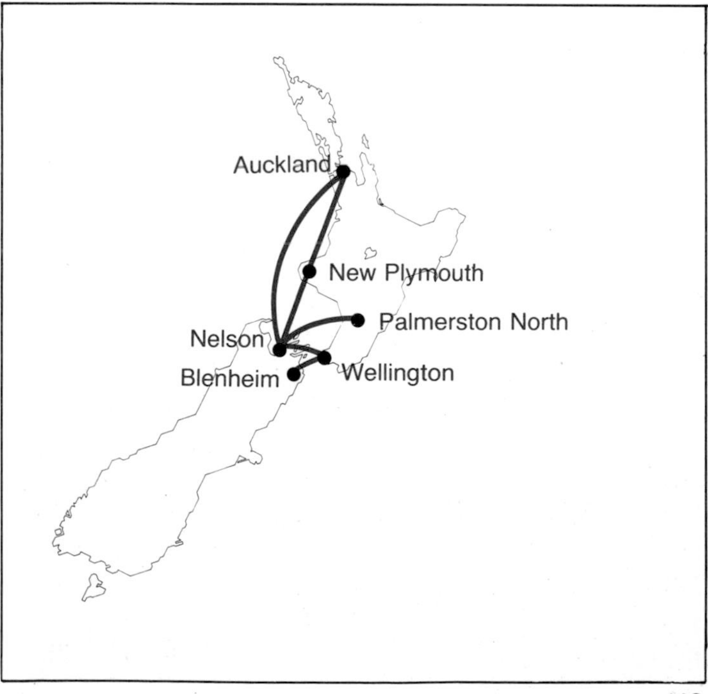

Map showing Air Albatross air routes.

Driving in New Zealand

Driving Licences

A current licence and/or an international licence are acceptable. Minimum age for rental-car hiring is 25 years. Front seat belts must be worn by law ($25.00 fine otherwise). In built-up areas speed limit is 50 km/h (30 mph); on open road and motorways, 80 km/h (50 mph). LSZ means Limited Speed Zone, in which the maximum is permissable only when conditions are ideal. If there are children, pedestrians, heavy traffic or bad weather, 50 km/h prevails. This sign is shown on the outskirts of towns and cities.

Traffic Officers (Ministry of Transport)

Traffic Officers enforce the speed limit and deal with accidents. They are separate from the Police Force and neither carry weapons. Report all accidents to the Ministry of Transport.

Petrol

High-octane gas is about NZ$ **4.30** per gallon (**96** cents per litre). No discounting, same price countrywide.

Maps and Driving Aids

The Automobile Association (AA) provides an excellent road-map and accommodation-guide service. Free reciprocal membership privileges are offered to members belonging to equivalent overseas organisations. Check with the telephone directory in each town or city for the local AA address. AA Head Office: corner of Lambton Quay and Willis Street, Wellington, P.O. Box 1053. Telephone: (04) 851-745.

Motor Homes

Now becoming a popular way to explore the back roads of New Zealand taking your accommodation with you. With few restrictions on where you can go and where you can stop, the wilderness can really be yours to enjoy – by a lake or near the beach.

There are more than 450 motor camps in New Zealand and, except at the peak summer season (December through February), there is no need to pre-book. Facilities generally include washing machines, dryers, showers and superettes. The average tariff is $3.00-$7.00.

Droving sheep on the Mt Cook Rd, Mackenzie Country. ***(Andris Apse Ltd)***

Touring in New Zealand

Cars and motor homes

Avis Rent A Car is New Zealand's largest rental car company with more than one hundred branches and service agents throughout New Zealand. A wide range of late model vehicles to choose from, ranging in size from small sedans and hatchbacks to large automatic sedans and station wagons. Also available are comfortable eight-seater mini coaches, perfect for the larger family or group. The spacious interior means plenty of room for luggage as well as ensuring travel comfort. All vehicles at competitive rates including unlimited mileage. To reserve your Avis Rent A Car in New Zealand, or for more information, write or telex direct or contact any Avis Worldwide location or NZ Government Tourist Office.

Avis Rental Cars
22 Wakefield Street
Auckland
Private Bag
Auckland
Telephone: (09) 792-645
Telex: NZ 2543

Avis offer late-model four-berth and six-berth Motorhomes, well appointed with cassette radio/stereo, gas cooker, battery/electric refrigerator and all cooking equipment and bedding. Avis Motorhomes are designed so that they can be plugged into mains voltage at any of over 300 well-equipped and site camping grounds and caravan parks throughout New Zealand, as well as being able to operate on battery when 'off the beaten track'. Avis Motorhomes are comfortable "homes away from home" and a great way to see New Zealand. All are supplied with a comprehensive map directory. To reserve your Avis Motorhome in New Zealand, or for more information, write or telex direct or contact any Avis Worldwide location or NZ Government Tourist Office.

Avis Motorhomes
105 Neilson Street
Onehunga
PO Box 13-314
Auckland
Telephone: (09) 662-168
Telex: NZ 2543

This company specialises in motor caravan rental, providing a wide range of top-quality and well-maintained vehicles, from 2-berth pop-tops to economical 4-6 berth diesel units. A special feature, offered exclusively, is a tape tour programme – your personal tour guide on cassette – giving you history, Maori mythology, places of interest and some little-known spots often missed by travellers. These cassettes cover a variety of routes, taking in New Zealand's main attractions. They are complimentary and can be retained for use with your movies or slides. All vehicles are fully equipped with bedding, cooking equipment and utensils, and heater. They are available for pick-up from either Auckland or Christchurch and one-way hires are available at no extra charge. From $350 per week. Book direct by mail or telephone, or through the G.T.B or your travel agent.

Adventure Vans
PO Box 13-427
Auckland 6
Telephone: (09) 665-737 or 642-905
After Hours: (09) 817-6452
Telex: NZ 2553 Attn: Adventure Vans

Motor-home holidays: Newmans offer a wide range of motor homes for your New Zealand holiday, accommodating in comfort two, four, or six people, depending on your requirements. These modern, easy-to-drive vehicles are superbly appointed – to make you feel at home, away from home. This is the ideal way to see New Zealand independently, going where you want to go, seeing what you want to see, stopping wherever you like – for as long as you like! With lots of storage for your clothes and equipment, you are free to make your itinerary as varied as you please. Stay in the great outdoors, by the beach, bush, stream and farmland; or use New Zealand's many excellent motor camp facilities. Newmans Motor Homes – the relaxed, carefree way to tour New Zealand.

Offices in: USA, Japan, Australia and Canada.

Newmans Tours Limited
PO Box 3719
Auckland
Telephone: (09) 31-149
Telex NZ 2478
Telegrams/Cables: 'Newcoach'
Christchurch: Telephone (03) 795-641

Bus travel – Scheduled and Regional

H & H Travel Lines Ltd.
PO Box 423
Invercargill
Telephone: (021) 82-419
Telex: NZ 5766

Offers a wide variety of coach-transport services throughout New Zealand. These include sightseeing tours, charter coaches, ski area connections, rent-a-coach and long-distance services.

Grayline sightseeing: A great variety of quarter-, half- or full-day sightseeing tours through areas of major interest to travellers.

Charters: If you've got a large group coming to New Zealand, enquire about H & H Luxury Cougar Coaches, which are available for charter.

Ski area connections: H & H Cougar Coaches operate from the main centres to the ski areas at Mt Ruapehu, Porter Heights, Treble Cone and Cardrona.

Rent-a-coach: 13 or 14-seater hire coaches are available on a 'drive yourself' basis.

Starliner: Provides daily services between Christchurch, Dunedin, Cromwell and Invercargill.

For further information: Contact a travel agent or any H & H Office. Auckland: (09) 792-426, Christchurch (03) 799-120, Dunédin (024) 740-674, Te Anau (0229) 7233, Queenstown 146.

Newmans Coach Lines Limited
PO Box 3719
Auckland
Telephone: (09) 31-149
Telex: NZ 2478
Telegrams/Cables: 'Newcoach'

Travel New Zealand with Newmans Coach Lines: operating regular daily services between many main towns, with offices nationwide. For visitors, Newmans Coach Lines are an ideal, flexible and inexpensive way to enjoy more of the country. No comfort is lacking, coaches are air-conditioned and each seat has its own sheepskin cover. Drivers are friendly and informative.

Sample routes (other connections arranged): North Island: Auckland – Hamilton – Waitomo Turn Off – New Plymouth – Hawera. Napier – Hastings – Palmerston North – Wellington. South Island: Picton – Blenheim – Christchurch. Picton – Nelson – Motueka – Takaka. Nelson – Westport – Greymouth. For free timetables/route guides and further information, telephone: New Plymouth (067) 75-482, Wellington (04) 851-149, Picton 687M, Nelson (054) 88-369, Greymouth (027) 6118, Christchurch (03) 795-641.

Offices in: USA, Japan, Australia and Canada.

Luxury Escorted Coach Tours
Mutual Holidays (division of the Mutual Group)
22 Wakefield Street
Auckland
PO Box 5913
Telephone: (09) 792-495
Telex: NZ 2804

Mutual Fourways operate their own fleet of luxurious tour coaches which are all fully air conditioned and specially fitted with exclusive toilet/restroom facilities. Experienced coach captains are chosen for their skill, courtesy and vast local knowledge, and every tour is accompanied by a charming hostess to ensure individual care and attention. A wide range of Luxury Escorted Coach Tours are offered, covering the North and South Islands of New Zealand, with selected regional areas of interest, and half-day Auckland sightseeing trips. Tours range from 3 days/2 nights, to 17 days/16 nights, and offer a choice of quality or superior accommodation. For more information, write or telex direct, or contact your nearest NZ Government Tourist Office.

Guthreys New Zealand Tours Ltd
126 Cashel Street
PO Box 343
Christchurch
Telephone: (03) 793-560
Telex: NZ 4243

With offices in Sydney, Melbourne, Los Angeles, Vancouver, Tokyo and London for your booking convenience, this company offers an extensive range of fully-escorted coach tours, covering the length of New Zealand. With a reputation for excellent service, itineraries range from four days to 19 days with regular, fixed departure dates throughout the year. A superior standard of accommodation and meals is provided. Comprehensive sightseeing with entrance fees included in costs.

Touring in New Zealand

Green Domain Coach Holidays: From three to 21 nights, Newmans offer a comprehensive range of New Zealand holiday options – holidays to suit time and budget considerations, incorporating all you want to see and do in one island or both. Holidays are fully escorted by courier drivers who pack every kilometre with interest and amusement. Choose a deluxe or standard tour – or join a Value-Pak holiday, where emphasis is on budget fun. Holidays can include dinners and breakfasts. Costs include numerous sightseeing trips, special excursions, internal air fares, and sometimes farm stays, or overnighting in New Zealand homes.
Offices in: USA, Japan, Australia and Canada.

Newmans Tours Limited
PO Box 3719
Auckland
Telephone: (09) 31-149
Telex: NZ 2478
Telegrams/Cables:
'Newcoach'
Christchurch: Telephone
(03) 795-641

Specialised Tours

Self-drive holidays and rental cars: Arrange your holiday with Newmans and have a three-way choice.
★ With Newmans and National car rental, drive a modern car of the size to suit your needs, with the entire country to tour.
★ Newman's Freewheeler self-drive holidays give you the freedom to go where you choose, staying where you please. There are two grades of accommodation: Best Western for the thrifty-minded (over 150 comfortable motel inns and motels); or Blue Ribbon, staying at any hotel or motel regardless of standard.
★ Newmans' pre-planned, self-drive holidays offer you confirmed accommodation reservations prior to arrival, with three grades of accommodation. Whatever your choice, Newmans make your holiday a marvellous adventure.
Offices in: USA, Japan, Australia and Canada.

Newmans Tours Limited
PO Box 3719
Auckland
Telephone: (09) 31-149
Telex: NZ 2478
Telegrams/Cables:
'Newcoach'
Christchurch: Telephone
(03) 795-641

This company offers a full range of great holidays. You can use self-drive rental cars, motor homes or eight-seater mini buses. Options are offered of either fixed itineraries or Freewheeler Tours, utilising superior or budget style hotel and motel accommodation. Motor homes sleeping up to six persons are available from either Auckland or Christchurch. Offices in Sydney, Melbourne, Los Angeles, Vancouver, Tokyo and London for your booking convenience.

Guthreys New Zealand
Tours Ltd
126 Cashel Street
PO Box 343
Christchurch
Telephone: (03) 793-560
Telex: NZ 4243

If you prefer a packaged holiday of New Zealand that includes accommodation and self-drive car, and require flexibility with time and the places you choose to visit, then Mutual Freewheel Holidays are the answer. A wide range of fixed-itinerary holidays are also available, varying in duration and covering the North, South, or both Islands. All holidays offer a wide choice of three grades of accommodation – standard, quality or superior – and all tours include free and discount admissions to some of the country's top attractions. Self-drive Ski Holidays also available. Mutual Holidays use New Zealand's largest rent-a-car company, Avis Rent A Car, giving a choice of vehicle size (including mini buses) with unlimited mileage. For more information, including a wide range of complimentary, attractive, four-colour brochures, write or telex direct, or contact your nearest NZ Government Tourist Office.

Self Drive Holidays
Mutual Holidays (division of the Mutual Group)
22 Wakefield Street
PO Box 5913
Auckland
Telephone: (09) 792-495
Telex: NZ 2804

Newmans Tours Limited
PO Box 3719
Auckland
Telephone: (09) 31-149
Telex: NZ 2478
Telegrams/Cables:
'Newcoach'
Christchurch: Telephone
(03) 795-641

Tear-away Adventure Holidays: If you're between 18 and 35 and feel like putting real adventure into your life, then try a Newmans Tear-away holiday. Take off around New Zealand with a group of singles or couples out to have a great time – boating, riding, flying, skiing, dancing, drinking, laughing, singing, eating – plus loads more! You'll stay in cabins, hotels, castles, and on a Maori marae (meeting place), travelling in style. Newmans' crazy fun buses have great stereo sound, and are really comfortable. Tear-away holidays are available all year round for sun or snow fun. Itineraries vary from eight to 21 nights. Most activities, entry fees and sights are included in tour costs, which makes Tear-away the best value for money anywhere. Offices in: USA, Japan, Australia and Canada.

CONTIKI

If you're aged between 18 and 35 and want to travel with people of your own age – Contiki has the answer. Their tours are designed especially for the budget-conscious, and with four different itineraries (lasting from 11 to 19 days), there's something to suit everyone! Traditional 'over-organised coach tours' don't apply with Contiki. Their philosophy is to include as much as possible of the fun and adventure available in New Zealand, as well as making sure there's plenty of free time to meet up with the 'locals'.

Accommodation with Contiki is quite different too. You'll stay in a combination of comfortable cabins, hotels and what Contiki calls 'Special Stopovers'. These are unique features of the tour, giving you the opportunity to stay in places you may not otherwise get the chance to see. There's a resort complex in the beautiful Bay of Islands, authentic log cabins at Orakei Korako (a thermal hideaway near Rotorua), or chalets at a mountain base camp at Makarora, where a special adventure awaits – fly by light aircraft into Mt Aspiring National Park, go bush walking and jet boat back to base!

From the city sights of Auckland to the year-round resort of Queenstown, Contiki provides the 18-35s with a really different experience. From $512 for 11 days plus $84 food kitty (covers breakfast and dinner every day).

For further information contact Contiki:
NEW ZEALAND
Atlantic and Pacific Travel, telephone: Auckland (09) 770-660.
AUSTRALIA
Contiki Travel, telephone: Sydney (02) 290-3622.
UNITED STATES OF AMERICA
Contiki America, telephone: Los Angeles (714) 937-0611.
GERMANY
ADAC Reisen GMBH, telephone: München (089) 76-760.

Guthreys New Zealand
Tours Ltd
126 Cashel Street
PO Box 343
Christchurch
Telephone: (03) 793-560
Telex: NZ 4243

In addition to coach and fly/drive tours, Guthreys offer a full range of camping, skiing, adventure and special interest holidays. Camping tours operate all year round, staying in cabins and chalets, with regular departures from Auckland and Christchurch. The skiing season runs from June through November, and Guthreys feature tour packages to Turoa (Mount Ruapehu), Mount Hutt, Mount Cook, Wanaka and Coronet Peak (Queenstown), with several grades of accommodation and travel by coach, rental car or motor home. Adventure packages include hiking, back packing, climbing, white-water rafting, canoeing, jet boating, trout and salmon fishing and scuba diving. A special interest department will plan any type of tour to suit your requirements, specialising in planning conferences and conventions. Offices in Sydney, Melbourne, Los Angeles, Vancouver, Tokyo and London for your booking convenience.

Touring in New Zealand

Specialised Holidays

ACTIVITIES COVERED:

River rafting	Caving	Fishing
Diving	Para-flying	Water skiing
Jet-ski	Sailing	Snow skiing
Hiking/Climbing	Hunting	Horse riding
Abseiling	Parachuting	

SCENIC TOURS:

Waterborne – Sea or lake, speed boat and launch
Airborne – Fixed wing, helicopter
Landborne – Large/small coaches, four-wheel-drive vehicles
Legborne – Pushbikes, walking.

Transport to and from the activities is arranged so that you participate alongside New Zealanders. Experience is unnecessary as tuition also offers equipment hire. Your safety, desires and enjoyment are paramount.

Live-Life New Zealand Ltd
Action Tours and Activities
CPO Box 4517
Auckland
Telephone: (09) 768-936

Discover the 'real' New Zealand – combining action with sightseeing the way YOU want it! Through 'Great Escape Plans', Rainbow organises whatever you want – superb sailing adventures, skiing, diving, fishing, tramping – then give you a car to roam the country! A range of accommodation can be pre-arranged or choose as you go – from staying on private farms, to hotels! From $825, 18 days/per person.
(US package: from $US1,699, flights inclusive).

Rainbow Adventure Holidays
PO Box 8327
Symonds Street
Auckland
Telephone: (09) 790-457
North America:
(800) 227-5317
(800) 722-2288

This four-day tour captures the scenic grandeur of Canterbury and Central Otago. Inland, via Mt Hutt, the first night's stop is Omarama, where flight-seeing around Mt Cook is available. Two nights in Queenstown give time for jet boating, river rafting, enjoying the history and scenery. Luxurious coaches with all facilities and informative driver. From $295 (bed and breakfast). Departs Tuesday/Saturday, September - May at 8.30 a.m.

Pacific Tourways Ltd
502A Wairakei Road
PO Box 14-037
Christchurch
Telephone: (03) 599-133

Highly personalised tours with a difference. A superb way to see New Zealand. You are welcomed and escorted south to Dunedin by Dick Skinner. Guides are caring, locally knowledgeable, and experienced. We feature homestays and visits, with hosts of interests like your own. Towering mountains and vast glaciers, sparkling lakes and native forests form a backdrop to lush farmlands and clean cities. Fishing, jet boating and ski-plane mountain landings for those who seek adventure. Express rail travel and deluxe air conditioned road coaches. Top line hotels. Most meals included.

Packages include three-day Fiji and eleven-day Australian options. Itineraries may be tailored for longer stays in New Zealand or Australia. Special interest groups welcome.

Costs: from USA $3,100 for 22 days in New Zealand (Portland Oregon return). Quote from any major city.

Winter sports tours at height of northern summer. Mt Cook, Wanaka, Queenstown. Cross-country, downhill and heli-skiing for all levels of competence. Well equipped ski fields, breathtaking scenery, top hotels. Eleven days in New Zealand plus Fiji stopover. July through September.

Enquiries and bookings in USA.
The Travel Bug, 208 S.W. 1st Ave., Portland 97204, Oregon, USA (503) 228-7455
Odessy Club, 2101 N.E. Flanders, Portland 97232, Oregon, USA (503) 233-9961
Travel at the Dorchester, 226 West Rittenhouse Square, Philadelphia, Penn. 19103 (215) 735-1513.

South Pacific Odyssey Ltd
PO Box 5427
Dunedin
Telephone: (024) 776-801
After hours: (024) 89-6377
Telex: NZ 5618 GOSPO

Accommodation

At the top of the scale are the luxury hotels that provide all the style, comfort and services expected of top international hotels – places such as the Sheraton in Auckland, the Hyatt Kingsgate in Auckland and Queenstown, and in Rotorua, the Parkroyal in Wellington, Noah's Hotel in Christchurch, the Queenstown Travelodge on the shore of Lake Wakatipu. Find hotels of this standard only in major cities or favourite tourist destinations.

Tourist Hotel Corporation, or THC, hotels are state-owned, luxury hotels in places of special tourist interest, often remote.

Find THC hotels at Waitangi, where the modern complex spreads along the shore looking out on the Bay of Islands; at Waitomo, near the caves, in a rambling Victorian country hotel; at Rotorua, right by steaming geysers and with an emphasis on Maori entertainment and culture; at Wairakei, set in 1,620 hectares, (4,000 acres) of parkland, including one of the best golf courses in the country; at Tokaanu, on Taupo's southern shore, with an emphasis on trout fishing; in the elegant splendour of the THC Chateau Tongariro on the lower slopes of Mt Ruapehu.

In the South Island there's the THC Hermitage, focal point of Mt Cook village, with balconied rooms looking out towards the mountain; the THC Milford Hotel on the shore of Milford Sound with views of Mitre Peak; THC Te Anau sits in a spreading parkland of lawns and trees on the edge of Lake Te Anau; balconied rooms at THC Wanaka look out past pines, firs and poplars and over Lake Wanaka; THC Franz Josef is surrounded by mountains and thick bush, and adjacent to the glacier that forces its way through the rain forest.

Also offering top accommodation are the exclusive, small, family run lodges, country resorts with first-class standards of comfort, service and informal sophistication. Activities here are organised to suit the individual's wishes and most specialise in fishing and hunting. Sites are usually superb, in garden seclusion on lake or river edge. (See the Lodges section.)

As well as a good range of up-market hotels, cities usually have modest, moderately priced hotels near the city centre, places such as the DB Royal International in Auckland, the Grand Establishment in Rotorua, St George in Wellington, the Clarendon in Christchurch, the Mountaineer Establishment in Queenstown. The Vacation Inns provide an excellent standard of accommodation in most of the main tourist centres, as well as in more remote areas such as Te Anau.

In country towns old hotels that have seen grander days often provide bargain accommodation for those trying to stretch their travelling dollar – expect to find a comfortable, simple room, usually with private bathroom, but without telephone or television (there will be a 'television lounge' for the use of guests). Some such hotels are privately owned; most will be brewery owned, by the DB or Lion chain. Both chains have some very smart hotels, such as the high-class DB Rotorua, and a good range of moderate hotels, but the budget-watching traveller should remember the small-town hotels – expect good plain cooking in the dining room and find lively hotel bars that are a local meeting place.

Hotels all have a licence to serve liquor, with a house bar for guests and public bars. A 'tourist licensed' hotel will be licensed to serve liquor to guests only – no public bar. A 'private hotel' has no liquor licence but can often provide good, economical accommodation – guest houses and private hotels are similar in style and function.

A 'motor inn' might also be labelled a 'motor hotel', 'motor lodge' or 'serviced motel' – generally anticipate modern quality accommodation, especially well suited to car travellers. At many you park your car by the entrance to your room. Expect a licensed restaurant and a house bar.

Motels are a feature of New Zealand travel – most motel units are, in fact, small self-contained apartments, with separate bedroom(s), bathroom, sitting/dining room and fully equipped kitchen. There's everything necessary for self-catering, from toaster to oven dish. Instant tea, coffee, salt, pepper and milk are provided – you must cook your own meals, make your own beds, but for a moderate price you have, in effect, got a suite.

Motels are usually small, family-run concerns, with six to 12 units, and so provide an individuality not found in major accommodation chains.

Travellers on a shoe-string budget will find youth hostels in main cities and towns and at prime tourist destinations. Camping grounds are prolific, on the outskirts of cities and towns, but particularly along the coasts and by lakes. Most also offer simple cabin accommodation. Take to the hills and mountains in National Parks and Forest Service Parks and you will find a unique system of 'huts', strategically placed in the remotest territory. Some provide the simple basic needs of shelter; others are large and modern with extra comfort, such as cosy armchairs to pull up around the huge stone fireplace. National Park huts charge a few dollars a night, Forest Service huts are free.

Air New Zealand Ltd
HOTPAC
ACCOMMODATION

There is a reservation system that puts you in touch with accommodation, a very simple way to pre-arrange your accommodation before visiting New Zealand. The preferred system is Hotpac. Designed by Air New Zealand. to make it easy for you to reserve hotels, motels and motor inns, their system contains a selection of 68 properties throughout all the most-visited areas of New Zealand. These range from well-appointed and serviced motels with kitchens, through to the more sophisticated hotels, available in resort areas and main centres. Air New Zealand reservations staff can advise on availability, rates etc. making your reservations at the same time they book your Air New Zealand flights. To secure the accommodation, Air New Zealand issues you with a pre-paid Hotpac voucher before you leave which you hand to the property on arrival.

If what you want is not available through Hotpac, Air New Zealand also have another 132 hotels, motels and motor inns available through the Instant Freeline System. These may also be booked with your Air New Zealand flights. Rather than being a pre-pay system. Instant Freeline makes the reservation and you pay upon checking out.

If you plan to stopover at any of the islands of the South Pacific enroute to New Zealand, Hotpac properties are available at all destinations on the Air New Zealand network. Contact your travel agent for details on the South Pacific's most comprehensive and easiest accommodation reservation system. Air New Zealand offices are located throughout Australia. in Canada, U.S.A., Japan and Europe.

Tourist Hotel Corporation
Level 28
Williams Centre
Plimmer Lane
Wellington
Telephone:
Auckland (09) 773-689
Wellington (04) 729-179
Christchurch (03) 790-718
Telex: NZ 3488

In every corner of the country – where civilisation gives way to wilderness, and sometimes in the middle of the wilderness itself – one can find first-class Tourist Hotel Corporation accommodation. The list of THC hotels reads like a 'Who's Who' of New Zealand tourist destinations – and in some places like Milford Sound and Mt Cook, THC offers the only possibility for enjoying first-class accommodation and cuisine, right in the midst of a National Park! Each hotel offers a variety of accommodation and selections of restaurants and bars. The taste buds are not forgotten in the feast of scenic splendour. (See the section on National Parks to learn more of the THC locations near the Fiordland, Mt Aspiring, Mt Cook, Westland and Tongariro National Parks, as well as the Bay of Islands Maritime Park). All these hotels are linked by a modern computerised reservation service needing only one call to make several reservations. The central reservations office is located in Wellington.

THC WAITANGI RESORT HOTEL, Telephone: (0885) 27-411 Telex: NZ 2200
THC WAITOMO RESORT HOTEL, Telephone: (0813) 88-227, Telex: NZ 2905
THC ROTORUA INTERNATIONAL HOTEL, Telephone: (073) 81-189, Telex: NZ 2427
THC WAIRAKEI RESORT HOTEL, Telephone: (074) 48-021, Telex: NZ 2223
THC CHATEAU TONGARIRO RESORT HOTEL, Telephone: (081223), 809, Telex: NZ 2213
THC TOKAANU RESORT HOTEL, Telephone: (0746) 8873
THC THE HERMITAGE, Telephone: (05621) 809, Telex: NZ 4308
THC GLENCOE LODGE, Telephone: (05621) 809, Telex: NZ 4308
THC MOUNT COOK MOTELS AND CHALETS Telephone: (05621) 809,Telex NZ 4308
THC FRANZ JOSEF RESORT HOTEL, Telephone: 719, Telex: NZ 4367
THC WANAKA RESORT HOTEL, Telephone: (02943) 7826, Telex: NZ 5636
THC TE ANAU RESORT HOTEL, Telephone: (0229) 7411, Telex: NZ 5335
THC MILFORD SOUND RESORT HOTEL, Telephone: (02298) 6, Telex: NZ 4300

1 WAITANGI
On the shores of the Bay of Islands and set in the grounds of the Waitangi National Trust.

2 WAITOMO
Set amid the green rolling hills of the lush King Country.

3 ROTORUA
Overlooking legendary Whakarewarewa with its abundance of thermal activity.

4 WAIRAKEI
Opposite the two Wairakei Golf Courses and near to the Huka Falls.

5 TOKAANU
A small fisherman's hotel at the southernmost end of New Zealand's largest lake – Lake Taupo.

6 CHATEAU TONGARIRO
Mountain resort hotel on the slopes of Mount Ruapehu, highest peak in the North Island.

7 THE HERMITAGE
High up in the Southern Alps in a small mountain village.

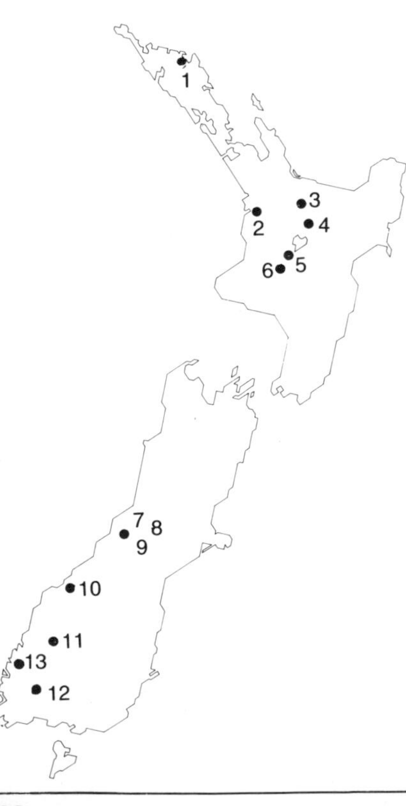

8 GLENCOE LODGE
An economy priced hotel, Glencoe Lodge has grand views of surrounding mountains and glaciers.

9 MOUNT COOK MOTELS AND CHALETS
Superb views of the surrounding mountains and glaciers.

10 FRANZ JOSEF
Located on the perimeter of Westland National Park with a grand view of mountains, glaciers and sub-tropical bush.

11 WANAKA
On the shores of Lake Wanaka with superb views of the Lake and surrounding mountains.

12 TE ANAU
Within views of Lake and mountains, Te Anau Hotel is on the doorstep of New Zealand's largest National Park, Fiordland.

13 MILFORD SOUND
New Zealand's most remote Hotel is located deep in Fiordland National Park at Milford Sound – views of the mile high Mitre Peak and the Sound itself.

Touring in New Zealand

With just one call, organise a superb first-class New Zealand holiday, staying at any of 20 individually operated retreats throughout the country. These are intimate lodges for a select few, and are personally hosted by the owner.

A Retreat Holiday makes possible a style of New Zealand living tailor-made for people whose needs are different and whose tastes are for the unusual. Even in well-known resorts, Retreat Holidays offer secluded places like Muriaroha, near Rotorua – a first-class homestead on a sheep station, overlooking the wild southern Pacific Ocean. There are lakeside and riverside resorts – for example, an Edwardian mansion nestled on the shore of an alpine lake. Each of them offers the full variety of activities available in New Zealand or the most peaceful and restorative holiday imaginable.

Whatever you require, a Retreat Holiday is an excellent way to experience the mágic that is New Zealand in a first-class manner. See the Lodges section, Living with New Zealanders section and Regional listings for a full description of these properties. Assistance is provided with itineraries and travel advice. A RHC video brochure and compendium is available on request.

PAPEETE OFFICE: RHC International, Retreat Holiday Company Ltd, BP 1366, Boulevard Pomare, Papeete, Tahiti, French Polynesia. Telephone: 29-501, Telex: FP253.

USA OFFICE: RHC International, Retreat Holiday Company Ltd, 3625W MacArthur Boulevard, Suite 310A, Santa Ana, CA92704, United States of America. Reservations: (California residents) telephone 800-227-8614; (USA general) telephone 800-874-7207. Telex 8874486.

OTHER COUNTRIES:
Contact head office, New Zealand.

RETREAT HOLIDAYS IN THE SOUTH PACIFIC EN ROUTE:

The Retreat Holiday Company is affiliated to RHC International, which also offers exciting stop-over possibilities :

'Island Resorts of The South Pacific' (nine island resorts on five islands through Tahiti).

For information, contact RHC head office – New Zealand, Papeete office, or USA office.

Retreat Holiday Company Ltd
Head Office: Regent Building
Cathedral Square
Christchurch
PO Box 4029
Telephone: (03) 799-126 or 799-127
Telex: NZ 4051

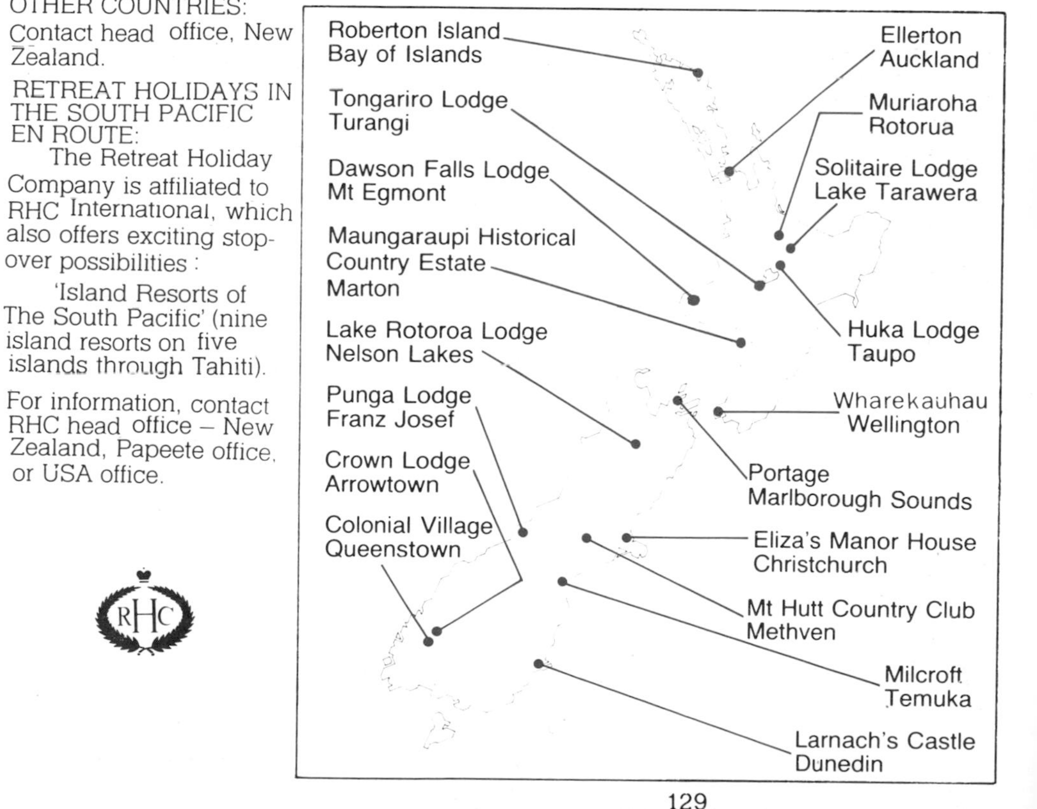

To make the most of eating in New Zealand, – to enjoy world-class gourmet delicacies at relatively low cost – it is a matter of knowing what to look for and how to find it.

Food

Surrounded by seas, there is an abundance of first-rate fish and shellfish – snapper, red snapper, tarakahi, hapuku, blue cod, orange roughy, John Dory, flounder and sole are all excellent white fish.

Fish smoking using aromatic manuka wood is a tradition in New Zealand. Smoked snapper roe is a true gourmet delight, spread on brown or rye bread, with a dash of lemon juice and a dusting of black pepper. Other smoked pleasures are smoked eel, smoked marlin and smoked salmon, but don't neglect the more prosaic smoked snapper, smoked trevally and smoked mullet.

The famous New Zealand crayfish is an exquisite luxury, known elsewhere in the world as rock lobster, spiny lobster or crawfish. It is usually sold ready cooked, which too often means over cooked. Realise that any restaurant prepared to get live crayfish and cook them on the premises is probably also fussy about correct cooking. For a perfect summer picnic buy a cooked crayfish from a good fish shop or local fisherman (in seaside towns and villages there are often well sign-posted backyard sales).

Two kinds of mussel are widely available – a small, blue-lipped mussel and a large green-lipped mussel. Both are equally delicious and usually well presented in restaurants. They can also be bought pickled in brine for picnics or snacks.

There are three varieties of oyster – small, sweet rock oysters, large Pacific rock oysters and the rich, distinctive Bluff oysters dredged from Foveaux Strait. Oyster connoisseurs will want to try the Bluff oysters, in season between March and August.

And then there's the tuatua, a relative of the famous toheroa, but more readily available, generally served in a creamy soup or as fritters but also wonderful simply steamed open in the shell.

Try also the whitebait, a tiny delicacy, unlike any other whitebait except that caught in the river mouths of Tasmania.

Game-food specialities to seek out are venison and wild pork; and don't pass up any opportunity to taste sweet spring lamb.

Given a climate that ranges from subtropical to almost subantarctic, local fruit and vegetables cover a wide range, and tropical fruit are flown in from the Pacific islands to the north. If you want fruit and vegetables very fresh, pick your own (P.Y.O.) in road-side gardens – a very popular phenomenon new in most major towns.

Local cheeses to try are cheddar (especially South Island mature cheddar), Epicure, Cheshire, Havarti, Colby, Blue Vein and Feta. There's good local Camembert and Brie as well.

In main centres, and a surprising number of minor ones, specialist food shops and delicatessans carry a full range of imported and local food – great places to select food for outdoor eating. In main cities find the best French bread and croissants outside France (one French baker in Christchurch sends fresh croissants by air daily to Australia). Other specialist breads include excellent wholegrain and farmhouse-style loaves – try Vogels bread, it really is a bread sensation.

Many New Zealand honey sources are unique and so provide unusual delights for honey connoisseurs. These include pale gold kamahi and tawari, light amber rewarewa, sweet, delicate pohutukawa and the rich, aromatic-ling heather honey. Bush honey is a dark, rich blend originating from forest flowers.

Where to eat? Starting at the bottom of the scale are the fast-food eateries, including the ubiquitous Kentucky Fried Chicken, Pizza Hut and MacDonalds. The traditional fast-food standby is fish and chips – ask a local where the best fish and chip shop is to be found or choose one with the longest queue (if the locals are prepared to line up for their order, the results should be worth it). Try meat pies – best from places proclaiming 'home cookery' or 'baked on the premises'.

Coffee shops provide good snack meals and poor coffee. If you relish good coffee, drink tea instead; or try the delicious apple juice. Also find milk bars, distinctly 1950s in style, using rich creamy milk in the milkshakes.

Dining out in the cities of Auckland, Wellington or, to a lesser extent, Christchurch, offers a sophisticated range of possibilities. Also find plenty of pleasant choice in tourist-oriented towns such as Rotorua, Taupo and Queenstown.

Restaurants are either licensed to sell wine or BYO (meaning bring your own wine). The latter are usually smaller and more informal but the quality of cooking may well be better than that of an elegant, more expensive establishment.

Off the beaten tourist track, where time and trends move more slowly, first-class stylish cooking can be hard to find although eating treats can turn up anywhere – an imaginative little restaurant with a superb tuatua soup or simply the best meat pie ever, wrapped in layers of light flaky pastry. Look for old-fashioned farm-style cooking and try mammoth morning and afternoon teas. Helpings are always large.

In a country that's small, with excellent communication systems, food is transported quickly from its source at one end of the country to a table at the other. You can dine on fresh Hawkes Bay asparagus in Queenstown or just-picked Nelson cherries in Auckland, but make the most of delectable produce by concentrating on specialities in their region of origin.

The standard of restaurants changes continually. For a selection of restaurants, read local newspapers and magazines like *Metro* (Auckland) and *Cosmo* (Wellington). Diners Club publish a restaurant guide (available from their offices in Auckland, Wellington and Christchurch), which covers a good selection of restaurants through the country (but not all). Each year, Diners Club conduct the 'Restaurant of the Year' competition, voted for by consumers. The Diners Club 'Restaurant of the Year' and top ten restaurants for 1983, plus progress results for 1984, in order of popularity are:

1983
Wheelers, Auckland
Bacchus, Wellington
Bonapartes's, Auckland
Bronze Goat, Auckland
Rogues, Auckland
Orsini's, Auckland
La Scala, Dunedin
Aorangi Peak, Rotorua
Camelot Room, Regency Hotel, Christchurch
Plimmer House, Wellington

1984
Rogues, Auckland
The Sign of the Takahe,
Camelot Room, Regency Hotel, Christchurch
Antoines, Auckland
Coachman, Wellington
Wheelers, Auckland
Jules, Auckland
Olivers, Tauranga
Paul Revere, Christchurch
Gainsborough House, Hamilton

Take home the culinary secrets of some of these chefs, or select your restaurant from the recipes offered by 50 chefs from around the country in *The New Zealand Restaurant Cookbook*, by Michael Guy and Digby Law (Lindon, 1983).

There's a distance of little more than 800 kilometres (500 miles) from Cape Reinga, in the far north of the North Island, to Wellington, the capital city that looks out towards Cook Strait and the South Island. But don't be misled – it may take longer than you think to travel around in New Zealand.

The North Island's main route, State Highway 1, runs almost all that distance, through major cities and towns, from Kaitaia, near magnificent Ninety Mile Beach, through hills and valleys to Northland's commercial centre of Whangarei, and south to Auckland, occasionally brushing by the coast.

From Auckland the highway leads straight into the heart of the Waikato dairylands, the city of Hamilton and the leafy town of Cambridge, continuing on to the Central Plateau – a region of thermal springs, geysers and vast Lake Taupo. Crossing the bleak desert lands east of the live volcanoes of Tongariro National Park, State Highway 1 descends into hill pastures and plains to the city of Palmerston North, a prosperous agriculture-oriented city surrounded by rich farmland. The highway then veers west to the coast, following the strip of lowland between rugged hills and sea before winding its way over windswept ridges to Wellington.

To explore the variety of the North Island, to discover the diversity of North Island life, diverge from the highway onto side routes and by-ways, and link up with other main North Island routes – one following the Pacific coast to the east, the other the wild Tasman to the west.

State Highway 2 branches off south of Auckland and leads down through coastal cities and towns, – such as Tauranga, Gisborne, Napier and Hastings – through forests, farms and orchards and by sheltered bays and long ocean beaches.

State Highway 3 swings away to the west just south of Hamilton, taking a route that leads near the Waitomo Caves and through to New Plymouth, Mt Egmont National Park and along the coast to Wanganui on the banks of the romantic, unspoilt Wanganui River. The route links up again with SH1 at Palmerston North.

A fourth state highway, SH4, leaves SH3 to run through the rugged King Country to Taumaranui, to the Central Plateau west of the Tongariro mountains, to link with SH3 again at Wanganui. And SH5 branches in a loop from SH1 to lead to Rotorua, then to Taupo and then away again to Napier and SH2.

Driving the North Island can be an adventure in itself, discovering how sparsely populated the countryside is, that little roads always lead somewhere, that traffic can be so light that drivers exchange a friendly wave as they pass.

These main routes are all two- or four-lane highways and all sealed, although road-surface conditions vary with topography.

Roads wind and intertwine between the three major routes, opening up fascinating possibilities when choosing a touring itinerary. Make the most of a countryside where the next turn of the road may open up entirely new vistas, where the small towns en route may offer as much, or more, than the main centre ahead.

Take these back roads and don't expect ideal road conditions – some will be excellent, wide, smooth-sealed roads, some narrow well-sealed lanes, others loose-metal winding hill roads.

Provincial highways bear double numbers such as 22 or 41; others are simply 'secondary roads'.

Between SH1 and SH2, east of Hamilton, for example, take provincial highways and secondary roads that spread out in a net across dairy pastures and horse-racing stud farms, through tiny villages that consist of little more than an aging community hall and rural school.

At Mangaweka head up into the hills on Provincial Highway 54 to reach Palmerston North by way of hill farms and great views over wide winding river valleys.

Take Provincial Highway 35 around the East Cape and be amongst the first in the world to greet the morning sun.

North Island Touring

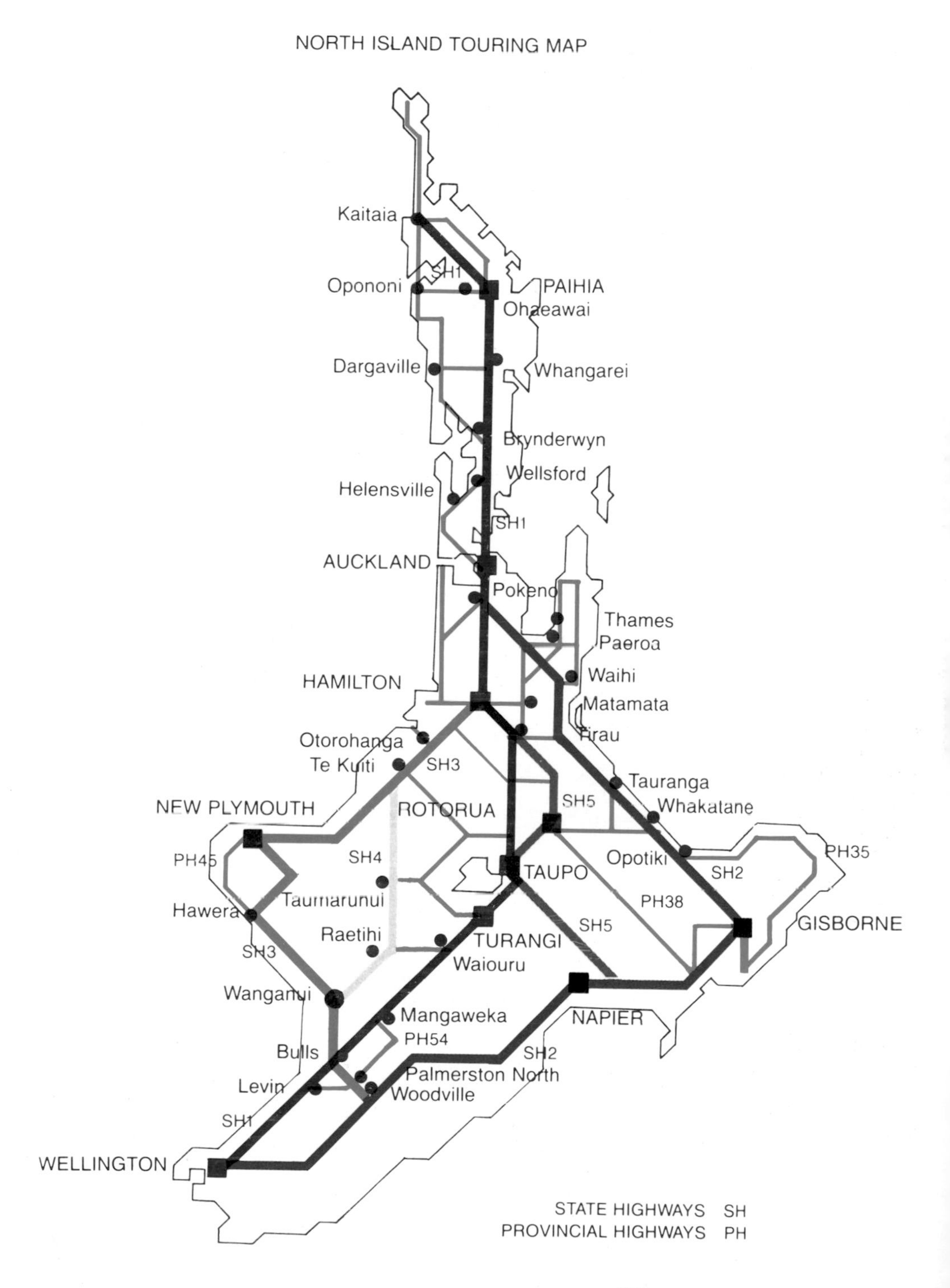

The sea dominates Northland. From the sheltered bays of the east and the long sweeping beaches of the west, the sea reaches deep inland with harbours, inlets and tidal creeks thick with mangroves.

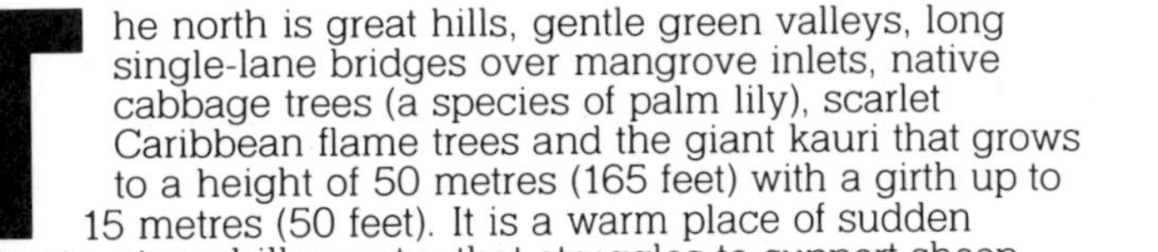

The north is great hills, gentle green valleys, long single-lane bridges over mangrove inlets, native cabbage trees (a species of palm lily), scarlet Caribbean flame trees and the giant kauri that grows to a height of 50 metres (165 feet) with a girth up to 15 metres (50 feet). It is a warm place of sudden contrasts, stony hill country that struggles to support sheep, cattle or goats, rolling green pastures where Friesian or Jersey cows graze, hillsides of white-flowering manuka scrub and occasionally pink-flowering manuka. There are dark green forests where the wild white clematis splashes over the treetops, vast peat swamps, mountainous sand dunes and lush subtropical orchards where tamarillos and oranges hang like bright globes, sheltered by high bamboo hedges.

History here stretches back over the centuries to the first Maori settlers. Legend has it that Northland was their first landfall – at Taipa in Doubtless Bay over 1,000 years ago. Many Northland communities today are predominantly Maori, and ancient pa sites, the fortified villages used in tribal warfare, can be seen as terraced hills. Ancient artifacts and tools used by the region's early fishermen and moa hunters can be seen in the museum at Kaitaia and the Wagener Museum at Houhora.

New Zealand's earliest European settlements also grew up along the edges of the bays and rivers, first with the arrival of sailors, who felled the tall kauri trees for spars for their sailing ships, and then with the missionaries, who arrived to preach the gospel and teach reading, writing, arithmetic, European agricultural methods and Victorian values.

Reminders of the mission days linger in many places, especially in the serene charm of Waimate North, the brooding isolation of Mangungu, the Kemp House and Stone Store at Kerikeri, the Williams Memorial Church at Paihia.

Kauris dominated the forests that grew over the hills and valleys of Northland – most of the forests have long gone, the trees felled for timber or burned to clear the ground for farming and digging kauri gum, the fossilised gum that made high-quality varnish.

See stands of kauri in the 9,000-hectare (22,000-acre) Waipoua Forest, in the Puketi Forest where the rare kokako bird lives in the forest canopy, in the Omahuta Kauri Forest, in the Ngaiotonga Scenic Reserve and in the small but superb Trounson Park.

The country's oldest town, Russell, began life as Kororareka, a wild settlement dubbed 'the hellhole of the Pacific', where whalers and seamen sought rowdy solace in the grog shops. Original buildings line the sea shore in today's tranquil town, now a major game-fishing port.

Further north is Whangaroa, a place to buy fresh oysters from the farms in the upper reaches of the harbour, drink in the harbour-side pub where commercial fishermen and game fishermen gather, and explore by boat the unspoilt, romantic outer harbour, still inaccessible by roads.

At Mangonui the town spills down the hill to the harbour, where buildings stand out over the water on stilts. At a small aquarium on the wharf giant packhorse crayfish and rare fish can be viewed. On the west coast harbour of Hokianga are Rawene and Kohukohu, once bustling timber towns but now villages of quiet charm and old buildings. A car ferry crosses the inlet.

In the far north the prosperous centre of Kaitaia began as a mission station, but owed much of its early development to the navigable Awanui River. Nearby Ahipara, a Maori settlement and small beach resort, was once larger than Kaitaia when gum from the rich gumfields was shipped out from Ahipara .

Bay. About 80 hectares (200 acres) of the gumlands have been kept as a special reserve where visitors can envisage the harsh life of Yugoslav gumdiggers, whose descendants now form a significant part of the population in the far north.

In the south the region's only city, Whangarei (pop. 38,000), owes its growth to the deep sheltered Whangarei Harbour, able to handle the world's largest oil tankers.

Roads came late to this region and the towns and villages relied on the sea and rivers for transport and communication. Don't be afraid of travelling down a gravel road to discover your own private cove.

NORTHLAND

National Parks
Bay of Islands Maritime & Historic Park.

Lodges
Roberton Island.

Outback Safaris

Fishing
Big Game
Other

River Adventures

Yachting/Cruising

Diving

Golf
1. Ahipara; 2. Kaikohe; 3. Kerikeri; 4. Waitangi; 5. Whangarei.

History
1. Kemp House; 2. Stone Store; 3. Waimate Mission House; 4. Pompellier House; 5. Waitangi Treaty House; 6. Ruapekapeka Pa.

Down on Farm

Live with NZ

Local
1. Far Northern Museum; 2. Otamatea Museum.

Driving Times within ½ 1 2 3 hours

Paihia

he holiday town of Paihia spreads along the foreshore, looking out across the Bay of Islands. Motels and hotels range from modest to luxury, tours leave for all parts of Northland, and down at the wharf side boats wait for the visitor.

Take off on the water on a launch trip around the bay or on a game-fishing expedition; hire a jet boat, sailing dinghy or row boat; charter a yacht with skipper or arrange a bare-boating holiday; take a barbeque cruise or a dinner cruise around the islands; rent a surf-cat or windsurfer; arrange a ski-tow boat for an afternoon's water skiing or take a water taxi service to an isolated island bay for a picnic, fishing, diving and swimming – the boat will return at a pre-arranged time. (Arrange similar boating pleasures across at Russell if you wish.) Take a scenic flight from Paihia and capture it all.

There are 144 islands and hundreds of coves, bays and beaches in the Bay of Islands, and nearly every one of them has a perfect spot for a picnic. Most islands are uninhabited so you may find not only a bay to yourself, you may find a whole island. Camping is allowed on Urupukapuka Island and others.

Back in Paihia, walk along the waterfront to find history, modern shops and motels clustered together on a short stroll. The Williams Memorial Church stands on the site of an 1823 mission station; a nearby Norfolk pine was planted by a missionary's wife in 1835. Walk towards Waitangi and pass the Waitangi National Marae, where Maori chiefs gathered in 1840 before crossing the river to sign a treaty acknowledging British sovereignty of New Zealand. (See In Touch with History section p.89).

The Treaty of Waitangi was much later adopted as the symbol of the birth of the nation. But these days the annual Waitangi Day celebrations at Waitangi are likely to be the occasion of demonstrations and protests that the treaty was a 'fraud'. Although initially seen by the British as a way of keeping the peace, the treaty was never ratified and protesters consider many of its provisions were never honoured. Many Maori leaders never signed it, and the slightly different meanings of the Maori and English versions caused considerable confusion over the years.

By Waitangi River bridge a three-masted barque is permanently moored – aboard is a shipwreck museum with intriguing displays of treasure retrieved from the deep.

Over the bridge is Waitangi, an area of 570 hectares (1,400 acres) centred on the Treaty House, built in 1833 on a headland overlooking the bay. There is also a Visitors Centre (with audio-visual displays on the Treaty of Waitangi), a Maori meeting house with carvings from many North Island tribes (a meeting house usually has carvings only from its own tribe) and, on the shore, a 36-metre (120-foot) ceremonial war canoe.

From Paihia take a passenger ferry or jet-boat taxi across to Russell to walk through a town of historic charm. Find old colonial buildings including elegant Pompallier House, the police station and jail, an 1835 church bearing musket-shot holes from a siege.

Also in Russell is the Captain Cook Memorial Museum with a 7-metre (23-foot) replica of his barque *Endeavour* and displays of local history. At the headquarters of the Maritime Park on The Strand audio-visual displays detail the Bay of Islands in the past and today.

Above the town is a hill where Ngapuhi chief Hone Heke four times cut down the British flagstaff before attacking the town in 1845.

Bay of Islands Community Public Relations Office Inc., Marsden Street, Paihia, P.O. Box 70. Telephone: Paihia 27683

1

Northland

Northland, with its favourable climate and fertile land and coast, was a centre of Maori population and thriving agriculture. However, coinciding with the arrival of the Europeans, inter-tribal warfare raged. The Maori population retreated under attack to massive fortresses called pa, built mostly on easily defensible high points and coastal headlands. The remains of pa sites, recognisable by their ridges, terraces and levelled hilltops, are mostly on private property, but at Ruapekapeka, 16 kilometres (10 miles) south of Kawakawa on State Highway 1, earthworks clearly show the huge scale of fortifications.

Ruapekapeka was the scene of the final battle in 'Heke's War', when 1,600 British troops under Governor Sir George Grey bombarded the palisades. Hone Heke achieved lasting fame by repeatedly chopping down the Russell flagpole as a political protest. His father-in-law, Hongi Hika, the leading warrior chief of the North's Ngapuhi tribe, returned from England in 1821 armed with 300 muskets and a suit of armour (a gift from the king). During Hongi's bloody incursions on enemy tribes, thousands were slaughtered before Hongi himself was shot when he forgot to wear his armour. Muskets and disease introduced by the Europeans reduced the Maori population dramatically from an estimated 150,000 when Captain Cook arrived in 1769 to just over 42,000 by 1896.

Entertainment. – The Bay of Islands in January shows a hint of its wild colonial past – holiday-makers converge on the bay for summer revelry that centres on the old Duke of Marlborough pub, Russell. With summer yacht racing and game fishing contests right through into autumn, the Bay of Islands is Northland's liveliest spot. Elsewhere the pace is slower, and small-town activities can include highland bagpipes at New Years Day (Waipu), Yugoslav folk dancing (Kaitaia and Dargaville), rodeo, agricultural fairs, arts and crafts festivals, or a beer and a game of darts in the pub.

Cruising in the bay.
(Courtesy Rainbow Yacht Charters)

Around Paihia

Kerikeri Stone Store.
(Courtesy Air New Zealand)

By road from Paihia visit Kerikeri, where rich soil and warm climate combine for an area of subtropical orchards – tour orchards and taste unusual fruit. Down by the tiny harbour is New Zealand's oldest building, a wooden mission house built in 1822, and the Stone Store, the first stone building, built in 1833. There's also an authentic reconstruction of a Maori village of pre-European times nearby.

The charm of Kerikeri attracts artists and craftspeople – music, arts and crafts thrive in Kerikeri and it is a village where quality handcrafts can be bought.

Yet another mission site awaits visitors at Waimate North. The house, built in 1831, has idyllic surroundings of wide lawns, old-fashioned English flowers, huge trees. Next to the house is the Church of St John the Baptist, built in 1871. Wander through a graveyard with wooden headstones and wild flowers under spreading oaks, the oldest planted in 1824.

And see the giants of the native forest, the kauri trees, in the Puketi Forest to the west of Kerikeri or in the Ngaiotonga Scenic Reserve east of Russell. For more splendid kauris, travel further afield to the vast Waipoua Forest.

Kawakawa has the oddity of a railway line running down the main street. Of greater interest nearby are the Waiomio Limestone Caves, with stalactites, stalagmites and a great gallery of glow worms, and Ruapekapeka Pa, a huge intensely fortified pa, with fortifications well preserved and spectacular views.

Paihia Taxis and Tours
PO Box 4
Paihia
Telephone: Paihia 27-506

Paihia Taxis and Tours provide local sightseeing by taxi or mini-coach to the many points of interest in this lovely region. Visit New Zealand's northernmost tip, Cape Reinga, or the famed giant kauri forests. Shorter tours include farm visits and a shipwreck museum, plus many places of historical importance, including Kerikeri. This is a personalised and friendly service, with full commentaries given. Service operates from Paihia, year around. From $20 per hour.

Kerikeri citrus orchards.
(Courtesy
Air New Zealand)

1

Northland

North to Kaitaia and Cape Reinga

From Kaitaia, the main commercial centre for the farming and tourist area, visit the many beach hideaways the Far North has to offer.

Try the local seafoods at the Albatross Restaurant at Ahipara, situated at the foot of Ninety Mile Beach; take a tour to Cape Reinga and see Spirits Bay, where the souls of the Maori depart this world. The beaches at Doubtless Bay, Cape Karikari and up to Houhora offer tranquility far from the crowded city. Houhora has the Wagener Museum, showing the history and collections of the Wagener family. The homestead was built by the Subritzkys, forebears of the Wageners and descendants of the Polish Royal House of Sobieski, who came to Houhora in the 1860s.

South from Kaitaia take the back roads to Kohukohu, the car ferry across the Hokianga Harbour to Rawene and down to Opononi. Read Maurice Shadbolt's short stories *The New Zealanders* to capture the essence of this area.

Far North Regional Museum
South Road
Kaitaia
Telephone: Kaitaia 892
Custodian: Miss J. Evans

A well-kept, progressive museum with displays covering the history and development of the Far North. Colourful exhibits include excellent photographic records illustrating this unique region. Learn about early Maori settlement, Kaitaia's Mission Station, the de Surville anchor and other maritime relics, plus many aspects of pioneer life. Find background information about kauri gum digging and Ninety Mile Beach, before your tour to Cape Reinga and the gumfields. Kaitaia is the perfect base for exploring beaches on three coasts, and the museum is ideally situated in the town's main street (on the walking route through town garden areas), handy to Golfland, cinema, swimming baths, Aqualand Aviary and lookout point. Foyer bulletin boards have information on various tours from Kaitaia, and friendly staff assist with all local information. Open daily, year round. Wheel- and push-chair access. From .50c adults, .10c children.

Travel around Northland by car to reach out-of-the-way places independently rental cars are available in main centres such as Paihia, Kaitaia and Whangarei. Fly from Kaitaia, Kerikeri and Whangarei to Auckland on scheduled services and charter flights from Paihia, Kaikohe, Dargaville, Kerikeri, Kaitaia and Whangarei. Use scheduled bus routes operated by N.Z.R. Road Services for economical wandering, or choose from the many coach tours.

SEE ALSO:

Yachting: Rainbow Yacht Charters (Opua).
NZ Historic Places: Pompellier House.
Yachting: Freedom Yacht Charters.
Diving: Paihia Dive/Hire/Charter (Fish).
Down on Farm: Bay of Islands Scenic Farm Safari Tours.
Live with NZ: Aspley House Farm Stays (Down on Farm) (Ohaewai).
Lodges: Roberton Island (Bay of Islands).
National Parks: Bay of Islands Maritime & Historical Park (Bay of Islands).
NZ Historic Places: Kemp House (Kerikeri), Waimate Mission House (Waimate Nth).
Water Adventures: Bay Beach Hire.

South via Hokianga and Dargaville to Auckland

Much of the land of the Hokianga lies idle, and there are visible signs of deterioration. For a long time land there was cheap and bought up by absentee owners and speculators. Communal ownership of Maori land once discouraged development, but Maori owners are now returning to settle on land previously used only for holidays and weekends.

While farmers' children leave for the city life, in the past 10 years a strong community of 'alternative lifestylers' have been attracted by the Hokianga's peacefulness, isolation (nearest towns Dargaville and Kaitaia are an hour's drive) and untamable vitality. On small farms and communes, these new settlers have built interesting houses – look out for their craftwork and delicious honey at roadside stalls. Forestry is now beginning to change both established and alternative lifestyles.

Local Government Centre, Hokianga Road, Dargaville. Telephone (0884) 7059

A town that was once one of the busiest ports in the country, when kauri timber and gum were loaded at the riverside onto sailing ships, the tiny port on the Wairoa River sees little commerce today. But the town makes a good base for exploring the wild west-coast beaches such as Bayley's Beach and Glink's Gully, and the Waipoua Kauri Forest. Travel out to the historic lighthouse on the Kaipara Heads and catch glimpses of old shipwrecks in the drifting sands, try surf casting from the beaches, visit the tiny perfect Kai-iwi Lakes, with white silica-sand beaches rimmed with pines.

Otamatea Kauri & Pioneer Museum (Off State Highway 12) Matakohe Northland Telephone: Paparoa 37-417 Curator: Merv Sterling

Superb museum (between Paparoa and Ruawai) built as tribute to pioneers, and nationally important for the 'Story of the Kauri' and unique kauri gum collection (over 1,500 pieces). The history is told with photographs, models, wall timber, early furniture (plus kauri bath!) and industry tools. Picnic amongst living kauris; refreshments available. Souvenir shop specialises in kauri/wooden novelties. Open daily 9.00 a.m. to 5.00 p.m.(closed Christmas Day). From $1.50 adults,.50c children.

SEE ALSO:
Live with NZ: Kai Iwi Lakes Farm Stay (Down on Farm) (Omamari).
Outback Safaris: Kauri Coaster Tours (Dargaville).

South via Whangarei to Auckland

Surrounded by steep, forested hills, the harbour city of Whangarei is the centre of the only significant heavy industry in Northland. There's little evidence in the city itself, however. The country's major oil refinery lies at Marsden Point, on the harbour's south head, where huge modern tankers make use of the deep anchorage, tying up only a few feet from shore. View Marsden Point from the north side of the harbour, while driving to Whangarei Heads via Onerahi to Parua Bay, McLeods Bay and Ocean Beach. Port Whangarei, closer to the city centre, also provides a deep natural anchorage, catering for ships up to 182 metres (600 feet) long and 9.5 metres (30 feet) draught. The oil refinery, fertiliser, glass and cement works all contribute to the city's prosperity, but don't impinge upon the pleasant 'small-town' quality of life.

Whangarei Public Relations Office, Forum North, Rust Avenue, Whangarei. Telephone: (089) 81079

In Whangarei, wander by the small town harbour, a boating anchorage in the heart of the city. Take a walk in Mair Park and up the Parahaki for a good view of the city. On the way south, stop at Lookout Hill for stunning views down harbour to Marsden Point, Mt Manaia and the sharply peaked Hen and Chicken Islands.

Northland

Accommodation. – Excellent hotel or motor-inn accommodation is available in Paihia, Waitangi, Russell, Kerikeri, Whangarei and Kaitaia. Motel units, with fully equipped kitchens for self-catering, are in all main towns and along the coast, sometimes right on almost-deserted beaches. Old-fashioned hotels, many now renovated, provide bargain accommodation in towns that have shrunk to villages – expect a comfortable bed, often a private bathroom, but no television or telephone in the room. Youth hostels can be found at Kerikeri, Kaitaia, Whangaroa, Opononi, Whangarei, with private hotels at Paihia. Camping grounds for those with tents or campervans are almost inevitably near the sea.

Food. – Surrounded by the sea, seek out the freshest fish and seafood such as snapper, hapuka, flounder, crayfish. Try smoked marlin in the region where marlin is caught. The shellfish tuatua is prolific on Northland beaches – try soup or fritters with tuatua straight from the shell, not the can. Also look for huge Pacific oysters or small sweet local rock oysters on the east coast. In the Bay of Islands sample fresh fruit, juices or preserves of goldfruit, tangelos, mandarins, tamarillos, passionfruit, babaco and kiwifruit.

North to Kaitaia

Pukenui Lodge Motel and Youth Hostel
(Adjacent to Pukenui Wharf)
PO Box 11
Houhora
Telephone: Houhora 837

Forty-nine kilometres (30 miles) north of Kaitaia, towards Cape Reinga, this is New Zealand's northernmost motel, scenically situated overlooking the Houhora harbour (good fishing from wharf). Six fully self-contained units (sleep four), with separate bedroom, colour television and well-equipped kitchens, plus a 15-bed hostel with all facilities – a friendly meeting place. Relaxed atmosphere, open all day. Cost: hostel, from $6 per person; units, from $36 double.

Adriaan Lodge
PO Box 320
Kaitaia
Telephone: Ahipara 888
Hosts: Esther and Ron Crabtree

Situated in spacious grounds, overlooking magnificent Ahipara Bay, southern end of the famous Ninety Mile Beach, and Shipwreck Bay. Comfortable one-, two- or three-bedroomed units offer sea views and are well appointed (kitchen optional). The Albatross Restaurant provides excellent dining, fresh seafood a speciality. Enjoy swimming or surfing at safe ocean beaches or dive for crayfish, mussels and paua. Located 13 kilometres (8 miles) from Kaitaia. From $40 (two persons).

Albatross Restaurant
Ahipara
PO Box 320
Kaitaia
Telephone: Ahipara 888
Hosts: Esther and Ron Crabtree

This great restaurant is only a 10-minute drive from Kaitaia, and overlooks famous Ninety Mile Beach. Dine in luxury while you watch the sun setting over the bay. Specialising in both fresh seafood and vegetarian cooking, the menu is complemented by a good selection of local and overseas wines. A relaxed and friendly atmosphere completes your dining enjoyment. Closed Sundays. Open from 6.00 p.m. Medium price range.

The Old Saddlery
Crafts and Teas
Main Road
PO Box 23
Kaeo
Telephone: Kaeo 64

the old saddlery

At the gateway to the magnificent unspoilt beauty of the Whangaroa Harbour, this comfortable and homely 100-year-old hostelry invites you to relax and sample great home baking, Devonshire teas, fresh brewed tea and coffee, plus a range of crisp, delicious salads. See the display of fine examples of local crafts available for puchase – superb homespun and hand-knitted pure-wool garments, unique wood-fired kiln pottery, woodware and bone carving.

Kerikeri

Adventure Park Motor Camp
Wiroa Road
Kerikeri
Telephone: Kerikeri 79-773

This facility offers a friendly base for your Northland holiday. It is rurally situated, adjacent to exciting adventure playground and 5 minutes from Kerikeri township, and offers 20 comfortable cabins, modern kitchens and ablution areas, games room, camp shop, courtesy van, plus unlimited tent sites (bedding not provided). Especially suited to young travellers, but comfortable for all. Cost: 20 December – 1 April, from $18 (double). At all other times, from $16 (double).

Riverview Motel
Kerikeri
Telephone: Kerikeri 78-741
Hosts: Angelika and Helmut Letz

On river bank in native bush setting, overlooking famous Stone Store, Kemp House and yacht harbour (no traffic noise). Six private, fully self-contained chalet units equipped with full kitchen facilities, and one paraplegic unit. Spa, sauna and swimming pool. Beautiful walks through surrounding reserves or swimming and boating on the river (rowboat is available). Be assured of a warm welcome. From $38 (two persons). 20% winter discount.

Spanish House Motel
PO Box 225
Kerikeri
Telephone: Kerikeri 79-311
Hosts: Tony and Sharon Churton

This is a motel of distinctive quality with two-bedroomed units set in 5 hectares (13 acres) of rural farmland with panoramic views of the historic Kerikeri inlet. All units fully self contained with additional facilities: outdoor swimming pool, spa and sauna, horse riding by arrangement, golf course and swimming beaches nearby. Four kilometres (2½ miles) from Kerikeri village you will find a warm welcome at this privately owned motel. From $30, single; $40, double.

Jane's Restaurant and Bar
State Highway 10
(5 kilometres south of Kerikeri)
Kerikeri
Telephone: Kerikeri 78-664
Hosts: Fred and Joy Zylstra

This restaurant is set beside the main road and open for lunches and evening dining. The ambiance is that of an English pub, with congenial hospitality and pleasantly intimate decor. Each meal is individually prepared and the menu takes full advantage of the wide range of local seafood, vegetables and fruit. Fully licensed, the wine list is extensive. Medium price range, open daily. Book for evening dining.

Kerikeri Stone Store Ltd
Kerikeri
Telephone: Kerikeri 78-194/78-479
Owner: David Stretton-Pow

This historic stone building is New Zealand's oldest, today supplying everything from petrol to food and souvenirs. Visit the interesting museum in the upper stories and then cross the road to the restaurant/tearooms, which provides delicious natural foods and good service at moderate prices while offering unparalleled views. During summer months enjoy verandah dining and outdoor concerts. Booking advisable for evening dining (occasionally closed during winter).

Paihia

Centabay Lodge
Selwyn Road
Paihia
Telephone: (0885) 27-466

This backpackers' hostel accommodates 36 persons in four modern, separate, self-contained flats, equipped with lounge and television. Comfortable, clean and spacious in quiet setting close to shops, amenities, activities and Marine Park walks. A warm welcome is assured. Bed linen is available for hire and your hosts will be happy to organise bicycle hire or yacht charter on *Druiana* at Youth Hostel Association discount rates. Bookings unnecessary. From $7 per person.

Smiths Holiday Camp, Cabins and Motel
PO Box 41
Paihia
Telephone: Paihia 27-678

This lovely, family-owned holiday resort is secluded in a sheltered bay, right on the water's edge on a bush-covered peninsula. Located 2 kilometres (1.2 miles) from Paihia towards Opua, it's a perfect spot for relaxing or catching an and shellfish (hiring a boat to catch your breakfast or pole-fishing for yellowtail). Your host will jet-boat you to your own island for an idyllic picnic or you can explore the many beautiful coastal walks. Enjoy a friendly atmosphere plus choice of accommodation, from completely self-contained motel units with fully equipped kitchens, to deluxe one bedroom/kitchen/lounge cabins (complete except for linen and blankets) or continental one-room cabins. Also offers 52 power-equipped tent and caravan sites. Facilities include showers/toilets, kitchen, laundry, games and television rooms. Cost: sites from $4, cabins from $20 (double) and motels from $32 (double).

Dargaville

Awakino Point Lodge
PO Box 168
Dargaville
Telephone: (884) 7870
Hosts: June and Wally Birch

This is a small family concern, minutes from Dargaville and set in attractive gardens on a peaceful farmlet. You are assured of a high standard of comfort in well-appointed, tastefully furnished two-bedroom suites, each with colour television. Cooking facilities not included, but a complimentary cooked or continental breakfast is available. Experience Northern hospitality. From $29 (single), $32 (double).

Parkview Motel
36 Carrington Street
Dargaville
Telephone: (0884) 8339
Hosts: Shona and Arthur Keoghan

Overlooking a 'child-safe', solar-heated swimming pool, these units are situated in a quiet location not far from town centre. Ground floor accommodation with parking at door. Self-contained twin/double and family units, centrally heated, with personal telephone and television. A restaurant provides à la carte menu, and breakfasts are available. Facilities include laundry, car wash, heated swirl pool and trampoline. From $44 (double). Major credit cards accepted.

Cameo Lounge
18 Beach Road
Dargaville
Telephone: (0884) 7133
Host: Gary Burnett

This is Dargaville's food and entertainment centre, a reception lounge offering a changing variety of live New Zealand performers and fine New Zealand food in comfortable and fully licensed premises. Dance to music by local and visiting artists. Conference and private functions catered for. Courtesy transport is available. Open seven days a week. Reservations essential. Treat yourself – book in advance for a champagne breakfast! Fine food, entertainment and service combined with Northern hospitality.

The Cottage Restaurant
Corner Victoria and Gladstone Streets
Dargaville
Telephone: (0884) 7761

Centrally situated, this teahouse and restaurant is open seven days a week, from 9.00 a.m. till late, serving delicious home-style, New Zealand country cooking. The restaurant is fully licensed and has seating for up to 60 people. Relax in the warm, friendly atmosphere and comfort of colonial architecture and tasteful decor. Evening reservations appreciated. Special rates available for children.

Whangarei

Timothy's Myth Licensed Restaurant
58 Vine Street
Whangarei
Telephone: (089) 87-849

Timothy's Myth

Menu: Traditional French cuisine, offering a range of seafoods, game, steaks and poultry with seasonal changes. Wine list: Superb range of New Zealand wines, including lesser-known vintners. Staff are knowledgeable about wines. An excellent cocktail selection also available, including local exotics! Feel at home, be well looked after. Friday/Saturday evenings, resident group plays old standards, jazz flavour. Luncheon 12 noon – 2.00 p.m. Tuesday to Friday; dinner from 6.00 p.m. (reservations necessary). Closed Sundays and Mondays. Children's meals by arrangement.

Auckland may be the country's most populated region, but for those who wish to escape the city the surrounding area provides extraordinary opportunities with its islands, beaches, hills and valleys.

entred on a narrow isthmus of dormant and extinct volcanoes, the region of Auckland sprawls out from the city over the hills and countryside. This is a region of people – about a quarter of New Zealand's population lives in this area – yet it feels more like a series of villages with a small city centre than a major metropolis.

The suburbs spread out in a vast web from the commercial centre on the edge of the Waitemata Harbour, through vineyards and orchards to the hills of the west where houses nestle in the native bush; along the beaches and tiny bays to the north and east and across green fields to the south.

At first glance it is a homogeneous collection of houses and trees strewn over hills and valleys, thinning at the green perimeters where the true countryside takes over. Yet the suburbs, the outlying country towns and villages all have their own distinct characteristics throughout the region.

Travel to the north of the region, through the pretty riverside town of Warkworth to the village of Leigh, where fishing boats and dive boats gather in the inlet. In a spectacular marine reserve along several kilometres of the shoreline divers can hand feed fish. Surfers head over the hill to the long, beautiful beach at Pakiri. From nearby Sandspit, boats leave for Kawau Island, where visitors can see through a grand mansion, once the home of a governor, Sir George Grey. Bush walks lead over a rugged, roadless island – walk quietly and you may find wild wallabies sharing the track.

Reach most islands of the Hauraki Gulf from Auckland City's harbour front – there are about 100 islands out there. Ferries, yachts, launches or sea planes open the way to the islands, right out to the furthest and largest of them, Great Barrier. This covers 28,000 rugged hectares (70,000 acres) and has a population of less than 500. Closest to the city is Rangitoto, an uninhabited, sharply defined volcano, formed a mere 800 years ago.

Safe, sheltered swimming beaches indent the coast of the gulf. Some, such as Snells Beach, Algies Bay, Waiwera, Orewa and Manly, are dense with holiday cottages and permanent homes, but also offer village shopping amenities. Others such as Wenderholm and Mahurangi Heads are special reserves where the natural beauty of the shoreline is unmarked by any buildings. All are popular but never crowded – an important distinction.

Aerial view over Westhaven marina and the harbour bridge. ***(Andris Apse Ltd)***

At Waiwera natural hot springs have been tapped and turned into an elaborate complex of hot-water swimming pools, with private dip pools and giant water slides – barely a towel's throw from the beach. Also find natural hot-water swimming to the west at Parakai, near Helensville.

The beaches of the west coast are wild and treacherous, favourites with surfers and those who like invigorating surf swimming – surf life-savers patrol the black-sand beaches of Muriwai, Piha and Karekare, ensuring visitors know the safe places to swim and surf.

Between the city of Auckland and the closest west-coast beaches rise the Waitakere Ranges, high forest-covered hills, threaded with walking tracks. Once dominated by kauri forest that was milled out last century, the bush remains thick enough to get lost in if you stray from the tracks. Stands of kauri remain in the hills, and an information centre on the Scenic Drive near Titirangi details the history, the walks, the flora and fauna of the ranges.

To Bombay at the south of Auckland the hills rise again,

rich, volcanic soils in the south west providing a patch-work of market gardens. To the south east there are more bush-covered hills, dipping down to pretty east-coast bays, the home of riding schools and the mini-estates of the wealthy.

Travel on towards the Coromandel Peninsula, across the edge of a flat plain where deep ditches border the road and divide the fields, and boulders keep river levels above the surrounding land. Ahead looms the extraordinary contrast of the sharp, raw splendour of the peninsula.

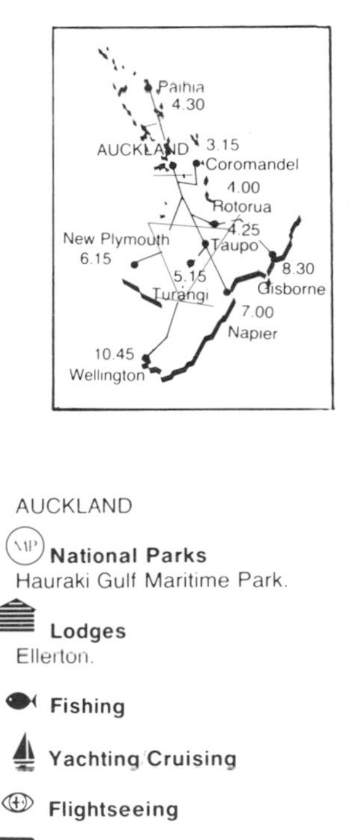

Travel around by car in Auckland. Fly by amphibian aircraft to islands or bays on the east coast, and fly on small land craft to Whitianga or Pauanui. Public buses, run by the Auckland Regional Authority, serve some beaches and villages outside the city limits. N.Z.R. Road Services buses have a regular service through the Coromandel from Auckland. Take tours, with a wide variety to choose from.

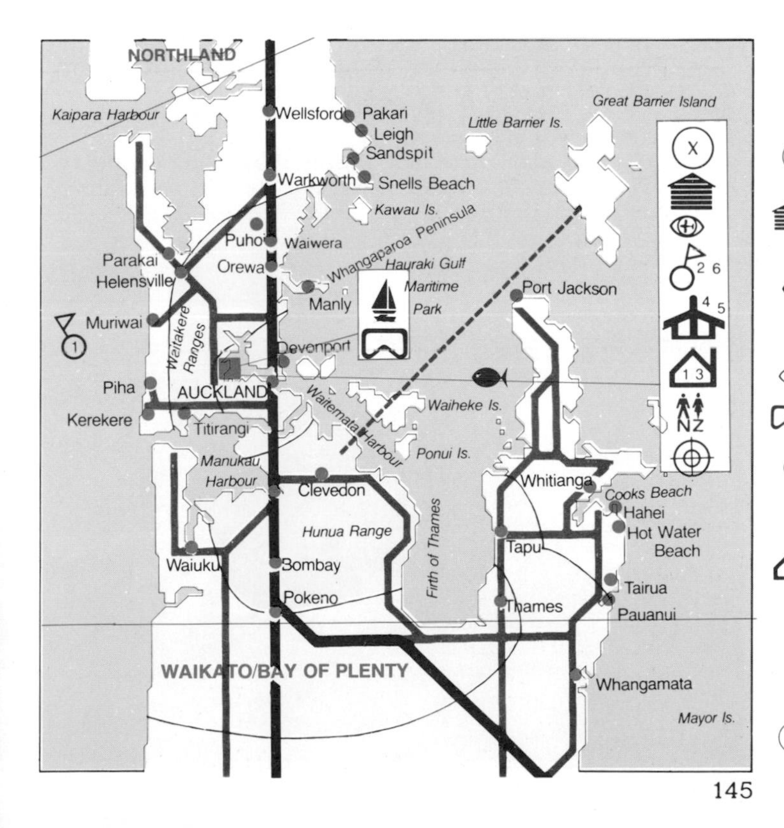

AUCKLAND

National Parks
Hauraki Gulf Maritime Park.

Lodges
Ellerton.

Fishing

Yachting Cruising

Flightseeing

Diving

Golf
1. Muriwai; 2. Chamberlain; 3. Grange; 4. Remuera; 5. Titirangi; 6. Manukau.

History
1. Ewelme Cottage; 2. Highwic House; 3. Alberton; 4. Mt Eden – Pa site; 5. One Tree Hill – Pa site.

Live with NZ

Local
1. Museum; 2. Zoo.

Sailing at Takapuna Beach. *(Courtesy Air New Zealand)*

Auckland is a city of views. From hilltops and ridges you can look down to the Waitemata Harbour on the east coast and the Manukau Harbour on the west. At the narrowest point there is scarcely more than a kilometre between the two coasts.

Generations of Maoris heaved and dragged their large and small canoes over these portages from harbour to harbour as a shortcut during wars or on fishing trips. Being surrounded by good locations for pa and two good harbours, Auckland was coveted by a number of Maori tribes. Although numbering up to 4,000 people in pre-European times, European guns and disease drastically reduced the Maori population before Auckland was founded in 1840.

About 800,000 people live in Auckland, mostly in single-storey houses each with its own garden – there is little high-density living. Drive to the top of One Tree Hill or Mt Eden and see houses and gardens spreading out through the valleys in an area the size of greater London. Filled with trees, freshened by sea breezes and showers, Auckland has little of the hazy pollution that plagues many cities.

For other perspectives of the city, drive around the Waitakere Ranges through thick native forest, or cross the harbour by bridge or ferry to Devonport and the twin cones of Mt Victoria and North Head.

On the North Shore residents relish a casual lifestyle in beachside suburbs. Visit beaches such as Takapuna, Cheltenham, Milford or, on the city side, minutes from the centre, swim at Mission Bay, Kohimarama, St Heliers.

Down at the waterfront find boats and sea planes that will whisk you away out to the islands of the Hauraki Gulf for fishing, sailing or sightseeing.

Back in the city, discover the many beautiful parks. Albert Park in the city centre is distinctly Victorian, with flowerbeds and band rotunda. The Auckland Domain ençompasses woods where daffodils grow, unusual trees, cricket grounds, tropical glass house, ponds and statuary. Cornwall Park merges with One Tree Hill into more than 120 hectares (300 acres), where sheep and cattle graze under old oaks, olives and Norfolk pines. A huge Edwardian-style afternoon tea taken at the kiosk provides an unusual time warp.

Old buildings also emphasise the city's Victorian origins. Down town is the old Customhouse. Further afield see through grand mansions, Highwic and Alberton, and the charming cottage, Ewelme Cottage and Kinderhouse (see the History section page 94)).

Auckland Region Visitor & Convention Bureau (Inc.), Aotea Square, 299 Queen Street, Auckland, P.O. Box 7048. Telephone: (09) 31889

A style of architecture known as 'Selwyn' dominates early Church of England buildings – find this romantic Gothic style in Parnell, especially the tiny St Stephens Chapel, at All Saints' in Howick and St Andrew's in Epsom.

Stroll or bus to Orakei state housing suburb, one of the areas where the state has housed low-income families. Over 70 years ago the first town-planning conference sponsored a competition for the design of a garden suburb. Orakei has been developed almost along the lines of the prizewinning model.

Discover the large ostentatious homes of Paritai Drive on one side of the valley and the unpretentious state houses of the Orakei marae on the other. Facing Okahu Bay, find the roughcast and brick houses with terracotta tiled roofs and Georgian proportions. Influenced by the English garden suburb, they represent the idealism of the 1930s.

Entertainment – Find out when the Symphonia plays by watching the ads in the back of both Auckland daily papers. Unearth jazz, blues and rock by reading the *Auckland Star* on Thursdays when there's a special entertainment and gig guide. For folk music check out the Poles Apart Folk Club in Newmarket, and just around the corner for jazz, the Royal George Inn. Rock lovers jam into the Windsor and the Gluepot. Those wanting a more sophisticated cabaret atmosphere should try Club Casa Blanca, Club 21, Club Mirage, Retro or Brandys.

Auckland boasts several theatre companies. For stimulating inventive productions, visit the Mercury or Theatre Corporate at night, or the New Independent, a theatre group that specialises in lunchtime shows. The Maidment Arts Theatre in the university grounds often features theatre, recitals and dance. Limbs Dance Company delights audiences there regularly.

Do not miss getting a copy of *Metro* magazine – one of the country's best. The Metrolog pages of the magazine give the most comprehensive entertainment guide and good reviews of restaurants are also provided. See too the Dining Entertainment Guide in the free, weekly *Auckland Tourist Times*, which is distributed nationally to hotels, car-hire firms and tourist booking offices.

A view from North Head across the Waitemata Harbour to the downtown area of Auckland city. *(Andris Apse Ltd)*

Parnell Village, Parnell. (Courtesy Air New Zealand)

useums detail the past. The imposing War Memorial Museum in the Domain has a splendid display of Maori and Pacific Island artifacts, and at Western Springs the Museum of Transport and Technology is a stunning collection of everything that whirrs, from music boxes to Lancaster bombers.

Adjoining the technology museum is the zoo, with an international collection in park-like gardens, and your chance to see the strange kiwi bird in a special nocturnal house. More animals? On the western outskirts of the city, at Massey, is a lion park – great fun for children, with camels that insist on being hand fed, a small water slide and a moated fort with paddle boats.

More spectacular youthful fun can be found in the complex at Rainbow's End, where there are water slides, bumper boats, mini racing cars. This is in the south at Manukau City (administratively Auckland splits itself into three cities and many boroughs).

For more grown-up pleasure, tour the vineyards of the western suburbs where grapevines spread over the gentle lower slopes of the Waitakere Ranges. Small or large, the vineyards welcome visitors and there is the opportunity to discover how good New Zealand wines can be. Some vineyards have pleasant outdoor restaurants where you can linger under a canopy of vines.

Browse through markets: at Cook Street and Victoria Park Markets find the fun and bargains of any big city bazaar; at the Mill discover a concentration of quality crafts; and out at the Otara Shopping Centre carpark each Saturday morning there's a distinctly Maori and Pacific Island market, where raw shellfish, melons, taro, rewena and kumi kumi are sold along with more durable wares.

In the city find further evidence that Auckland is the world's largest Polynesian centre in Karangahape Road, and also Ponsonby, where chic boutiques are side by side with shops selling cheerful island cottons and food such as yams, taro and green coconuts.

Over 60,000 Polynesians live in Auckland; more Niueans, Tokelauans and Cook Islanders live here than in their own islands. Large Samoan and Tongan communities also bring vitality to city life.

For up-market, sophisticated shopping, visit Parnell and find exclusive fashion boutiques, excellent pottery, glassware, jewellery, wood crafts, books, antiques, hand-made sweets. If you long for pastrami, Parma-style ham, pumpernickel or simply a good cup of coffee, you should find it here.

There is far more variety in Auckland than that first glance might imply.

Highwic house, Epsom. *(Anthony Henry Photography)*

Auckland

Auckland Zoological Park
Motions Road
Western Springs
Auckland
Telephone: (09) 761-415

Two of the world's most fascinating creatures – the flightless kiwi bird and the tuatara (sole remaining link with the dinosaurs) are included in Auckland Zoo's collection of exotic and native species, numbering 1,500 mammals, birds, reptiles and fish. Though located only five minutes' drive from the city's heart, the zoo is also one of Auckland's finest parks. Covering 18 hectares (45 acres) of varied terrain, it has superb trees, streams and ponds as well as flora from the high-rainfall areas of the tropics to the extremes of alpine districts and desert areas; and, of course, native specimens abound. The kiwi nocturnal house, where 'day' is turned into 'night', enables visitors to see the kiwis move during the daylight hours in their native setting of New Zealand bush. Breeding herds of animals are exhibited wherever possible, rather than small groups or pairs. It is also the zoo's policy to acquire only animals born or reared in captivity, not taken from their natural habitat (except for endangered kiwis). An example is the 'family' of four Bornean orangutans – the only orangs in New Zealand – from which it is planned to establish a breeding colony. The zoo is a haven for kiwis rescued from bush-clearing, or injured in traps, but it has also established breeding pairs and has an impressive record of 30 hatchings in the last 10 years. Because of Auckland's temperate climate, almost all of the animals can be kept outdoors throughout the year, and wherever possible they are displayed in spacious enclosures where they can be viewed to best advantage. Examples are the large, grassed enclosures where the giraffe and antelope gallop freely. Souvenir shop and cafeteria. Open daily from 9.30 a.m. to 5.30 p.m. Admission: from $3.50 adults, $1.50 children.

Auckland City Art Gallery
Cnr Wellesley and
Kitchener Streets
Auckland
Telephone: (09) 792-020
After Hours: (09) 792-069

The Auckland City Art Gallery boasts one of the most notable public art collections in New Zealand. Occupying a fine building in the French Chateau style, it possesses excellent collections of historical European art, contemporary international prints and New Zealand art, past and present. The gallery is superbly situated in a central city location; the bustling heart of the city on one side, the green slopes of Albert Park on the other. It opened its doors to the public in February 1888 with a fusion of the private collections of Sir George Grey (a former Governor of New Zealand), and James Tannock Mackelvie, a once prominent New Zealand merchant. While those collections are still a feature, the city's own holdings have grown and expanded to the point that they are without rival in New Zealand.

Auckland Winter Gardens
The Domain
Auckland
Telephone: (09) 792-020

A fascinating range of plants of the South Pacific awaits the visitor to the Winter Gardens, located in the Domain. The complex consists of a Cool House, displaying about 10,000 pot plants each year; the heated Tropical House; the Fernery; and the 'old world' Courtyard, with its pergolas, massive vases, a sunken pool, statues and benches.

Varieties in the Cool House include calceolarias, begonias, primulas, gloxinias, cyclamen and chrysanthemums, as well as the hardier orchids such as papiopedilums and cymbidiums. There is a striking contrast in the Tropical House, with permanent residents such as the ravenala (the traveller's palm), banana and carludovica (the Panama Hat palm), as well as 2,000 more temporary inhabitants on display through the year. An Auckland City Council amenity, the Winter Gardens are open from 10.00 a.m. to 4.00 p.m., daily. Admission is free.

Chamberlain Park Public Golf Course
Linwood Avenue
Mount Albert
Auckland
Telephone: (09) 866-758

Chamberlain Park Golf Course is unique in Auckland because it is the only one that welcomes all golfers, male or female, young or old, seven days a week – and without any membership fee. The cost for 18 holes is probably the cheapest in the world – from $5 during weekends, with a reduced fee weekdays. There are special rates for juniors and senior citizens. Clubs, trundlers, shoes and other gear can be hired. All that is required is the urge to play a round. The course is only eight minutes from town by car. The club has a modern clubhouse, complete with cafeteria and golf shop run by a leading New Zealand professional golfer, Terry Kendall. Terry (known throughout the South Pacific for his big drive) also conducts regular clinics.

Chamberlain Park (administered by the Auckland City Council) is located in the Western Springs area, close to the Zoological Park, the Stadium – which is the venue for major speedway events throughout the summer – and the Museum of Transport and Technology (MOTAT). If you are pressed for time, you can combine your round of golf with other activities. You do not have to be a good golfer to tackle the course, but if you are, you are playing on a park which has hosted such celebrities as Gary Player, Australia's Peter Thomson, and Bill Dunk. The important thing is that you don't have to be 'introduced' to get on the course; and because there are no regular tournaments and no 'club days', it is available to you at any time. One of the best-drained courses in Auckland, it is open literally throughout the year – seven days a week – dawn to dusk.

Customhouse Woolshed
Old Auckland Customhouse
Corner of Custom and Albert Streets
Downtown
Auckland
Telephone: (09) 399-006
Owners: Judy Donovan and Garth Cumberland

Wool crafts in the city – The Downtown Auckland branch of Clevedon Woolshed in the historic and beautiful Customhouse, is packed with an exciting range of wool crafts too vast and diverse to describe. Knitwear, weaving, sheepskins and accessories are carefully chosen to represent the consistently high quality of New Zealand's craftspeople and the sheep industry. A great range of pure wool knitwear, fashion garments and gift items.

Mutual Fourways
C/- Downtown Travel
8 Lower Queen Street
Auckland
Telephone: (09) 793-591

For those whose time in Auckland is limited, Fourways Pacific offers inexpensive half-day and full-day sightseeing coach tours, encompassing the major attractions of Auckland. See the city in the comfort of a hostess-escorted luxury coach with on-board toilet/restroom facilities. The morning tour skirts the beautiful harbour and brings you the best of the eastern suburbs and central Auckland. The afternoon tour incorporates the rich wine-making area of the west and the picturesque northern suburbs. For those taking both tours, a return ferry trip on historic MV *Kestrel* to the charming suburb of Devonport is provided during the lunchtime break. From $14 adults, $5 children.

The Clevedon Woolshed
(Opposite Post Office)
PO Box 88
Clevedon
Telephone: (09) 2928-615
Owners: Judy Donovan and Garth Cumberland

Pure wool and New Zealand crafts in the country. Just 30 minutes' pleasant drive southeast of Auckland city, in the heart of Clevedon Village, set amongst beautiful farmland, discover an exciting range of pure wool products – quality knitwear, fashion garments, weaving, sheepskins, yarn and toys. See also superb New Zealand Crafts – pottery, woodware and glassware – made by talented local craftspeople. An innovative and everchanging shop.

Auckland

Gold is the history of the Coromandel peninsula. A brief but wildly successful gold rush began in 1867, with one mine producing more than a ton of gold in one month in 1871. The town of Thames became a boom town, with a hotel on every street corner – many of the buildings remain, some still as hotels. Find historical reminders of the gold-rush days in the towns of Thames and Coromandel and in the hills where guided walks lead through old mine shafts and tunnels.

The peninsula is a favourite with hikers – more than 30 major tramping tracks and many short walks lead deep into the ranges throughout the Coromandel Forest Park. Track information can be obtained from an information centre in Thames' Queen Street or from the Forest Park headquarters in the beautiful Kauaeranga Valley.

Rock hounds who can recognise semi-precious gemstones in their raw state find the peninsula New Zealand's most productive area. There's agate, jasper, onyx, carnelian, chalcedony, amethyst, quartz crystal, sinter and chert to be found in the streams and along the beaches. Polished stones and jewellery can be bought at crafts shops, which often sell excellent potttery as well – some of New Zealand's best potters have chosen to live on the peninsula and sell their work locally.

The peninsula is the southernmost limit of kauri forests. The forests were ravaged in the early nineteenth century, but some splendid ancient trees survived and can be reached today by well-defined tracks. Through much of the forest the kauri trees are regenerating in their natural environment.

But it is the beaches, perhaps even more than the hills, that make Coromandel a spectacular and special area. Long golden beaches with rolling surf, tiny perfect bays surrounded by gnarled pohutukawa trees, great rocky promontories where the sea crashes in. It is a place for swimming, surfing, sailing, windsurfing, water skiing, fishing, diving.

Every beach has its own charms and character: Hahei, with its pink-tinged sands, ancient pa sites and excellent diving; Hot Water Beach, where hot springs seep through the sand at low tide and swimmers can leave the sea to scoop out hot pools in the sand; Whitianga, where dive boats and game-fishing boats congregate in a deep, sheltered harbour; Pauanui, a long golden beach where a carefully designed holiday town nestles in the pines.

Waiwera Hot Pools Leisure Resort
(Highway 1 between Orewa and Warkworth)
PO Box 26
Waiwera
Telephone: (0942) 65-369

Spend a day or a week having fun at this superb resort. Adjoining the Waiwera Hotel, the complex offers hot pools (small and large, public and private, with varying temperatures), private saunas, suntan beds, sun lounges, barbecues and picnic areas, mini golf, a snack shop, party pools, seven exciting stainless steel water slides, children's water slides and the Paradise Spa Pool Video Games Room. Towels, bathing suits, bathing caps and goggles are available for hire. Resort is open every day, till late evening. Great fun for the family, private functions or groups. Daily cost: from $5 adults, $2.50 children. Set against a backdrop of native bush-clad bluffs, the village also offers a range of accommodation and shops plus safe swimming in this sheltered bay. Just 45 minutes north of Auckland by car or take an ARA bus from Auckland City.

Walkways, Parks and Reserves

Walkways

The Auckland Isthmus – where only 9 kilometres (5½ miles) separate two oceans – is latticed with sign-posted walkways.

Urban Area: The Coast To Coast Walkway

This is a great way to get to know Auckland. Linking both harbours, it is a permanent route through parks, gardens, past historic barracks and buildings to the summits of both Mt Eden and One Tree Hill. Starting from Queen Elizabeth Square, the total distance of 13 kilometres (8 miles) takes about four hours, and a guide map is available from the Auckland City Council Visitors and Convention Bureau.

Nature and Historic Walks

Aucklanders and visitors can explore the city with experienced guides provided free by the city council. Sunday walks in the Domain (nature and historic walks leave at 1.30 p.m. from museum steps) go all year round, other walks summer only (November to the end of May). Leaflets available from the city council or the Visitors Convention Bureau, Aotea Square. Other walks, most of which take two hours, explore markets, galleries, historic places, the suburb of Parnell, theatres, arts and crafts, and architecture and leave from a variety of gathering points.

The Waterfront Walk

There are other mapped walks you can follow on your own, taking from 15 minutes to two hours, along the beautiful Auckland waterfront from the Harbour Bridge to Mission Bay. Brochures from the Visitors Bureau have maps and points of interest.

Devonport and North Head

Cross the harbour by ferry to quiet Devonport. The historic North Head Reserve is a short waterfront walk away past yacht moorings and quaint old houses. North Head, once a volcano, was an old military fort built in 1885 and further strengthened with successive 'Russian scares'. In World War I it was an internment camp, in World War II its gun emplacements protected the channel and city.

The Point England Walk

The Point England Walk, about 8.7 kilometres (5½ miles), takes about three hours. Take a bus to the end of the

Pastoral scene in Cornwall Park *(Andris Apse Ltd)*

waterfront, Tamaki Drive to St Heliers. From there walk to Achilles Point for harbour views. Hugging the shoreline, the walk passes two ancient pa sites, an old volcanic crater and 600-year-old pohutukawa trees before descending to the Tahuna-Torea nature reserve, bird sanctuary and sand spit. (Tahuna-Torea is well worth a visit on its own – take a Glendowie or Glen Innes bus from the city terminal. A thoughtful walk right round takes just over an hour.) The walk continues through greenways and reserves to St John's Ridge for panoramic views of the isthmus, Rangitoto and the Tamaki Estuary.

Parks and Reserves

Within driving distance of Auckland are many large parks, bushlands and farms open to the public. Auckland Centennial Memorial Park is the largest of the Auckland Regional Authority's 10 regional parks, and is a reminder of the heavily forested landscape that greeted the first Europeans. Within its 8,400 hectares (20,000 acres) of forest are many nature trails, peaceful picnic stops and varied coastlines. Stands of kauri and a profusion of other native trees and plants, as well as relics of the kauri sawmills and steep bush railway, are only 40 minutes drive from the city centre. Stop at the Information Centre on the Scenic Drive, 5.5 kilometres (3½ miles) from Titirangi, for leaflets, displays and information. From there join the identification trails (20 minutes, 40 minutes or 75 minutes) to numbered stations giving plant and forest information, the story of the forest's regeneration, growth, maturity and decay. There are also over 185 kilometres (115 miles) of walking and tramping tracks in the park and Waitakere Ranges (maps from the information centre).

Muriwai Beach Regional Park

Muriwai Beach Regional Park has wild surf and west coast scenery 45 kilometres (28 miles) from Auckland. For good views take the Mitchelson Track on the main hillside overlooking the beach. The Maori Bay Track follows the cliffs to a disused quarry with unusual lava rock and views of an island bird colony.

Parks and Reserves

Tawharanui Regional Park

Tawharanui Regional Park, 90 kilometres (55 miles) from Auckland, is a coastal and marine park. A three-hour walk along the beach shows historic Maori terraces and pits; a one-hour walk along clifftops offers views of Kawau and Little Barrier Islands.

Wenderholm Regional Park

Wenderholm Regional Park is a favourite family picnic spot with an old-world charm, 48 kilometres (30 miles) from Auckland. It features walks through coastal bush, where native wood pigeons and tuis can be seen feeding on berries and flowers. Visit the historic Couldrey House.

Long Bay Regional Park

Long Bay Regional Park is only 25 minutes from Auckland (26 kilometres or 16 miles) and can be reached by a regular bus service. A coastal walk leads to two smaller bays.

Shakespeare Regional Park

Shakespeare Regional Park, at the tip of the Whangaparaoa Peninsula (56 kilometres or 35 miles from Auckland), has a regular bus service from the city terminal. Sign-posted trails through a wooded stream valley emerge into open paddocks at the Park's summit, with views of the gulf and Auckland. Swamps are homes for pukekos, waders and an Australian green frog.

Omana Regional Park

Omana Regional Park, on the east coast 42 kilometres (26 miles) south of Auckland city, between Beachlands and Maraetai, was once a profitable kauri gum-digging area. Perendale sheep and Hereford cattle now roam the paddocks, open to the public. A perimeter walk passes an old Maori pa site.

Waharau Regional Park

Waharau Regional Park, 70 kilometres (44 miles) from Auckland on the Firth of Thames, is coastal forest, with some abandoned farms gradually reverting to forest. Walking tracks (4-5 hours, 1½ hours, 1 hour or 30 minutes) are colour coded and sign-posted.

Awhitu Regional Park

Awhitu Regional Park, 90 kilometres (55 miles) from Auckland, is on the southern shores of the Manukau Harbour, and is another Auckland Regional Authority farm. It includes tidal mudflats and birdlife – featuring the migratory godwit and pied oystercatcher, the rare fernbird and banded rail.

The Regional Botanic Gardens

The Regional Botanic Gardens, 23 kilometres (14 miles) south of Auckland, just off the motorway at Manurewa, has informative and attractive walks specialising in plants growing best in the Auckland region.

Hunua

Brochures about the regional parks can be obtained from the Auckland Regional Authority or the Visitors Bureau. In the Hunua Ranges in Auckland's water-catchment area, walking tracks link dams and reservoirs (information from the ARA Water Department, Moumoukai Depot, phone 292-5870).

Hauraki Gulf Maritime Park

The Hauraki Gulf Maritime Park is made up of dozens of islands, many easily reached by ferry or small plane. The Park forms a maritime playground for visitors while protecting wildlife. Rangitoto Island is the cone of a volcano that last erupted 250 years ago. Tracks go round and to the summit of the island. Island roads were built from crushed lava by prison labour during the Depression. A ferry leaves weekends at 9 a.m. from the ferry building downtown. (A pamphlet is available from the Lands and Survey Department or the Visitors Bureau.)

Motutapu Island

Motutapu Island connects with Rangitoto by causeway at Islington Bay. A ferry leaves town from Princes Wharf (contact Blue Boats, phone 34-478) and passengers can be dropped off at Rangitoto to combine a hike to the summit with a Motutapu excursion. Walk from Islington Bay to Home Bay, and across farmland to the highest point (about 3 hours). A shorter route is from Home Bay to Administration Bay (1¼ hours), with an option of a walk to Billy Goat Point (1½ hours from the main track) past World War II fortifications.

Wenderholm Reserve near Waiwera. *(Andris Apse Ltd)*

Motuihe Island

Motuihe Island, with a daily ferry service from Auckland, has sandy bays, steep cliffs, gentle hills, pockets of forest and rock pools. Walks all over the island give sweeping views – from the wharf to Calypso Bay return is about 2 hours; around the island, about 3 hours.

Waiheke Island

Waiheke Island, an hour by ferry and 10 minutes by air from Auckland (vehicle ferry from Half Moon Bay, air service from Ardmore and Mechanics Bay), is the gulf's largest and most central island. Towns and beaches are an easy walk apart, and there are 4 kilometres (2½ miles) of bush trails at the Royal Forest and Bird Society's reserve at Onetangi (by bus from the wharf). At the far end of Waiheke is Stony Batter Historic Reserve, with gun emplacements linked by underground tunnels. To reach farmland walks there, take the bus from the wharf or travel from Onetangi on the Man o' War Bay road. From the entrance to Stony Batter itself takes 30 minutes (2 kilometres); from Stony Batter to Hooks Bay about 45 minutes (2.5 kilometres or 1½ miles); to Opopo Bay, about 45 minutes (2.5 kilometres or 1½ miles).

Kawau Island

Kawau Island, with its historic Mansion House (open daily from 9.30 a.m. to 3.30 p.m.), has numerous walking tracks, colour coded and easy to follow. From Mansion House to the look-out, with views of the gulf and old copper mine, takes one hour. Leave from Sandspit, near Warkworth.

Accommodation – Auckland city has a full range of accommodation from luxury hotels at one end of the scale down to youth hostels. You can choose according to your pocket and inclination. Outside the city, motels offer the traveller the best accommodation, often right by beautiful beaches. Find youth hostels also on Great Barrier Island, Waiheke Island and Opoutere Beach on the Coromandel. Well-serviced camping grounds, many with cabin accommodation as well, exist throughout the region. Four huts provide free overnight accommodation in the Coromandel Forest Park, and there are several camping areas in remote bays on farm parks on the Coromandel Peninsula.

Food – Eat as well as you wish and spend as much or as little as you wish in the city's proliferating restaurants. You can dine elegantly with fine china, fine silver and the best French-style cooking or in casual, bistro-style informality. Ethnic restaurants offer Greek, Lebanese, Italian, French, Japanese, Chinese, Indonesian, Indian, Thai and Vietnamese cooking.

To sample the best of local produce, look for sea food such as snapper, orange roughy, John Dory, smoked snapper roe, crayfish, mussels, squid, whitebait, oysters. Find baby lamb cooked to pink perfection or large venison steaks. Local fruit and vegetables are superb when well presented – globe artichokes, zucchini, kumara, nectarines, melons, strawberries, kiwifruit. Travel out of town and the standards vary wildly – you may find an exciting little restaurant in a seaside township, you may find fish and chips. Picnic on delicious fare – buy freshly cooked crayfish from a fisherman, peaches and melons from a roadside stall and you have the basis of a perfect picnic.

SEE ALSO:

Golf: Chamberlain Golf Course.
Live with NZ: Growse House.
Lodges: Ellerton.
National Parks: Hauraki Gulf Maritime Park.
NZ Historic Places: Ewelme Cottage, Alberton, Highwic.
Skiing: Live-Life NZ, Newmans Skihomes.
Water Adventures: Live-Life NZ Promotions "Go raft".
Yachting: Katena Sailboat Charters, South Seas Yacht Charter.

Vacation Inn
187 Campbell Road
Greenlane
Auckland
PO Box 17-042
Auckland
Telephone: (09) 661-269
Telex: NZ 2781

Set in quiet peaceful surrounds, close to the rural beauty of Cornwall Park Reserve and less than 10 minutes from the city centre, this comfortable hotel offers 222 guestrooms, each well appointed with all facilities, (including in-house video). Private spas are available plus a heated outdoor swimming pool. The two restaurants are popular dining places with locals and visitors. Conference facilities are available. From $75 single. Major credit cards accepted.

Hyatt Kingsgate Auckland
Waterloo Quadrant
PO Box 3938
Auckland
Telephone: (09) 797-220
Telex: NZ2298

Situated on a hill overlooking Auckland city and its beautiful harbour, each of this hotel's 325 rooms commands a great view. Experience first-class accommodation and renowned Hyatt service and hospitality, with bars and restaurants to match — from gourmet dining at 'Top of the Town' to relaxed casual dining and coffee breaks in the Gallery Care Restaurant. Conference facilities available. From $75 single. Major credit cards accepted.

This is a wide region of forests, hills, plains, river valleys, lakes and marshes. Around Rotorua is extraordinary thermal activity, where subterranean heat bursts through the earth's thin crust with geysers, hot springs, boiling mud and steaming fissures.

Boiling mud, Rotorua.
(Andris Apse Ltd)

n high ridges, giant ferns grow under a shady canopy in forests of tawa, rimu and totara. Across former wastelands, man-made forests of pine march in straight lines as far as the eye can see. Down in the gentle valleys, willows, elders and poplars edge streams, hedgerows of box and hawthorne divide rich green pastures. In remote gorges of the Waikato River, huge hydro-electric stations straddle the river creating long, tranquil lakes.

To the west towards Waitomo, where sheep and cattle graze on hill farms, there's steep limestone country with peculiar outcrops and deep caves. To the east on the warm coast from Katikati to Te Puke are subtropical orchards crowded with kiwifruit vines, orange and avocado trees.

Travel from the north toward the remarkable volcanic area of Rotorua and discover en route great wetlands (Whangamarino is 10,000 hectares (24,700 acres) of wild swamp sheltering 50 species of birds), marshy lakes where mists lie low, rich dairylands and lush pastures where great racehorses are bred. Find out about dairying around Hamilton; visit stud farms around Cambridge and Matamata.

Find too memories of fierce battles between British troops and Maori defenders in the land wars of the 1860s. Riverside communities from Mercer to Cambridge began as garrison towns at the end of the war in 1864. At Meremere there's a terraced hilltop where the Maoris halted the British advance for three months; at Rangiriri a plan of a battlefield is displayed in a tiny cemetery where British soldiers were buried. History of the land wars is well displayed in the Waikato Art Museum in Hamilton, where there's also a famous 140-year-old war canoe.

By the riverbank at Ngaruawahia travellers can sometimes see great ceremonial canoes moored by Turangawaewae Marae, a splendid complex of buildings and home of the Maori queen.

Travel to the west of the region into the limestone country that contains the Waitomo Caves and glide on a punt through underground caverns studded with thousands of glow worms. Nearby at Otorohanga a bird park concentrates on native birds, featuring the kiwi. Not far away too is a specially created village demonstrating traditional Maori crafts – authentic, unusual souvenirs can be bought.

Travel east to the coast for long ocean beaches and orchards of kiwifruit, feijoas, tamarillos, oranges and avocados, around the city of Tauranga and the kiwifruit 'capital' of Te Puke. Here, at Tauranga and Whakatane, game-fishing boats leave for offshore islands.

Discover also more memories of bitter fighting in the land wars, at Tauranga's Gate Pa battleground, and visit an elegant early mission house, 'The Elms', surrounded by spreading lawns and gracious gardens. At Whakatane discover a town rich in pre-European Maori history and legends, where archaeological excavation has revealed settlement stretching back for centuries. Inland in the southern part of the region, immense forests of pine cover the country. Planting began on unproductive land before World War I, was increased in the 1930s and by the 1940s the pine forest of the central North Island was the largest man-made forest in the world. Tour the giant pulp, paper and board mills at Kinleith, Kawerau, Whakatane. At Kawerau, underground energy is harnessed with deep bores, providing natural steam for the milling process.

Waikato — Bay of Plenty

Travel around by car rented in Rotorua, Auckland, Hamilton, Tauranga. Small planes flit around the region from the airport in Rotorua or from Lake Rotorua for amphibian flights. As well as the ubiquituous N.Z.R. Road Services buses, there are coach services travelling out of Rotorua to various points, operated by Mt Cook and Newmans. Many tours are available from Auckland, especially through Newmans, Guthries and Mutual Holidays.

WAIKATO/B.O.P.

National Parks
Urewera National Park.

Tramping

Lodges
1. Solitaire Lodge;
2. Muriaroha.

Outback Safaris

Hunting

Fishing
Big Game

Other

River Adventures

Flightseeing

Diving

Golf
1. Matamata; 2. Okoroire Springs; 3. Hamilton; 4. Cambridge; 5. Mount Maunganui; 6. Tauranga; 7. Waitomo; 8. Arikikapakapa.

History
1. Rotorua; 2. Ohaki Maori Village.

Down on Farm

Live with NZ

Local
1. Pioneer Museum; 2. Waikato Art & History Museum; 3. Clydesdale Museum; 4. Firth Historical Museum; 5. Kiwi House & Native Bird Park; 6. Waitomo Caves.

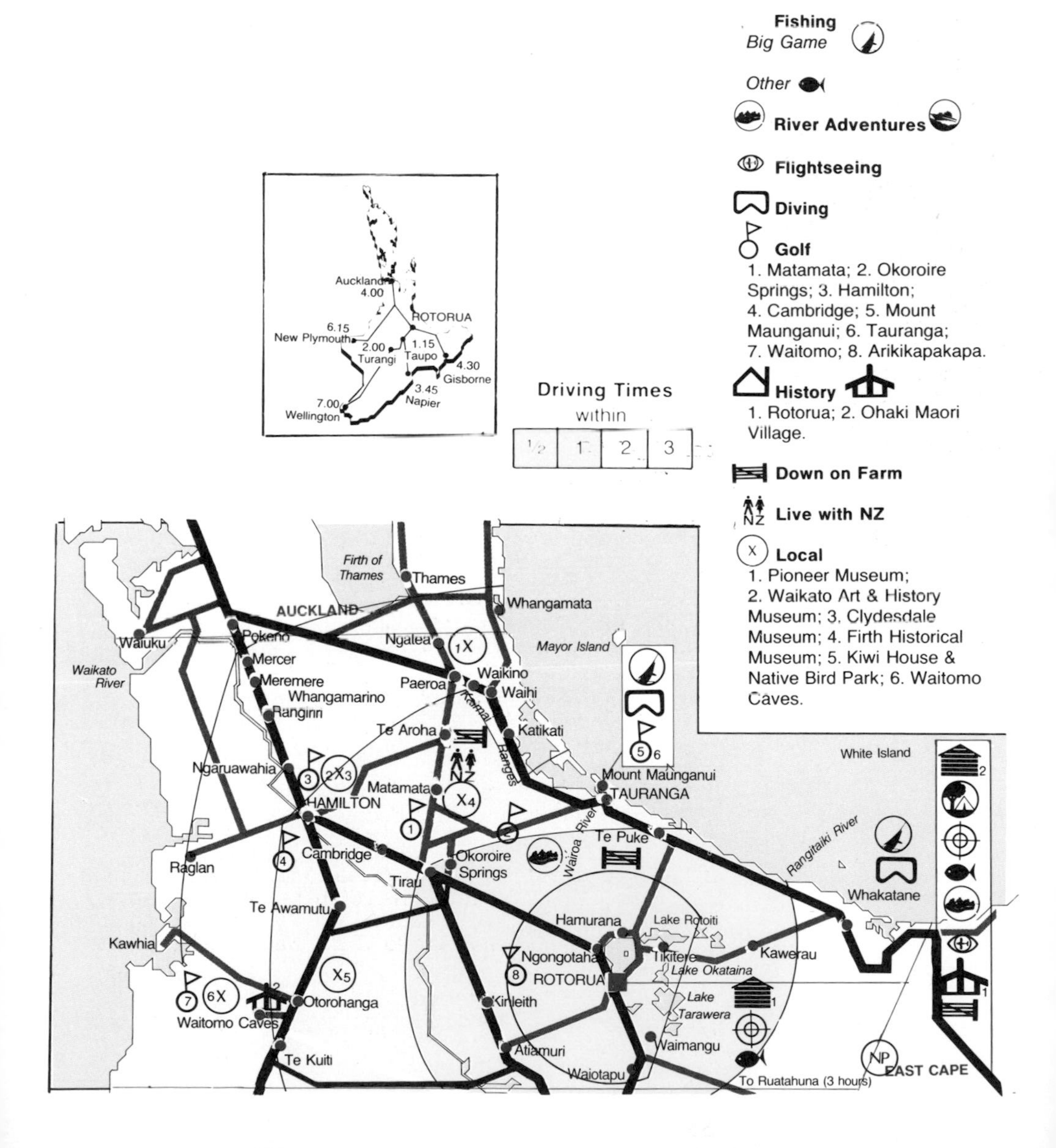

Rotorua

Rotorua is one of New Zealand's best-known tourist centres for the simple reason that there is so much to see and do – the area is crammed with unusual sights, experiences and spectacular scenic surprises.

or a start, the whole town seems to be steaming. Steam pours up, not just in the areas of intense activity, but in backyards, along pavements, on golf courses. The smell of sulphur hangs heavy on the air – not the balmiest of perfumes, but one soon gets acclimatised and ceases to notice it.

To see thermal activity at its fuming best, visit concentrations of erupting geysers, boiling mud and multi-coloured silica terraces: at Whakarewarewa, Maori villagers use the hot water for bathing, cooking, washing and heating; at Waiotapu the thermal area includes over a hectare of rainbow-hued terraces; at Waimangu there's a 4-hectare (10-acre) boiling lake and also the startling colours of a turquoise lake backed by blood-red cliffs; at Tikitere (also known as Hell's Gate) fiercely boiling pools contrast with picturesque warm waterfalls.

Maori pa entrance, Ohaki Maori Village (near Waitomo Caves)

If you want more evidence of subterranean violence, take a four-wheel-drive tour to the crater of Mt Tarawera. In 1886 the mountain, believed extinct, erupted with sudden devastating force. Ash and volcanic debris were strewn over 16,000 square kilometres (617 square miles), three Maori villages were obliterated and 153 people died. There's a fast way to the mountaintop – by small aircraft that lands on the crater rim.

Take flight-seeing trips from Rotorua over the thermal areas, lakes, forests and mountains and over White Island, the constantly active volcano off the coast near Whakatane (a round trip over White Island takes little more than an hour).

In the nineteenth century Rotorua was a spa town where visitors sought the invigorating, curative, hot mineral waters. The Elizabethan-style Tudor Towers in the Government Gardens was once a magnificent bath-house, and is now a complex of art gallery, museum and restaurant.

Rotorua's waters have been claimed as a remedy for many ailments, from rheumatism to skin complaints. Whether or not you wish to test the health-giving properties, there are plenty of opportunities to enjoy a good hot swim.

Should you tire of all the hot-water springs, visit cool freshwater springs in pretty parkland settings at Rainbow and Fairy Springs, Taniwha Springs, Paradise Valley Springs, Hamurana Springs. All have sparkling springs, streams and trout pools where monster trout, as big as 10 kilograms (22 pounds), crowd in the clear water. Each has its own special charms such as a magnificent fernery or grove of redwoods, ancient pa site or native bird aviary.

And then there are the lakes. Take a launch cruise to Mokoia Island on Lake Rotorua, an island imbued with a romantic love story. There are 4 kilometres (2½ miles) of bush walks on the island. Also hire a jet-cat, speed boat or children's mini-jet for self-propelled fun on the lake.

Cruise Lake Rotoiti where holiday cottages dot idyllic bays surrounded by dark bush. Take a cruise on perfect Lake Okataina or hire a boat and explore the unspoilt lake shores yourself – dense forest dominated by giant tree ferns surrounds the lake, unmarked by roads or buildings. Secluded sandy beaches spread out from under the ferns; ancient pa sites, birds and wild deer hide in the bush.

The Blue and Green Lakes, side by side, are actually blue and green, and can be found on the way to serene, bush-fringed Lake Tarawera, spreading under the shadow of Mt Tarawera.

Go trout fishing, even if you have never held a rod before. Fishing guides provide all the equipment and take you to the

Rotorua District Council Public Relations Office, Haupapa Street, Rotorua, Telephone: (073) 84067

best fishing places on lakes or streams.

Rotorua is also a centre of Maori life and culture. At Whakarewarewa find the Maori Arts and Crafts Institute, a prestigious centre of traditional carving and weaving, and Rotowhio Model Pa, a reconstruction of a pre-European fortified village. At Ohinemutu Maori Village on the lake edge there's an outstanding Maori meeting hourse, Tama-te-kapua, built in 1878, with some magnificent carvings dating back to 1800. A concert of traditional songs and dances is held regularly in the meeting house. Similar performances are held at several hotels and theatres in Rotorua, often combined with a 'hangi', food cooked Polynesian-style in a pit of steaming stones. (In Rotorua nature simplifies the cooking process.)

Entertainment. – In Rotorua the Maori concert and 'hangi' dinner is a novel variation on theatre and dinner. Dine and dance is a feature of some restaurants and hotels provide pop, jazz or rock entertainment. Around a region obsessed with horses, discover country race meetings, polo, show jumping, hunt club meets (no foxes, they chase hares) and sales of yearling thoroughbreds (in Hamilton). In Rotorua there's the Agrodome, a vast agricultural entertainment with 17 breeds of sheep, some of which perform a song and dance routine! And there are A & P Shows – in Rotorua (late January), Te Puke (mid-February), Whakatane (early March). Tauranga has highland games in January, A & P Show in February and an orange festival in August. And at Ngaruawahia in mid-March at Turangawaewae there's a special kind of Maori regatta with a grand parade of huge ceremonial war canoes, canoe races and performances of songs and dances by many tribes.

Rotorua thermal area.
(Andris Apse Ltd)

Rainbow and Fairy Springs
Fairy Springs Road
Rotorua
PO Box 25
Telephone: (073) 81-887
Host: Max Martin

A winner of tourism awards, this lovely park of native bush will delight young and old. Interests range from a nocturnal aviary housing the rare kiwi, underwater viewing of trout, to a free-flight aviary of native birds. Among the exotic species wandering freely around are ponies, farm pets, deer, goats, peacocks and doves. Guided tours are available, the staff are friendly and some speak German and Japanese. An excellent shopping complex provides variety from genuine Maori carvings and selections of hand-knitted wool, suede and fur garments, to jewellery and inexpensive souvenirs. Complete your experience with Devonshire teas or a full meal from the Springs Cottage Restaurant (functions a speciality). The selection is appealing, the setting superb, prices reasonable. Park entrance costs: $4 (adults), $1 (children). Limited family accommodation available.

Ruihana Woodcarvings
35 Lake Road
Rotorua
Telephone: (073) 477-174
Hosts: Louis and Mere Phillips

See the very fine tradition of Maori woodcarving at its best; watch and learn as Maori carvers demonstrate their art. Louis and Mere explain carving techniques, Maori culture and history and demonstrate traditional Maori poi dances. A range of souvenir items is available – from traditional carvings and greenstone to novelty items and T-shirts. Open daily.

SEE ALSO:

Fishing: Bryan Colman Trout Fishing, Dennis Ward Fishing Guide.
Flightseeing: Floatplane Air Services, Helitours.
Hunting: Tarawera Deerland.
Lodges: Muriaroha, Solitaire (Fish).
Outback Safaris: Rough Rider Rafting Co. (Water Adv), Te Rehuwai Safaris (Tramping) (Urewera NP).
Down on the Farm: Agrodome.

Marakapa Falls, King Country. *(Andris Apse Ltd)*

Waikato – Bay of Plenty

West via Te Kuiti and Waitomo Caves

Otorohanga Kiwi House & Native Bird Park
Alex Telfer Drive, Otorohanga
Telephone: (08133) 7391

It can be difficult and sometimes impossible to identify many New Zealand birds in the wild. The breeding and display centre at Otorohanga offers natural surroundings and a chance to see some of New Zealand's rarest birds. View kiwis in their nocturnal habitat. A guide (and graphic display) explains this strange ancient genus of which the large spotted, little spotted, and the North Island brown kiwi species are kept at the park. A huge dome-shaped aviary complete with native rain forest, is the home of native birds including bellbird, tui, pigeon, red-fronted parakeet, kingfisher, piedstilt, shoveller, scaup duck and the kaka. The rarest are a breeding pair of shore plovers, of which only 150-200 remain in their Chatham Island habitat. Two species of rare New Zealand ducks are on display – breeding pairs of the blue ducks and brown teal.

Ohaki Maori Village
(near Waitomo Caves)
PO Box 123
Te Kuiti
Telephone: (0813) 86-610
Hosts: The Te Kanawa Family

Ohaki was set up as a family enterprise in order to build a centre dedicated to the preservation of the weaving skills of 92-year-old Mrs Rangimarie Hetet (MBE) and her daughter Mrs Digger Te Kanawa. Because very few people still practise this ancient art form, using authentic materials and techniques, these women have become renowned internationally. Away from tourist routes, members of this family guide visitors around the model village. Some visitors spend a day, listening to the stories of pre-European Maori life, watching the weaving, being incorporated into the family life, and admiring the work display which includes several priceless feather cloaks. There is no set talk, each day is different. At the head of a long and beautiful valley, Ohaki is a place apart for those who want to learn about the Maori.

Matamata

In the heart of the rich Waikato pastures, Matamata is surrounded by farms – dairy farms, sheep farms, cattle farms and race-horse stud farms. Go to the races for first-class country racing meetings.

Once part of the huge Firth Estate, the farms and town were sub-divided in 1904. Longlands Farm, a farm-visit location, was once part of this estate.

The grassy airfield at Matamata is one of the best known venues for gliding in the North Island, making use of conditions created by the almost-flat plains and the Kaimai Ranges rising immediately to the west. Drive to the Kaimai Lookout on a ridge of the ranges for a view stretching out across the Waikato as far north as Auckland's Bombay Hills.

Matamata Public Relations Assn. Inc., Hetena Street, Matamata, P.O. Box 93. Telephone: (0818) 7260

Farm Highlights Tours
Burwood Road
Matamata
Telephone: (0818) 6588
Host: Mr Kerry Simpson

Join this half-day, escorted, agricultural tour of the varied farms of the Matamata region. Included are a thoroughbred horse stud (home to some of the finest-bred horses in the world), a sheep and beef farm (discover why livestock agriculture is responsible for a high percentage of New Zealand's overseas revenue), the Firth Tower (an important historical feature of the area), a kiwifriut orchard (see the source of this world-famous little fruit), a dairy factory (a guided tour around the perimeter of the largest butter factory in the world) and, finally, Longlands Dairy Farm (milking demonstrations and comprehensive commentary). End the tour with a superb lunch of barbecued lamb and fresh salads, with New Zealand beer, wine and fruit juices. Cost: $30 per person.

Totara Springs
Taihoa Road North
(5 kilometres, 3 miles, from Matamata)
RD 3
Matamata
Telephone: (0818) 8970
Hosts: Malcolm and Judy Barrow

Tucked away in a bush and farm setting, this wonderful facility is renowned as a Christian and educational retreat for children, groups and conventions, and is one of the few inviting casual visitors. Walk through pools, grottoes and gardens, amongst beautiful bird species in an open aviary, and housed small animals such as opossums, deer, rabbits and wallabies. Ride horses, abseil from the man-made mountain or go bush walking along the little railway tracks to the natural diving pool. Swim in the hot pool and visit the auditorium (fully equipped for indoor sports) with its beautiful mural. Other facilities include trampolines, archery, flying fox, rifle range and sports fields. Note: Excellent motel units and meals available at nominal rates, during weekdays only and not school holidays. Please telephone or write in advance.

Matamata Racing Club
PO Box 22
Matamata
Telephone: (0818) 8898 or 6222
President: Jack McAnnalley

Situated in the central Waikato area, mid-way between Tauranga, Rotorua and Hamilton is one of the centres of the horse-breeding industry in New Zealand. The Matamata Racing Club is one of the leading clubs in the country and holds races in February, May, July, August, September and October. This club stages the Matamata Breeders Stakes each February, being the richest race in the country for two-year-old fillies. Many studs in the area are renowned and welcome visitors with a genuine interest in thoroughbreds. Race going cost: $1, Stand badges and race books are available. Enquiries by mail.

Firth Tower and Historical Museum
Tower Road
Matamata
Telephone: (0818) 8369

This unique tower was built in the late 1800s as a defence post/lookout. The accompanying homestead has been maintained 'as was', and collections create a 'lived-in' look. Complex includes old post office, church and school, historical and railway displays. See also art gallery and workshop, displaying/selling local pottery and paintings. Admission: from $1.20 adults, 50c children. Group concessions. Open 10.00 a.m. – 4.00 p.m. daily.

Waikato – Bay of Plenty

Hamilton

'The Fountain City' borders the mighty Waikato River and is set in the heart of one of New Zealand's richest agricultural areas; it is also the junction of all major highways in the central North Island.

Organisations such as the Dairy Herd Improvement Centre of New Zealand and the Ruakura Research Centre, leaders in agricultural research, are centred here. The city is world famous for its field days held at Mystery Creek in early March, June and November. These attract crowds in excess of 130,000 people annually and are a great way to see the development of agricultural, industrial and sporting activity in New Zealand, and also to meet with people from all over the country. The area is also famed for its thoroughbred horse studs, some of which may be visited by appointment.

Hamilton City Council Public Relations Office, Barton Street north, Hamilton, P.O. Box 1100. Telephone: (071) 392065

The Clydesdale Museum offers the traveller an insight into the agricultural history of New Zealand. The complex is owned by the National Fieldays Society Inc. and has developed from humble beginnings to now feature: a working blacksmith's shop, a wildlife lake, swimming pool and barbecue area, Clydesdale horses, vintage vehicles, dairy museum, native trees, and colonial village (complete with church, school and garage). Regular 'live weekends' or field days are held, when horses are worked, sheep are shorn and butter is made. The famous Clydesdales are prize-winners at all A & P shows, and a breeding programme ensures that foals are born each year to keep the Clydesdale interest for years to come. Unique local crafts, souvenirs and refreshments are on sale. Can be very busy on holidays or field days. Admission: from $2 adults; $1 children. Group discounts.

Clydesdale Museum
(Close to airport)
Mystery Creek
Private Bag
Hamilton
Telephone: (071) 437-090
After Hours: 296-839

Dairy herd, Waikato.

(Courtesy Air New Zealand)

Waikato Museum of Art and History
150 London Street
Hamilton
Telephone: (071) 392-118

This City Council funded and operated museum features art and Maori and European history collections, illustrative of things New Zealand. Important collections include the most extensive collection of Waikato historic prints; paintings, letters and curios of soldier/adventurer Major G.F. von Tempsky; the Ferrier-Watson collection of the early New Zealand watercolour paintings of the Rev. John Kinder (1819-1903); permanent Hamilton Centennial Exhibitions and the Turangawaewae Maori war canoe 'Te Winika', entrusted to the care of the city. Other temporary exhibitions are changed regularly. New multi-million dollar premises for the museum are under construction from 1984, on a magnificent and historically significant site at Grantham Street. Admission is free. Hours: Tuesday to Saturday from 10.00 a.m. to 4.30 p.m. Sundays and Public Holidays from 12.00 noon till 4.30 p.m.

Hamilton Arts Centre
Cnr Victoria and Marlborough Streets
Hamilton
Telephone: (071) 390-685

Take time to visit the gallery and see changing exhibitions of contemporary art. Visit also the Left Bank Theatre, bar, cafe and restaurant complex.

Van der Sluis Pottery Studio
11a Hamilton Parade (ext. Rostrevor Street)
Hamilton
Hosts: Melis and Ruth Van der Sluis

In Hamilton's centre, see this master craftsman at his wheel creating beautiful pottery. Inspect the kilns and gallery, purchasing as desired from the fine range of individually handcrafted, high-quality, stoneware pottery. Functional and special 'one-off' pieces, all created on site. There is no charge for enjoying this facility. For groups over six, book in advance if refreshments required (nominal charge).

Hereford Fine China International Ltd
Corner Euclid and Norris Avenues
PO Box 10-010
Te Rapa, Hamilton
Telephone: (071) 493-973
Telex: C/- NZ 2772

Hereford Fine China is unique in the Southern Hemisphere, creating fine bone china birds, animals and figurines – equal to the best in the world. From the life-like 'Bird in the Hand' (fledgling sparrow) to beautiful 'one-off' pieces presented to Royalty, the sheer and delicate perfection of this wonderful range will take your breath away! Don't miss this rare opportunity to view a working studio, talking with the artists who create these fine models. The number of staff is suprisingly small (more like a family), and all are dedicated and pleasant craftsmen and women. A 20-minute video presentation explains the intricate details of Hereford Fine China, and also outlines the company's history. Following the studio tour, view the extensive showroom at your leisure. The showroom contains Hereford's current, closed and unique model editions, including the Royalty models. Many pieces are of native New Zealand birds and animals, including tuis, famous horses and the Hereford bull. Two guided tours are scheduled daily, Monday to Friday, at 10.30 a.m. and 2.30 p.m. (approximately 90 minutes duration, including a complimentary cup of tea or coffee). You are welcome to view the showroom at any time: weekdays, 10.00 a.m. to 4.00 p.m.; Saturday, 10.00 a.m. to 1.00 p.m. Closed Public Holidays and no scheduled tours Christmas to mid-January. Numbers are restricted for daily scheduled tours, so advance notice is preferable. Large groups and tour parties are requested to advise by telephone. Most current models are available for purchase from the showroom, packing and posting undertaken by request. Cost: scheduled tours from $3 adults. Children under twelve must be accompanied by an adult and will be admitted free of charge. (Note: take a scheduled tour. This is the very best way to gain a true appreciation of this remarkable facility.)

Hilldale Zoo Park
(8 kilometres from city centre)
Brymer Raod
Hamilton
Telephone: (071) 495-157

Well signposted from Te Rapa, on State Highway 1 from Auckland, these 14 hectares (35 acres) of developed zoo complex contain an extensive display of native/introduced birds, parrots and waterfowl. See zoo animals in a setting where deer, llama, wallabies, and even a camel will eat from your hand. Species include pumas, jaguars, zebras, South American agouti, and a bison. A farmyard contact area delights children with donkeys, pigs/piglets, sheep, goats, rabbits and a pigeon loft. Don't miss the New Zealand keas, with their brilliant plumage and cheeky manners! The theme of the complex is conservation and public education plus recreation, preserving our natural resources for the pleasure and enjoyment of all. A barbecue area is available; bring your lunch. Open each day (except Christmas Day and Good Friday) 1.00 p.m. to 5.00 p.m. (longer in summer). From $2.50 adults, $1 children. Group discounts available.

Hamilton Gardens
Cobham Drive
Hamilton

These gardens cover many hectares and feature numerous varieties of native and imported flora in a park-like setting. The main attractions are a tropical house, a cacti house and a tropical (flowering) plants display house. All these houses are open to the public each day, from 10.00 a.m. to 4.00 p.m. (free of charge) and are administered by the City Council.

See also the 'Little Bull', a bronze statue created by Mrs Molly MacAlister and given to the city in 1964 to commemorate the centennial of the founding of Hamilton.

Rogers Rose Gardens are a main feature of the outdoor gardens, bordering the Waikato River and laid out over 1½ hectares (3½ miles). There are more than 4,000 rose bushes of named varieties. The best time to see the roses blooming is from November through to April.

Hamilton Centennial Pools
Minogue Park
Garnett Avenue, Te Rapa
Hamilton
Telephone: (071) 494-389

Not far from the city centre, find one of the most modern competition and recreation swimming complexes in Australasia – open all year round with fully air-conditioned indoors facilities. The indoor heated pool complex consists of: 50-metre x 21-metre (8-lane) competition pool, 25-metre x 11-metre learner's pool and toddlers pool. It provides spectator seating for 1,000, numerous dressing rooms, meeting rooms, a conference room and well-appointed cafeteria. Outdoors, in lovely surrounds, are the lido and toddlers' pool, with picnic and barbecue areas available. The outdoor pool is open from October to March (weather permitting). Additional attractions include a double hydroslide, play area with trampolines, 9-hole putting green and shop. Pool admission is inexpensive. Towels, swimming costumes and clothes lockers available for hire.

SEE ALSO:

Down on Farm: Longlands Farm.
Live with NZ: The Homestead.

East to Te Puke and Mt Maunganui

Te Puke

It is hard to believe that until the 1920s the grazing of animals in this area was a discouraging business. Although aptly named the Bay of Plenty by Captain Cook because of the plentiful supplies of pork and kumara, a cobalt deficiency in the soil caused 'bush-sickness' in cattle.

These days the coast around Te Puke is known as the kiwifruit capital of the world and the sheep and dairy farms are now becoming highly productive orchards. Every year in mid-May a kiwifruit festival is held.

As a bonus, there are excellent beaches on the coast nearby.

MacLoughlin Orchards Ltd
No. 3 Road
Te Puke
Telephone: (075) 38-480/ 38-859
Host: Peter MacLoughlin

Take advantage of this opportunity to tour a kiwifruit and avocado orchard, personally escorted by Peter MacLoughlin. View the oldest commercially planted kiwifruit vines in the world (also New Zealand's largest development of kiwifruit from nursery stage). These vines are forty years old, and were planted by Peter's father – a leading figure in promoting international awareness of this unique fruit. The export operation is explained in detail, and in season (May-June) the packhouse is fully operational. You are invited to a complimentary tasting of kiwifruit wine and fresh fruit, in season. Let Peter know in advance and he arranges a barbecue lunch for you to enjoy around his pool. The orchard also grows avocados and squash for export, the latter for the Japanese market. You are sure to enjoy both the tour – available year through – and meeting 'Mac'. Please telephone in advance. Large and small groups welcome. Tour cost: from $2.50 (lunch excluded).

Mount Maunganui
Borough Hot Pool
Complex
Adams Avenue
Mount Maunganui

This is the only natural hot-water pool complex in the Southern Hemisphere, right beside the motor camp and ideal after a windsurfing lesson or a long swim. There is one main open pool and four private pools, operated by the Borough Council and open daily from 8.30 a.m. to 10.00 p.m. Water is brought to the pools through a bore 40 metres below the ground and the water changes completely four times per day. Temperatures are maintained at 39 degrees Celsius.

Windscene Windsurf Shop
School-Hire
19A Pacific Ave
Mount Maunganui.
P.O. Box 5116.
Telephone: (075) 57-831
(after hours 420-465)
Owners: Glen and Wendy Bright

Whether experienced or novice this windsurf shop is fully geared to handle your needs . . . and repairs! Tuition is offered (including a dry-land simulator) by NZ Yachting Federation qualified instructors, also hire of windsurfers, surf boards, body boards, wetsuits, harnesses, bouyancy aids and equipment for women and children. Bring your towel and relax in hot pools after your experience. Tuition from $5, Hireage from $2. Hours vary – call first.

North of Mt Maunganui

Waikino Pioneer Museum
Poland Street
Waikino
Telephone: (08163) 5974
Host: Peter Davison

This museum houses a collection of restored Gasoline Stationary Engines (both local and imported), used from late 1800s till circa 1925, in cowsheds, woolsheds and for driving many other machines. See also collections of cream separators, vacuum pumps, polished gum, mineral rocks, gem stones (polished and uncut), plus many other interesting pieces. Open Sunday to Friday, 9.00 a.m. to 4.00 p.m. Admission: from $1 adults, children free. Restrooms available.

Waikato-Bay of Plenty

Accommodation. – In Rotorua the range covers every possibility. Large luxury resort hotels overlook lake or steaming geysers, exclusive fishing lodges shelter in the seclusion of bush by lake or stream. The city is crammed with motels, grand, average and humble – many in all categories have private hot mineral pools. Budget travellers find accommodation in simple motels, old hotels that have seen better days, an excellent youth hostel, cabins at camping grounds on the edge of town. Elsewhere in the region find a choice of excellent quality motels and motor inns in Hamilton and Tauranga, a charming old THC hotel at Waitomo. Along the coast from Waihi to Ohope, motels and well-serviced camping grounds serve the beaches. Find youth hostels also at Te Aroha by the high Kaimai Ranges, at Tauranga and nearby Mt Maunganui, at Whakatane, Hamilton and Otorohanga. Off the beaten tourist track the choice narrows – accommodation often caters for the utilitarian needs of foresters, hunters and trampers.

Food. – In Rotorua dine on ordinary 'international' cooking, special New Zealand fare, plain home-style cooking or every kind of fast food. Catch a rainbow trout and a hotel or restaurant kitchen will cook it for you. Look for New Zealand specialities such as lamb, venison, wild pork, avocados, tamarillos and, of course, kiwifruit. (Buy kiwifruit by the kilo from the orchard gate in Te Puke.)

Esperanto Restaurant
Matamata
Telephone: (0818) 7169
Hosts: Sue and John Doel

Don't miss a fine dining experience – this licensed restaurant has a seven-year reputation for quality and excellence and is well-reviewed by dining guides. It has a warm, busy and friendly atmosphere, and is popular with the locals. Extensive seafood and steak menu, winelist with emphasis on New Zealand vintners. Try smoked marlin, venison stroganoff, or Steak Esperanto. Cocktail lounge, live music at weekends. Open daily. Lunch: 12.00 noon – 2.30 p.m.; dinner from 5.00 p.m. (reservations recommended).

Aorangi Peak Restaurant
Mountain Road
Rotorua
PO Box 43
Telephone: (073) 86-957
Hosts: Bill and Shirley Barry

This superb restaurant commands unequalled 180 degree views of the panoramic Rotorua area, from the summit of Mount Ngongotaha to the Pacific Ocean – with the horizon becoming a myriad of sparking lights at night. Bill and Shirley are justifiably proud of their reputation, offering fresh and beautifully prepared food, a well-balanced wine list and attentive service in an atmosphere enhanced by tasteful decor and natural timber. Whether anticipating an intimate dinner for two or entertaining 130 guests at a conference banquet, you'll be delighted. Enjoy a pre-dinner cocktail in Ihenga's Lookout Lounge and read the lovely Maori legend of this mountain on your place-mat. (Should a wisp of mist drift by, listen for the voices calling for their lost warrior.) Drive up or fly in by helicopter. Open daily 12 noon – 2.00 p.m. and from 6.30 p.m.Evening reservations essential.Easy access for wheelchairs.

Pineland Motel
245 Fenton Street
Rotorua
Telephone: (073) 86-601
Hosts: Jenny and Warrick Mason

This motel offers eleven spacious, self-contained and centrally heated units, sleeping from one to nine persons in one-, two- or three-bedroomed comfort. Additional facilities include waterbed suites, private mineral pools, heated swirl and spa pools, and videos in each unit. Short walk to shops and restaurants. Courtesy car to airport and NZR Travel Centre. From $40 double. Book through Best Western chain or direct. Credit cards accepted. Member of Motel Assn. of New Zealand Inc.

Mount Maunganui Domain Camp
1 Adams Avenue
Mount Maunganui
Telephone: (075) 54-471
Hosts: Win and Marie Cox

Fronting on to both a rugged ocean beach and a calm inner harbour, the camp is sited at the base of a beautiful mountain. Wake to the surf gently rolling in only metres from your camp site, with white sand inviting that early morning stroll. Excellent facilities for self-contained living. Food facilities close by. Offers tent sites, on-site vans and caravan sites. Book well in advance by mail.

Hyatt Kingsgate Rotorua
Eruera Street
PO Box 1044
Rotorua
Telephone: (073) 477-677
Telex: NZ2210

Beside tranquil, trout-filled Lake Rotorua – the heart of New Zealand's unique thermal wonderland – this new Hotel offers luxurious hospitality in fine Hyatt tradition. Two hundred and thirty-three well-appointed rooms include 6 suites with spas. Superb recreational fitness centre offers private/communal spas, steam rooms, heated pool. Terraces Cafe, Brent's Piano Bar and Lobby Lounge Bar provide relaxation and entertainment. Conference facilities available. From $84 single. Major credit cards accepted.

Blue Lake Holiday Park
Tarawera Road
Rotorua
PO Box 292
Telephone (073) 28-120
Hosts: Mary and Peter Topham, Gail and David Denton

This park on the shores of the Blue Lake offers beautiful sites for a campervan and well-appointed cabins, some with wonderful lake views. Facilities include modern ablution block, barbecue area, games room and children's playground. Stroll through tranquil bush and listen to the native birds, ride a horse, go fishing or canoeing. From $3.50 to $20 per person.

Te Puke Holiday Park
State Highway 2
Te Puke
PO Box 10
Telephone: (075) 39-866
Owners: Paul and Karlene Redding

This lovely facility is set among avocado, feijoa, walnut, grapefruit and macadamia trees. It is spacious, private and peaceful. Bring your own campervan or stay in the on-site caravans, cabins or hostel for up to 24 people. Amenities are beautifully maintained by Paul and Karlene and include full laundry, swimming pool, half-size tennis court, private spa, games room, barbecue, refrigerated lockers, good kitchen, telephone and TV. From $5 to $20 per person.

Te Puke Country Lodge
PO Box 44
Te Puke
Telephone: (075) 39-983
Telex: NZ 21744

Overlooking the 'Kiwifruit capital of the World' this peaceful lodge combines old English design with new world comfort and decor. Superb facilities include guests' library, billiard room, outdoor pool and private spas, licensed restaurant/cosy bar, luxurious accommodation, and conference facilities for 200; plus heliport and car parking. Free access to squash courts/golf course close by. Enjoy fishing, deer hunting, horticultural visits and duck shooting. From $58.00 upwards. Special rates for extended stays/group bookings.

Waikato-Bay of Plenty

Maori meeting house. *(Courtesy Air New Zealand)*

Captain Cook monument, Gisborne. *(Courtesy Air New Zealand)*

This is a region of distinct and dramatic contrasts. In the north the few roads twist and wind over hills of primeval forest and around the coast to reveal one of the most spectacular coastlines in the country, with beautiful bush-fringed coves and long empty beaches. Tiny communities, often little more than a hotel, general store and church, cling to the coast.

It is a place apart, where time can move very slowly, where children ride to school on horseback, where drivers stop while a large flock of sheep pass by.

The Urewera and Raukumara ranges, with mountain beech on the highest hills and almost impenetrable forest reaching down into the valleys, formed the character of the East Cape, enforcing an isolation on the inhabitants. European influence came to the Cape, making less impact on the Maori way of life than in many other parts of the country.

Travel the coast road between Opotiki and Gisborne for 335 kilometres (208 miles) and discover idyllic picnic spots and camping places by sandy bays, long beaches and rocky inlets that can be completely deserted. Find settlements that were once busy whaling stations, see simple, beautiful Maori churches and elaborately carved meeting houses, and quench your thirst in the most easterly pub in the world (at Te Araroa or Tikitiki – both claim the distinction).

Wander through general stores that might have escaped from a 'western' – bare board floors, old shop counters, everything on sale from sunhats, lanterns, haberdashery, food and fishing lines.

Take the overland road from Opotiki to Gisborne through the spectacular Waioeka Gorge, a wild and sparsely populated area. A route recommended only for the adventurous and competent driver, in fine weather and with a sturdy, reliable vehicle, is an old coach road through Motu and Toatoa, from Matawai to the coast. It looks like an hour's drive on the map, but it will take half a day and will take you back 50 years in time.

At Gisborne you are in the commercial centre of Poverty Bay. Realise that the name is a misnomer as you pass by vineyards, orchards, cornfields and prosperous sheep farms. Captain Cook made the mistake after his first landing in New Zealand here in 1769, but the bay enjoys the irony. Gisborne enthusiastically commemorates Cook's historic landing with memorials on Kaiti Hill and on the shore below.

In the deeply indented Hawkes Bay, there is another rich coastal area patch-worked with market gardens, orchards and vineyards. Sheep stations spread into the high hills behind the bay, farms that have often remained with the same family for several generations. Màny pioneer sheep farmers built grand, elegant houses, colonial versions of English country houses with sweeping driveways, croquet lawns and English trees.

The English 'county' lifestyle mimicked by the early run-holders lingers on among their descendants around Hastings and Havelock North and the small towns to the south – tweed, cavalry twill and cashmere sell well here, and horse show-riding is a popular pastime.

Perhaps the most spectacular 'sight' of the region is the excursion to Cape Kidnappers, the world's only mainland gannet colony, where about 15,000 gannets congregate from late July to February each year. The setting here is dramatic, with sheer barren cliffs dropping into the ocean in a series of sharp-edged hills. The area is open to the public from the end of October, when egg-laying and hatching is over.

East Cape – Hawkes Bay

Travel around independently by car – rent a car in Gisborne, Napier or Hastings; railway runs between Gisborne, Napier and Hastings, heading south through the region towards Wellington. N.Z.R. Road Services, Newmans and Hawkes Bay Motors provide bus services. Flight-seeing trips available from Gisborne and Napier.

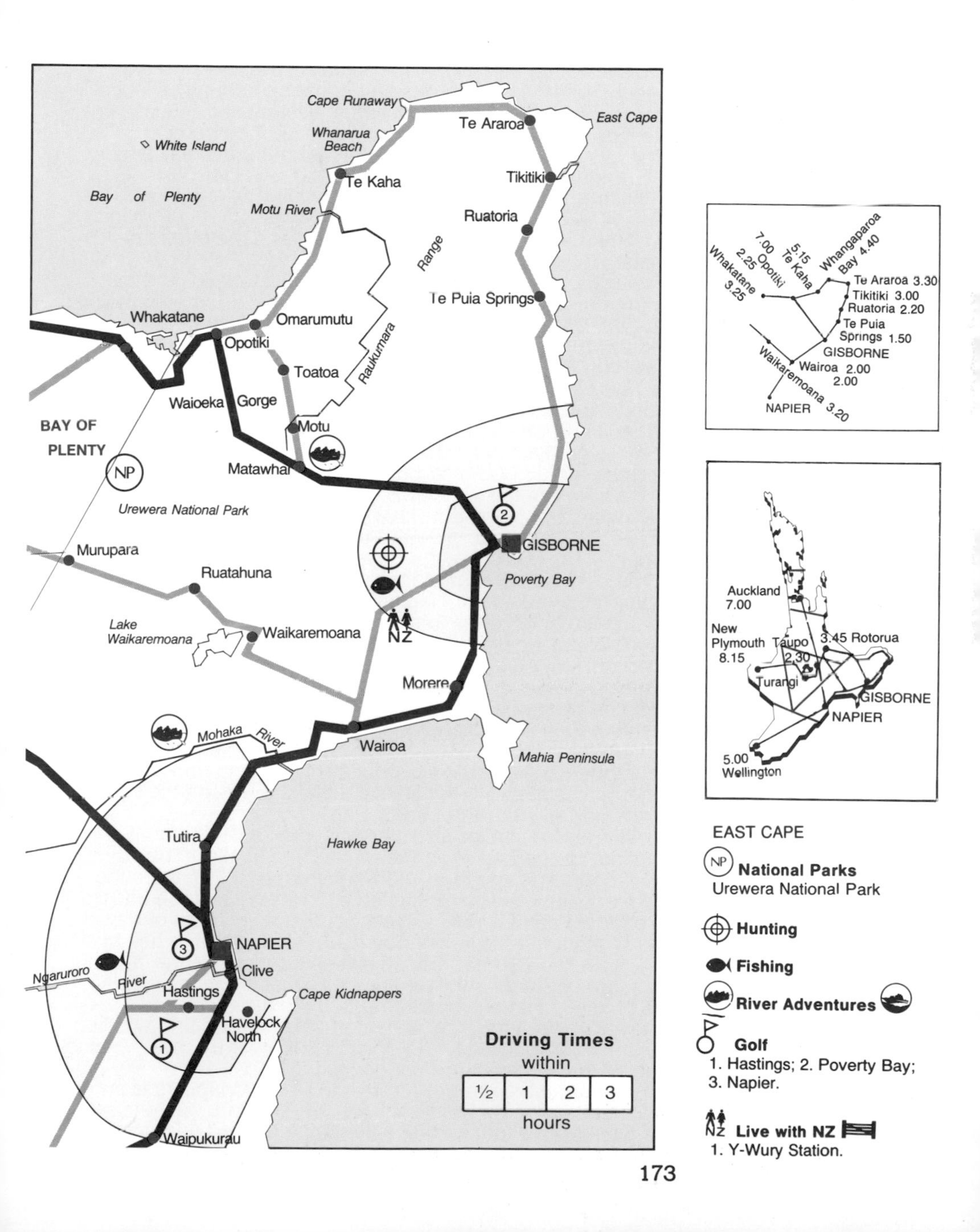

Napier/Hastings

The main centre for Hawkes Bay, Napier makes an excellent base for travel in the surrounding region.

The city owes its present appearance to a massive earthquake that shook the area back in 1931 on a hot February morning. Almost every building in Napier and neighbouring Hastings was destroyed or badly damaged when the towns were reduced to rubble in less than five minutes. Cliffs collapsed into the sea, a lagoon lifted itself out of the sea to create 3,340 hectares (8,250 acres) of new land and 258 people died.

If disasters on a grand scale fascinate you, visit the city museum where photographs and contemporary newspapers detail the devastation. The museum also houses an excellent collection of Maori artifacts from the moa-hunter period.

The city today, almost completely rebuilt immediately after the earthquake, is a celebration of 1930s Art Deco architecture. Walk the streets of the small City and absorb the styles, in particular hotels such as the Masonic, the Provincial, the Central and the Rothmans Building and the Municipal Theatre.

Along the sea front is the Marine Parade, edged with tall Norfolk pines. Here find an aquarium, oceanarium, marineland with performing dolphins, roller-skating rink, gardens, paddling pools, illuminated fountain, a kiwi house.

On Bluff Hill look out along the coastline of Hawkes Bay and also find cottages that survived the earthquake. Botanic gardens spill down the hillside and not far away is the Centennial Rock Garden featuring native shrubs and plants. For more gardens, visit the Kennedy Park Rose Garden, which has more than 3,000 rose bushes.

Take a tour of the vineyards, independently or organised. Vines were first planted in Hawkes Bay in the 1850s, in a climate that is similar to that in the best grape-growing areas of Europe. Combined with the Poverty Bay vineyards around Gisborne, this region produces most of New Zealand's wine grapes. Vineyards near Napier and Hastings range from large commercial enterprises to small family-run wineries. The country's first vineyard established by the brothers at a Catholic mission is here. Another, the first commercial vineyard, still uses the original cellars.

Around Hastings there are tours of local industries – this is the major food-processing area, with the largest cannery in the Southern Hemisphere and frozen-food plant. Discover where the ubiquitous frozen pea begins its journey, to turn up on dinner plates from North Cape to the Bluff, around the Pacific Islands and even in the Middle East.

Hastings is a similar size city to Napier, a commercial and industrial centre based on the region's horticulture, but also a city of parks and gardens, old English trees. From there the road leads through the pretty town of Havelock North and up to Te Mata Peak for one of the most dramatic views of Hawkes Bay. The hill rises abruptly above a river valley to a height of 1310 metres (4297 feet) giving sweeping views of the curving coast, the orchards, vineyards and market gardens, with the hills of sheep stations spreading into the distance.

Travel out into the foothills around Napier and find winding rivers in valleys lined with Poplars and Silver Birches – perfect riverside picnic spots are not difficult to find.

The remarkable gannet colony at Cape Kidnappers is an essential item on an itinerary here, whether you take the safari four-wheel-drive tour or brave the elements and tides and approach along the beach independently.

Napier Public Relations Office, Marine Parade, Napier. Telephone: (070) 57182

East Cape – Hawkes Bay

Entertainment – On the East Cape, head for the nearest pub – one way or another it will be entertaining. Find a little more sophistication in Hawkes Bay and Gisborne, though no less fun. Annual events include the excellent Hastings A & P Show in October and at Easter in Hastings the unusual spectacle of highland games with bagpipes, highland dancing, tossing the caber and even hurling-the-haggis contests.

SEE ALSO:

Live with NZ: Y-Wury Station (Down on Farm).
National Parks: Urewera National Park.

Cape Kidnappers, Napier.
(Courtesy Air New Zealand)

North to Gisborne and Opotiki

Just north of Napier on the coastal route (Highway 2) to Gisborne, is the Lake Tutira bird sanctuary, originally part of a sheep station owned by Guthrie-Smith, an early conservationist. Guthrie-Smith meticulously documented the spread of weeds and pests in his book *Tutira, The Story of a New Zealand Sheep Station*.

Nearer Gisborne, take a break at Morere Springs – bathe in the curative waters and picnic in the 200 hectare (500 acres) bush reserve.

If you're feeling tired on arrival at Gisborne, reflect on the stamina of Elizabeth Colenso, a missionary who walked to Gisborne for the birth of her child. It took 11 days in the 1840s.

Gisborne

The first Europeans to step ashore landed on Kaiti Beach in 1769. A series of unfortunate incidents led to the death of six Maoris, after which Cook named the area Poverty Bay, 'because it afforded us no one thing we wanted'. Others who followed Cook found the reverse, establishing orchards and vineyards on the rich flats around Gisborne. New Zealand's first winery was founded here by French Brothers of the Society of Mary to produce altar wine. Other links with Gisborne's past can be found in the local museum, where local craft work can be purchased. To the north stretch a string of beaches, excellent for swimming and fishing.

The trip around the East Cape combines spectacular coastal scenery with a sense of the past. Maori culture flourishes, the isolation splendid. Some highlights are:

Te Puia Springs – An oasis of thermal activity.

Ruatoria – A charm of its own and centre of the great Ngati Porou tribe

Tikitiki – An Anglican church incorporating Maori design.

Te Aroroa – A long narrow bay and small settlement beneath the cliffs. The world's largest pohutukawa tree and the remote but well-appointed Kawakawa Hotel.

Whangarua Bay – One of the prettiest on the coast – secluded beaches, fishing, swimming, waterfalls and glow worms (at Whanarua Creek).

Te Kaha – A popular resort with a beautifully carved meeting house – Tukaki – plus remains of an old pa and redoubt.

Omarumutu – The enterior decoration of the Omarumutu War Memorial Hall belongs with the finest Maori art in the country. Nearby Tutamere meeting-house reveres the ancestral chief of the Ngatirua sub-tribe.

Gisborne Community Public Relations Inc., 209 Grey Street, Gisborne, P.O. Box 170. Telephone: (079) 8613

Opotiki

Sheltered from cold southerly winds and with some of the highest sunshine hours in the country, Opotiki offers an all-year-round interest. The sea, the rivers, the mountains, history and horticulture offer a great variety of things to do. Opotiki is not a tourist mecca, but an isolated escape from the world, where one spends time joining in with the locals – fishing, boating, sailing, swimming, rafting, jet boating or just walking.

Long an area of Maori Settlement, the Europeans established occupation for fishing and whaling. Tribal warfare decimated the local Maori tribes, especially after the Ngapuhi of Northland obtained muskets in the 1820s and raided the area. The pressures of European settlement led to open warfare.

East Cape – Hawkes Bay

Accommodation – Motor inns, hotels and motels in Gisborne, Napier and Hastings especially. In out-of-the-way places, find old hotels that can offer bargain accommodation and old-fashioned roast dinners. There are motels and camping grounds along the East Cape coast as well as opportunities for camping wild. At Whanarua Bay, one of the prettiest on the coast, 160 hectares (400 acres) have been reserved for holiday-makers. Youth hostels are at Gisborne, Tutira (a sheep farm near Napier) and Clive, near Napier.

Food – Look for fresh fish and shellfish such as paua, mussels, tuatua, pipis and crayfish around the cape. Getting it cooked to perfection may be more difficult – this is not haute cuisine territory. From Gisborne through Hawkes Bay enjoy fresh fruit and vegetables – apples, peaches, melons, avocados, grapes and, around Hastings especially, the best green asparagus in the country. Dine and wine well in Hawkes Bay.

Maori carving on the pataka at Te Araroa School, East Cape. *(National Publicity Studios)*

Mts Ruapehu and Ngaruahoe Volcanic Plateau. ***(Courtesy Turangi Scenic Flights)***

About 1,800 years ago a massive eruption, greater than Mt St Helens, Karakatoa or Santorini, rocked the earth. Debris was thrown 55 kilometres (34 miles) into the air and the land around for 20,000 square kilometres (7,722 square miles) was devastated. (Mt St Helens threw up a column 23 kilometres (14 miles) high and demolished 550 square kilometres (212 square miles) of forest.).

Look on the vast tranquil Lake Taupo today and it may be hard to imagine that the lake once exploded with one of the biggest volcanic eruptions in human history. But look more closely and evidence of the massive blast lies all around the Volcanic Plateau – in the pumice soils that dominate the plateau, in cliffs of white pumice on the lake's eastern shore, in beaches of white pumice stone, in charred remains of trees protruding from banks on the Desert Road.

This is a region of wild expansive beauty. Lake Taupo covers 619 square kilometres (238 square miles); in the west thick bush and waterfalls edge the isolated bays, in the east the landscape has been tamed with small parklands where deciduous trees provide brilliant colour in the crisp autumn air. At the southern end of the lake, beyond the fishing and tourist township of Turangi, a cluster of volcanic mountains rise to 2,706 metres (8,875 feet) with one, Ngauruhoe (2,290 metres or 7,500 feet), constantly belching steam. These mountains, a mere 3 million years old, are the southernmost link in a volcanic chain that stretches around the perimeter of the Pacific.

Travel around the region and find roadsides edged with purple and white heather or yellow broom, see red-tussock grasslands stretching out to meet pine forests, native beech forest spilling down the Kaimanawa Ranges (mountains that are 300 million years old) and great totara, matai and rimu trees in stands of rainforest.

In a region of startling contrasts, discover the Tongariro National Park encircling the mountains Ruapehu, Ngauruhoe and Tongariro. Within the park's 76,198 hectares (188,000 acres) are glaciers, a hot crater lake, hot springs, barren desert, alpine herb-lands, ski fields.

The neighbouring Kaimanawa Forest Park attracts trampers, rafters, fishermen and hunters seeking red and sika deer, wild pigs and goats.

The Tongariro River which flows between the national park and the forest park, is world famous for the fighting rainbow trout that battle the fast glacier-fed waters. By the Tongariro, visitors can see a trout hatchery and view wild fish through windows cut in the side of a tributary stream. Fry raised at the hatchery are not destined for Taupo or its surrounding rivers but for other parts of New Zealand and other countries.

At nearby Tokaanu there's a small, unspoilt thermal area – paths through manuka scrub lead to hot springs, a small geyser, boiling mud pools and silica deposits.

A great delta of reeds stretches out into the lake around the mouth of the Tongariro, near the township of Turangi and the village of Tokaanu. Birds abound here – black swans, cormorants (known as shags in New Zealand), bitterns, pukekos, white-faced herons, ducks, dab chicks, fernbird.

At the western edge of the delta, where the lake road ends, is Waihi, a Maori village of quiet charm, nestling on the lake edge beneath cliffs that exude steam. On the Taumarunui road that rises above the lake behind Waihi are splendid views of the lake and the Tongariro delta.

Another superb lake view may be gained from the Pihanga Saddle Road, leading from near Tokaanu across to the Tongariro National Park. Further over the saddle a short but superb bush walk leads to a tiny bush-fringed crater lake, Rotopounamu.

Head south along State Highway 1 and pass by the mountains, travelling across the desolate Rangipo Desert. Prevailing westerly winds lose their moisture on the far side of the mountains, sweeping around to help create a strange, inhospitable desert of drifting sand and gravel. Out of the desert and tussock lands the road dips and climbs through deep gorges and over high, rolling hills that form large sheep farms.

The Volcanic Plateau is a region for swimming in hot pools or cold lake, water skiing, sailing, boating, fishing for incomparable rainbow trout, rafting, canoeing, climbing, skiing, tramping, hunting; or a place to take a picnic to a quiet lake or riverside spot where bellbirds and tuis sing in the surrounding trees and trout leap in the clear water below.

Travel around best by car. The wildness of the region is its attraction, with its rivers, lake, forests, desert and stark mountains most easily experienced to the full with independent transport. The main Auckland-Wellington railway line runs through the west of the region, with stops made at Taumarunui, National Park, Ohakune. Buses of N.Z.R. Road Services, Newmans and Hawkes Bay Motors serve main points in the region.

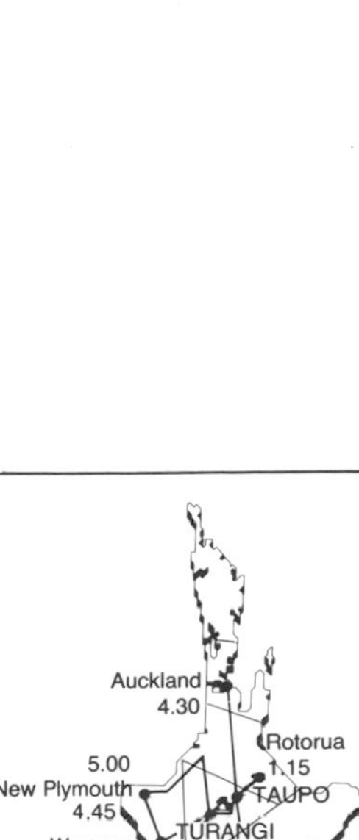

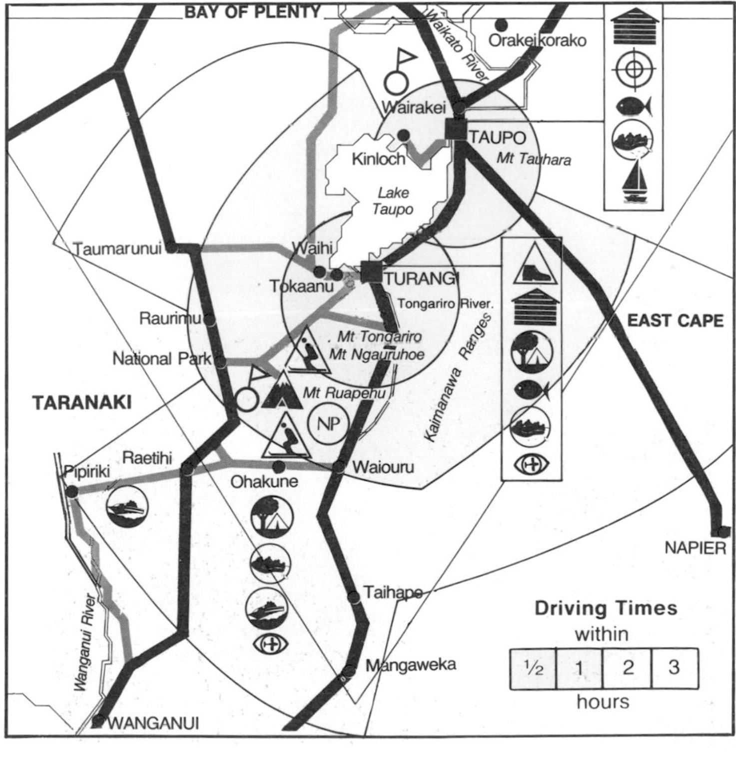

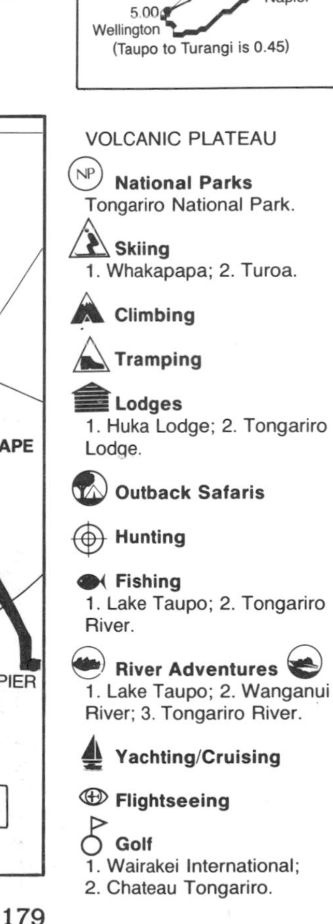

Taupo

Taupo grew up from a small military outpost in 1869 to a town designed to serve holiday-makers. The warm mineral waters and nearby thermal sights drew nineteenth-century visitors, who stopped over in the town before taking the lake steamer south to Tokaanu. Then came the rainbow trout, released in the late 1880s, and the lake became a mecca for anglers.

Take a cruise on the lake – sightseeing launches and charter boats leave from a pretty river bank jetty where the Waikato River leaves the lake. Hire paddle boats, windsurfers and row boats on the lake front.

Swim in the lake – where hot-water streams enter the lake one can enjoy swimming in hot and cold water. Swim in the large thermal pools at the A.C.Baths or De Brett Thermal Pools.

Take walks of extraordinary variety: through the Waipihihi Botanical Reserve, a mixture of rhododendrons, azaleas, alpine herb garden, and bush walks of rare and unusual ferns and trees; to the Opepe Graves, deep in a sombre stand of bush, where British cavalrymen were ambushed in 1869; to the top of an extinct volcano, Mt Tauhara, 1,099 metres (3,600 feet) high; beside the Waikato River along an official walkway from the Huka Falls to Aratiatia, through wild flowers and grasses.

The Huka Falls have been a tourist attraction since soldiers at the Taupo redoubt cut a rough track through to the river bank. Here the Waikato River surges through a narrow chasm, changing colour from deep green to milky turquoise as it fans out in a churning mass at the base of the falls. Drive to the falls or take a tour, and go on to Aratiatia where the river crashes through a zig-zagging drop of 28 metres in 0.8 kilometres (9 feet in 2,600 feet). The natural drop supplies a power station, and the rapids are switched on twice a day for the benefit of visitors.

Between the Huka Falls and Aratiatia is Wairakei, the site of a huge geothermal power station. Visit the power station on the river edge and the valley of steam and pipes behind. There is also a thermal valley of hot springs and bubbling mud pools. Here too is the famous Wairakei golf course.

Further afield, travel out to the thermal region of Orakei Korako for a concentration of geysers, hot springs, terraces and the amazing colours of sinter and algae. Drive to lakeside bays such as Acacia Bay and Kinloch, to the west of the town, or drive along the eastern shores to discover a string of pretty lakeside picnic places stretching the length of the lake. Get to the remote and beautiful bays at the far west of the lake by boat only.

Taupo Borough Council Community Affairs Office, P.O. Box 142, Taupo. Telephone: (074) 84100

Wairakei steam bore. *(Courtesy Air New Zealand)*

Turangi

A town built to serve the complex Tongariro power projects, Turangi now serves holiday-makers. By the swirling glacier-fed Tongariro, a river with a world-wide reputation for magnificent fighting rainbow trout, and also close to the shores of Lake Taupo, Turangi is a splendid base for anglers.

There's boating and swimming in the lake from nearby beaches, bird watching in the vast marshy Tongariro delta that attracts numerous waterfowl, tramping and hunting in the hills, skiing only 45 minutes away by car on Ruapehu's Whakapapa ski field, and walks by the lake shore, riverbanks or through deep bush.

At nearby Tokaanu is a small, intriguing thermal area of geysers and mud pools.

With the Tongariro River, Lake Taupo, the Kaimanawa Ranges, the mountains of Ruapehu, Tongariro and Ngauruhoe all within easy distance, Turangi can offer a perfect holiday. If you have any time to spare, don't neglect the excellent tiny museum for information on the geological past, the forests, the Maori history and an explanation of the electric power schemes that use canals and tunnels to divert water around the edges of the mountains.

Entertainment. – It's an outdoor region – find yacht races, speed-boat races, fishing contests. In the evenings there's dinner-dance or live entertainment at restaurants and hotel bars that range from quietly relaxed to rough and raucous.

Wairakei International Golf Course and THC Wairakei Hotel
Telephone:
Auckland (09) 773-689
Wellington (04) 729-179
Christchurch (03) 790-718
Telex: NZ 3488
Telephone: Taupo (074) 48-152

The golfer's golf course, Wairakei offers more than a challenging 18-hole round. Playing Wairakei is an opportunity to really experience what a country course is all about – clear, crisp air and miles away from city limits or bustling industry. In a magnificent setting somewhat reminiscent of Gleneagles in Scotland, the links lie 9 kilometres (5½ miles) north of Taupo near the junction of State Highways 1 and 5. Adjacent to the first-class Tourist Hotel Corporation complex, the site selected for the Wairakei Course was a designer's dream – a gently rolling contour over pumice and volcanic cinder. The well-drained fairways and greens, designed by John Harris, are a fair but demanding test for everyone. As well as an automatic underground watering system, Wairakei has several other innovative features including subtle variations in the shape of greens and three sets of tees for each hole. This effectively creates three courses of varying difficulty within the one 18-hole links. Wairakei has no club membership and is green at all times. Green fees from $5.

SEE ALSO:

Flightseeing: Turangi Scenic Flights.
Lodges: Tongariro Lodge, Huka Lodge.
Outback Safaris: Turangi Trail Rides.
Tramping/Trekking/Walking: Central Safaris.
Fishing: South Pacific Sporting Adventures.
National Parks: Tongariro National Park (National Park).
Skiing: Whakapapa (National Park).
Water Adventures: Pipiriki Jet Boat Tours (Raetihi).
Outback Safaris: Ruapehu Outback Adventures (Water Adv/Flightseeing).
Skiing: Educational Tours Unlimited.

Once upon a time Ohakune was known as a timber town that diversified into market gardening, concentrating on carrots; but not any longer. Today Ohakune is known as one of the country's best centres for mountain sports and adventure activities.

With the development of the magnificent Turoa ski field, Ohakune blossomed into a lively mountain village with hotels, motels, lodges, chalets and restaurants. It's not merely a skiers' town but a base for all-year-round activities such as canoeing, rafting, trekking, jet boating and trout fishing.

Ruapehu Outback Adventures
PO Box 51
Ohakune
Telephone: (0658) 58-733, 58-733 (after hours)
Hosts: Sue &'Don Allomes

A great way to explore the variety of the wonderful Volcanic Plateau on one- or two-day tours: with 4-wheel-drive safaris' heli-jetting, river rafting, flight-seeing over the volcanoes of the National Park, jet-boating tours, horse trekking, canoeing and hunting. Expert tuition offered in skiing and rafting. From $20 to $120. Accommodation at Ruapehu Homestead from $25.

'Discovery'
PO Box 55
National Park
Telephone: 744

From 'Discovery', go white-water rafting, horse trekking, hiking, hunting, trail-bike riding, jet boating, trout fishing and skiing in the Tongariro National Park, depending on season. Accommodation in motel suites with cooking facilities, in bed-sitters or caravan park with service amenities. Enjoy communal or private spa pools, indoor heated swimming pool, games room and restaurant. From $40 double, meals inclusive. $99 for three days.

Skiers at the Whakapapa skifield, Mt Ruapehu, look out to Lake Taupo in the background. The active smoking volcano is Mt Ngaruahoe. ***(Scott Lee)***

The Volcanic Plateau

Accommodation. – At Taupo the choice is wide – exclusive, luxury lodges, spartan fishing lodges and cabins, luxury motels and motor inns on the lake shore, older traditional hotels, modest motels with self-catering, or motor camps with space for tents or caravans. Turangi has similar accommodation, but less of it because it is a smaller town. However, Turangi does have an extraordinary budget camp with 144 cabins, basic shelter that served large hydro-electric projects. Ohakune also offers travellers good accommodation, geared especially to house skiers. Youth hostels are at Taupo and Ohakune. Accommodation in the national park is at one grand THC hotel, a motel-lodge, camping ground and park huts on tramping routes; some huts also in the Kaimanawas.

Food. – In Taupo you can dine on Bluff oysters or Australian prawns; but for the best taste treats look for game food – venison, wild pork, pheasant, rabbit. Catch a trout and lodge, restaurant or hotel kitchen will cook it for you. Plenty of fast food includes Chinese, hamburgers, fish and chips. Find a great cup of coffee in an espresso coffee shop in Heuheu Street; get picnic food in the little delicatessen nearby – the range is really surprising; buy local fresh cottage loaves with poppy seed or cheese topping. Elsewhere in the region it can be a matter of taking what you can find – not always disappointing. A humble meat pie, homebaked with layers of flaky pastry, takes on a new look when you are hungry.

Taupo - Turangi

Courtney Motel
15 Tui Street
Taupo
Telephone: (074) 88-398
Hosts: Grant and Jan Bremner

Set in a quiet garden, this motel offers homely New Zealand hospitality. Units are well appointed with one or to bedrooms, separate from lounge and fully-equipped kitchen. As well as colour TV, heating and telephone in each unit, general facilities include laundry, spa pool, trampoline and swings. Grant will organise fishing, hunting or sightseeing. Cooked breakfasts available. From $38 double.

Tauranga-Taupo Lodge
State Highway 1
Turangi RD2
Telephone: (0746) 8385
Hosts: Heather and Michael Sadlier

Relaxing fishing or skiing base. Accommodation ranges from caravan park and cabins to comfortable luxury motels (suites accommodate up to 8 persons) with television/video, telephone, full kitchens, double and twin beds. Facilities: laundries, drying room, paraplegic unit, spa pool, fishing tackle for sale and hire, trampoline, barbecue and breakfasts by arrangement. Cost: sites from $9, cabins from $20, motels from $45 (for two persons).

Judges Pool Motel
92 Taupehi Road, Turangi
Telephone: (0746) 7892
Hosts: Chris and Margaret Plummer

A great stop for action-seekers, this motel offers tasteful decor with units accommodating from four to six persons. Additional facilities include fish-cleaning room, laundry and spa pool. Units are self-contained with full cooking facilities, telephone, colour TV and bedrooms separate from living area. Rafting, scenic flights, fishing and skiing trips can be arranged through Chris.

Tokaanu Lodge
PO Box 75
Tokaanu, via Turangi
Telephone: (0746) 8572
Hosts: Betty and Derek Ingram, Jo and Rex Gudopp

This attractive complex has 14 self-contained and beautifully appointed units (with lofts), which accommodate up to ten persons. Decor is particularly tasteful and caring hosts have created real 'home away from home' feeling. Facilities include: fish cleaning/smoking rooms, laundry and drying room, ski maintenance bench and mineral pools. Continental breakfasts available, or supplies to cook your own light meals provided. Moderate tariffs, party or group concessions available.

The west coast swerves out into the Tasman Sea here, creating a region dominated by the symmetrical shape of Mt Egmont, a lone perfect mountain rising to 2,518 metres (8,260 feet) above the lush dairylands of Taranaki.

From the top of Mt Egmont, an easy walk in good weather, Taranaki spreads out below like a vast trim parkland – an illusion that carries some truth, for the rich volcanic soils created by the dormant mountain form not only gentle green pastures but parks and gardens with ferns, trees and flowers.

In the National Park that encircles the mountain, the wild flora has developed in isolation from other alpine areas, often producing features unique to the region. Below the stark snow-capped summit is a wilderness of mosses, alpine herbs, waterfalls and thick forest with giant rata trees.

At lower levels, find a variety of parks and gardens such as New Plymouth's Pukekura Park, regarded as a superb formal park of Victorian charm with flower gardens, fernery, waterfall, fountain and artificial lakes; or the large Pukeiti Rhododendron Trust, a 360-hectare (890-acre) springtime spectacle of rhododendrons and azaleas mingle with the soft green of native bush; or a very special commercial nursery, Duncan and Davies, with rare plants from all over the world and a huge collection of evergreen shrubs and trees – you don't need to be buying to enjoy the 40 hectares (100 acres) of greenery.

Along the region's sweeping coastline are wild seascapes with surf beaches attracting surfers and fishermen. In the north sandstone cliffs have been eroded into extraordinary shapes, and tiny fishing settlements nestle by river mouths. In the south are beaches of black iron sand.

But it is the gentle pastoral charm of the landscape, spreading out from below the massive mountain, that remains the most distinctive feature of Taranaki. Travel through Taranaki, taking a route that encircles the mountain, and you will discover that this charm belies the past. Many of the tranquil rural towns and villages began life as stockades and blockhouses, as Taranaki endured 12 years of battles and bloodshed from 1860. There are tales of fraudulent land dealings by the colonial government that initiated these years of conflict; and tales of settlers and British soldiers ambushed, shot or tomahawked, of towns under siege.

At New Plymouth's Taranaki Museum, ancient sacred stone sculptures echo the monuments of Easter Island. Former pa sites are found on hilltops throughout the region. Koru Pa near Oakura Beach has shown evidence of occupation stretching back a thousand years.

In the 1880s, with friction between European and Maori at an end, the Taranaki Region developed into one of the richest dairylands in the world – today more cheese is said to leave New Plymouth than any other port in the world. Visit dairy farms and butter and cheese factories in the region. At Eltham some of the best New Zealand cheeses are made in the European tradition – for example, Blue Vein (similar to Danish Blue or Roquefort), Danbo, Havarti, Erbo and Gouda.

In the last 15 years a new wealth has appeared in the region to boost the prosperity – natural gas. Great complexes rise on the rural landscape as the energy is tapped and converted to various uses from fields at Kapuni and the off shore Maui Field, one of the top 20 such fields in the world. Energy projects at Kapuni, Oanui and near Waitara all have information centres.

Lake Rotokare Walk

(4.2 kilometres (2½ miles) – approximately two hours) Location: signposted in Eltham Township. Turn off at Rawhitiroa Road, then Sangster Road. Beautiful and easy walk around Lake Rotokare (Rippling Lake) with native trees named and explained. Also good location for native birds.

Hawera

A well-preserved ancient pa site of Turuturu-Mokai (heads on stakes), which was deserted before European settlement following tribal war. A short walk from Turuturu-Mokai is the site of a garrison outpost, sacked by the Maori during the land wars of the 1860s. Take the by-pass (Glover Road) to Turatura Road.

From New Plymouth

Drive inland and onto the slopes of Mt Egmont – it is a mere 25 kilometres (15½ miles) from New Plymouth to the end of a road at North Egmont, 936 metres (3,000 feet) high on the mountainside. From here there are various alpine walks, one leading to the 30 metres (100-foot) Bell Falls. From North Egmont it's also possible to walk to the summit – it takes about four hours from the road end to the top of the mountain. The walk is not difficult, but park rangers always stress the need to be sensibly clad and prepared for weather changes. Guides are available from alpine clubs.

On a sharp, clear day the mountaintop views are extraordinary, across dark bush and radiating mountain streams, over a patchwork of green fields spreading to the coast or towards the high heathlands of the Central Plateau and the cluster of volcanoes, Ruapehu, Tongariro, Ngauruhoe.

Legend suggests that Egmont (its Maori name is Taranaki) once formed part of the Tongariro mountains, but left after an argument with Tongariro, banished to the far coast. At times it is not difficult to believe that Egmont gazes back wistfully toward to the distant group of mountains.

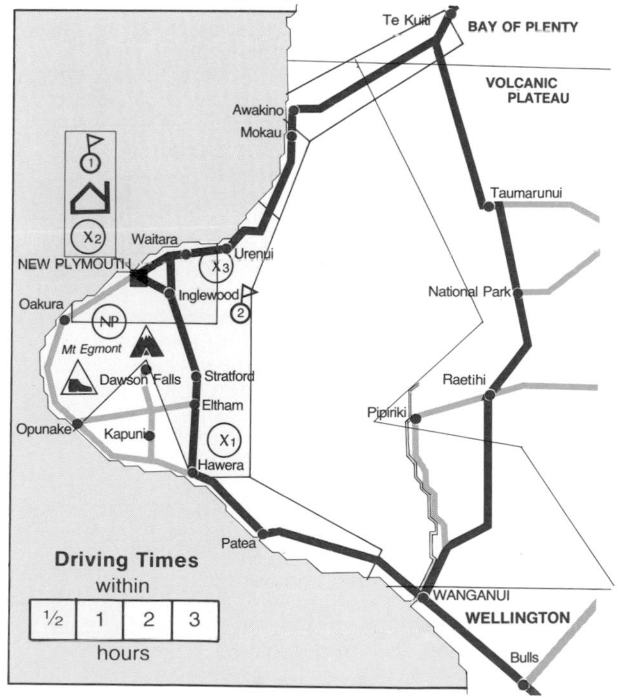

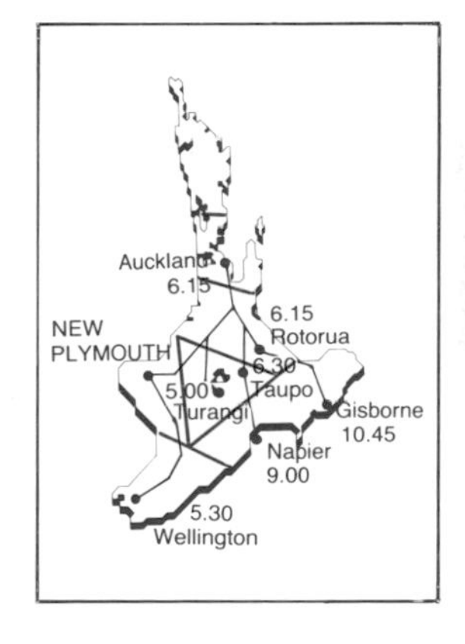

New Plymouth

The main port and service centre of the region, the city of New Plymouth (pop. 44,000), makes an excellent base for touring. a round-the-mountain tour from here makes a leisurely day's travel, with time to pause in the most scenic places.

In the city itself, however, visit the parks – a fifth of New Plymouth's land is devoted to public parks and gardens. First and foremost is Pukekura Park, with paths that lead through mossy arcades to glasshouses of tropical ferns and orchids, through formal flower gardens, beside two artificial lakes and through native bush. At night the fountain provides a multi-coloured, flood-lit, 45-minute performance. Adjoining the park is Brooklands Park, with bush, sweeping lawns, immense trees and a natural amphitheatre where crowds up to 17,000 can enjoy outdoor concerts. From the grassy slopes of Mt Moturoa, rising above a bushy parkland fringe, look out across the city towards Mt Egmont and the distant Tongariro mountains, or along the coast across the North Taranaki Bight.

For the region's most spectacular floral sight, travel out of town to Pukeiti between September and November, when thousands of rhododendrons and azaleas colour the 360-hectare (900-acre) park and bird sanctuary.

At the Taranaki Museum in New Plymouth see an excellent collection of very old and unusual Maori artifacts. The city's Govett-Brewster Art Gallery is one of the most exciting small public galleries in the country, with a superb collection of works by New Zealand-born avant-garde artist and film maker, Len Lye. The gallery contains the two largest Len Lye kinetic sculptures in the world: 'Trilogy' (a flip and two twisters), high-tensile stainless-steel ribbons that whip and scythe the air; and 'Fountain', a great spray of trembling steel rods. Lye, who lived most of his life in New York, explored the power of energy through film and, later, kinetic sculpture. He believed the artist tunes into the human 'old brain' to express emotional truth, unlike the scientist who uses the 'new brain'. He was so pleased with the gallery's 1977 exhibition of his work that he bequeathed to it his collection of papers, works and famous films.

In New Plymouth there's also the charming 'Selwyn' Church of St Mary, the oldest stone church in the country, built in 1842 when the settlement of New Plymouth was only a year old (the settlers came from Devon and Cornwall). The church is as beautiful inside as it is from the outside – don't merely admire the exterior. Also walk through the old churchyard, where many of those first settlers are buried.

At Hurworth, a few kilometres from the city, a young English settler in the 1850s cut and sawed the timber to build himself a simple, elegant cottage and surrounded his new home with trees such as chestnuts and oaks. The settler, Harry Atkinson, later to become Sir Harry, was to be prime minister of New Zealand four times. The house is beautifully restored and some of the original trees remain in an enchanting rural setting.

At Waitara to the north, the Te Atiawa tribe were dispossessed of their land by government troops in 1860, heralding the beginning of many years of bitter fighting. Today visit Waitara to see the Manukorihi Pa, a superbly carved meeting house built in 1936 as a memorial to Sir Maui Pomare, a distinguished and revered politician.

Near Waitara, see also the Pukerangiora Pa site, a dramatic vantage point above the Waitara River for the Te Atiawa people to retreat to in times of tribal warfare.

Continue north to Urenui, once heavily populated with forts on many surrounding hills. Here at Okaki Pa is an impressive memorial to another Maori knight, Sir Peter Buck, politician and internationally acclaimed anthropologist.

New Plymouth Public Relations Office, 81 Liardet Street, New Plymouth. Telephone: (067) 86086

Entertainment. – One doesn't go to Taranaki for sophisticated night life. However, bands and cabaret singers often entertain in hotels and motor inns. In New Plymouth in summer check what's offering at Brooklands Park outdoor theatre – it could be a pop singer or symphony orchestra. As well as A & P Shows, look out for local horticultural shows.

Travel around the region and literally travel around the mountain by car or coach. N.Z.R. Road Services and Newmans provide scheduled bus transport. For flight-seeing around the region and over the mountain, contact aero clubs in New Plymouth.

Food. – In the region of cheese stock up with local varieties and take a picnic on the mountainside, in a park or on a beach. Restaurants cover a wide range in the two cities, from large and licensed to small B.Y.O. For basic economical sustenance of steak and chips or fish and chips, look in New Plymouth's Devon Street. Oddities can turn up anywhere in New Zealand – you can eat Indonesian in New Plymouth.

Accommodation. – Find the best selection in New Plymouth, with hotels and first-class motor inns. On the slopes of Mt Egmont itself accommodation ranges from a stylish Swiss-inspired lodge at Dawson Falls to spartan bunkhouses and trampers' mountain huts. Hotels and motels are also found in Awakino, Mokau, Urenui, Waitara, Inglewood, Hawera, Oakura, Opunake, Stratford, Eltham and Patea. Youth hostels and camping grounds (some with cabins) provide budget accommodation in New Plymouth and most small towns.

This restored lodge dating from 1896 is set on the slopes of Mount Egmont, overlooking splendid scenery to Tongariro National Park. Peaceful and restorative, its nearest neighbours are eight kilometres (5 miles) away and the silence is broken only by birdcalls. Accommodation is sumptuous in well-appointed rooms with Swiss alpine influence and private facilities. Enjoy great cuisine, relaxed atmosphere, wonderful walks and a variety of diverse and interesting day trips. Cost: $50 per person, per night (includes dinner and breakfast).

Dawson Falls Tourist Lodge
Dawson Falls
Taranaki
R.H.C. Reservations
Telephone: (03) 799-126/7
(USA: 800-874-7027)
Telex: NZ 4051
(USA: 8874486)

Mt Egmont and pastoral scene. *(Courtesy Air New Zealand)*

The capital city, Wellington, perches on the windswept southwest tip of this region, its satellite suburbs and towns spreading up the valleys behind.

ravel north from the city, however, and soon discover that the overriding characteristics of the region are distinctly rural, not urban.

Massive ranges of hills, first the Rimutakas and then the Tararuas, run the length of the region, like a mountainous backbone dividing east from west. As you move out of the urban sprawl, the decision must be made to go east or west – straight ahead the rugged Tararuas bar the way, uncrossed by roads for another 130 kilometres (80 miles).

Go west and there are long, pleasant beaches backed by sand dunes, stretching up the coast to the South Taranaki Bight. Here lies the river city of Wanganui, a river that gives access into the interior; its source is in the Tongariro Mountains. Further south, the low-lying coastal countryside, with its market gardens and rich pastures, is peppered with small beach resorts and rural towns. At McKay's Crossing, memorial gates remember a World War II U.S. Marine Corps Camp and there's also a museum of vintage public transport. Otaki is a rewarding stop for those interested in Maori culture and history, in particular for the Rangiatea Maori Church with its superb interior.Levin is a centre of horticulture research and Palmerston North is a city with a university concentrating on agriculture and special research establishments.

The west-east connection can be made from Palmerston North through the Manawatu Gorge. The road follows the tortuous course of the Manawatu River, which rises on the eastern side of the Ruahine Ranges and then turns to flow westward towards the sea. Such are the physical characteristics of the gorge that when the road was cut in 1871 workmen had to be lowered down cliff sides on ropes.

On the east side there's a broad inland valley sweeping the length of the region from Dannevirke (settled by Scandinavians in 1872) through to Masterton and Martinborough. With an eye for geology, you can see fault lines extending through the edges of the valley, defining an area of instability that reaches down to the city of Wellington.

Hills rise again on the east coast, forming high-country sheep and cattle farms that are top dressed by small aircraft. The planes operate from small farm landing strips and perform hair-raising feats, swooping close to hills. On farms too steep for machinery,aerial top dressing has proved the most practical and economical method of spreading fertilisers and·lime – a method that is now a vital part of hill-country farming.

Travel up into the Tararuas onto the slopes of Mt Bruce, a native bird reserve in rich native forest, where rare birds are cared for, studied and bred. The primary purpose of the reserve is to provide protection for the birds; some of them, such as the takahe and black stilt, are among the rarest birds in the world. Here too are the kakapo, saddleback, kiwi, blue duck, as well as more common native birds.

The Tararua Forest Park covers 98,400 hectares (243,000 acres) of sharp hills and dense forest, threaded with tracks for trampers and hunters. On the edge of the park the Mt Holdsworth Reserve attracts less-dedicated outdoor folk – those fit enough scramble up a well-marked track to the mountaintop for a superb view of beech forests, valley farms, distant hills and the Pacific Ocean beyond.

In this sheep-farming district of Wairarapa, visit Martinborough, where it all began – the first sheep stations in New Zealand were established around here in 1844. Continue on past Lake Wairarapa to Cape Palliser if you have a taste for wild, savage coastlines.

7

WELLINGTON

Accommodation. – Wellington is a cosmopolitan city, although not large by world standards. It is the centre of government and head office for major commercial businesses. Accommodation can be tight, especially during the week, and it is wise to book ahead in Wellington. There is top-class hotel accommodation and there are also motor inns, and some old hotels for those on a tighter budget. There is a youth hostel in Wellington and also at Kaitoki and Palmerston North. Don't expect to find camping grounds in Wellington, but elsewhere in the region, including nearby Lower Hutt, there are plenty of camping grounds.

Food. – Eat very well indeed in Wellington at some of the country's best restaurants, where high-quality New Zealand food is cooked with the best European skill. Find excellent French, Italian and Greek restaurants; also Asian cooking at Indonesian, Mongolian, Burmese and Chinese restaurants. Pub food at old hotel bars is a bargain institution.

Travel around the region by air from Wellington to Palmerston North on scheduled flights. Hire a car in Wellington or Palmerston North. N.Z.R. Road Services and Newmans provide bus transport to most main points in the region. This is also one region where it is feasible to travel by train, either along the west coast to Palmerston North or along the eastern route towards Napier. Reach outlying suburbs and western-coast beaches on the good commuter rail service.

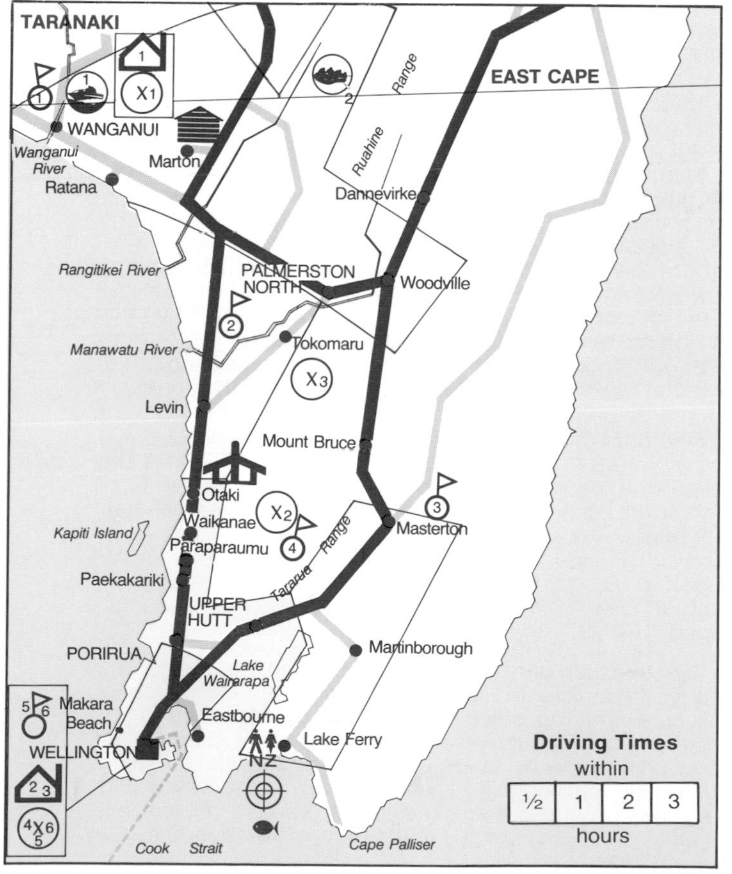

Wellington City

ellington has a reputation for being the 'windy city'. Southerly gales from the Antartic region sweep in through Cook Strait to batter the city. Fortunately this is not often, but these and the fogs that roll in from the straits give the city a reputation that other New Zealanders love to exaggerate.

But in peerless or perilous weather, Wellington is a city of architectural surprises – quaint old wooden houses, tall and narrow, huddle together behind or beside stark new buildings. Walk along Tinakori Road and side streets such as Glenbervie Terrace and Ascot Terrace for charming reminders of Wellington's past. Visit too the gabled cottage of Plimmer House (now a restaurant), Antrim House (headquarters of the Historic Places Trust) and the Nairn Street Colonial Cottage.

Not all new buildings lack grace or charm – see in particular the whimsical, innovative Wellington Club building and the stylish Michael Fowler Centre, a superb convention-theatre complex. In the main entrance foyer are twin carved poles known as the 'Pillars of Peace'. These carvings trace the history of the resident Te Atiawa tribe, before the arrival of the Europeans.

A walk around the vicinity of Parliament Buildings provides some interesting architectural contrasts – the dome-shaped 'Beehive' executive building, the solemn old stone Parliament House and the Gothic-style General Assembly Library. Not far distant are the Government Buildings, the second largest wooden building in the world. In Mulgrave Street is Old St Paul's, a graceful Gothic-style 'Selwyn' church.

Those who have an interest in art and culture should visit the National Art Gallery, which has an excellent collection of British paintings, Italian prints, works by Rembrandt and Dürer as well as works by New Zealand artists. The National Museum features Maori and Pacific exhibits. The Alexander Turnbull Library has an outstanding collection of books, maps, letters, and documents of historical interest.

Rise above the buildings to take in the city view from Kelburn, travelling there by a small cable car rising out of the commercial area, past the university, through gardens and by hillside houses in a four-minute ride. Walk back down through the Botanic Gardens and the Lady Norwood Rose Gardens.

Get out of town almost as quickly with a drive around the bays and beaches of the Miramar Peninsula. Start with Oriental Bay, less than a kilometre from the central area, and follow a road that winds around the shoreline, past the airport, by the pleasant beaches at Scorching Bay and Worser Bay and around to Lyall Bay on the far side of the airport. Continue on through Island Bay to Owhiro Bay. From here a shoreline walk of about 6 kilometres (4 miles) leads, in winter, to a seal colony.

Back in the city centre find shopping concentrated in Lambton Quay, Lower Willis Street, Cuba Street Mall and Manners Street.

For collectors of historical reproductions, the Turnbull Library offers pictorial images of the land and the people of early New Zealand, selected from the national research collections of paintings and photographs. Over sixty exceptional prints are offered for sale, in presentation sets or individually – from $2.50 and ready for framing. Illustrated postcards and books are also sold. A complete catalogue is available. Open 10.30 a.m. – 5.00 p.m. weekdays; Saturday, 9 a.m. – noon.

Houses perch on hilltops and spill down the steep slopes in tiers towards the high-rise buildings clustered on the harbour shore – look down on the city from Mt Victoria, Tinakori Hill or the hillside suburb of Kelburn on a clear, fine, still day, and the spectacular view of Wellington and its harbour is an exhilarating sight.

Looking up from the boat harbour past St Gerard's to the summit
(Courtesy Air New Zealand)

Wellington City Council Public Relations Office, 2 Mercer Street, Wellington, P.O. Box 2199. Telephone (04) 735-063

Alexander Turnbull Library
44 The Terrace
Wellington
Telephone: (04) 722-107

7

WELLINGTON

Serving from 1866 for nearly a century, Old St Paul's is now preserved as a historic place, used for occasional services and as a setting for music and drama. It is a particularly fine timber Gothic church, with superb interior, stained-glass memorial windows and brasses. Open daily (except Christmas Day and Good Friday), 10.00 a.m. to 4.30 p.m. Sundays 1.00 p.m. to 4.30 p.m. Admission free, donations accepted.

Old St Paul's
Mulgrave Street
Wellington
Contact: NZ Historic Places Trust
Private Bag, Wellington.

Entertainment – Wellington is not renowned for nightclub entertainment. The city has a reputation for social activity based on the small intimate dinner party and the diplomatic social round. But do not despair – the city has excellent restaurants and many other attractions for travellers.

Permanent exhibitions include the National Museum (Buckle Street, City 1), Colonial Cottage (Nairn Street,.City 1), Antrim House (63 Boulcott Street, City 1) and, of course, guided tours of Parliament Buildings. The visual arts are well catered for, as well as theatre – visit Circa, Downstage and the New Depot. Check out what's in *Cosmo*, Wellington's 'Who, What, Where, Why, When' magazine. If shopping is a form of entertainment, Wellington offers some of the country's best: Manners Plaza and Cuba Mall; Upper Cuba Street for curiosities; Willis Street, and the ultra-modern complexes of Lambton Quay. Don't forget the boutiques of Kelburn Village, and Marbles Restaurant, worth a lunch-time drive through the university.

On a fine day, especially in the weekend, take a walk around Oriental Bay and catch the character of some little city cafes. Further around in Evans Bay is the Shorebird Restaurant and the Greta Point Tavern, an unusual corrugated-iron structure.

Festival in January is something to get out and enjoy. Local papers have all the details. While signs of life may not be too apparent, you will discover that many Wellingtonians will be visiting these places too – and maybe a chance meeting will see you at one of those small intimate dinner parties.

Looking across the city from the top of Mt Victoria.
(Courtesy Air New Zealand)

North to Wanganui via Kapiti Coast or Palmerston North

This rich coastline around Waikanae and Otaki is known for its warm climate, horticulture, local holiday and retirement facilities.

The richness of the area is more than in the soil. Here the arts flourish. One of New Zealand's better-known contemporary artists, Malcolm Warr, lives and works on the coast. The feeling of calm and peace in his work comes from the beach coastline and seabirds found on the coast. Visit Malcom's studio gallery (corner Parata and Kapanui Streets, Waikanae). It's a bonus to find an orchid nursery of 20,000 plants opposite (flowering July to October). Waikanae, with its established homes and beautiful gardens, is also the location of the Nga Manu Bird Sanctuary. Over 50 species of birds use or visit the sanctuary, which combines an impressive array of natural habitats from giant kahikatea to fern-lined walks and ponds (Ngarara Road off Te Moana Road, Waikanae – closed Mondays).

The coast is home to many potters, amongst them Mirek Smisek, near Te Horo (State Highway 1), who displays his work in a garden setting.

For a collection of a different kind, visit the Southward Museum and Theatre Trust at Otaihanga Road, 2 kilometres (1 mile) north of Paraparaumu on State Highway 1. This is one of the largest privately owned collections of veteran and vintage cars in the Southern Hemisphere.

North in Otaki find Rangiatea Church, in Te Rauparaha Street. One of the finest of the Maori churches in New Zealand, the interior includes carvings and beautiful tukutuku wall panels. (The ashes of Inia Te Wiata, international opera star, are buried in the grounds.)

Te Rauparaha was a famous chief of the area, and his war parties were responsible for the nineteenth-century Wairau Massacre near Blenheim. Kapiti Island, whose distinctive form is ever present along this coast (often featuring in Malcolm Warr's prints), was his stronghold. The island is now a bird sanctuary, which can only be visited by special arrangement with the Forest and Bird Society, 26 Brandon Street, Wellington.

For those interested in geology, Kapiti Island has another significance. The island is the northernmost land of the tectonic plate on which the South Island rests. Like other areas in the Pacific Basin, for example the San Andreas Fault in California, which delineates two tectonic plates, the North and South Island are on two separate plates. Moreover, the plate on which the South Island lies is moving under the North Island at an estimated 6 centimetres (2½ inches) per year and is one of the causes of the region's 200 plus earthquakes per year.

Along the coast, stop and 'pick your own' (P.Y.O.) fruit and vegetables, berries, stone and pip fruits of all varieties, beans, peas, tomatoes, zucchini, aubergine, capsicum, and artichoke – a veritable garden of Eden.

Tokomaru Steam Engine Museum
Tokomaru
Telephone: (063298) 853 or 867
Owner: Mr Colin Stevenson

This unique museum has working engines operating on steam and driven by a master boiler. Range includes a ship-winching engine (Appleby Bros, London 1869); a 70-ton compressor (Filer & Stowel Coy, Wisconsin, USA); a Shand Mason horse-drawn steam pump, a collection of early steam rollers, plus an operating railway. Static displays open daily (9.00 a.m. – noon and 1.00 p.m. – 3.00 p.m.). Operational 'open days' held most holiday weekends (1.30 p.m. – 4.00 p.m.) or by special arrangement.

Wanganui

thriving area of Maori settlement before the Pakeha arrival, Wanganui maintains its historical links. At Wanganui's Regional Museum (Watt Street, Civic Centre) find an excellent collection of Maori artifacts presented with style and imagination. One of the famous exhibits is a 23-metre (75-foot) war canoe built in 1810. Also see ancient carvings and tools, plus one of the finest collections of greenstone artifacts and Lindauer paintings in the country.

See also Putiki Church (Anaua Street, Putiki), noted for its magnificent Maori carvings and tukutuku wall panels.

At Operiki Pa, on the left bank of the Wanganui River, find the remaining earthworks of a great pa with commanding views of the river.

Now the centre of a wealthy farming community, Wanganui is also the entry point to the wild beauty of the Wanganui River, flowing from its source on the Volcanic Plateau. In the upper reaches a rapid churning mass of water twists through steep, bush-covered gorges, the lower reaches gliding gently between willow-fringed banks.

Many places have biblical names, for example Jerusalem; others are amended to Maori, like Atene (Athens) and Korinti (Corinth). Navigable to Taumarunui and with 240 rapids, the river is noted for summer canoeing and jet-boat safaris.

From Wanganui it's possible to drive along a winding road beside much of the river, but see the river at its best from the water – by sightseeing launch, jet boat, canoe or raft.

For a restful stop on the way north to Hawera, visit Virginia Lake and take a walk through the beautiful gardens.

Kawana Mill, near Wanganui. *(Historic Places Trust)*

Wanganui Regional Museum
Cnr Watt Street & Maria Place
Wanganui
Telephone: (064) 57-443

Largest regional museum in New Zealand. Famous Maori Court contains 23-metre (75-foot) war canoe and extensive collection of rare greenstone artefacts, as well as displays illustrating the Maori way of life. The natural history section includes an extinct American passenger pigeon. Open weekdays, 9.30 a.m. to 4.30 p.m.; weekends/holidays, 1.00 p.m. to 5.00 p.m. Admission: $1.50 adults, .50c children.

Kawana Mill
Matahiwi
Wanganui Valley
Contact: NZ Historic Places Trust
Private Bag, Wellington.

This flour mill was the longest operating, most successful of those on the Wanganui River in the 1900s. Machinery was given to the Poutana people by Governor George Grey, who practiced a policy of self-sufficiency and education for the Maori people. Operational from 1855, production later became spasmodic, finally closing 1912-13. Reconstruction saw the mill reopened in 1980. The interior can be seen at all times through viewing windows.

The Rock Shop
93A Guyton Street
Wanganui
Telephone: (064) 57-502
Owner: Mrs Moana Henry

You are guaranteed a friendly reception and a happy smile when you visit Wanganui's leading greenstone and paua specialists. Located next to Hurleys Grand Hotel in the town centre. Fine range includes: lapidary supplies, quality New Zealand souvenirs and many novelty gift lines. Open weekdays, 9.00 a.m. to 5.30 p.m. Moana will be happy to open the shop after these hours, by arrangement, for tours and conferences.

SEE ALSO:

Live with NZ: Wharekauhau Station (Down on Farm/Hunting) (Wairarapa).
Lodges: Maungaraupi Country Estate (Marton).
NZ Historic Places: Old St Pauls, Kawana Mill, Antrim House.

The New Zealand Parliament

Parliament buildings are prominent on a knoll in downtown Wellington.

Beside the neo-Gothic General Assembly Library is the central building of Takaka marble, completed in 1922. It contains the rimu-wooded legislative chamber, laid out in the British tradition. Visitors can sit in the gallery and watch parliament in action. You can join a guided tour and learn how parliament works or visit by yourself. A guard may ask who you are, but there'll be no grilling by a hefty watchdog bristling with weapons. Even this is relatively recent. In 1979 the media nostalgically noted the introduction of staff IDs and 25 uniformed guards to replace the elderly messengers affectionately known as 'dad's army'.

The legislative building is dwarfed somewhat by the 72-metre (236-foot) high Beehive. Designed by Sir Basil Spence, it lives up to its name with its circular construction and appearance of many tiny cells. It is here that cabinet meets, ministers have their offices and state receptions are held. On the way to the reception hall you pass Joan Calvert's huge woven wall hangings in the foyer. Holes cut through the vivid orange, turquoise and yellow wool reveal the soft grey marble of the building's interior walls.

Glory of the Beehive is the John Drawbridge mural, which wraps itself round the curved wall of the reception hall, covering 42 metres (140 feet) in length and rising to 5 metres (16 feet). Drawbridge won a national competition for this commission. He wanted to show the atmosphere of New Zealand – the strong light-blue skies, the sea, the weather. He designed a three-dimensional aluminium mural with fin-like extrusions echoing the surface treatment of the building's exterior. Each surface is treated as a continuous theme so that the mural reveals itself to the viewer differently from different angles. Drawbridge himself suggests walking up the main stairs, through the reception hall doors and continuing in this direction. It cannot all be taken in at once except when viewed from the street outside while spectacularly lit at night.

For New Zealanders, Parliament buildings are often a gathering place for demonstrations and a focal point for protest marches. Groups have even slept on the steps or camped in the grounds, as one group did at the end of the historic Maori land march from the far north in 1975.

Parliament Buildings and the Beehive. ***(National Publicity Studios)***

WELLINGTON

Every three years New Zealanders over 18 years old turn out to elect the new government. Even the pubs stay shut to encourage a sober choice. For decades they've chosen between the conservative National Party and the traditionally union-oriented Labour Party, but in the 1970s and 1980s new parties – Social Credit, Mana Motuhake, New Zealand Party – have emerged.

New Zealanders can be on familiar terms with their member of parliament. Many MPs hold regular 'meet the constituents' mornings and it's often possible to phone an MP direct, especially a back bencher or opposition member, without having to foil a battery of secretaries.

For 24 years from 1852 New Zealand had a kind of federal system with a national parliament drawing representatives from six provincial councils. Canterbury is the only province that has preserved its provincial chambers, a stone and wood Gothic-styled cluster of buildings square around a courtyard in central Christchurch.

From the abolition of provincial governments until 1950, parliament, based on the British Westminster system consisted of the House of Representatives, members from designated regions and areas, and an elected upper house, the Legislative Council. However, the upper house was stacked with elected supporters of the ruling party, so its only function, in effect, was to rubber-stamp the government. From 1951 New Zealand has had a one-house system, headed nominally by the Governor General as Queen's representative.

New Zealand has no written constitution, nor bill of rights, making, some say, citizens' rights uncomfortably vulnerable to the whim of whoever is in power. Major law changes can be made by the governing party no matter how slim its majority. Fears have been expressed too that the increasing power of the cabinet of government ministers takes decision making away from public scrutiny. The possibility of constitutional reform has been widely discussed.

Although New Zealand was the first country to grant the vote to women only a fraction of the 95 members of parliament are women; few women have ever risen to cabinet rank. The four Maori seats in parliament are traditionally Labour and linked to the Ratana church. Maori voters may register as Maori or on the European roll.

'Social security' has been of central concern to New Zealand governments since the turn of the century, leading to New Zealand being at one time seen as the 'social laboratory of the world'. Premier 'King Dick' Seddon introduced one of the first old-age pension schemes in the world in 1898; widows were provided for in 1906. The first Labour Government, coming into power in 1935 during the Depression, built on this base to introduce a national health service, a universal old-age pension (the first in the world), state rental housing and free milk for all school children (this continued till 1967). Today coal mining, bulk electricity, postal and telegraph services, education and rail transport are just some of the services and industries controlled by the state. Of course this requires an enormous bureaucracy, making the New Zealand Government the largest single employer in the country. Around 190,000 New Zealanders are in the civil service, 38 per cent of the workforce.

Parliament in session is indicated by the New Zealand flag flying; at night by three white lights on the flag pole. A visit to Parliament should not be missed.

Four major highways provide the main touring routes around the South Island. There's SH1 again, which began its southward journey in the north of the North Island.

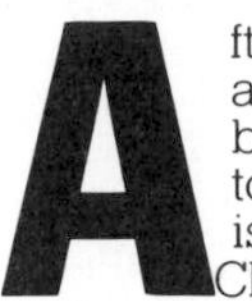

fter an enforced break at Cook Strait, SH1 picks up again at Picton, where the inter-island rail ferry berths. It runs through the wine country of Blenheim to hug the wild Kaikoura coast on the east of the island, and then over the Canterbury lowlands to Christchurch,the South Island's largest city. The highway never strays far from the east coast as it continues south, over the Canterbury plains, across wide, braided rivers, through the leafy town of Ashburton, the coastal port of Timaru, the town of Oamaru with its buildings of distinctive white limestone to the city of Dunedin. From there SH1 travels inland to the southernmost city, Invercargill.

SH6 leaves SH1 at Blenheim, veering west through Marlborough to the city of Nelson and then turning south through hills and mountains to the west coast and Westport. SH6 runs the length of the wild west coast, through Greymouth, Hokitika, and the glaciers at Franz Josef and Fox, finally branching inland again at the Haast River, crossing the alps at Haast Pass, on the edge of Mt Aspiring National Park. From there this spectacular highway leads by Lake Wanaka and Lake Hawea to the township of Wanaka and through to Queenstown. From Queenstown, the road runs between the mountain range, the Remarkables, and the lake, and on toward Invercargill through the green pasture downs of Southland.

SH7 is another spectacular route, running off SH1 north of Christchurch and climbing into the hills toward the wooded town of Hanmer Springs before crossing to the west coast through the Lewis Pass and Reefton, down to Greymouth and SH6.

Provincial highways (double numbers) link with state highways to provide a surprisingly good network of roads in country often wild and mountainous.

SH8 is a great inland loop from SH1 at Timaru, across to SH6 between Wanaka and Queenstown and then back through the grand, stark Central Otago country to SH1 near Milton, south of Dunedin. On its long route the highway leads through Burkes Pass to Lake Tekapo and then Lake Pukaki, where a provincial road branches off to Mt Cook, through Twizel, the centre of the hydro-electric schemes, Omarama, a small resort popular with anglers, and on across wild mountain country to the Southern Lakes region.

Secondary roads vary from reasonable to excellent in low-lying coastal land. In back-country mountainous areas they may be treacherous although always spectacular – check with locals if you have any doubts about a chosen route.

Travelling south from Nelson towards the west coast, take time out to visit Motueka or Kaiteriteri on the edge of Abel Tasman National Park and explore the villages of the river lowland.

The reward of exploring the countryside and the small communities along the way, rather than taking the quickest route between two points, will be discovering that the scenic variety and beauty of New Zealand stretches far beyond the well-travelled tourist routes.

Cut across country from Murchison on SH6 to Springs Junction on SH7. The road from Murchison to Frog Flat, like many secondary routes in the mountains, is not recommended in wet weather. But on a fine day follow a mountain road winding up beside the Matakitaki River through superb scenery and old gold workings.

Or instead of travelling from Balclutha to Invercargill by way of SH1, travel closer to the coast on a rough PH92 through the lovely Catlins district, by rivers, through wooded valleys, by splendid beaches and through tiny villages.

On the way North from Invercargill take PH99 along the wild south coast, with spectacular views to Stewart Island, through rich farmlands that give way to the lush vegetation of Fiordland. Leave PH99 at Clifden and take the backdoor route to Manapouri and Te Anau through Blackmount – isolated and splendid.

South Island Touring

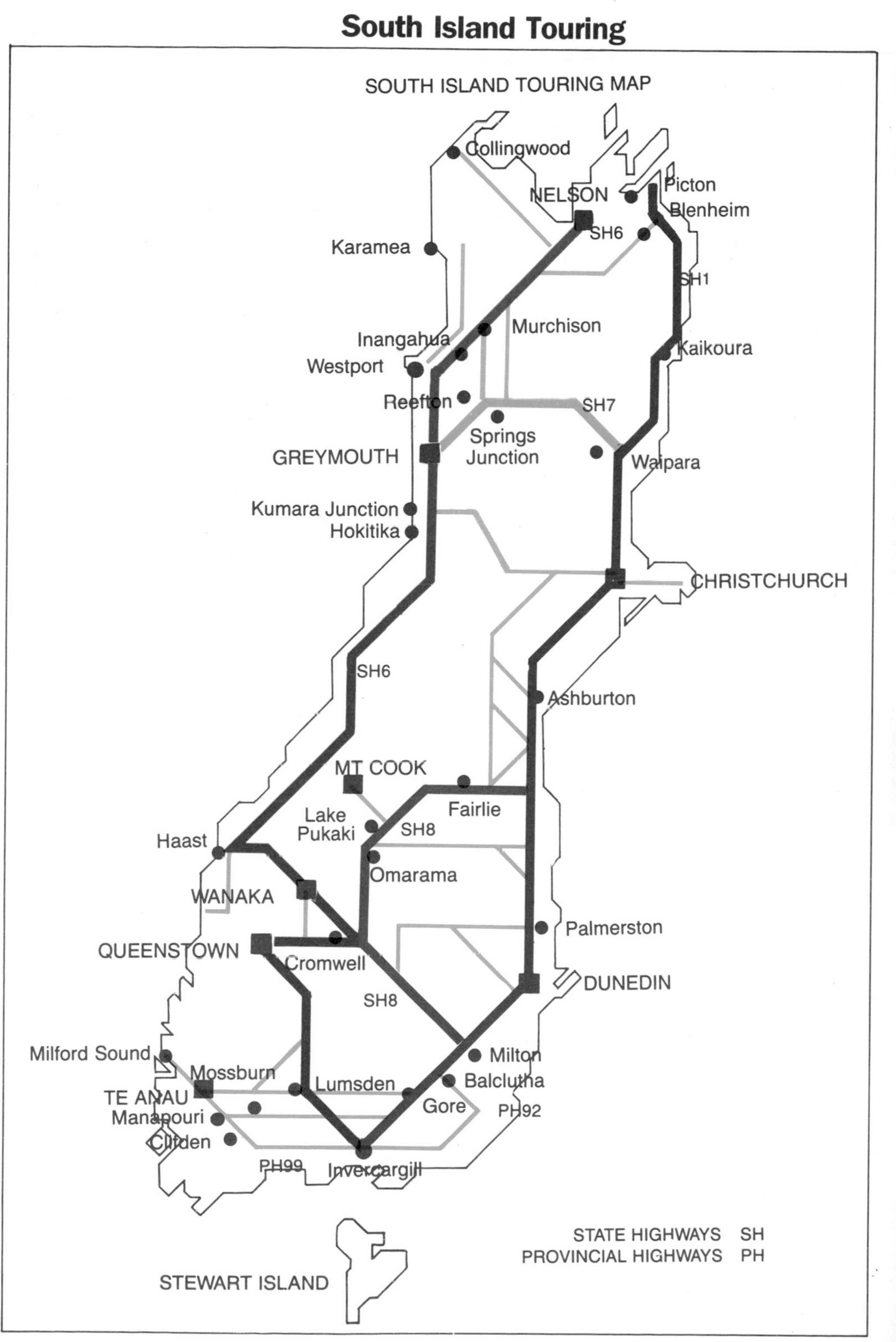

Yachts at anchor, Queen Charlotte Sound. ***(National Publicity Studios)***

Arrive in the region by sea, as many do, sailing up the deep, green waters of Queen Charlotte Sound. The coastline unfolds before you, with bush-covered hillsides plunging down into the sea.

From Picton you can travel straight to Canterbury along the Kaikoura coast, with a rugged chain of mountains to the west and a wild, rocky shore to the east; or you can linger awhile in the Nelson-Marlborough region and discover that this is the place to 'get away from it all'.

From Picton and Havelock, boats leave for all parts of the sounds – charter yachts, line-fishing boats, game-fishing boats, water taxis, mail boats, sundowner cruises, luncheon cruises, picnic cruises. Arrange for a boat to take you to a remote bay for a day or a week of Robinson Crusoe living; or to a beach-front lodge with all the comforts but none of the hassles of modern life.

The whole northeastern tip of the region is gashed with deep inlets and dotted with white sandy bays, coves and islands in a vast system of drowned river valleys – there's a total of 1,000 kilometres (620 miles) of coastline in the sounds, most of which can only be reached by boat.

You can see some of the splendour of the sounds from the road. Travel from Picton to Havelock and detour along the Queen Charlotte Drive that rises above the Queen Charlotte and Pelorus Sounds.

The intricate, beautiful sounds are only part of the region. Elsewhere, mountains and high hills frame warm slopes where apples, pears, grapes, hops, tobacco and garlic grow. Small towns are surrounded by towering hills, which are threaded with tracks and walkways leading to high lakes, deep caves, fast rivers and forests of mountain beech, splashed in summer with the red-flowering southern rata.

In the Nelson Lakes National Park, tracks lead near the glacial Lakes Rotoroa and Rotoiti and over alpine passes. Roads encroach briefly into the area to the lake-side townships of St Arnaud and Rotoroa. At St Arnaud is the headquarters of the park, and there are plenty of picnic places on the beech-fringed shores, and a backdrop of mountains that rise sharply on every side.

Bordering on the western shores of Tasman Bay is another national park, the Abel Tasman National Park. Take off by boat from Takaka or Kaiteriteri to explore the sandy bays and granite headlands of the park; take short walks or take a three- or four-day trek along the coast above lagoons, white-sand beaches, and estuaries crowded with wading birds.

In the west there's another large wilderness area, the Northwest Nelson Forest Park, with 376,000 hectares (930,000 acres) of mountains, forest and alpine meadows. The many tracks include one of the country's best known, the Heaphy Track, a five-day trek linking Golden Bay and the West Coast.

The curve of Golden Bay originally bore the name Murderers Bay, when Abel Tasman, the first European to see the coast of New Zealand, anchored here in 1642. After four of his crewmen were murdered by Maoris, he gave the bay its name and hurriedly left. The physically descriptive name of Golden Bay suited later settlers better.

Here, golden sand beaches lead out to Farewell Spit, a slim bar of sand 35 kilometres (22 miles) long, which turns inward sheltering the bay. From Collingwood, four-wheel-drive tours take visitors along the treacherous sands where seabirds gather.

You don't need to be an outdoors person to revel in the scenic variety of Nelson-Marlborough, but if you are, the region offers extraordinary opportunities – climbing, skiing and ski touring, caving, hunting, fishing, trekking, sailing, diving; and this is New Zealand's sunniest region as well.

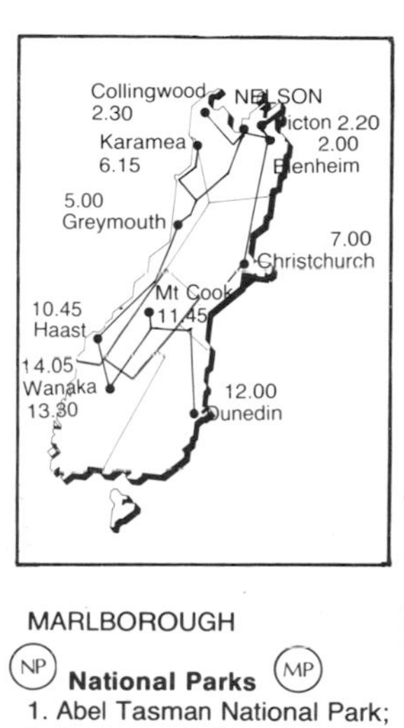

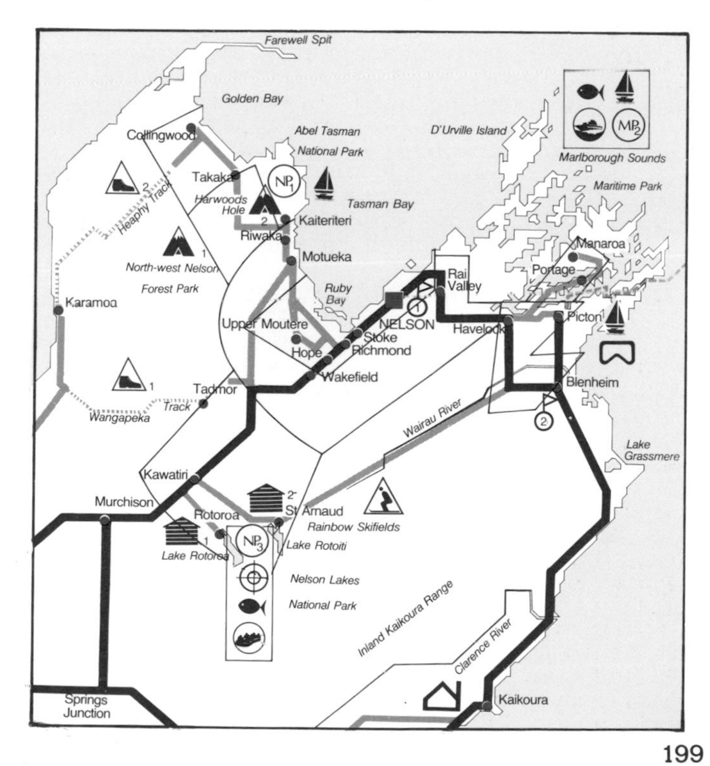

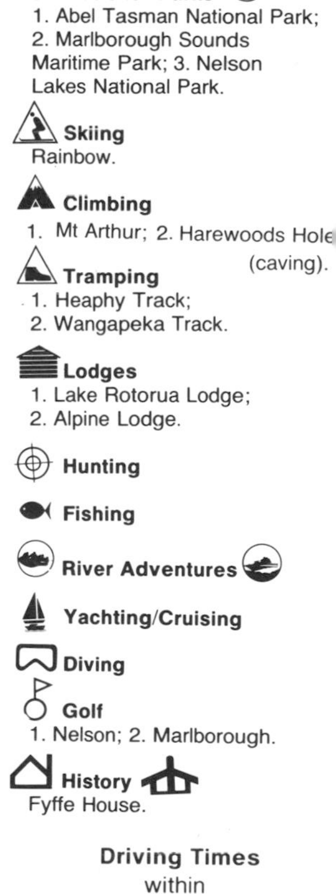

Nelson City

Backed by bush-covered hills, the city of Nelson is a city of walks – walk up hill and down dale, through parks, along walkways and tramping tracks. There are dozens of walks to choose from.

or a stunning view over Tasman Bay, walk to the top of Flaxmoor Hill. Another city walk leads out of town, through open country and native bush to Dun Mountain. Around Nelson there are gentle family walks and walks for the dedicated tramper.

In the city there are even walks that focus on grand colonial houses – they can, of course, be reached by car or coach tour as well. Early settlers built elegant houses, filled them with stylish furniture and planted splendid gardens to remind them of England. See especially Isel House, a solid timber and stone Victorian house set in 5 hectares (12 acres) of exotic trees, rose gardens, rhododendrons and azaleas. Behind the house is Nelson's Provincial Museum, which emphasises the early European settlers. See also Broadgreen, an 1855 two-storey cob farmhouse, nostalgically modelled on the style of farmhouses in England's West Country. The house is elaborately furnished in period. Wander through the sweet-smelling Lavender Hill Herb Garden, a traditional herb garden set around a century-old cottage.

Arts and crafts obviously thrive in Nelson – the city is crammed with shops selling quality pottery, ceramics, glasswork, woodcraft, weaving and jewellery, all made locally. The high-quality Nelson clay and the pleasant quality of life have led to flourishing cottage industries. Everywhere you turn there's a shop, studio or gallery. On the outskirts of the city, potteries with showrooms attached are prolific – drive out through Hope, Brightwater and Wakefield in particular to visit potteries and perhaps see craftspeople at work.

To the west of Nelson, the rich agricultural land spreads in a patchwork of apple orchards, then fields of tobacco and hops – in spring, fruit trees blossom against a background of snow-capped mountains. Village names have a suitable charm; names such as Redwoods Valley, Pigeon Valley, Spring Grove, Dovedale and even Pretty Bridge. Picturesque old churches and cob cottages nestle in the valleys, and each place seems to have a different, intriguing history. Hope began its life as a German Lutheran settlement called Ranzau. Brightwater was the birthplace of Rutherford, the first person to 'split' the atom. In the less idyllically named Pig Valley, find the South Island's oldest church, built in 1846.

Visit vineyards at Redwoods Valley, Ruby Bay and Upper Moutere. At Ruby Bay there's a pleasant sandy beach and several picnic places, and from the nearby Observation Point there's a superb view of Tasman Bay out to D'Urville Island. Upper Moutere was originally a German Lutheran community and the valley once bore the name Schachtstal.

For New Zealand's largest spread of vineyards, travel through to Blenheim, where thousands of hectares of vines reach out in straight lines toward the surrounding high, grass-covered hills, which turn a contrasting yellow-brown in dry summer weather.

For those who want to stay close to town in Nelson, there's a well-signposted circular drive that takes in some of the best sights the city has to offer: the Cawthron Institute Museum, with excellent scientific and agricultural displays; the Botanical Reserve, with views over city and bay; the pretty Queen's Gardens and Suter Art Gallery; the simple elegant building of Bishopdale, Isel House and its parkland, Broadgreen; Tahunanui Beach, with a foreshore promenade; Princes Drive, with remarkable views; and the Cathedral, which dominates Nelson's city centre.

**Nelson Public Relations Office,
Corner Trafalgar & Halifax Streets,
Nelson,
P.O. Box 194.
Telephone: (054) 82304**

Nelson — Marlborough

Entertainment. – Summer beach carnivals at popular beaches. Arts and crafts festivals, wine and food fairs, fishing contests, yacht races, horse racing, stock-car racing, motorcycle speedway, A & P Shows, horticultural shows. The Suter Gallery, rebuilt in 1979, has a collection of the works of Gully and Weber. The gallery also has a restaurant, film screenings, plays and recitals.

Food. – With rich seas, soil and climate, the produce of Nelson-Marlborough is superb. From the sea come scallops and mussels; for white fish try the sweet-flavoured butterfish. Apples, pears, boysenberries, blackberries, loganberries, cherries, kiwifruit, tomatoes and broccoli all grow to perfection here. Roadside stalls sell garden-fresh produce for do-it-yourself meals. In Rai Valley, local cheese and bread are famous.

Accommodation. – Modern first-class hotels, motor inns, motels, private hotels, guest houses, camping grounds; lodges and cabins in secluded bays reached by sea; youth hostels at Nelson, Havelock, Kaikoura; camping, caravan sites, park huts in Nelson Lakes National Park; casual camping in remote bays of Marlborough Sounds, also camping in Titirangi Farm Park in the sounds. Forest Service huts in Northwest Nelson Forest Park and Mount Richmond Forest Park.

North to Takaka

Sixteen kilometres (10 miles) past Motueka, turn off and see the Riwaka River source, where the river flows out from a limestone cavern in bush surroundings. Picnic downstream at the Moss Reserve before setting off across the 'Marble Mountain' to Golden Bay. At 20.6 kilometres (13 miles) from Motueka, turn right along the Canaan Road and drive through a blasted landscape to a 40-minute bush walk leading to the edge of Harwoods Hole. Experience the best vertigo in the Southern Hemisphere as you gaze down 370.6 metres (1,215 feet). From Takaka itself explore the springs at Waikoropupu, where 2,160,000,000 litres of water well out of the ground daily – one of the largest freshwater springs in the world.

SEE ALSO:

Tramping/Trekking/Walking: Abel Tasman National Park Enterprises (Motueka).
National Parks: Marlborough Sounds Maritime Park.

Travel around by car, renting a car in Nelson, Picton or Blenheim. Nelson suburban buses service the town and immediate countryside. Newmans buses cover Nelson to Picton, Blenheim, Golden Bay, Motueka. Flight-seeing and charter aircraft are available from Nelson, Blenheim and Motueka. Charter an amphibian taxi for flight-seeing from Picton. Boat charter and cruises from Nelson, Havelock, Picton, Kaiteriteri and Motueka.

Goat Bay, Abel Tasman National Park, Nelson. ***(Andris Apse Ltd)***

South to Christchurch via Picton, Blenheim and Kaikoura

Marlborough Public Relations Assn. Inc., Market Place, Blenheim, P.O. Box 199. Telephone: (057) 84480

Drive east from Nelson to Havelock and take the scenic Queen Charlotte Drive across to Picton. If time permits, use Havelock as a base for exploring the Sounds by mail-boat, or take the Kenepuru road from Linkwater past the Portage, around the shores of Kenepuru Sound across to Manaroa on Pelorus Sound. Wild swans and wading birds live in profusion along the estuaries.

The last 20 kilometres (12 miles) of the road from Linkwater to Picton winds along the coast of Queen Charlotte Sound through bush with spectacular views of the deep blue waters of the Sound.

Picton

Once the rival of Blenheim for capital of the old Marlborough Province, Picton is a quiet, picturesque village, a centre for water-based recreation at the head of Queen Charlotte Sound. A summer yachting and cruising paradise for New Zealanders, Picton is also the rail head into the South Island from the inter-island ferries.

Blenheim Wairau Valley

Blenheim's original name of Beaver, because of a flood experienced by an early party of surveyors, belies its position as the 'sunshine capital'. However, local vintners aim to capitalise on this climatic advantage. The most extensive acreage of grapes in New Zealand is planted in the Wairau Valley. This valley is part of the earthquake-faulted landscape that extends north across Cook Strait to Wellington. Before the big earthquake of 1848, the area at the river mouth was noted as birding ground by the Maoris.

Lake Grassmere

Before reaching the wild seascape of the Kaikoura coastline, the eye is struck by the pale pink and red ponds of Lake Grassmere. These are evaporation ponds for salt-making; the brine becoming strained reddish-pink by microbes as it concentrates.

Around Kaikoura stop and enjoy freshly cooked crayfish, advertised 'at the gate' on the roadside.

Gem Resort
Bay of Many Coves
PO Box 85
Picton
Telephone: Picton Sounds 39-245
Hosts: Ruth and David McConnell

In the heart of the Marlborough Sounds, beautiful gateway to the South Island, lies Gem Resort, amid unspoiled bushclad hills, clean and sparkling water and magnificent shoreline. The only access to this retreat is by launch or floatplane from Picton, 20 kilometres (12½ miles) away, and it remains a well-kept secret to honeymooners, families and fishermen who steal away from it all for some peace and relaxation. Facilities include cabins, share or private ablution and cooking amenities, a well-stocked general store, small boats, canoes and outboard motors for hire, and charter sightseeing, fishing and diving trips – with gear supplied by arrangement. You will be met in Picton and taken to the resort by launch. Note: accommodation is on hillside and may be unsuitable for elderly or disabled. From $30 double per night as per requirements.

Portage Hotel
Marlborough Sounds
R.H.C. Reservations:
Telephone: (03) 799-127/6
(USA: 800-874-7207)
Telex: NZ 4051 RHCHOT
(USA: 8874486)

The Portage Hotel in the Marlborough Sounds, not unlike the Mediterranean Coast, is only a floatplane or ferry ride from Wellington, or launch trip from Picton. This resort is a favourite spot for small groups, conferences or individuals seeking company or solitude. The fishing, swimming, tennis, launch trips around the Sounds and lounging about are as perfect as you could find. Hosts: Graham Kain and his wife Thelma. Cost: from $58 per night (including dinner and breakfast).

Nelson — Marlborough

SEE ALSO:

NZ Historic Places: Fyffe House (Kaikoura).

South to Christchurch or Westland via Nelson Lakes

The Nelson Lakes' National Park area (see the National Parks section) is one of New Zealand's undiscovered scenic jewels. The beautiful alpine lakes of Rotoiti and Rotoroa, the source of the Buller River, nestle at the foot of the northernmost reaches of the Southern Alps. Both summer and winter activities are available. Good walking tracks and huts are serviced by the park board. A range of activities are possible, though few are commercially developed – it's mainly a do-it-yourself area. Fishing, hunting (permits to be obtained from park headquarters), tramping, mountaineering, white-water rafting and also skiing. There is a choice of two small ski fields: Mt Robert – August/September, weekends and school holidays (check with park headquarters, St Arnaud, Phone 806); Rainbow Valley – a new field, partially developed, offers a wide range of terrain and magnificent views over the Rainbow Valley, Lake Rotoiti, the Waimea and Wairau Valleys.

For an action-packed holiday, this facility offers great variety. From your base at Alpine Lodge, where you can enjoy luxury and great cooking, go skiing, transported by four-wheel-drive vehicle to Mount Robert or Rainbow Valley (August/September). Try guided trout fishing in nearby rivers and Lake Rotoiti, or lake exploring by water taxi. Hunt for small game (rabbit and quail) or for red deer and chamois, with guide. Try the excitement of white-water rafting on the Buller River. There is tramping and mountaineering to suit all ages and experience. Popular trips of four to six days through valleys with alpine passes (guides available). Enjoy a farm visit with sheep dogs working, pony rides for children and Devonshire teas served at a homestead set in acres of beautiful gardens. From $80 to $120 per day (meals/activities).

Alpine Lodge, (Rotoiti)
C/- Post Office
St Arnaud
Nelson Lakes
Telephone: (05436) 869
Host: Mr Bill Mitchell

SEE ALSO:

Lodges: Alpine Lodge (St Arnaud), Lake Rotoroa Lodge (Rotoroa).
National Parks: Nelson Lakes National Park.

Westland is a region apart, a wild land separated from the rest of the South Island by high mountains. A climate of heavy rainfall creates distinctive dense forests and the freshest air and water.

Nikau. *(Dept of Lands & Survey)*

Huge waterwheel used for machinery operation in the Reefton Quartz Mine. ***(Courtesy West Coast Historical Museum)***

The winter is relatively mild with clear fine days and settled weather. As the rain falls mostly at night, the coast matches Auckland for sunshine hours. But don't forget your raincoat. The mood, the manner, the style of Westland are distinctly its own. Learn that many of the early settlers were Irish, bringing their own national characteristics to the coast, and you will understand that the idiosyncracies and charm of the coast are more than geographical.

Between the mountains and the sea, the habitable land is never more than 50 kilometres (30 miles) wide. Towns and villages that lie by river mouths have often diminished in size from boom towns of gold -- or coal-mining days – see deserted, once-thriving gold towns at Charleston and Barrytown, former coal-mining towns at Denniston and Stockton. Gold changed this countryside. In three years after 1864, the population climbed to 30,000 and Hokitika became the busiest port in the colony.

In limestone country at the north of the region the erosion of wind and sea has created weird coastal shapes at Punakaiki. Ashore, startling gorges of deep green forest sweep inland where there are deep and often unexplored caves.

All along the coast, low-level forest with nikau palms, tree ferns, toi toi grasses and flax alternates with areas of pasture and wasteland known as pakihi, a local peculiarity created by the interaction of decomposing vegetation and the high rainfall. Behind lie rain forests with rimu, miro, beech and southern rata, rising to forests of mountain beech that reach up into the snowcapped peaks of the alps.

It is a land of grey mists, ink-dark rain clouds, white snow, fresh green forests and ice-blue glaciers. The Franz Josef and Fox Glaciers, in the Westland National Park, plunge from heights of 2,600 metres (8,530 feet) to near sea level, fringed by green tree ferns in the lower reaches.

There are beautiful small lakes all along this West Coast, all abundant with brown trout and salmon – Lakes Mauapiurika, Paringa, Ianthe, Wahapo. Bird life is also abundant – fantails, tuis, greywarblers, bellbirds, weka, wood pigeons – and includes a variety of sea-birds – black-backed and black-billed gulls, blue and black shags, oyster catchers and occasionally Australian gannets and caspian terns.

At the one-time boom town of Charleston, there's an operating goldmine, still using an original stamp battery, but the town's 80 hotels have long gone. Visit Shantytown to the south of Greymouth for a splendid reconstruction of a gold-mining town.

In Hokitika, visit the West Coast Historical Museum, which emphasises gold-mining history, and nearby see the old Blue Spur Gold Mines with hand-dug shafts reaching deep into the hillsides.

Greenstone, the local name for nephrite jade, was sought by Maori tribes, who risked perilous journeys over the alps from all parts of the country to gather greenstone around Hokitika. It was used to make adzes, chisels, weapons and ornaments. Today, boulders of greenstone are brought out of the rugged mountain valleys by helicopter to factories in Hokitika. Visitors can watch the process that turns rocks into jewellery.

In a region of fast mountain rivers, high alps, thick forests and tranquil lakes, there are countless opportunities for climbing, tramping, fishing and hunting.

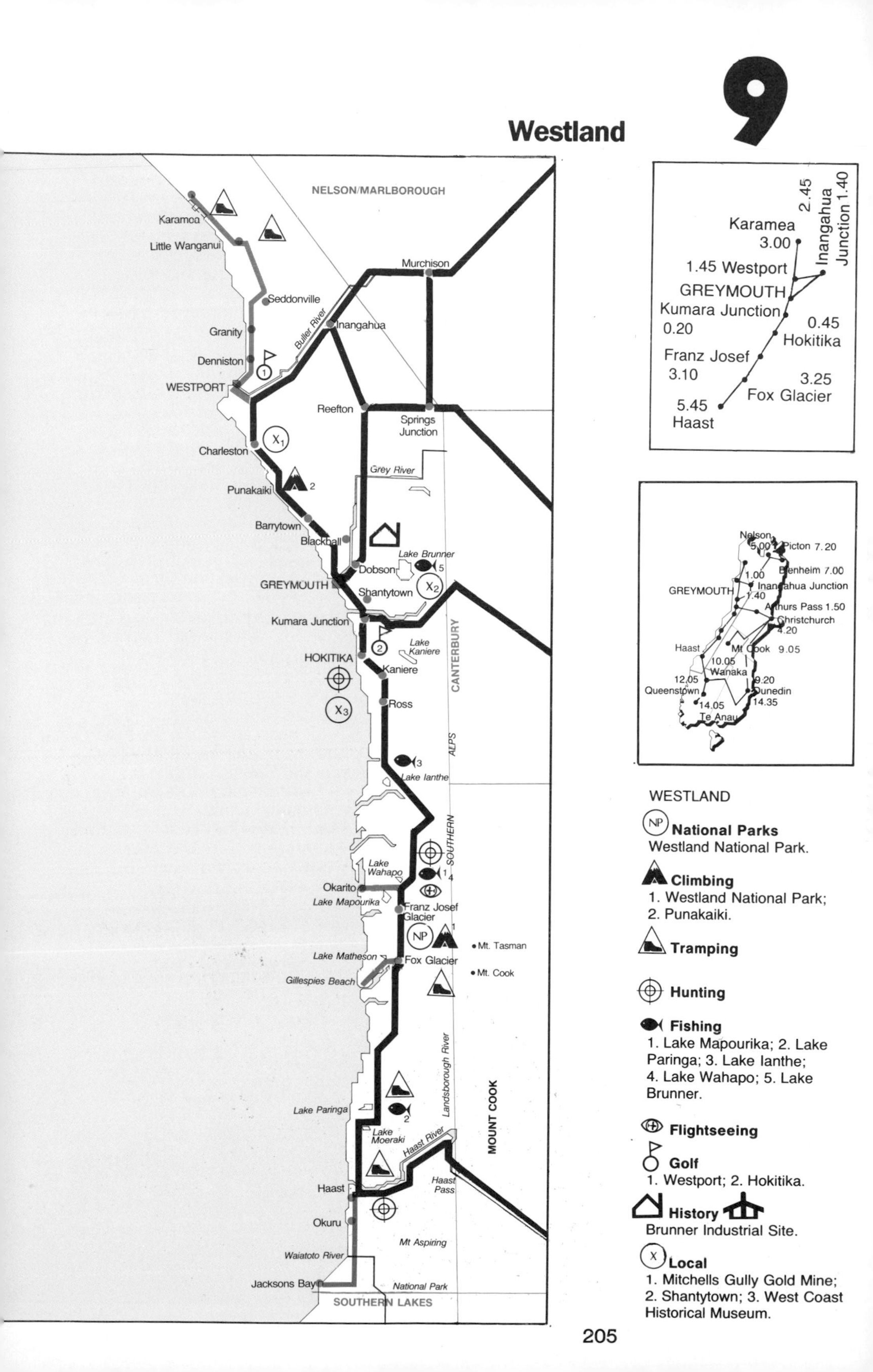

Westland
9
NELSON/MARLBOROUGH
Karamea
Little Wanganui
Seddonville
Granity
Denniston
WESTPORT
Buller River
Murchison
Inangahua
Reefton
Springs Junction
Charleston
Punakaiki
Grey River
Barrytown
Blackball
Lake Brunner
Dobson
GREYMOUTH
Shantytown
Kumara Junction
Lake Kaniere
HOKITIKA
Kaniere
Ross
CANTERBURY
Lake Ianthe
SOUTHERN ALPS
Lake Wahapo
Okarito
Lake Mapourika
Franz Josef Glacier
Mt. Tasman
Lake Matheson
Fox Glacier
Mt. Cook
Gillespies Beach
Landsborough River
MOUNT COOK
Lake Paringa
Lake Moeraki
Haast River
Haast
Haast Pass
Okuru
Mt Aspiring
Waiatoto River
National Park
Jacksons Bay
SOUTHERN LAKES
Karamea 3.00
2.45 Inangahua Junction 1.40
1.45 Westport
GREYMOUTH
Kumara Junction 0.20
0.45 Hokitika
Franz Josef 3.10
3.25 Fox Glacier
5.45 Haast
Nelson 5.00
Picton 7.20
Blenheim 7.00
1.00
Inangahua Junction 1.40
Arthurs Pass 1.50
Christchurch 4.20
Haast
Mt Cook 9.05
10.05 Wanaka
12.05 Queenstown
9.20 Dunedin 14.35
14.05 Te Anau
WESTLAND
National Parks
Westland National Park.
Climbing
1. Westland National Park; 2. Punakaiki.
Tramping
Hunting
Fishing
1. Lake Mapourika; 2. Lake Paringa; 3. Lake Ianthe; 4. Lake Wahapo; 5. Lake Brunner.
Flightseeing
Golf
1. Westport; 2. Hokitika.
History
Brunner Industrial Site.
Local
1. Mitchells Gully Gold Mine; 2. Shantytown; 3. West Coast Historical Museum.

West Coast

Banking: Before leaving Hokitika, ensure you have good cash reserves. There are no banks at Fox Glacier or Franz Josef and other small areas. Petrol: Available only at main service villages (Haast, Fox Glacier, Franz Josef Glacier) and towns (Hokitika, Westport, Karamea).

Greymouth, Hokitika and Around

The town of Greymouth is not large, although it is the most populated centre on the west coast. Squeezed between hills, sea and river, it began as a government depot for surveyors, and developed into a river port as gold, coal and then timber were brought down from the hills. It's a functional town that grew to serve the needs of gold miners, coal miners and bushmen in an area where life can be harsh.

From the end of the breakwater at the southern mouth of the Grey River, the surf can be seen crashing along the curving coastline with the alps sweeping into the distance behind. The Grey and its surrounding rivers, streams and lakes, such as the beautiful bush-fringed Lake Brunner, offer superb fishing for brown trout.

Travel up the Grey Valley to the former coal town of Blackball – on a misty day the town has a bleakness that accentuates the hard life of miners on the coast. Buy a gold-pan in Greymouth and head off up the Grey Valley at Moonlight Creek and up the Moonlight Valley for picnics, stream swimming and gold panning. At Reefton, an old gold-mining town surrounded by wooded hills, walks lead to old mines along former packhorse trails and by boulder-strewn streams where old batteries lie rusting. In Reefton's town museum, in an old church, the history of the town and its quartz mines are detailed. At Reefton's School of Mines Museum there's an excellent exhibition of the coast's mineral wealth – gold, coal, garnets, uranium, mica are all found in Westland.

West Coast Historical Museum
Tancred Street
Hokitika
PO Box 155
Telephone: Hokitika 418

Excellent display of authentic gold-mining equipment and West Coast goldfields history dating from 1864-5. A superb 20-minute audio-visual programme has been installed in a seated theatre, bringing this era to life. Friendly and knowledgeable staff welcome your questions. Allow 40 minutes' viewing time to appreciate this facility. August-May: open weekdays 9.30 a.m. – 4.30 p.m.; weekends, 2.00 p.m. – 4.00 p.m. Note: Times vary June and July. From $1.50, adults, .50c children. Group discounts.

Lake Brunner, Westland. *(Andris Apse Ltd)*

West Coast Public Relations Information Centre,
Corner MacKay & Herbert Streets,
Greymouth,
P.O. Box 95.
Telephone: (027) 5101

Westland

Just 11 kilometres (7 miles) from Greymouth is Shantytown, a unique replica of a West Coast gold-mining town at the turn of last century, complete with sluicing claim. As you approach the entrance and reception building you'll see the massive thirty-foot, overshot water wheel. An 0-6-0 side tank locomotive and an American geared "Climax" steam engine operate on a railway line, which threads its way through the beautiful native bush surrounds. On the main street, 'Memory Lane', see many interesting historical buildings, including a licensed restaurant and tearooms. A horse-drawn vehicle operates most fine days but the stage coach operates only in school holidays. Great fun for all the family. Bookings not required. Entry fee: $2 adults, 50c children. Gold panning $2 per head. Train rides less than $1. NZR Road Services bus six days per week from Hokitika and Greymouth.

Shantytown
C/- Post Office Shantytown
Via Greymouth
Telephone: (02726) 634
Hosts: The West Coast Historical and Mechanical Society Inc.

Watch skilled Swedish craftsmen blowing and forming objects of beauty from clear and coloured glass. Many pieces are free form and there is a wide range of colours used. All pieces are available for sale in the showroom. Glass blowing occurs weekdays only (7.30 a.m. to 4.00 p.m.); only the showroom is open Saturday 9.30 a.m. – 5.00 p.m. During June – August hours are 7.30 a.m. to 5 p.m. weekdays and 9.30 a.m. to 3.00 p.m. Saturdays.

Hokitika Free Form Glass Factory
130 Revell Street
Hokitika
PO Box 185
Telephone: Hokitika 1261
Hosts: Ove Janson & Mike Coll

A unique working gold-recovery system, this operational goldmine offers an educational look into the past, with bush walks, miles of original tunnels and test shafts, and a water-driven stamping battery producing on ounce of gold weekly. Twenty-two kilometres south of Westport on State Highway 6, the mine is open daily. Cost: Adults-$2, Children-.50c.

Mitchell's Gully Goldmine
C/- Post Office
Charleston
Telephone: 6804 (after hours)
Hosts: Valentine and Carol Currie

Entertainment. – On the coast you go to the pub. The pubs of Westland are a legend – in the days of 6 p.m. closing the licensing laws were blithely ignored. The laws have changed but the atmosphere of the pubs hasn't.

Hokitika Public Relations Office,
29 Weld Street,
Hokitika,
P.O. Box 171.
Telephone: Hokitika 1115

Most of the land on the west coast is publicly owned (except for the fertile river valleys and coastal plains). Entry permits are not required for public land unless you want to hunt.

Mist can descend quickly on this plateau; take care when exploring. As well, do not go out on to the glaciers without a guide.

A variety of walking tracks around Fox Glacier introduce glacial phenomena and Westland's rain forest. Lake Matheson offers outstanding forest walks and the most famous of reflections. Some of the major peaks of the Southern Alps – including Mt Cook and Mt Tasman – are captured in the mirror of the lake's black waters. Walk around the lake in 1 hour 20 minutes. ***(Andris Apse Ltd)***

North of Greymouth to Karamea

Again, this is a land apart – forest-clad mountains, extensive basins of lowland forest rich in native bird life, swamp lands, desolate coal plateau, plummeting gorges and endless sandy beaches; and the area around Karamea has a subtropical micro-climate. Take the Heaphy Track, one of New Zealand's most popular walks, 70 kilometres (45 miles) long, towards Collingwood. This is a four-day walk, which begins along the beaches and luxuriant subtropical, lowland forest. The track climbs through beech forest and the subalpine tussock grasslands of the Gouland Downs.

In the fertile, sheltered basins near Little Wanganui, find some of the largest rimu, kahikatea, matai and beech trees in the country (well over 5 metres or 16 feet in girth).

Denniston, located 600 metres (1,969 feet) above sea level on the distinctive coal plateau, is good base for exploring the old coal workings. Of particular note is the Denniston 'incline', now being restored. An engineering feat in its time, this almost perpendicular rail track delivered coal to the coast. Once a thriving town of 3,000 people in 1910, it is now almost a ghost town.

The Granity-Millerton area combines the working Stockton mine with the history of past efforts. The drive to Millerton passes a burning mine covering 81 hectares (200 acres), which has resisted all attempts to extinguish it over 70 years.

For Summer Guided Walks programmes (January), contact Department of Lands and Survey, Government Buildings, Palmerston Street, Westport. Telephone 7869.

Charming Creek Walkway (32 kilometres (20 miles) north of Westport): follow an old bush-railway through bush between Ngakawau and Seddonville and see some of the finest scenery in the North Buller – rugged country, high bluffs, immense boulders and the spectacular Mangatini Falls. This is part of the National Walkway system, suitable for family groups. About 3 hours.

The Glaciers – Westland National Park

Franz Josef

The great ice wall of the Franz Josef makes an almost impenetrable barrier to those wishing to walk onto the glacier. However, the five hour THC walk to this grand glacier, climbing up the valley floor, is most rewarding. Daily heli-hikes and ski planes provide plenty of opportunity to do so.

Excellent walks from 5 minutes to 4 hours include: Sentinel Rock – 5 minutes to a spectacular view of the Glacier Valley Terrace; Tatare Track – an hour walk climbing the terrace behind the village to visit a sluice face and gold-mining relics; Alex Knob – 4 hours, 1,290 metres (4,230 feet), a moderate climb through lowland and subalpine forest to alpine grasslands and herb fields. Superb views of glaciers, mountains, forest and sea coast.

The glaciers can be visited with ease – visitors' centres at the National Park's headquarters at both glaciers are well stocked with valuable information, maps, and, in the evenings, offer illustrated lectures on the geological history of their area.

Fox Glacier

Dominating the valley – a breathtaking panorama of mountains and snowfields towering above the deep green bush – is the huge white tongue of the Fox Glacier. There is easy access by road, though stop and take time. Take a guide and walk onto the glacier – one of the few opportunities in the world to do this so easily. Try the 10-minute heli-flight, which leaves from the village, over the glacier.

A glow-worm grotto – a short 10-minute walk just south of the village – and Gillespies Beach, where gold and gemstones are to be found in the black sands; seals add to the bevy of natural attractions. For other activities, try hunting, fishing and mountaineering.

Note: It is dangerous to walk onto the glacier without a guide.

Punga Lodge
PO Box 23
Franz Joseph Glacier
Westland
Telephone: Franz Josef Glacier 721
Host: Derek Williams

Fishing and hunting safaris arranged to some of the best locations on the West Coast. Try lake fishing: Lake Mapourika (quinnat) salmon, sea/run salmon, brown trout: Lake Paringa (sea-run salmon, brown trout); Lake Wahapo (brown trout) – or river fishing with spinner or fly. Guides, boats, rods and transport supplied. To really get off the beaten track, heli-fishing will take you to a complete wilderness. Hunting safaris for red deer, chamois and thar arranged on request. For those who like the wilderness without hunting or fishing, scenic photographic tramping trips are offered. A good way to find the spots only the locals know about. Personal car tours can also be arranged including Franz Josef, Fox Glacier and Lake Mathieson. If desired Gillespies Beach seal colony and Okarito Beach can be included. Costs on enquiry.

When visiting National Parks, always report to the park headquarters for information and inform them of your plans to go into the park; check road conditions also. For further information contact: Lands and Survey, Westland District Office, Sewell Street, P.O. Box 123, Hokitika, Phone 585. Forest Service, Central District H.Q., Weld Street, P.O. Box 138, Hokitika, Phone 1224.

South of Haast settlement is the west coast 'in the raw'. Along each side of a flat, treeless, straight road, between sand dunes and a swamp, is a classic exhibition of recent ramshackle architecture – none of it spoiled by footpaths or kerbs. Bleached peeling wood, iron, desolate yards, the odd upturned can

This is not a 'ghost town'. Stop and talk to the garage manager (who left university to return to the family business) and he will introduce you to the store manager, Ian, who left the Orkney Islands 22 years ago. If you're interest in staying, Ian will tell you where and how to fish, surf cast or whitebait. And note: Haast is famous for whitebait (see food section).

The commercial fishermen at Jacksons Bay may even take you out crayfishing. It's a harsh pioneering area, with a history of past settlers, like the German and Polish families whose dreams were lost in the Smoothwater River Valley in 1878 (now a walking track 1 kilometre (½ mile) before reaching Jacksons Bay).

Seal, blue penguins and Fiordland crested penguins inhabit rocky portions of the coast. Rimu and kahikatea dominate the forest around Haast, giving way to silver and mountain beech in Jacksons Bay. The exception to the scrubby vegetation of the pakihi flats is a forest of kowhai just south of the Haast Hotel – masses of yellow flowers each spring.

Waitangi River, near Haast, Westland. *(Andris Apse Ltd)*

DB Westland Hotel
2 Weld Street
Hokitika
Telephone: Hokitika 411
Telex: NZ 4310

This warm, comfortable hotel offers a choice of 35 rooms to suit your needs. A lounge bar has open log fires, and there is a choice of bistro or à la carte meals served in the restaurant from 6.00 a.m. – 9.30 p.m. daily. On Friday and Saturday nights a disco is held – the focal point of the town's social scene – where you can meet the locals. From $15 (single) to $40 (double). Budget single rooms from $10.

The Seafood Shop
51 Weld Street
Hokitika
Telephone: Hokitika 1644
Owners: Gary and Hendrika Searle

Select your favourite fish or try something new from this display. Gary and Hendrika will cook it for you, or you can prepare it yourself in a favourite seafood recipe. The shop also provides a complete range of New Zealand shellfish, cooked or raw (crayfish, scallops, oysters, mussels and paua). International travellers have commented on this seafood's freshness. Have your own fishing trophy cleaned or cooked for you here. Located on the main street.

Westland

Accommodation. – Some hunting and fishing lodges; THC hotel at Franz Josef; motor inns, motels, old hotels (and West Coast old hotels often look battered as well as aged), guesthouses; youth hostels at Greymouth, Franz Josef and a shelter hostel at Okarito (a swamp reserve renowned for nesting white herons and royal spoonbills); camping grounds.

Food. – If you are in Westland between September and November, feast on whitebait – tiny delicacies caught at river mouths, generally served in a fritter. Also try local venison. With few exceptions, meals on the coast are likely to be old-fashioned grills or roasts, not cordon bleu.

Charleston

European Hotel and Tavern
Highway 6
Charleston
PO Box 285, Westport.
Telephone: (0289) 7504
Host: Kevin Sheldon

This licensed hotel has offered friendly Westland hopitality to travellers for over 100 years. Overlooking the ocean, the hotel has eight units (double and twin), each equipped with refrigerator, toast- and tea/coffee-making facilities, colour television, heating and radio. A restaurant provides simple meals at excellent prices, with a choice of two bars. From $35 (two persons), children half rates. 20% reduction June – 15 August.

Greymouth

Ashley Motor Inn
74 Tasman Street
Greymouth
Telephone: (027) 5135
Telex: NZ 4927

This lovely facility is located just 3 kilometres (2 miles) from Greymouth town centre, just off the main south highway, and offers the ultimate in comfort amid quiet and relaxing surroundings. Accommodation consists of 61 self-contained units (including 15 with full kitchen facilities), four executive suites and six family units. They are all attractively furnished, with telephone, colour television, music, tea/coffee-making facilities, heating, power and shaving points and easy chairs. Choice of units from bedsitters (sleeping two) to five-star suites. accommodating up to six persons. These latter have spacious lounge rooms, with separate double and single bedrooms. Additional amenities include a licensed restaurant with comprehensive à la carte menu, house bar, enclosed heated swimming pool, spa pool and sauna, and a fully equipped guest laundry. From $38 (single), $48 (twin).

Kings' Motor Hotel
Mawhera Quay
PO Box 80
Greymouth
Telephone: (027) 5085
Telex: NZ 4279

Owned by the King family and renowned for providing excellent accommodation, this is the town's social centre (meet 'locals' in any of three bars). Waterfront location; offers superb suites or well-appointed, tastefully furnished budget rooms at reasonable rates. Facilities include guest and valet laundry service, spa and sauna, on-site shopping, plus parking. Excellent restaurant caters to all requirements, from local seafoods and grills, to coffee shop and children's menu.

South Beach Motel
318 Main South Road
Greymouth
Telephone: (02726) 768
Hosts: Bev and John Patchett

Centrally situated for visits to Shantytown, forest walkways, historic goldfields, plus excellent surf casting, beachcombing and trout fishing; the South Beach motel is 5 kilometres (2 miles) from Greymouth. Adjacent to the ocean beach in a quiet country setting, offering 10 fully self-contained family units, including a waterbed suite and paraplegic unit. Additional facilities include laundry, barbecue area and electric blankets. Breakfasts available. Tavern, store and restaurant close by. From $32 double.

Glacier View Motel
PO Box 22
Franz Josef Glacier
Telephone: Franz Josef Glacier 705
Owners: Peter and Lee Nolan

In spacious and peaceful grounds beside the Tatare stream, 2 kilometres (1½ miles) north of Franz Josef this motel offers 13 fully self-contained units (choice of one or two bedrooms) and a Honeymoon Suite. Facilities include colour television, central heating, electric blankets, food supplies and souvenir shopping, games room, spa pool and squash racquets for hire. Breakfasts are available. Courtesy transport is offered from Franz Josef. From $38, children's rates.

Punga Lodge
PO Box 23
Franz Josef Glacier
Westland
Telephone: Franz Josef Glacier 721
Host: Derek Williams

Set amongst world-famous scenery, Punga Lodge offers well-appointed ensuites, spa pool, cuisine and West Coast hospitality, accommodating eight persons. Derek specialises in organising fabulous hunting and salmon- and trout-fishing trips and safaris for you. Other excursions include bush walking, ski-plane/helicopter flights to snowfields or scenic car tours viewing seal colonies and glow worms. From $20 per person, bed and breakfast. Book direct by telephone or mail, or through RHC. Major credit cards accepted.

Rata Grove Motels
Cron Street
Franz Josef Glacier
Telephone: Franz Josef Glacier 741
Hosts: Elaine and Ray Barron

Caters for the weariest of travellers with the best of home comforts and traditional West Coast hospitality. Well-appointed units are warm and close to all amenities – centrally situated in the village. The scenery is beautiful with magnificent views of snow-clad mountains from each unit. Elaine and Ray provide glacier and other sightseeing trips in a vintage car! From $38 (two persons) per night.

T.H.C. Franz Josef Resort Hotel
(2 kilometres, 1.2 miles, north of Village)
Franz Josef Glacier
Telephone: Franz Josef Glacier 719

This T.H.C. Hotel offers top-class accommodation in a luxurious native bush setting. Featured highlights are the splendid viewing gallery (for coffee breaks) and the fern room, a fully licensed restaurant renowned for its excellent cuisine, specialising in legendary West Coast whitebait, mussel chowder, venison steaks and other delicious dishes. Cost: young children free, rooms from $53 to $71 (double). Book through Southern Pacific Hotel Corporation, Travelodge, Hotelex, Flag Inns or travel agent.

DA's Restaurant
Franz Josef Glacier
Westland
Telephone: 721

For the hungry traveller with time to stop and relax, or no time to waste, DA's Restaurant is open until late every day. It offers full meals – with specialities such as venison and seafood – in addition to a wide range of take-out foods and a coffee shop. Bring your own wine. The reasonable prices and informal atmosphere make this restaurant a must when you are visiting Franz Josef Glacier.

Glacier Motors Ltd
Franz Josef Glacier
Telephone: Franz Josef Glacier 725
Owner:Brian McLennan

Open seven days a week, all year round, this service facility will ensure motoring is a pleasure. The garage offers full mechanical services, staffed by an A-grade mechanic. A 24-hour breakdown service is available, and all requirements from petrol and oil to tyres, spare parts and accessories are stocked. Brian is also a sub-agent for Avis Rent A Car and can organise local sightseeing trips.

Glacier Store and Tearooms
PO Box 8
Franz Josef Glacier
Telephone: Franz Josef Glacier 731
Hosts: Ralph Fegan and Lynne Wyber

These lovely alpine-style tearooms offer ideal refreshments: fresh-brewed tea and coffee, hot soup, pies and savouries, danish pastries, deliciously different sandwiches and a range of cakes. The accompanying general store caters for all requirements, supplying food, outdoor clothing (woollen and wet-weather gear), hardware supplies, stationery, haberdashery, fresh seasonal fruit and vegetables. Clean toilet facilities available. Open every day (along with souvenir shop), all year through, from 7.45 a.m. to 6.30 p.m.

Westland

Fox Glacier

Owned and operated by descendants of early New Zealand pioneers, this hotel offers 'home away from home' comfort. Well appointed with central heating, open log fires, and a games room for your leisure enjoyment. The restaurant serves an interesting *table d'hôte* menu and is open for casual diners as well as hotel guests. Arrangements made on request for excursions to Fox Glacier and Lake Matheson. From $41.

Fox Glacier Hotel
PO Box 1
Fox Glacier
Telephone: Fox Glacier 839
Telex: NZ 4356

An informal, relaxed holiday experience, amid the scenic grandeur of New Zealand's spectacular glacier region. The 51 comfortable and modern guest rooms are equipped with ensuite facilities, and the hotel is centrally heated throughout. There is a private guest lounge, a sumptuous cocktail bar, and a restaurant which highlights local specialities such as tender venison and delicious whitebait. From $55 single. Major credit cards accepted.

Vacation Inn Fox Glacier
Main Highway
Fox Glacier
PO Box 32
Telephone: Fox Glacier 847
Telex: NZ 4212

Lake Paringa

At beautiful Lake Paringa 70 kilometres (43 miles) south of Fox Glacier and 50 kilometres (31 miles) north of Haast, this motel offers brown trout and salmon fishing, bush walks, hire boats and canoes, plus shop and restaurant serving refreshments or full meals. Variety of accommodation, well appointed with heating, electric blankets, double or single beds and showers, some with kitchenette. Services operate year through. From $30 double. Off-season rates June to September, no charge toddlers.

Lakeside Motels
Private Bag
Hokitika
Telephone: Fox Glacier 894
Hosts: Toni and Ron Hoglund

Haast

In lovely South Westland, this company offers all you need for a great holiday – accommodation in the friendly atmosphere of a nine-unit, spacious, well-appointed motel, plus a store (open any time for guests) providing food, outdoors clothing, outfitting for fishing and hunting adventures, sporting information, licences and ammunition. In addition, a garage offers a 24-hour breakdown service, spare parts and A-grade mechanical servicing. Motel units from $35 per night, bedsitters (single) from $25.

Erewhon Motel
South Westland Tourist Services Ltd
Haast
Telephone: Haast 825
Hosts: June and Shane Johnston

Offering inexpensive accommodation in lovely surroundings, this facility has 34 caravan/campervan sites, 15 cabins of differing grades, one fully equipped 'tourist' flat and a bunkroom. Facilities include two communal kitchens, shower blocks, automatic laundry and camp store. Fishing tackle/whitebait nets available and bed linen can be hired. From $6 (tent site, two persons) to $16 (cabin, two persons).

Haast Motor Camp
Haast
South Westland
Telephone: Haast 860
Hosts: Brian and Phillippa Glubb

Situated on a private farm, beside a river and close to the ocean, 13 kilometres (8 miles) from the Haast turn-off and 1 kilometre (½ mile) left from the Okuru Bridge. Offers three large units, spacious bedsitters, and one double bedsitter. Comfortable, heated and well-appointed. Ideal stop for fishermen (surf casting and fly, trout and whitebait). Bush walks, farm animals, trampoline, rods and whitebait nets available for use. From $32 double, $3 children.

Riverside Motel
C/- Post Office
Haast
Telephone: Haast 814
Host: Des Nolan

SEE ALSO:

Hunting: Westland Guiding Service (Fish).
NZ Historic Places: Brunner Industrial Site (Grey Valley).

Wide plains of wheat, high snow-capped mountains, broad rivers – the Canterbury region is New Zealand on a grand scale.

Across the plains travel roads that run straight, as far as the eye can see, over long bridges crossing tumbling, braided rivers, through crop fields and pasture land where lambs are fattened for market, the fields defined by the dark green of pine shelter belts.

Travel on into the golden-brown tussock-covered foothills of the alps. Here are the sheep stations – much larger than most other New Zealand farms and often isolated with a self-contained way of life. Visit Mt Peel, where the grand homestead is set among spreading 100-year-old English trees – the stone family church is open to visitors. Nearby is Peel Forest Park, an unusual pocket of forest in a tussock landscape, with ferns growing thickly under the shelter of matai, totara and kahikatea. Also close by is Orari Gorge Station, a cluster of restored station buildings including an impressive 1862 homestead, 1859 cottage and smithy.

Molesworth, the largest of the stations, spreads for 1,800 square kilometres, (450,000 acres) straddling the northern boundary of the Canterbury region and the Nelson-Marlborough region. On the station's southern perimeter is Hanmer Springs, a nineteenth-century spa that today offers visitors horseback riding, jet boating, skiing, trout fishing, golf, tennis, walks in a magnificent forest of deciduous trees, as well as hot-spring bathing and crisp mountain air.

The mountains of Canterbury offer far more than spectacular alpine scenery – there's superb skiing at Mt Hutt and several less-developed ski fields, and there's excellent climbing and tramping in the Arthur's Pass National Park. The park falls across both sides of the alps, with rainforest to the west, beech forest, tussock and scree to the east. There's tramping tracks suitable for beginners or family groups and there's serious climbing for dedicated 'alpinists'. Find the park's headquarters in the mountain village of Arthur's Pass on the road that crosses to Westland.

The towns of the Canterbury plains and foothills are essentially market towns, serving the outlying farming districts. Filled with English trees – elms, oak and planes – planted last century, these leafy towns also serve the visitor. Towns such as Ashburton, Geraldine, Oxford, Waimate and the small coastal city of Timaru are all surrounded by rivers and streams that offer trout and salmon fishing, jet boating and canoeing. The farming centre of Methven also now serves as the base for the ski fields on Mt Hutt, as well as the centre for the summer and autumn activities of fishing, trotting and rodeo.

The rivers plunge down from the alps, often through dramatic gorges such as the Waimakariri Gorge or the Ashley Gorge, and then fan out across the alluvial plains in ribbons through the stones, shingle and sand of the river beds. The Rakaia River reaches 1.6 kilometres (a mile) wide on the plains, crossed by the country's longest bridge.

Huge hydro-electric power stations harness the energy of the rivers high in the tussock hills – on the Waitaki, see the immense Benmore Dam, 109 metres (357 feet) high, creating the country's largest man-made lake. Jet boats make sightseeing and fishing trips on the lake.

Other natural lakes in glacial bowls ringed by mountains offer rainbow trout and land-locked salmon for anglers and remote lake and mountain scenery for others.

Trampers pause to admire the "Devil's Punchbowl", Arthur's Pass National Park. ***(Andris Apse Ltd)***

Canterbury

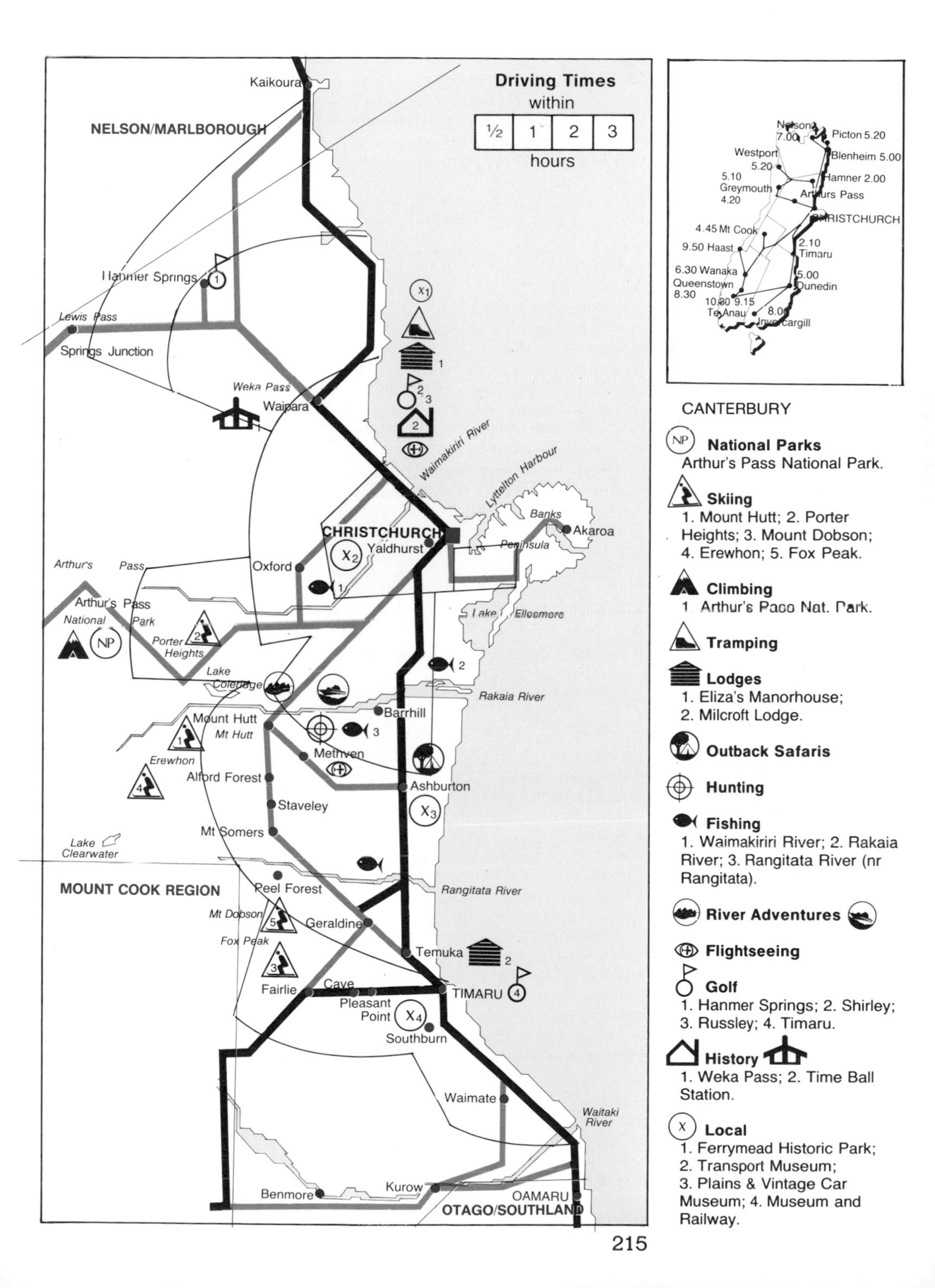

Driving Times
within
½ 1 2 3
hours
Kaikoura
NELSON/MARLBOROUGH
Hanmer Springs
Lewis Pass
Springs Junction
Weka Pass
Waipara
Waimakiriri River
Lyttelton Harbour
Banks
Peninsula
Akaroa
CHRISTCHURCH
Yaldhurst
Oxford
Arthur's Pass
Arthur's Pass
National Park
Porter Heights
Lake Ellesmere
Lake Coleridge
Rakaia River
Barrhill
Mount Hutt
Mt Hutt
Methven
Erewhon
Alford Forest
Ashburton
Staveley
Mt Somers
Lake Clearwater
MOUNT COOK REGION
Peel Forest
Rangitata River
Mt Dobson
Geraldine
Fox Peak
Temuka
Fairlie
Cave
Pleasant Point
TIMARU
Southburn
Waimate
Waitaki River
Benmore
Kurow
OAMARU
OTAGO/SOUTHLAND
Nelson 7.00
Picton 5.20
Westport 5.20
Blenheim 5.00
5.10 Greymouth 4.20
Hamner 2.00
Arthurs Pass
CHRISTCHURCH
4.45 Mt Cook
9.50 Haast
2.10 Timaru
6.30 Wanaka
Queenstown 8.30
5.00 Dunedin
10.30 9.15 Te Anau
8.00 Invercargill
CANTERBURY
National Parks
Arthur's Pass National Park.
Skiing
1. Mount Hutt; 2. Porter Heights; 3. Mount Dobson; 4. Erewhon; 5. Fox Peak.
Climbing
1. Arthur's Pass Nat. Park.
Tramping
Lodges
1. Eliza's Manorhouse; 2. Milcroft Lodge.
Outback Safaris
Hunting
Fishing
1. Waimakiriri River; 2. Rakaia River; 3. Rangitata River (nr Rangitata).
River Adventures
Flightseeing
Golf
1. Hanmer Springs; 2. Shirley; 3. Russley; 4. Timaru.
History
1. Weka Pass; 2. Time Ball Station.
Local
1. Ferrymead Historic Park; 2. Transport Museum; 3. Plains & Vintage Car Museum; 4. Museum and Railway.

Christchurch

hristchurch, the third largest city in New Zealand, is imbued with a surprising tranquillity, rare even in many smaller cities or towns. The pace is so gentle you must remember to watch for traffic and office workers. Take picnic lunches to the grassy banks of the meandering Avon River.

It is often said that Christchurch is the most 'English' city outside of England, an impression easily gained from the dominance of stone Gothic-style buildings, the willow-fringed Avon and spring daffodils flowering under the oaks in Hagley Park. Catch sight of uniformed Christ's College schoolboys wearing straw boaters, and the impression is enhanced.

The planners of Christchurch began with high aspirations for a model Church of England settlement with a carefully structured social system. Not all their hopes were realised as egalitarian ideas progressed and prevailed. However, the city still remains very aware of its origins.

Christchurch's best-known landmark is the cathedral, dominating the central square. You can't miss seeing the decorative stone Gothic-style building, inside which panels commemorate early missionaries, bishops and members of the church. Take the increasingly steep stairway up to the balcony of the bell tower for a view that reaches over the city to the distant mountains.

Traffic has now been banned from the square around the cathedral. Instead, it has become a lively area where people gather – it's the favourite haunt of the city's resident wizard. (Christchurch also has a reputation for tolerating, even encouraging, eccentricity.)

Other Gothic-style stone buildings to see include Christ's College and the Arts Centre. The Arts Centre buildings originally formed part of the University, but the University outgrew its space and moved out of town. Now the medieval-style complex arranged around two quadrangles provides accommodation for a theatre, cinema, ballet, crafts shops, restaurants and gallery.

The Provincial Government Buildings enjoy a ponderous title that gives little indication of their architectural delights – a fascinating combination of Gothic-style buildings including stone, timber and brick, and inside, ornate ceilings, stained-glass windows and mosaic walls.

However Christchurch isn't all Gothic stone. The city's Roman Catholic community branched into 'high renaissance' for their splendid basilica built at the turn of the century. In the city centre, solid Victorian buildings line up alongside modern office buildings, and on the banks of the Avon the modern town hall complex is a delightful tribute to architectural flair.

Take lunch in the Town Hall's restaurant by the Avon River – few town halls anywhere could offer a more pleasant setting and stylish design. Other examples of modern Christchurch architecture include buildings at the university and the Queen Elizabeth II Park.

Walk in Hagley Park, under the lofty trees by the river. Within the vast park are playing fields, riding tracks, woodlands and the city's botanic gardens.

Catch up with cultural pursuits at the McDougall Art Gallery, by the botanic gardens, where there are excellent exhibitions of painting, sculpture and ceramics. Next door is the Canterbury Museum – as well as Maori and pioneer history there is a splendid section devoted to Antarctic exploration and studies, in fact, the only Antarctic exhibition gallery, library and theatrette in the world. Special items on display are Scott's

**Canterbury Information Centre,
75 Worcester Street,
Christchurch,
P.O. Box 2600.
Telephone: (03)
799629**

sledge, a ski used in his 1904 expedition and Shackleton's 1914 motor sledge. The world-renowned botanic gardens also deserve particular mention. Established in 1863, the 30 hectares (75 acres) accommodate a wide variety of exotic and native species. Guided tours are run daily at 12.00 p.m. and at 4.00 p.m. in fine weather. In wet weather, visit the five conservatories housing tropical plants, cacti, ferns, succulents, native and exotic alpine and insectivorous plants.

Drive southeast out of Christchurch and over the Port Hills, or through the long road tunnel to Lyttelton (the energetic can walk the Bridle Path over the hills from Heathcote). The town spills down the steep hillside to the port below. Of special interest is the Time-ball Station, a fort-like building used until 1935, now restored and open to visitors.

Further on explore an unusual village, Akaroa. Founded in 1840, the country's only French settlement echoes its origins in French colonial buildings, place and street names. Visit particularly the Langlois-Eteveneaux House and Museum.

Entertainment. – In a city that prides itself on culture, find lively music, theatre, dance and art. Check what is offering at the Town Hall's theatres and visit the Arts Centre. Watch a cricket match, go to the races, or go to the night trotting races.

Travel around Christchurch on a rented bicycle – or try the bus service. Buses for many destinations leave near the main square. Several car-rental agencies provide sturdy four-wheel-drive vehicles for back-country touring. Flight-seeing, air charter and scheduled flights leave from Christchurch airport. Trains run north to Picton, west to Greymouth and south to Dunedin. Long-distance bus transport is by all major companies: N.Z.R. Road Services, Mt Cook Landlines, Newmans, Guthries, H & H. Plenty of organised tours available, from conventional sightseeing to high-adventure tours.

Christchurch city surrounds beautiful Hagley Park, seen here against a backdrop of the Southern Alps. ***(Andris Apse Ltd)***

Christchurch

Pacific Tourways Ltd
502A Wairakei Road
PO Box 14-037
Christchurch
Telephone: (03) 599-133

From Christchurch, enjoy a day tour to Akaroa, driving over the Cashmere Hills to Banks Peninsula with panoramas of the Canterbury Plains and Southern Alps. See the old-world French charm of New Zealand's oldest town and watch traditional cheeses being produced. A Devonshire tea is included. Half-day sightseeing tours in Christchurch are also offered in comfortable buses with courteous, knowledgable drivers. From $20 (half-day) and $38 (full day).

Ferrymead Bridge Gallery
1061 Ferry Road
Christchurch 8
Telephone: (03) 849-566, after hours, (03) 849-994
Owner: Paul O'Donnell

Just 15 minutes from the city centre, this unique art and craft shop operates from an old factory complex which made soap and candles in the late 1800s (when Ferrymead was in its zenith as a transportation centre). The gallery specialises in local pottery, arts, weaving, woodworking, furniture pieces, cane and willow basketware and crafts. Standard of work is high, the cost maintained at a very reasonable rate, and each contributing artist has a display area. Orders taken for commissioned pieces. Tea, coffee and a lounge area with open fire provided for relaxation. Pottery is created by members of the Mount Pleasant Potters group and members staff the shop on Sundays. The introduction of a working wheel and on-site kiln is planned. Open 7 days (except Good Friday and Christmas Day), 9.30 a.m. (10.00 a.m. weekends) – 5.00 p.m. Special openings arranged for groups.

Ferrymead Historic Park
269 Bridle Path Road
Heathcote
Christchurch
Telephone: (03) 843-376

One of New Zealand's largest man-made tourist attractions this complex offers 40 hectares (100 acres) of park, incorporating a vintage township plus museums of yesteryear's vehicles and equipment, all operational! Several collections are of world-standing – for example, 'The Hall of Flame' (with 45 fire engines) is reputed to be the largest and most wide-ranging collection in the world. The Kitson Steam Tram (regular mode of transport around the township) is the only one of its kind in the world. The railway operates with examples of diesel, steam and electrified systems. The 'Hall of Wheels' is an impressive collection of vintage motor cars, motor cycles and bicycles. Don't miss the Museum of Rural History, containing a working steam-driven sawmill, plus model railway, military and aeronautical displays. The 1910-vintage township is complete with everything from a printing shop and blacksmith to a bakery and tobacconist, every building open and operational! The facility had been developed for the education, recreation and pleasure of all by the Ferrymead Trust, which represents eighteen voluntary organisations and five local bodies. The area is historically important as the site of the ferries that took the Canterbury Pilgrims (walking over the Bridle Path from Lyttelton) across the Heathcote River. During the mid 1800s, the area developed as a transportation centre, with ships, coaches, ferries and a hotel. Trams operate each day, steam trains operate at weekends, during holidays or by special arrangement. Use your own transport or catch a Number 3 bus from Cathedral Square. Admission: from $2.50, adults; $1.50, children.

Yaldhurst Transport Museum
School Road
Yaldhurst
Christchurch
Telephone: (03) 427-914
Host: Grant Cooper

A superb, private family collection – vintage cars, fire engines, motor cycles, racing cars and more – in garden setting. Included is one of the Southern Hemisphere's finest collections of horse-drawn vehicles, dating from 1810. Also – gift shop, tearooms, picnic area, a Penny Arcade, plus free rides on original machines (weekends/holidays). Guides accompany large groups by arrangement. Admission: from $2.50 adults, $1 children. Group discounts available. Open daily. Suitable for wheelchairs.

Riverside Walk (90 minutes). Cathedral Square, Avon River and Victoria Square – numerous historical buildings and city features. (For guided walks, phone 68-243.)
The Bridle Path (90 minutes one way). Take the path first used by settlers travelling from Port Lyttelton to the Canterbury Plains. Start from the Christchurch end of the Lyttelton Tunnel and walk over the hills.
Coronation Hill (30 minutes). Begin at the Sign of the Kiwi, and follow the harbour around until Marleys Hill, or continue to Kennedys Bush (2 or 2½ hours return).
Quail Island in Lyttleton Harbour. A half loop (1 hour) or full (2½ hours) across grassland, wooded areas and basalt cliff tops. Once a quarantine station, it is now a pleasant retreat in this dramatic harbour landscape.

For excellent detailed information on city walks and other regional attractions, visit the Canterbury Information Centre, corner Worcester Street and Oxford Terrace. Telephone 799-629. Hours: Monday-Friday 8.30 am.-5.00 p.m.

SEE ALSO:

Lodges: Eliza's Manorhouse.
NZ Historic Places: Lyttelton Time-ball Station (Lyttelton).
National Parks: Arthurs Pass National Park (Arthurs Pass).
Tramp/Trek/Walk: Women Walk.

Waimakiriri River and the Southern Alps, North Canterbury ***(Andris Apse Ltd)***

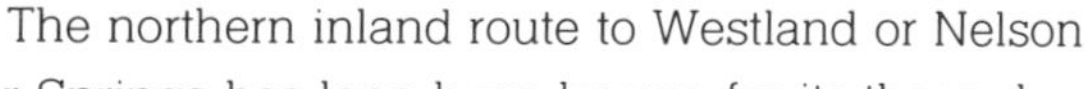

The northern inland route to Westland or Nelson

Hanmer Springs

Hanmer Springs has long been known for its thermal springs, its invigorating climate and its magnificent setting enhanced by man-made forests.

In 1859 William Jones of the St Leonard's Station found several hot springs in thick scrub near the Jollies Pass Track. The waters are saline and alkaline, and the temperature varies from 36 to 40°C. In 1883 Hanmer was declared a Government Resort and a Government Sanitorium was built in 1897, at the same time as the original Lodge Hotel. In 1916 the Queen Mary Hospital was opened.

There are many walks to choose from, in both exotic and native forest. A track leads to the top of Conical Hill, where there are excellent views of the surrounding countryside. The Mt Isobel Track is of special interest for its magnificent subalpine plants and fine panoramas. The Nature Trail and the Waterfall Track take visitors through mountain-beech forest, while the Woodland Walk and the Forest Walk are located close to the Information Centre on Jollies Pass Road, from which further information on all these walks, and a Forest Drive, may be obtained.

Ice skating on a frozen mid-Canterbury lake. ***(Courtesy Four Seasons Scenic Tours)***

South via the inland route through Methven and Mount Hutt

Nestling at the foothills of the Southern Alps, this area is rapidly developing as an all-year-round recreation area.

Access is gained by Provincial Highway 72, which runs parallel to the alps – an alternative scenic route from Christchurch, through to Mackenzie Country and Mt Cook.

Once a coach stop between Alford Forest and Rakaia, Methven doubles as the service centre for local agriculture and the summer and winter activities.

Its recent development has been assisted by the growth of the Mt Hutt Ski Field, internationally recognised as having the longest season in the Southern Hemisphere.

Within 1½ to 2 hours of Methven, there are seven other smaller club ski fields: Erewhon, Mt Dobson, Mt Olympus, Porter Heights, Mt Cheeseman, Broken River and Craigieburn.

There is, however, more than skiing. The Rakaia River, with its spectacular gorge, provides not only thrilling jet-boat rides but also some of the best salmon fishing in the country. Each February a fishing competition with $30,000 in prizes is held.

At Easter a marathon begins in Methven and finishes at Ashburton. Spring is time for the floral festival (October) and the rodeo (September), both in Methven. As the area is known for breeding some top trotting horses (many exported to the U.S.A.), enquire whether your visit coincides with one of the local trotting meetings.

Being part of the Canterbury Plains means villages and the influence of England. See little villages like Alford Forest and Staveley (where there are interesting bush walks across a swing bridge to the Sharplin Falls, skating and curling). Barrihill Village (20 kilometres (12 miles) from Methven) nestles amongst beautifully established English trees. Planned as an old English village, it has an attractive church, Church of St John, built in 1877.

Mount Hutt Country Club
PO Box 55
Methven
Telephone: (053) 28-721
Telex: NZ4997
Host: Stephen Cohen

The Country Club offers a luxurious standard of comfort and the staff's objective is to make your stay a pleasantly memorable one. Facilities include 26 ensuite rooms, superbly furnished and individually heated. A first-class restaurant provides à la carte dining and features beautifully presented New Zealand cuisine. Relax in the well-appointed bar or large lounge around the open log fire. For your convenience a spa is provided and the Country Club is right in the heart of Methven Village. For excitement – go rafting, fishing, skiing (in winter), bicycling, hunting, horse riding; play tennis, squash, bowls, croquet or golf, go tramping, jet boating; take a boat cruise or a scenic flight. All arrangements made for you. From $50 per room, depending on season/requirements. Book well in advance by letter, telephone, telex, or R.H.C. Reservations, telephone (03) 799-127/6, telex NZ 4105. A hire car service from Christchurch airport provided as required.

SEE ALSO:

Fishing: Mount Hutt Country Club.
Hunting: Mount Hutt Country Club.
Skiing: Mount Hutt Ski Field.

South via the coast – through Ashburton and Timaru

Once a stark featureless arid land of shingle fans spreading to the east from the Southern Alps, Ashburton is now the centre

of one of the country's most prosperous agriculture areas. Irrigation, wheat, sheep, cropping and determination have led to prosperity, all achieved in the past 130 years.

For the traveller, this quiet garden town offers a good base for exploring the area. The northern and southern boundaries of the county, the Rakaia and Rangitata Rivers, are nationally important angling rivers, especially for quinnat salmon (season, February and March).

In total there are 24 species of fish in these rivers. A rarity in New Zealand, American brook trout, can be found in the Hinds River, 20 minutes to the south. Try fishing for rainbow trout or land-locked salmon in Lake Clearwater.

The rugged alpine grandeur of the hinterland, up the Ashburton Gorge, past mineral-rich Mt Somers and Lake Clearwater, provides a marked contrast with the massive patchwork of paddocks and farmhouses of the plains.

Ashburton is also another trotting and horse-racing centre of considerable note.

Fishing for trout at the Rakaia River-mouth, near Ashburton. ***(Andris Apse Ltd)***

Luxury, reasonably priced motor inn, close to town centre, set in 5 hectares (12 acres) of landscaped grounds. Fifty-three well-appointed units (colour television), some with kitchens; paraplegic facilities; excellent à la carte and bistro restaurants plus full range of bars; heated pools, sauna, spa, games room, trampoline, golf course, all-weather tennis court; conference facilities; ample parking. From $40 single, off-season rates available. Book through travel agents, Instant Freeline, Best Western or direct.

Hotel Ashburton
Racecourse Road
PO Box 70
Ashburton
Telephone: (053) 83-059
Telex: NZ 4598

Re-live the past – see an old working steam railway, plus (up Maronan Road) a vintage car museum. The 'Washington' locomotive (built U.S.A. 1879) was dumped in a river in 1927. Restored, it now runs on a section of what was the original Mount Somers branch line. See old locomotives, fire engines, vintage horse-drawn agricultural machinery and tractors, printing presses and steam cranes. A rare N.Z. exhibit is the sole remaining Kemp Electric tractor (built Ashburton 1930s). Museum is operational every second Sunday from October – May.

Plains and Vintage Car Museum
Tinwald Domain
C/- PO Box 5051
Tinwald

Pastoral scene near Fairlie, South Canterbury. *(National Publicity Studios)*

Timaru

One of New Zealand's more scenic cities, set around a harbour. Close to the city centre is Caroline Bay, a safe, sandy beach with extensive lawns and gardens, play areas, tennis courts, aviary and restaurant.

The Public Relations Office has details of many scenic drives but first see the Aigantighe Art Gallery, Historical Museum and the Botanic Gardens. For relaxation there is a heated indoor and outdoor olympic pool, golf course and modern library.

The Lovelock Oak can be seen in the grounds of Timaru Boys' High School; this specimen is the only tree still standing of those given to gold medallists by Adolf Hitler at the 1936 Berlin Olympics.

A drive should include Hadlow Game Park and Pleasant Point Railway and Museum, as well as the old rock drawings of the moa hunters, signposted on the road between Cave and Southburn.

Public Relations Office,
corner Stafford and Sefton Streets, Timaru.
Telephone: (056) 86163

Skinworld
The Sheepskin Shop
200 Stafford Street
Timaru
PO Box 580
Telephone: (056) 84-811
Owner: Trevor Snook

Right in the main street of Timaru, this sheepskin shop carries a wide range of stock: natural-wool jerseys, skeepskin rugs, slippers, gloves, boots, tailored sheepskin jackets, and genuine leather goods, plus a full range of paua jewellery, souvenirs and luggage. Trevor will parcel and post anywhere in the world for you. Open weekdays from 9.00 a.m. – 5.30 p.m. (Fridays till 9.00 p.m.) and on Saturdays, from 9.30 a.m. – 12.30 p.m. After hours: telephone (056) 84-760.

Pleasant Point Museum and Railway
Pleasant Point Railway Station
near Timaru
Telephone: (056) 27354
Host: Russell Paul

Take a trip back in time to days of steam. Ride on the 'Fairlie Flyer' steam loco (AB 699), resplendent in 1920s brass livery/steam dome, running through Pleasant Point. At the 106-year-old railway station, find local historic exhibits; parts from the first aeroplane built by pioneer aviator Richard Pearse, railway equipment, printing press, old dolls, phonographs and more. Open Sundays and Public Holidays (1.30 p.m. – 4.30 p.m.). Cost: $1, adults; 50c, children.

Hadlow Game Park
Wai-iti Road
RD4
Timaru
Hosts: Bryan and Jocelyn Bassett-Smith

Set in the gentle rolling South Canterbury countryside, 10 kilometres (6 miles) from Timaru; Hadlow Game Park is a 30-hectare (74-acre) wildlife reserve. The animals are free-ranging and the design of the park permits visitors close contact with them. The collection is varied, including the largest and tamest groups of Bennetts wallabies, Himalayan thar and Captain Cook pigs in the world, plus chamois, Arapawa Island sheep and goats. Red deer, wapiti (elk) and fallow deer are also bred. Exotic species include jaguar, South American golden spider monkeys, bison and llama, plus many species of birdlife. Be sure to see the red (or lesser) panda, a gift from the People's Republic of China. It's a great place for a picnic, and for the children there is a playing area. Open all year through. From $3, adult; $1.25, child.

Food. – Excellent restaurants in Christchurch, both licensed and B.Y.O. Range includes French, Italian, Chinese, Greek and British (roast beef and Yorkshire pudding). Pub meals can be pleasant, low-cost eating. In Canterbury look for Canterbury lamb, cooked to pale-pink perfection. If lamb can't be found, don't ignore the rich flavour of hogget. (When everyone lives on lamb and hogget down on the farm, restaurants are less inclined to serve it.) Try the salmon, fresh or smoked. Discover tearooms serving delicious large afternoon teas, including scones thick with jam and cream.

Canterbury

Accommodation. – In Christchurch there are luxury to modest hotels, motor inns, motels, budget private hotels and two youth hostels. Comfortable traditional hotels and motels serve towns of the region.

This hotel is situated in the heart of the 'Garden City' of Christchurch, overlooking beautiful Victoria Square and the tranquil Avon River. Each of the 86 guest rooms and 5 suites is appointed with all facilities, including in-house video. Two fine restaurants, cocktail bars and a lounge offer excellent relaxation, wining and dining. Staff are renowned for their friendly service. Conference facilities available. From $75 single. Major credit cards accepted.

Vacation Inn
776 Colombo Street
PO Box 1896
Christchurch
Telephone: (03) 795-880
Telex: NZ4523

Treat yourself to dine in this historical home, 100 years old. The decor is tasteful period setting, candlelit, warm and cosy, enhanced by soft French background music. This is a B.Y.O. restaurant, but you are offered a complimentary sherry upon arrival. The table is yours for the evening to relax and enjoy superb à la carte French cuisine. Open daily (except Tuesday) from 7.00 p.m. Reservations essential. Medium price range.

Leinster House Restaurant
158 Leinster Road
Merivale
Christchurch
Telephone: (03) 558-866
Host: Julie Adams

In cheerful surroundings with red tablecloths and fresh flowers abounding, enjoy warm and friendly service, excellent New Zealand game food and Continental cuisine. The widely experienced chef prepares specialities like roast saddle of rabbit or the dish of the house, Pork Martini, as well as a range of superb sauces. B.Y.O. Open Monday to Saturday, casual lunching from 12.00 noon – 2.00 p.m., dining from 6.00 p.m. Supper served from 10.00 p.m. Main courses from $10. Reservations advisable.

Martini's Restaurant
128A Oxford Terrace
Christchurch
Telephone: (03) 69-363
Hosts: Lois and Rex Smith

Christchurch's leading seafood restaurant is in the city centre (near Noah's Hotel), overlooking the Avon River. Relaxed casual dining for intimate twosomes or large groups. Wide range of fresh local and imported seafood, steaks and a great salad bar. Alan even prepares/cooks your own catch by arrangement. Air-conditioned, blackboard menu – food is delicious. B.Y.O. Inexpensive, reservations not essential, but popularity makes them advisable. Credit cards accepted. Open for lunch (weekdays), dinner (Monday to Saturday).

Spratts Restaurant
182 Oxford Terrace
Christchurch
Telephone: (03) 67-817
Host: Alan Wilkie

Enjoy the 'best steak in town' in Colonial America. The staff are servant boys and wenches, complete with tricon hats and mob caps, and in a restaurant that is unique to the city, you can dine in the drawing room, scullery or stables. Service is friendly, fast and good. Fully licensed with cocktail bar, plus resident band for dancing Fridays and Saturdays. Open Tuesday to Saturday, from 6.00 p.m. Reservations advisable. Medium price range.

The Paul Revere Licensed Restaurant
813 Colombo Street
Christchurch
Telephone: (03) 799-099

This historic Gothic stone house, with its stained-glass windows and intricate wood detailing was built as a resting place for Port Hills travellers in early 1900s. Visit and learn its history (10.00 a.m. – 5.00 p.m.), enjoying Devonshire teas and smorgasbord lunches (12 noon – 2.00 p.m.). Panoramic views over the Canterbury Plains with the backdrop of the Southern Alps. At night dine in these exclusive and beautiful castle-like surrounds, enjoying great French cuisine from 7.00 p.m., Tuesday – Saturday. Evening reservations essential.

The Sign of the Takahe
Cashmere Hills
Christchurch
Telephone: (03) 324-052
Host: Mr T. Hadjichristos

SEE ALSO:

Lodges: Milcroft (Skiing) (Temuka).
Skiing: Fox Peak (Fairlie), Mount Dobson Ski Field (Fairlie).

Mt Tasman, Southern Alps. ***(Andris Apse Ltd)***

t Cook the region is mountains and more mountains. Mt Cook, the highest mountain in New Zealand at 3,764 metres (12,349 feet), and Mt Tasman are the focal points of a national park in the west of the region, and is surrounded by a further 140 peaks over 2,300 metres (7,550 feet) – a lot of mountains.

Between the mountains of the park are glaciers, great walls of ice with permanent snow covering, remnants of a time when glaciers gouged out the great valleys through the region. These glaciers include the Tasman, the largest outside the Himalayas or Antarctica, 29 kilometres (18 miles) long, 3 kilometres (1.8 miles) wide.

Outside the park there are still more mountains, great rounded mountains reminiscent of Scotland, and classic alps rising above glacial valley floors.

Travel into the region from the north and drive through long U-shaped valleys of the Mackenzie Country, named after a legendary sheep-stealer who first passed this way. It is country where hardy Merino sheep withstand the rigours of winter, beef cattle graze, and great steel pylons carry electricity across country from hydro-electric schemes.

It is also country where the lakes have a startling beauty. From the north one suddenly arrives at Lake Tekapo and the burst of colour is a visual shock – a brilliant opaque turquoise, edged with grey shingle and red-brown tussock with a backdrop of snowy mountains sprawling across the horizon.

On the shore of the lake the tiny Church of the Good Shepherd stands alone between the road and the lake, looking out across the serenity of water and mountains. Enter the church and find the window behind the altar is clear glass, a recognition that nature here provides more than stained glass could ever achieve. To appreciate the effect at its best, visit the church in the early morning or late afternoon when the interior is shadowy but the lake and mountains etched in brilliant light.

It is an area of clear light and cloudless skies, so much so that at nearby Mt John high above the lake there is an international observatory and also a United States satellite-tracking station.

Whether approaching from the north or from the south, the road to Mt Cook village takes the traveller by Lake Pukaki, another milky blue-green lake. From the eastern end of the lake the view leads up the glacial valley along the lake to the Southern Alps, rising in a cluster around Mt Cook – at times the mountains are mirrored perfectly in the lake waters. The lakes Pukaki, Tekapo and Ohau all occupy the end of glacial valleys, drawing their water from the glaciers above. Fine dust, ground by the action of the glaciers and held in suspension by the lake waters, is responsible for the remarkable colours.

Skiing is one of the region's major attractions, with diverse skiing possibilities. At Mt Cook there's glacier skiing, ski planes, heli-skiing, alpine ski-mountaineering, downhill ski touring and, especially in spring, Nordic ski touring. Lake Ohau offers a conventional field looking down on the incredible blue waters of the lake and heli-skiing in the long Ben Ohau mountain range. The Tekapo slopes above the northwest end of the lake provide an excellent family field, with heli-skiing from the adjacent ridges for the more adventurous.

Mt Dobson is one of the newest fields, with wide slopes looking out across lakes to Mt Cook and the Southern Alps.

11

Mt Cook

Runs are excellent, facilities as yet limited but improving with every season – the learners' area is one of the best. Fox Peak offers plenty of variety, with long exciting runs, but it lacks sophisticated equipment and facilities – rewarding for skiers who don't mind good rope tows instead of high speed lifts.

Travel around by air (flight-seeing and charter ski plane, light aircraft or helicopter are a regional feature); by car (rental car can be arranged by major hotels); by bus, especially Mt Cook Landline services; by tour – take conventional coach tours or four-wheel-drive safaris that go to 'the back of beyond'. Tours can be arranged from Christchurch through Guthreys, H & H, Fourways Pacific.

SEE ALSO:

Climbing: Alpine Guides Mt Cook (Skiing).
National Parks: Mount Cook National Park.
Climbing: Mountain Guides NZ (Skiing).
Flightseeing: Air Safaris Lake Tekapo.
Hunting: Lilybank Safari Lodge (Lodges).
Skiing: Tekapo Ski Field.

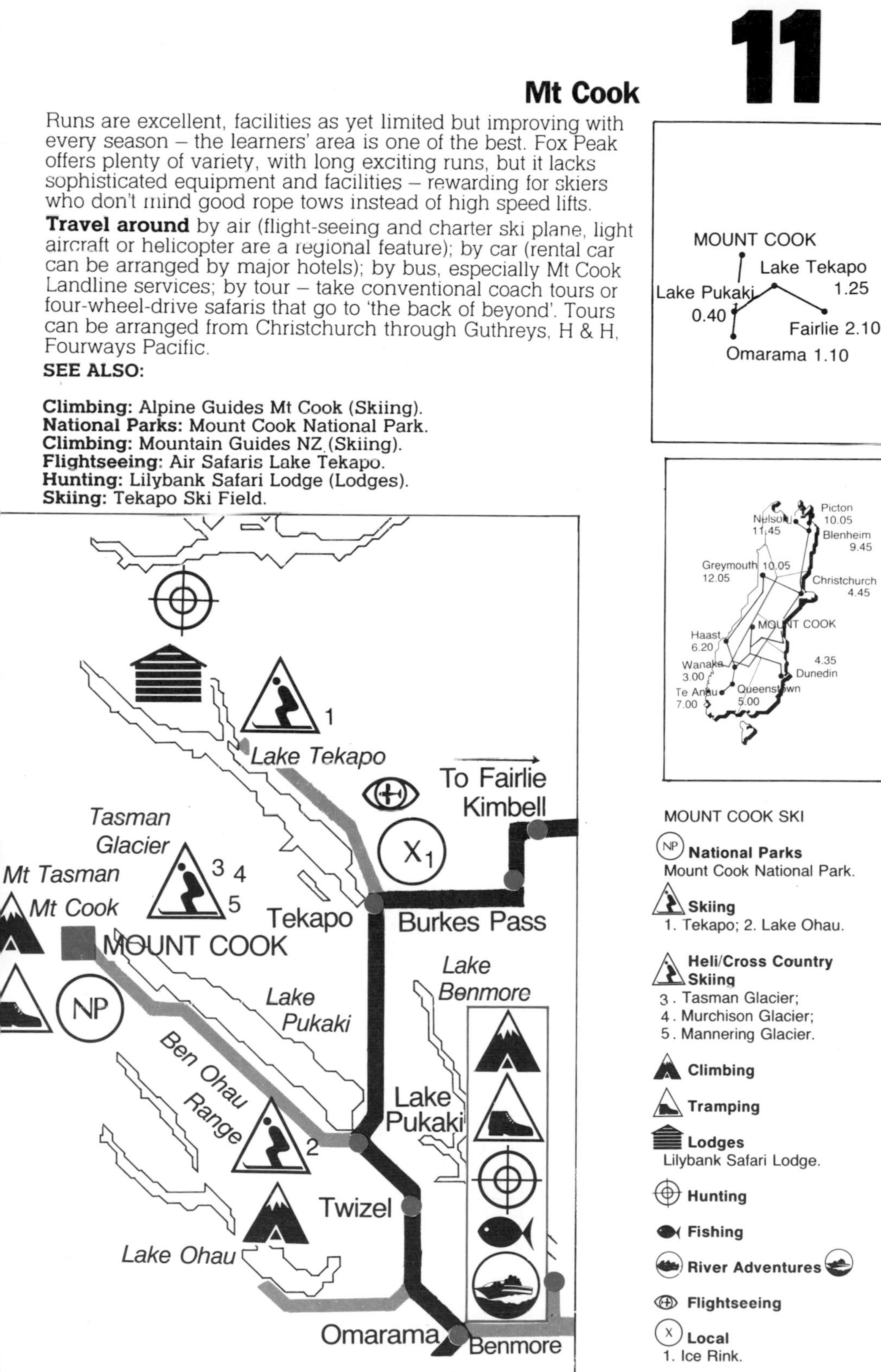

The few towns and villages of the region are really outposts, devoted to the tourist, the adventurer, the climber, tramper, skier and angler.

Omarama, on the southeastern edge of the region, is a centre for excellent trout fishing (the Ahuriri River is world famous), jet boating, skiing, flight-seeing and gliding – every summer pilots and gliders congregate at Omarama where ideal gliding conditions exist, away from sea breezes.

Lake Ohau Lodge serves anglers in summer and skiers in winter. It is also the base for tramping into the Hopkins, Hunter and Dobson mountains.

Twizel was built in the 1970s to house construction workers on power projects that redirect water from Tekapo, Pukaki and Ohau in a series of dams and canals. The workers have gone, the town has dwindled but retains the look and mood of a construction town – find out about the big hydro-electric schemes here. The information centre at Twizel has a good display and film on the hydro system.

Tekapo is a village devoted to the holiday-maker, catering for skiers, trampers, campers, boaters and anglers and offering flight-seeing over lakes, mountains and glaciers. The tiny settlements of Burkes Pass and Kimbell also serve skiers at Tekapo, Fox Peak and Mt Dobson fields (Burkes Pass is little more than a hotel, motel and tiny church on the border of green rolling hills and wild tussock country). Fairlie, on the eastern perimeter of the region, is the service centre for surrounding sheep runs but also offers a base for skiers and other holiday-makers.

Deep in the mountains of the Southern Alps is Mt Cook village. The village groups itself around the sprawling splendour of The Hermitage, a luxury hotel overlooked by towering mountains.

There's a school of mountaineering, guides for climbing, tramping, glacier skiing, heli-skiing, ski touring and ski mountaineering. Those who don't wish to ski or climb can be whisked into the heart of the mountains by ski plane to land on the perpetual snows of the Tasman Glacier. In winter the emphasis here is on skiing, in summer on climbing, but all year round there is some of the most spectacular, most accessible alpine scenery in the world. At the park headquarters, find detailed information on the many walks, from the 10-minute Bowen Track through alpine shrubs to the three-day alpine crossing over the Copland Pass to Fox Glacier in Westland.

Accommodation. – First-class hotels and motor inns at Mt Cook village, Tekapo, Omarama. At Mt Cook there is also a moderately priced lodge, motel and chalets and a youth hostel. Nearby Glentanner Park has a camping and caravan park, caravan and cabin accommodation. All Mt Cook accommodation should be booked in advance – it is a long way back if there's nothing available. As well as hotels and motels, Omarama has a caravan park and cabins. Tekapo has camping grounds with cabins and cottages and a youth hostel. Hotels, motels and camping ground with cabins are available at Fairlie. Twizel offers hotel, motel and camping ground with cabins.

Food. – First-class restaurants attached to the top hotels and inns. Otherwise food tends to reflect the needs of outdoors enthusiasts – hearty and filling. You won't go hungry with meals in traditional country hotels.

Mt Cook

Omarama Motor Lodge
PO Box 20
Omarama
Telephone: (02984) 805
Telex: NZ 5227
Hosts: Rob and Jan Perriam

This superb resort complex is situated in the heart of the Mt Cook Ski Region, offering excellent facilities including totally self-contained units accommodating from two-six persons. The Barn licensed restaurant has a lovely decor and a cuisine to match – with mouth-watering local and international delights such as Venison Omarama, Salmon Steaks and French-style scallops. The emphasis at the lodge is on comfort – enjoy a drink in the spacious Dalranchey lounge bar, watch a movie in the Television Room, play a game of pool, or pamper yourself in the luxurious Finnish Sauna complex. A hairstylist for both men and women is available by appointment. Through the lodge, you can arrange a multitude of different activities: water skiing, boating and fishing on Lake Ohau, gliding, abseiling and climbing, four-wheel-drive excursions and tandem bike riding. Take a scenic flight over Mt Cook with breathtaking views of mountains and glaciers; or charter an aircraft for hunting, heli-skiing or tramping trips (guides are available for outback trips). Enjoy a horse and wagonette ride – the wagonette is a 100-year-old delight. And then there is the skiing! The lodge is a well-known base for skiers and is only an hour's drive from prime ski slopes. These slopes have lots of powder snow and facilities, including canteen, equipment-hire service, tuition and tows for both the beginner and expert. Transport to and from the slopes is organised for you. Whether you want a restorative laze in comfort or an action-packed holiday to remember in New Zealand, this lodge is a complete holiday destination for all ages. From $52, double; children $5.

Entertainment. – In the evening activity centres on the nearest bar, whether in a smart modern hotel, a rough-and-ready dam-workers' bar or a hotel that began life as a coaching stop last century.

Lake Tekapo skifield, Mt Cook ski area, with Lake Tekapo in the background.
(Andris Apse Ltd)

Omarama

Stage Coach Inn
PO Box 70
Omarama
Telephone: (02984) 894
Telex: NZ 5247
Hosts: Keith and Karin Stirling

This beautifully designed facility offers 50 comfortable units, each with private facilities (some with telephone) and distinctive decor. Three luxury suites also available. Excellent restaurant caters for in-house guests and the casual diner. The à la carte menu includes many traditional New Zealand dishes, specialising in lamb and seafoods. As fishing is excellent in this area, the chef will gladly prepare and cook your own catch! The tasteful decor throughout includes cedar shingles and distinctive murals depicting local scenes. A cosy house bar provides open log fires, and additional facilities include spa pool, games room, television and video room. Omarama is the centre for many outdoor activities, which can be arranged for you by Keith and Karin's friendly staff. These include fishing, hunting, hiking, guides, scenic flights and water activities. From $50 (double). Special ski rates available from June to August.

Country Crafts
Omarama
Telephone: (02984) 844
Owner: Aileen Woods

Aileen Woods, who has lived in Omarama most of her life, stocks her shop with a wide variety of hand-made crafts – any of which will make the perfect souvenir of your visit to this lovely back-country region of New Zealand. Hand-knitted and crocheted items include jerseys, hats, shawls and mittens. The wide range of crafts includes paintings, Maori crafts, basketry and woodware, greenstone and paua jewellery, leather work and sheepskin rugs and tailored jackets. Aileen also stocks the now famous Ashford spinning wheel, which she is happy to pack and post to you, anywhere in the world. Take time out to browse. In winter, a pot-bellied stove and Aileen's hospitality are guaranteed to keep you warm. The shop is open Monday through Saturday, from 9.00 a.m. until late (depending on demand).

Omarama Caravan Park (1981) Ltd
PO Box 34
Omarama
Telephone: (0298 4) 875
Hosts: Pat & Bruce McDuff

Bordered by the Omarama Stream and set in 4 hectares (10 acres) of sheltered grounds, this complete camping facility offers thermostatically heated cabins with power points, modern kitchen, showers and automatic laundry facilities. For children, a play area and trampoline. Close by, enjoy a variety of leisure activities including fishing (tackle for hire), boating on rivers or lakes, skiing, tramping, gliding. Cabins from $6 per adult, camping from $3.50 per adult.

Lake Ohau

Lake Ohau Lodge
Lake Ohau
Telephone: (02984) 885
Telex: NZ 5297
Host: Ian Healy

This lodge, a complex of 72 units, comprises both luxury and budget accommodation. Most rooms have private bath and shower, tea/coffee-making facilities and extensive views over Lake Ohau and surrounding mountains. Additional facilities include fully licensed lounge bar and restaurant, games room, guest laundry and drying rooms, as well as a seven-day service station with a mechanical workshop. If you have a caravan or campervan, there are power-appointed sites available. The lodge is situated 20 minutes' drive from State Highway 8, between Twizel and Omarama, and is set amid the splendid isolation of this lovely lake and mountains. Enjoy friendly hospitality and a wide range of outdoor activities, from tennis, climbing, walking and horse riding to ice skating, water skiing, swimming and scenic flights. From $31.95 (dinner, bed and breakfast).

Twizel

56 kilometres (35 miles) State Highway 8 from Tekapo, 63 kilometres (40 miles) SH 80 from Mount Cook, 30 kilometres (18 miles) SH 80 from Omarama. Closest town to Mount Cook and regional service centre for MacKenzie Basin. Service station, hotel, bank, post office, restaurant, food and clothing stores, doctor, dentist, chemist, hardware, dry cleaning, rural services. Library, squash/tennis courts, swimming pool (hydro-slide), roller rink. Information centre: Adjacent SH 8, open daily. Displays, maps, information. Centre Mackenzie hydro lakes: Fishing, camping, canoeing, boating, water skiing, swimming, yachting, windsurfing, hang-gliding, trail-bike riding, tramping, mountaineering. Centre Mount Cook ski region: Ohau, Tekapo, Mount Dobson fields; heli-skiing, glacier skiing, ice skating, ski-skate hire. Lake Ruitaniwha: International rowing course, camping ground, water-ski slalom, power-boat racing.

Twizel Community Council
PO Box 4
Twizel
Telephone: (05620) 636

Lake Tekapo

Near the famous Church of the Good Shepherd, overlooking this superb lake and surrounding mountains, the inn offers both budget and superior accommodation for 200 guests, including rooms or motel units. Facilities include tea/coffee making, colour television/video, radio and telephone. Also two licensed restaurants, house bar, conference facilities, gift shop, guests' lounge and games room, laundry, heated swimming pool and spa pool. From $45 twin/double.

Lake Tekapo Alpine Inn
PO Box 8
Lake Tekapo
Telephone: (05056) 847 or 848
Telex: NZ 4313
Hosts: Diane and Barry Ferguson

This unique, natural ice-skating rink is set by the shores of beautiful Lake Tekapo and provides great fun for all, with tuition and full equipment hireage available. Facilities include indoor heated observation room, two rinks, flood-lit evening skating and canteen serving hot drinks. Open winter only: 10.00 a.m. – 4.00 p.m. and 7.00 p.m. – 10.00 p.m. daily. Cost: $5 for adults all-day skating, plus children's rates. You will need warm clothing.

Lake Tekapo Ice Rink
Lakefront
Tekapo
PO Box 78
Telephone: (05056) 827
Owner: Mrs Joan Thomlinson

This camp is nestled amongst fir trees overlooking Lake Tekapo, with snow-clad mountains completing the picture-postcard scene. Variety of accommodation includes motel units, cottages, cabins and caravans, only a short walk from the village shops or ice-skating rink and a 30-minute drive to ski fields. Facilities include ample power points, well-maintained shower and kitchen blocks, and a boat ramp. From $6 to $32.

Lake Tekapo Motor Camp
PO Box 43
Lake Tekapo
Telephone: (05056) 825
Hosts: Peter and Anne Brass

Right in the centre of Lake Tekapo Village, this facility is well equipped to supply all your motoring needs and shopping requirements, including petrol, motoring accessories, ice, fishing tackle and basic sporting goods. The full grocery store supplies fresh fruit and vegetables, dairy products, fresh and frozen meat, as well as books, stationery, hardware etc. A great place to stock up when travelling or staying at the motels or camping ground here at Lake Tekapo. Open every day except Christmas Day, from 8.00 a.m. to 6.00 p.m.

Tekapo Services Ltd
PO Box 1
Lake Tekapo
Telephone: (05056) 809
Owners: Peter and Gillian Maxwell

Enjoy friendly hospitality, cosy atmosphere and tasteful decor, while you relax over morning/afternoon teas, lunches and evening meals (superb views over Lake Tekapo). Inexpensive and delicious, evening meals specialise in New Zealand roast meats/salad bar (roast lamb always available). Robin and Gillian also provide delicious takeaway foods. Robins Nest is adjacent to Tekapo Services in the village. Open every day (except Christmas Day) from 8.00 a.m. till 8.00 p.m.

Robins Nest Restaurant
PO Box 31
Lake Tekapo
Telephone: (05056) 886
Hosts: Gillian and Robin Muir

Mitre Peak, Milford Sound, Southland. ***(National Publicity Studios)***

This is 'champagne' scenery, the region that contains New Zealand's best-known, most-photographed tourist destinations – Milford Sound, Queenstown, Lake Wakatipu, Lake Wanaka, Lake Te Anau. The scale, the colours, the juxtaposition of mountains, lakes, rivers, forests and fiords combine to create unsurpassed, unforgettable scenery.

It is a region where visitors come to absorb the scenery, to tramp, climb, hunt, ski, raft, canoe or fish. Then they come back to do it all again, returning to the region each year, not merely from other parts of New Zealand, but from all over the world.

Lakes and mountains dominate the area. See mountains sharply etched against the skyline, rising from wide valley floors, abruptly from the edge of lakes or sheer from the sea, in the deep fiords. Here you can see, or travel on, rivers such as the Shotover, which rushes in a wild torrent through steep, barren canyons, or the Landsborough, which flows through a trackless wilderness approachable only by expert trampers or by helicopter transport.

In the Southern Lakes Region you can walk the famous Milford, Hollyford or Routeburn Tracks or any of the hundreds of lesser-known tracks.

The Milford Track is acclaimed as 'the finest walk in the world', a five- or six-day trek from the head of Lake Te Anau to Milford Sound, leading alongside and across clear green rivers, over an alpine plain, across a high mountain pass, by the Sutherland Falls (third highest in the world at 580 metres or 1,900 feet) and down to the sea at magnificent Milford Sound.

The Hollyford walk begins in the Hollyford Valley at the road's end and follows the blue Hollyford River through to Lake Alabaster, Lake McKerrow (once a fiord) and the sea at Martins Bay, where there is a colony of fur seals. The experience is varied, with jet-boat travel on river and lake, and transport out by light aircraft.

The Routeburn is a high track leading from the head of Lake Wakatipu over the Harris Saddle Pass, by tiny mountain lakes, through red-beech forest, over alpine meadows full of flowers in late spring and early summer and with spectacular views down glacial valleys.

The coast of the region is deeply indented with immense gashes gouged out by glaciers that finally disappeared as recently as 15,000 years ago, leaving behind sheer granite walls that drop hundreds of metres into the dark-green sea. At Milford Sound, Mitre Peak rises in serene splendour straight from the mirror-calm waters of the fiord – a scene that has become a symbol of New Zealand. Reach Milford Sound the energetic way, on the Milford Track, by road from Te Anau along one of the world's great alpine drives, or by air on what is probably the most spectacular scenic flight in the world.

Milford Sound is the focal point for most visitors to the 1.2 million-hectare (3 million-acre) Fiordland National Park, but it is only one aspect of an amazing area. Here, there is not only one of the world's highest waterfalls, but also one of the world's highest rainfalls – up to 7,600 millimetres (300 inches) in places. With this rain come forests that seem almost magical; giant totara, rimu, matai, red and silver beech grow in precarious places, clinging to humus gathered on rocks; ferns, mosses and vines engulf the trees and lichens hang in drifts, like immense lace curtains; shafts of sunlight glance through the forest in muted colours; glow worms display their

Kea.

Southern Lakes

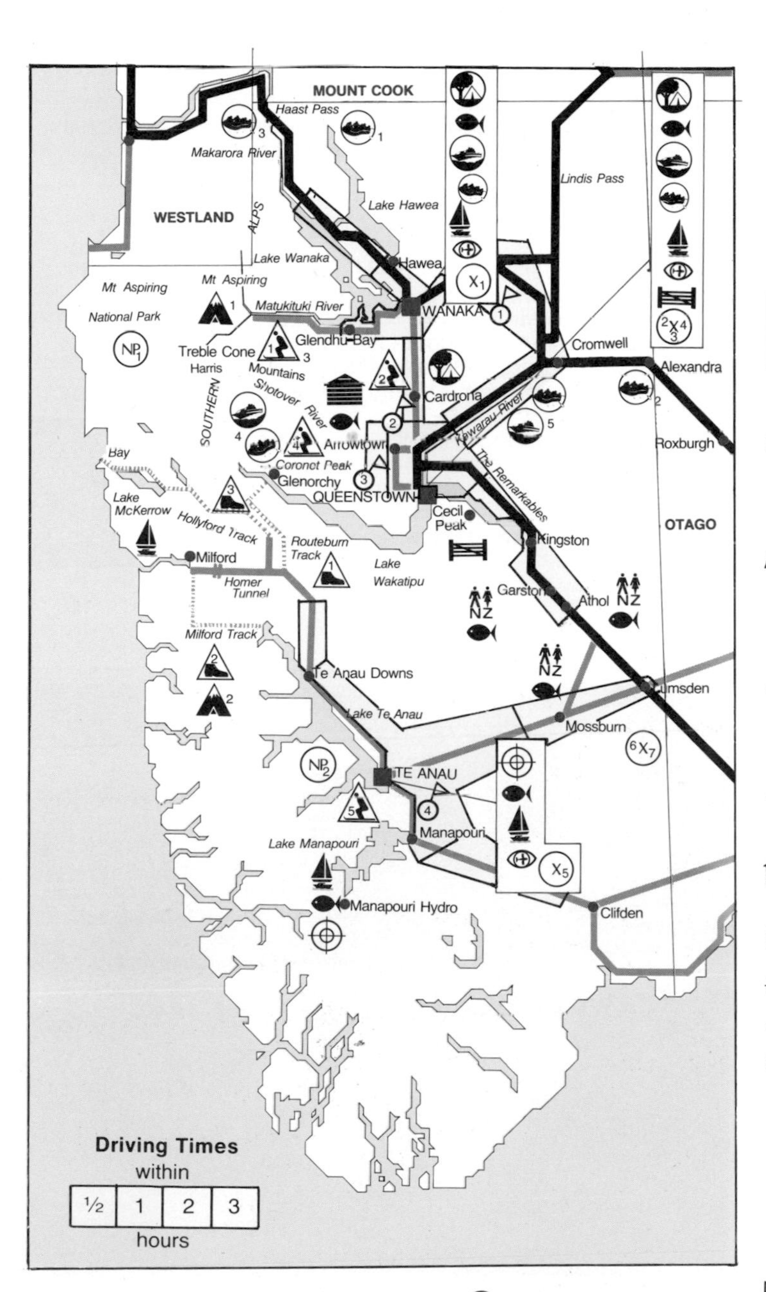

SOUTHERN LAKES

National Parks
1. Mount Aspiring National Park; 2. Fiordland National Park.

Skiing Heli/Cross Country
1. Treble Cone; 2. Cardrona; 3. Harris Mountains; 4. Coronet Peak. 5. Mount Luxmore.

Climbing
1. Mount Aspiring National Park; 2. Fiordland National Park.

Tramping
1. Routeburn; 2. Milford Track; 3. Hollyford Track.

Lodges
Crown Lodge.

Outback Safaris

Hunting

Fishing

River Adventures
1. Hunter River; 2. Clutha River; 3. Landsborough River; 4. Shotover River; 5. Kawarau River.

Cruising

Flightseeing

Local
1. The Maze & Puzzle Centre; 2. Motor Museum; 3. Sound & Light Museum; 4. Art Gallery; 5. Milford Track Audio-Visual; 6. Matuku Engine Museum & 7. Bee Bazaar.

Golf
1. Wanaka; 2. Arrowtown; 3. Queenstown; 4. Te Anau.

Down on Farm

Live with NZ

tiny lights on damp, mossy banks.

Bush life includes forest birds such as tuis, bellbirds, cuckoos, kakas, and robins. The park is also home to the rare takahe and kakapo. There's wapiti, red deer, chamois, rainbow and brown trout; on the shores, seals and penguins.

In the north of the region, Mt Aspiring National Park draws dedicated mountaineers, trampers and adventurers to an area that includes classic alps, more than 50 glaciers, the headwaters of seven major rivers, rainforest, beech forest, alpine meadows and wide, tussock river flats. It is wild, difficult, intensely beautiful terrain, sought out by experts, unchanged from the days when the mountains earned names such as Mt Awkward, Mt Awful, Mt Dreadful and Mt Defiant. See the park in comfort on flight excursions.

The gateway to Mt Aspiring National Park is through Wanaka (the park's headquarters are in Wanaka). On the edge of the long twisting Lake Wanaka, the town is a centre for skiing, trout fishing, boating, canoeing, rafting, flight-seeing and horse trekking.

A similarly wide range of activities awaits visitors to Queenstown, the top South Island tourist destination on the shores of Lake Wakatipu. On the edge of Lake Te Anau, the largest South Island lake, there is the town of Te Anau, yet a third excellent base for exploring the region, and gateway to dramatic Fiordland.

Mt Talbot and reflection, Fiordland National Park. ***(National Publicity Studios)***

Southern Lakes

Accommodation. Excellent quality accommodation in hotels and motor inns at Queenstown, Wanaka and Te Anau. Milford Sound has one high-class THC hotel and one hostel (prior booking advisable). Also find excellent accommodation in exclusive hunting and fishing lodges and on high-country sheep stations. Plenty of motels. Queenstown has seven camping grounds with cabin accommodation within reasonable distance of town. Camping grounds also at Wanaka, Glendhu Bay, Te Anau, Hollyford Valley, Manapouri. Find budget accommodation in bunkhouse lodges, guest houses and youth hostels.

Food. Queenstown offers a full range, in fact the highest number of restaurants per capital of any New Zealand town, of stylish licensed restaurants, informal bistros and plenty of snack bars for people in a hurry. Less to choose from in Wanaka and Te Anau, but excellent quality. Look for New Zealand specialities such as lamb, venison and salmon. For something different, try some locally made fruit wines – apricot, elderberry, plum, cherry – at the Key of the Lakes near Te Anau.

Entertainment. Queenstown is small but one of the liveliest towns in the country. Excellent restaurants, convivial bars, good live entertainment. Most night life centres on the hotels with music, cabaret or dancing. In Te Anau or Wanaka, after an enjoyable outdoors day a relaxing dinner and early night are usually the rule. Good hotels have spas or saunas to soothe weary limbs.

Travel around the Southern Lakes region with the most spectacular alpine flight-seeing in the world. Light aircraft, float planes, amphibians and helicopters leave from Queenstown, Wanaka, Te Anau. Travel by car, remembering that mountain roads off the beaten track may test your motoring skills. (Rental car insurance does not cover travel on the Skippers Canyon road, so take a tour bus.) All major bus companies serve the region well – buses to Milford coincide with launch tours. Plenty of tours are available to suit all tastes, from outback four-wheel-drive to conventional sightseeing.

Wanaka

From Wanaka, the gentle township on the edge of Lake Wanaka, explore the lake's bays and beaches, fringed with willows, maples, kowhai and poplars.

A favourite boating lake with little road access, Wanaka is long and twisting, winding its way through peninsulas and islands with mountains often mirrored in the lake's calm surface. Take a launch cruise on the 390-square-kilometre (240-square-mile) lake, leaving from the Wanaka waterfront and stopping off at lake islands, perhaps for a barbecue or picnic lunch. Go jet-boat touring, water skiing, para-sailing or windsurfing on the lake. Hire a sail boat, power boat, row boat or canoe and explore the bays independently.

Go swimming too, if you enjoy a dip in ice-cold mountain water (the town beach, Sunshine Beach, is one of the best for swimming). Swimmers find the lake's water refreshingly welcome on a hot summer's day. Summer in Wanaka can be very hot indeed, with cloudless sunny days, in a suntrap valley where temperatures soar to 38°C.

A successful day's fishing on Lake Wanaka. ***(Courtesy Paul Miller)***

There's superb fishing in Lake Wanaka, neighbouring Lake Hawea and surrounding rivers. Local guides ensure visitors find the best spots for brown trout, rainbow trout and land-locked salmon, and provide all the necessary equipment. Even if you're not going fishing, visit the trout hatchery in Stone Street, where trout and salmon make a fascinating study.

Other around-town diversions include a one-kilometre maze, an elaborate mini-golf course, a puzzle centre, hire bicycles and tandems.

But it is the recreational variety of lake, hills, mountains and valleys that draws thousands of visitors to Wanaka each year. As well as the magnificent boating and fishing, holiday-makers come to play golf, take high-country safari tours, go tramping, climbing, hunting, horse trekking along old mining trails, rafting and canoeing on fast rivers; all these activities are based at Wanaka.

In winter, Wanaka becomes the centre for skiing at the Treble Cone and Cardrona ski-fields. Both fields have fabulous views over distant lakes and with new facilities are one of the country's fastest growing ski areas. For heli-skiing try the Harris Mountains, where over 30 runs provide intermediate and expert slopes of 600 to 1,200 vertical metres (2,000 to 4,000 feet). There's also ice skating on Diamond Lake, a small sparkling lake set in the hills above Lake Wanaka's Glendhu Bay.

Take flight-seeing excursions from Wanaka's airfield or lake front, over the lakes and the wilderness of Mt Aspiring National Park or further afield to Milford Sound or Mt Cook; there are chicken and champagne breakfast flights over mountains and lakes.

Horse-trekking by the Cardrona Hotel ***(Courtesy Gin & Raspberry Stables)***

Enjoy the splendour of Wanaka's scenery from boat or plane, but also travel out from town by road; drive along the fringe of Lake Hawea to The Neck, and then to the Makarora Valley by Lake Wanaka, through to the edge of Mt Aspiring National Park. Continue through to Haast Pass for constantly changing alpine views.

Travel west from Wanaka township to Glendhu Bay, with the dramatic landscape softened by willows and poplars.

Confident drivers who enjoy mountain roads can take the Cardrona Valley – Crown Range Road. (On a map it looks like a short cut between Wanaka and Queenstown – it's not.) This is exciting mountain territory, an old gold-mining route where

Southern Lakes

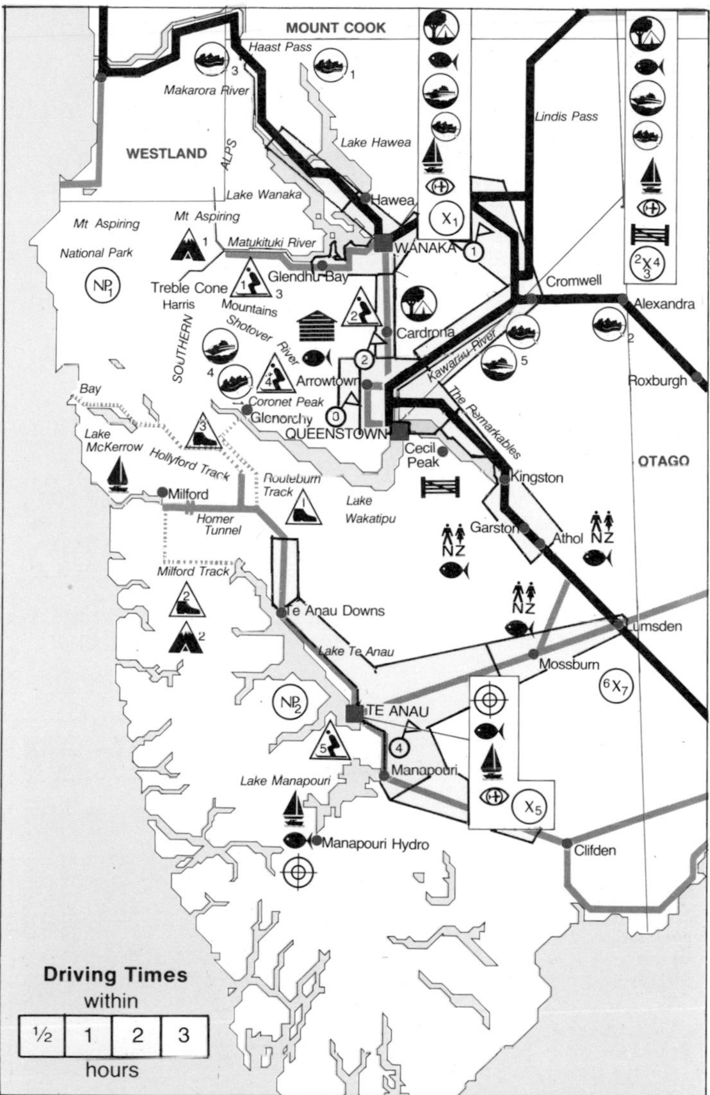

SOUTHERN LAKES

National Parks
1. Mount Aspiring National Park; 2. Fiordland National Park.

Skiing Heli/Cross Country
1. Treble Cone; 2. Cardrona;
3. Harris Mountains;
4. Coronet Peak.
5. Mount Luxmore.

Climbing
1. Mount Aspiring National Park; 2. Fiordland National Park.

Tramping
1. Routeburn; 2. Milford Track;
3. Hollyford Track.

Lodges
Crown Lodge.

Outback Safaris

Hunting

Fishing

River Adventures
1. Hunter River; 2. Clutha River; 3. Landsborough River; 4. Shotover River; 5. Kawarau River.

Cruising

Flightseeing

Golf
1. Wanaka; 2. Arrowtown;
3. Queenstown; 4. Te Anau.

Down on Farm

Live with NZ

Local
1. The Maze & Puzzle Centre;
2. Motor Museum; 3. Sound & Light Museum; 4. Art Gallery;
5. Milford Track Audio-Visual;
6. Matuku Engine Museum &
7. Bee Bazaar.

decaying stone cottages stand as reminders of bygone days. At Cardrona, find an old gold-mining pub and the quaintly named 'Gin-and-Raspberry Stables', offering guided horse-treks deep into the mountains.

Take walks beginning with tracks leading from the town's waterfront around the shore of the lake. From the Glendhu Bay Road you may take a walk to the top of Mt Roy for spectacular views of sharply ridged ranges spreading out into Lake Wanaka. Drive on up the Mt Aspiring Road to Raspberry Creek, and from there take walks up the Matukituki River valleys, with forests, mountain and glacier views; the road can be grim but the tracks are well worth the drive. Intrepid walkers should visit the Mt Aspiring National Park Headquarters in Wanaka for all information on the mountain wilderness of Mt Aspiring.

Wanaka

The Wanaka Maze and Puzzle Centre
Wanaka-Cromwell Highway
(2 kilometres, 1.2 miles, from Wanaka)
Telephone: Wanaka 7489
Hosts: Jan and Stuart Landsborough

This maze has won national awards for enterprise – find out why! The first of the world's mazes, it is a three-dimensional maze with 1.5 kilometres (1 mile) of confusing over-and-under passageways, through which you must make your way to the lovely Rose Garden terminal. This is great fun for adults and children alike, and there are emergency gates for those with limited time or energy! Sit in the garden and watch and listen to your friends still making their way out. The other major attraction not to be missed is the Puzzle Centre. This centre contains one of the largest displays of puzzles and puzzling things in the world. There are jigsaw puzzles, puzzles made from wood, wire and string, optical illusion prints, incredible three-dimensional holograph photographs, to name but a few. You are invited to try these puzzles for yourself, and demonstrations are held to show you how to solve them. There is also a shop where you can buy puzzles to take home.

Having happily bewildered and bemused yourself, enjoy a game of lawn croquet or mini-golf and then relax amid all this excitement over a delicious devonshire tea. For those of you interested in the art of maze design, talk with Stuart, who has designed mazes around the world, including the United States and Japan, and is known as a foremost authority in the field.

This is an all-seasons entertainment and since it opened a decade ago has been enjoyed by over a third of a million people. Maze fee: adults $2, children $1. The Puzzle Centre is free of charge and there is a nominal charge for the croquet and mini-golf.

Looking across from Scar Burn area to Lake Wanaka and beyond to Mt Gold, Central Otago. *(National Publicity Studios)*

Southern Lakes

A warm and friendly welcome is extended to all of Jim and Cecille's guests. The motel has twelve sunny, comfortable, fully self-contained units. Facilities include colour television, continental breakfast, two-bedroomed units and a spacious children's playing area; handy to shops, post office and golf course, and lake- and river-fishing guides arranged for you on request. From $39 double.

Alpine Motel
7 Ardmore Street
Wanaka
Telephone: Wanaka 7950
Hosts: Jim and Cecille Haley

Uninterrupted views of Lake Wanaka, inexpensive and comfortable accommodation, Hillary's licensed restaurant, and above all, friendly and courteous service make this an ideal base for summer or skiing holidays. Colour television/video plus radio in each room, guest laundry and drying rooms, lock-up ski racks and ski maintenance bench, sauna and plunge pool. Hillary's is open for breakfast – 8.00 a.m. to 9.30 a.m., (lunch pending) and dinner – 7.00 p.m. to 9.00 p.m. From $34.

Pembroke Inn
94 Brownston Street
PO Box 149
Wanaka
Telephone: Wanaka 7296
Telex: NZ 5344
Manager: Graham Parker

This restaurant is set upstairs in the Pembroke Village Mall, giving unsurpassed views of Lake Wanaka and surrounding mountains, with optional verandah dining. Decor is pine and cane with pleasant table appointments. Menu is innovative, international and includes a range of delicious vegetarian and New Zealand dishes. A B.Y.O., serving lunches, dinners and, in winter, breakfasts. Open seven days in mid-winter and mid-summer, otherwise closed Mondays. Medium price range.

Ripples Restaurant
PO Box 150
Wanaka
Telephone: Wanaka 7413
Host: Colin Sutherland

Centrally situated 1 kilometre (half a mile) from township, sheltered by trees, with great views over Lake Wanaka, this camp offers tent and caravan sites, cabins and tourist flats. Additional facilities include modern laundry with dryer and kitchens. Close to golf course/squash courts. Go canoeing, for launch trips or fishing at the lake; or walking, tramping and mountaineering. Great base for skiing holiday. From $4 (tent sites), $7 (powered campervan site), $14 (double) cabins.

Wanaka Motor Camp
212 Brownston Street
Wanaka
Telephone: Wanaka 7883

Three kilometres (2 miles) from Wanaka township, this motel offers seven fully self-contained units (two with fireplaces) with choice of one or two bedrooms: all units equipped with lounge, full kitchen, heating, shower/tub. Also children's play area, guest laundry and breakfast upon request. The grounds are park-like in a country setting. Splendid views of Lake Wanaka and mountains. Easy walk to lake and township. From $40 (two persons). Major credit cards accepted. Member Golden Chain group.

Bay View Motel (formerly Hawthenden)
Glendhu Bay Road
PO Box 11
Wanaka
Telephone: Wanaka 7766
Hosts: Margaret and Gerald Scaife

SEE ALSO:

National Parks: Mount Aspiring National Park.
Outback Safaris: Gin & Raspberry Stables.
Skiing: Ski Guides NZ Ltd, Treble Cone.
Cruising/Yachting: Wanaka Hovercraft.
Fishing: Paul Miller Fishing Guide.
Flightseeing: Aspiring Air.

Queenstown

In Queenstown the emphasis is on action, whatever the season, whatever the time of day. Yet the town also has a dream-like quality, a faultless setting of mountains and lake; a charm based on the days when it catered to miners seeking their fortunes on the Shotover, Arrow and Kawerau Rivers. All these qualities combine to make Queenstown the perfect place for a complete holiday.

From hotels and motels you can look out on the splendour of the glacial Lake Wakatipu. To further savour the view, take a gondola ride straight above the town, a four-minute ride to the top of Bob's Peak (466 metres, 1,530 feet), through dark pine woods; at the top is a glass-walled restaurant and magnificent views. Take a walk up Queenstown Hill, from York Street to the top of a 900-metre (3,000-foot) hill overlooking the town.

On the wooded peninsula that forms the west side of Queenstown's almost square bay (formed by a glacial moraine), find a garden reserve, rimmed with fir trees concealing wide lawns, rose gardens, lily ponds, skating rink and tennis courts. Stand on the peninsula looking back on the town with Bob's Peak looming above. Look in the other direction to the Remarkables, unfolding into the distance along the lake shore.

See further views by travelling a little out of town to Deer Park Heights, a game reserve near Frankton, where wapiti, red deer, chamois, thar and mountain goats surround you and the lake spreads out below. Ride a chairlift to the top of Coronet Peak – in winter one of the country's top ski fields with some of the best facilities and skiing in the Southern Hemisphere.

Experience more views and excitement with flight-seeing; there are 10-minute flights over mountains and lake; half-hour flights that can encompass several mountain ranges, rivers, lakes and high-country sheep and cattle stations; flights further afield reach Milford Sound quickly and spectacularly. Take a helicopter ride to the top of the Remarkables.

Queenstown is a town eminently suited to wandering; stroll through tiny, narrow streets where shops, boutiques, restaurants and century-old buildings of timber and stone cluster. At the corner of Ballarat and Stanley Streets, the flavour of old Queenstown is encapsulated in the 1876 courthouse and library buildings.

Present-day Queenstown centres on the mall at the lake end of Ballarat Street. Here find quaint shops selling hand-knitted woollen garments, jewellery, crafts and leatherwork. The Wakatipu Trading Post is an arcade of small shops created out of historic buildings.

There are also information and tour offices, offering dozens of excursions in and around town and further afield into the region. Find out all you want to know about jet-boat trips on the Shotover River, white-water rafting and canoeing, horse trekking along old mining trails, safaris into the back country, or tours to the spectacular Skippers Canyon.

On the lake front, have a drink at Eichardt's Hotel, a pub that's been in business since 1871, and contemplate a lake excursion.

Pride of the lake is the *Earnslaw,* a steamer that has been plying the lake since 1912. At one time its prime purpose was to carry supplies to sheep stations around the lake. Today its interior is more sophisticated, with a licensed restaurant and room for 1,000 passengers. Luncheon cruises serve chicken and champagne while steaming by the Remarkables mountain range. Other *Earnslaw* cruises include visits to high-country

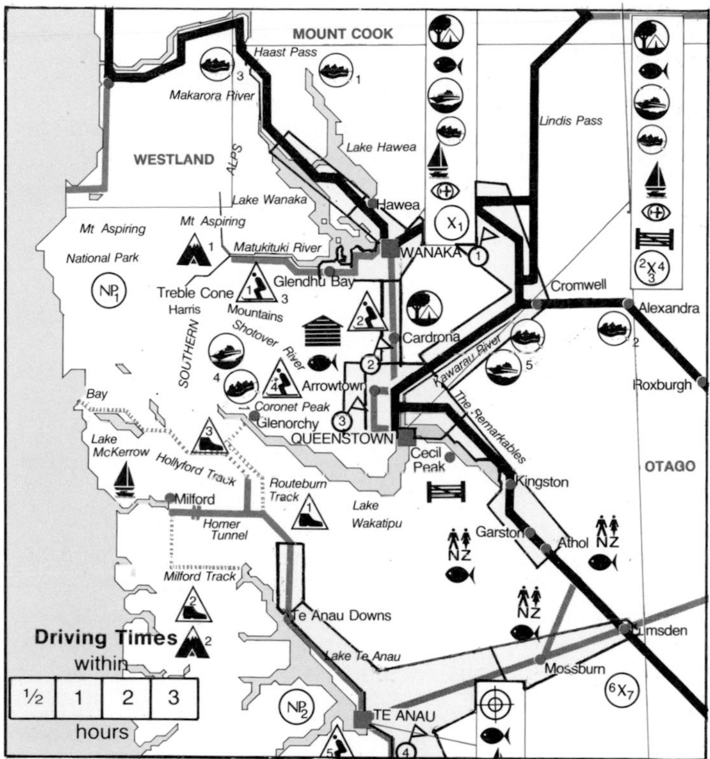

SOUTHERN LAKES

National Parks
1. Mount Aspiring National Park; 2. Fiordland National Park.

Skiing Heli/Cross Country
1. Treble Cone; 2. Cardrona;
3. Harris Mountains;
4. Coronet Peak.
5. Mount Luxmore.

Climbing
1. Mount Aspiring National Park; 2. Fiordland National Park.

Tramping
1. Routeburn; 2. Milford Track;
3. Hollyford Track.

Lodges
Crown Lodge.

Outback Safaris

Hunting

Fishing

River Adventures
1. Hunter River; 2. Clutha River; 3. Landsborough River; 4. Shotover River; 5. Kawarau River.

Cruising

Flightseeing

Golf
1. Wanaka; 2. Arrowtown;
3. Queenstown; 4. Te Anau.

Down on Farm

Live with NZ

Local
1. The Maze & Puzzle Centre;
2. Motor Museum; 3. Sound & Light Museum; 4. Art Gallery;
5. Milford Track Audio-Visual;
6. Matuku Engine Museum &
7. Bee Bazaar.

sheep and cattle stations and dinner-dance cruises.

Lake excursions also include hydrofoil, hovercraft and jet-boat cruises, and launch tours to sheep and cattle stations; watch sheepdog, shearing and spinning demonstrations; walk through historic farm buildings and enjoy a high-country morning or afternoon tea. In the fishing season the options extend to charter boats and fishing guides for rainbow-and brown-trout fishing.

Back on dry land, visit the Cattledrome on the Arrowtown Road for a stage show featuring live beef cattle and dairy cows. (There's the chance, too, for you to try hand-milking a cow.)

For journeys into the past, visit the motor museum, an excellent collection of vintage touring cars, racing cars and motor cycles; or visit Colonial Sounds, an audio-visual display of gold-rush days, which recreates the past superbly.

Relive the gold-mining days further at a recreated village, Golden Terrace Mining Town, near Frankton, which includes 1860s-style general store, sweet shop, book shop, mining company office, bank, stables, barber shop and, of course, the pub; or travel to nearby Kingston to take a memorable journey on the Kingston Flyer, a picture-book steam train that travels to Fairlight and back.

When is the best time to visit Queenstown? The answer is in summer, when the town and lake are caught in a hot, dry, sun trap; in winter, when it turns into a skiers' town with the liveliest aprés-ski life in the country; in spring, when wildflowers, hawthorn and may trim the roadsides; in autumn, as the crisp mountain air turns leaves bright yellow and red.

Queenstown

Central Art Galleries Ltd
PO Box 159
Queenstown
Telephone: Queenstown 1025 (after hours: Queenstown 1255)

You are warmly invited to browse through the Central Art Gallery in the Queenstown Bay Centre. Available for purchase are the works of well-known New Zealand painters, such as Dr M. Soper, Garrick Tremain, John Husband and Da Vella Gore. Work is representative of all media. A selection of reproductions and limited print editions are also available. The gallery is open Monday through Saturday. All major credit cards are accepted.

Queenstown Motor Museum
25 Brecon Street
Queenstown
Telephone: Queenstown 752
Hosts: John and Glenys Taylor

Just 5 minutes' walk from the town centre, this beautiful display of vintage, veteran and classic vehicles dating from 1861, is reputed to be one of Australasia's best. Included are cars, motor bikes (two- and three-wheelers), aircraft exhibits plus wonderful motoring memorabilia. Set in a warm, enclosed building, ideal for wet-day activity. A souvenir shop specialises in motor themes. From $3 adults, $1.25 children. Open daily, except Christmas Day.

The Sound and Light Museum
Beach Street
Queenstown
Host: Mr Angus Watson

The Sound and Light Museum is an audio-visual, continuous 20-minute show, where Queenstown's historic past – from 1860s gold rush to present day – is dramatically recreated. Walk-through 'film sets' and simultaneous slide/movie show, all with sound effects, guarantee fun entertainment for everyone. Have a sepia photograph taken of yourself in nineteenth-century period costume. From $3, adults; and $1.50, children. Photographs additional.

H & H Travel Lines Ltd
PO Box 423
Invercargill
Telephone: (021) 82-419
Telex: NZ 5766

H & H Travel Lines offer a wide choice of sightseeing tours in the Queenstown area including a 3-hour tour along the historic road to the site of the Skippers Goldfield. For further information, see your travel agent or any H & H Office in New Zealand. Auckland: (09) 792-426, Christchurch (03) 799-120, Dunedin (024) 740-674, Te Anau (0229) 7233, Queenstown 146.

Kawarau River, near Queenstown. *(Andris Apse Ltd)*

Southern Lakes

Cecil Peak High Country Sheep Station
Private Bag
Queenstown
Telephone: Queenstown 491M
Host: Dennis Rogers
Telex: C/- NZ 4315

Isolated amid spectacular scenery, this station is home to 9,500 sheep, 300 cattle, 50 deer and several thoroughbred horses. Take a 25-minute relaxing lake cruise on the station's luxury launch to this world of peace, tranquillity and absolute beauty. See sheep dogs working, visit the 100-year-old original stone cottage, watch a sheep-shearing display and enjoy a 'high-country' tea with fresh-baked scones and berry jam! Launch departs twice-daily (9.30 a.m. and 2.15 p.m.) from Cecil Peak Jetty, in Queenstown Bay. Cost: $14. Accommodation is available in the exclusive lodge, offering comfort and style with friendly personal service. Enjoy trout fishing in the world-famous Lochy River, ride the thoroughbred horses, or just relax – absorbing the glorious scenery. From $87.50 per person, per night (meals, transport, tour included – liquor additional).

SEE ALSO:

Cruising/Yachting: Fiordland Travel, Hydrofoil Cruises, Queenstown Waterski and Sail.
Down on Farm: Expo Cattledrome.
Fishing: Queenstown Trout Safaris.
Flightseeing: Heli Jet Adventures (Water Adv).
Live with NZ: Riverview (Outback Safari/Fishing/Down on Farm/Water Adv.), (Athol), Birch Hill/RHC (Garston).
Outback Safaris: Hillandale Rides (Dalefield), Moonlight Stables, Danes Back Country (Water Adv/Tramping/Fishing/Flightseeing).
Water Adventures: Airborne Hovercraft Services, Marine Enterprises (Cruise/Tramp).

Queenstown under snow. *(Ray Dustow)*

Al Queenstown Motel
13 Frankton Road
Queenstown
Telephone: Queenstown 289
Telex: NZ 5334
Hosts: John and Glenys Bax

In peaceful surroundings near the Botanical Gardens and the town centre, this motel offers 10 spacious units, all fully equipped, including kitchens. Facilities include colour television/video, radio and central heating in each unit, outdoor heated swimming pool and private spa. Courtesy transport is available on request. Enjoy friendly service and assistance with arrangging ightseeing trips. From $45 (two persons). Present this book and receive a 10% discount!

Colonial Village
Queenstown
R.H.C. Reservations:
Telephone: (03) 799-127/6
(USA: 800-874-7207)
Telex: NZ 4051
(USA: 8874486)

Overlooking beautiful Lake Wakatipu with a superb view of the Remarkable Mountains, the Colonial Village is a beautifully comfortable facility, with generous-sized rooms – all offering this same breathtaking view from your private balcony. Fitz Roller is both host and international chef, ensuring not only gastronomic experiences in his restaurant, but a pleasurable and relaxing stay. An ideal base for your Queenstown experience. From $51 (including breakfasts).

Vacation Inn – O'Connels Hotel
Beach Road
Queenstown
Private Bag
Telephone: Queenstown 286
Telex: NZ 5704

Centrally located in one of New Zealand's most popular resort towns, O'Connels is an established name, offering charm and atmosphere for locals and visitors alike. The hotel offers 65 guest rooms, two restaurants, a house bar, lounge and games room, plus excellent service. All rooms are equipped with private bathrooms, telephones and tea/coffee making facilities. From $50 single. Major credit cards accepted.

Hyatt Kingsgate
Queenstown
Frankton Road
Private Bag
Queenstown
Telephone: Queenstown 940
Telex: NZ 5704

This hotel offers a magnificent panorama of mountains and lake combined with traditional Hyatt service. The attractions of Queenstown are mere minutes away. Eighty-three comfortable and well-appointed guest rooms have ensuite facilities, including individual temperature controls. The Hunt Room, overlooking the lake, specialises in distinctive New Zealand cuisine – local meats and game. From $75 single. Major credit cards.

The Goldfields Motel and Breakfast Inn
41 Frankton Road
Queenstown
Telephone: Queenstown 221
Hosts: Noel Edward and Pat Cleland

A friendly and comfortable bed-and-breakfast place, located on the main road into Queenstown, just a stroll from the village. Choose from warm guest rooms with delicious dining-room breakfasts, balconied chalets with light breakfasts and own facilities (overlooking lake and mountains), or kitchen flats (fully equipped). All have heated beds. Guest laundry facility. Courtesy car, airport bus stop at gate. From $18 single (guest rooms), $36 double (flats), $42 double (chalet).

The Mountaineer Establishment
Rees Street
Queenstown
PO Box 236
Telephone: Queenstown 307
Telex: NZ 5286

The Mountaineer Establishment, operating since 1863, is situated in the centre of Queenstown. This licensed hotel offers 62 well-appointed rooms at reasonable tariffs, with a warm and friendly atmosphere incorporating the charm of old England. The hotel is a hub for locals and travellers alike, featuring two bars where regular and varied entertainment is provided, including a Cobb & Co. Restaurant, that serves tasty and inexpensive meals.

Turner Heights Townhouses
Turner Street
Queenstown
PO Box 435
Telephone: Queenstown 319-S
Owner: David Bradford

Commanding sensational views of Lake Wakatipu and surrounding mountains, these architecturally designed townhouses are set in gardens close to the towncentre. Each is three-storied, luxurious and quiet, with two double bedrooms accommodating up to six people in spacious comfort. Beautifully appointed with large living and dining areas. From $55 (double). Book through G.T.B. or write direct. 20% deposit confirms booking.

Queenstown Motor Park
Man Street
Queenstown
PO Box 49
Telephone: Queenstown 164

Facility is beautifully sited with lake-mountain views. Offers 300 power sites, 100 tent sites (set among trees), 11 tourist flats and self-contained cabins (occupants supply linen and blankets), tourist lodge (18 rooms – private facilities/communal cooking), 26 units (own equipment necessary). Bedding for hire, coin-operated automatic laundry, television room, store.

Beefeater Steakhouse
Shotover Arcade
PO Box 490
Queenstown
Telephone: Queenstown 1047
Hosts: Noel and Ailsa Cleghorn

'Queenstown's steak specialist' provides every type of steak from the minute' variety through to huge cuts of delicious Texas rump steak, as well as complimentary serve-yourself salad bar. Range of main courses includes lamb, pork and seafoods, plus juices, garlic bread, desserts and great coffee! Surroundings are natural wood, with cubicle seating. Open every day, lunch 11.30 a.m. to 2.00 p.m. and dinner 5.00 p.m. till 9.30 p.m. Reservations unnecessary. BYO and inexpensive.

Da Vina's Pizzeria Restaurant
Plaza Arcade
Beach Street
Queenstownn
Telephone: Queenstown 1385
Host: Lindsay Foley

Dine any evening from 6.00 p.m. onwards, in this cheerful and friendly restaurant atmosphere, with its intimate booth dining and cosy log fires. Although specialising in superb pizzas, the restaurant also serves a variety of delicious Italian dishes at very reasonable prices. BYO. Reservations are not necessary. Find the restaurant upstairs in the Plaza Arcade.

Packers Arms Restaurant
(Skippers Road, 10 minutes from town)
RD 1 Queenstown
Telephone: Queenstown 929
Hosts: Nick and Sally Costas

Make dining out one of the highlights of your Queenstown visit at this restaurant, which has received awards for excellence and consistency, serving an international and New Zealand speciality à la carte menu. Each meal is individually prepared and enhanced by the use of fresh seasonal fruits and vegetables. Enjoy historical setting, open fire and nightly live entertainment. Open Monday to Saturday, from 7.00 p.m. Garden barbecue lunches available for groups, by arrangement.

Westy's Restaurant
The Mall
PO Box 447
Queenstown
Telephone: Queenstown 609
Hosts: Ainsley Evans and Kevin Templeton

This homely and bustling little restaurant is situated at the rear of the Trading Post. The food is wholesome, varied and delicious. Fresh bread is baked on the premises daily and a range of vegetarian dishes are especially prepared. Join Ainsley and Kevin for lunch (Monday through Friday) or dinner (Monday through Saturday). The decor is fun, the background music lively and the prices inexpensive.

Treetops Seafood Restaurant
Sunshine Bay
PO Box 243
Queenstown
Telephone: Queenstown 1238
Host: Leon Udy

Queenstown's premier up-market restaurant. A 'dining event' at Treetops is judged by many to be a highlight of their New Zealand experience. To make it so for you, reserve in advance, be nice to your taste buds and do consider forgoing lunch!

This restaurant offers elegant and leisurely evening dining* and a gourmet experience. Treetops has a reputation for serving New Zealand's finest seafood cuisine. Leon Udy, and chef, Gail Thomson, acquired their knowledge and experience through contact with ethnic foodstuffs and kitchens on every continent, throughout the decade of the '70s. Added to this the quality of local seafoods from the cold waters off New Zealand's southern coastline, 2 hours' drive from Queenstown.

Menu is à la carte and non-seafood alternatives are included. There is full cocktail service and the wine list is both extensive and select. During daylight hours there are lake and mountain views to absorb. After dark, the ambiance is superb – candlelight highlights the crystal and lace, and classical music sets the tone.

*(When the requirement is for more abbreviated dining, this may be requested when reserving your table.)

Hours: Vary by season but normally are from 6.00 p.m. or 6.30 p.m., until late (closed Tuesdays).

ARROWTOWN

Arrowtown is a trip into the past, a town that once bustled with life when thousands of miners from all over the world converged on the area to seek their fortunes in gold. Gold fever diminished, the town's heyday was over, but the town didn't die. It remained to become one of the prettiest villages in the country, with old wood and stone cottages lining the street, nestling beneath great sycamore trees, a brilliant display of yellow in autumn. The pub and the shops that served the miners are still open for business.

Cobb cottage, Central Otago. ***(Ray Dustow)***

There's a splendid museum outlining the gold-mining history of the area and an old stone jail with heavy iron doors. If you wish, take a gold pan and try your luck in the nearby Arrow River. Flash floods on this river caused many miners' deaths, evidence of which survives in the tombstones in the local cemetery. Chinese tombstones show the cultural diversity of the area.

From Arrowtown, follow the trails of miners across country on four-wheel-drive, horseback or walking tours, to Mace Town, a mining town that didn't survive – old mining equipment, stone walls, garden trees and hedges mark the site.

Gold mining.

In 1862, when two prospectors panned up a large amount of gold from the Shotover River at Arthurs Point (near Queenstown), swarms of fortune hunters surged and flooded into the towering mountains and unexplored creeks. The solitude of a few run holders was lost as numbers mushroomed when the stories of fabulous rich finds spread – daily finds reckoned in pounds weight rather than mere ounces.

Makeshift canvas towns of miners' tents, stores and grog shops sprang up overnight, establishing Queenstown and Arrowtown and many small encampments on the lower reaches of the swift-flowing Shotover River.

The way to the source of the Shotover was impossible because of the sheer precipitous rocks that hemmed it into a long gorge. Undaunted by this, the miners invaded the mountain ranges that confined the river. The way was rough and often in deep snow.

To reach the upper part of the 'richest river in the world', the most spectacular and dangerous Skippers Road winds around precipitous bends, following the bridle track that the miners carved through this wild empty landscape. This is tussock country with huge rock outcrops. Chimneys and stone walls remind tourists of the numerous hotels that lined the road.

After the descent from Long Gully, the Shotover lies deep between its canyon walls. Marvel at the engineering ingenuity at Pinchers Bluff, where Chinese workers armed with hammer and chisel were lowered down a cliff face to forge this part of the road. There are parts of the road where, even today, cars have to reverse back and have two attempts, so sharp are the bends.

The gentle sloping terrace of Maori Point once held a busy mining population of over 2,000 people, complete with bakery, several shops, bank, courthouse to curb lawlessness, library and police camp and even a race track.

Though gold mining still goes on in the river below using sophisticated techniques, the town has totally disappeared. Nearby Skippers, once the largest town on the river, is now a ghost town with a cemetery full of those who lost the battle for gold through hardship, disease, severe winters and flash floods.

Life on the Shotover was excessively hard for miners, and by the 1870s large companies' dredges replaced the prospectors, but without the same dramatic success.

SEE ALSO:

Lodges: Crown Lodge.

Jade Shop
Main Steet
PO Box 106
Arrowtown
Telephone: Arrowtown 654
Owners: Cyril and Natalie Win

Situated in one of Arrowtown's original buildings, this company mines its own jade, and manufactures and retails jewellery and figurines. Watch craftsmen at work, shaping traditional and contemporary designs. Nephrite jade has long been prized by ancient Chinese and Aztec carvers and Maoris discovered this jade (greenstone) early in New Zealand's history. Competitively priced jade, jewellery, paua shell and Australian opals; plus unique hand-made jewellery, natural gold nuggets mounted in 14-carat gold as earrings, pendants and charms.

Lake County Press and Exclusive Crafts
PO Box 152
Arrowtown
Owners: Rosemary and Colin Jack

This establishment stocks a top-quality range of apparel from New Zealand's finest pelts, including 'Mistral' (washable) suede, leather and lambsuede, wool and furs. In addition, find après-ski boots, exclusive hand-knitted garments, natural and beautiful tweed fabrics, Bowron's graded sheepskins and accessories, plus a large range of Oroton handbags and jewellery. Great buying for yourself or friends. Open daily. Major credit cards and currencies accepted. Daily mailing overseas for customers.

The Stone Cottage
PO Box 10
Arrowtown
Telephone: Arrowtown 860

'The Devonshire Cream Tea Specialists'. The Stone Cottage, built in 1876, provides delicious cakes, pastries, light meals and refreshments – all served in the nostalgic and gracious atmosphere of yesteryear. Well worth a visit, just to view the wonderful display of early blue and white china. Situated on the famous avenue of trees (opposite the museum), the Stone Cottage is open daily, from 9.30 a.m. until 4.30 p.m.

Jet boating on the Shotover River, near Queenstown. *(National Publicity Studios)*

Te Anau

The *Milford Haven* passing the Stirling Falls, Milford Sound, Southland. *(National Publicity Studios)*

The lakeside township of Te Anau declares itself 'the gateway to Fiordland' and, as such, is the obvious base for more than a passing glimpse of the great Fiordland wilderness.

Make your first stop at the Fiordland National Park Headquarters at the southern end of the lake-front road for information on the park, its tracks and trails and outdoor activities. The park's rangers also organise summer field trips and special evening programmes. There are displays of the park's unusual plant and birdlife and explanations of the geological history.

Get your first hint of Fiordland's beauty with a cruise on the lake. Surrounded by bush and mountains, Lake Te Anau offers isolated coves, bays and islands; to the west, the lake branches into three land-locked fiords of its own. Take a launch trip to the Te Ana-au Caves, discovered only in 1948. At the limestone caves, visitors transfer to a punt that glides along on an underground river, where the cavern ceilings are covered with glow worms.

Other launch trips offer scheduled excursions to bays and islands for picnics, swimming and bushwalks. There are jet-boat rides, fishing charters and a water-taxi service for sightseeing, tramping, hunting and fishing. Arrange for a boat to drop you at a remote bay and return at a pre-arranged time; or hire a sail boat, outboard-motor boat, row boat, canoe or pedal boat. For travel on fast water, arrange for rafting or jet boating on the Waiau River.

Take walks – Te Anau is the base for the grand walks, the Milford and Hollyford Tracks, but less energetic, short walks are within easy distance of the township. Nature and lake-shore walks lead away from the centre; or combine lake travel and short bush walks with lake cruises to Glade House and Brod Bay.

In town, hire bicycles for pleasant around-town travel. Visit the wildlife museum – a display of stuffed animals and native birds. At an underground trout observatory, get a side view of rainbow, brown and brook trout – trout food is available for visitors to feed the fish.

Drive further afield to Milford Sound (2½ – 3 hours), by way of the Eglinton and Hollyford Valleys and Homer Tunnel, through red-beech forest with mountains looming closer on every side. En route, visit the Mirror Lakes, so calm and reflective that you may never know which is the right way up in subsequent photographs. Stop off at other lakes along the way – Lake Gunn, Lake Fergus and Lake Lochie. At Gunn's Camp on the Hollyford Road, find an intriguing little museum of mementoes and relics from the days when hardy pioneers tried, and often failed, to carve out an existence in this wild land.

On a day visit to Milford from Te Anau, take a cruise on Milford Sound right by Mitre Peak, rising 1,695 metres (5,560 feet) straight from the sea, past waterfalls that plummet from sheer mountainsides and past colonies of fur seals basking on the rocks.

Southwest from Te Anau is Lake Manapouri, often regarded as New Zealand's most beautiful lake – high praise in this land of beautiful lakes. It is also the country's deepest lake at about 450 metres (1,500 feet). The dark, still surface of Manapouri reflects the dense forest that grows down to the water's edge, tiny sandy bays appear as a flash of white, 36 forested islands dot the lake and three immense coves take the water deep into the mountains. Take a launch tour from Pearl Harbour. The

Te Anau,
Telephone: (0229) 646,
Information Officer:
C. Tauri

most spectacular tour takes you to West Arm to visit a hydro-electric power house, 184 metres (600 feet) deep down in a granite mountain. From there a bus takes visitors to the sea at Doubtful Sound.

The sounds of Fiordland are one of the most remarkable areas of New Zealand. It was here in Dusky Sound in 1769-70 that Captain James Cook of the *Endeavour* stopped for provisions and exploration. In this untouched wilderness you can still see where he cut spars for the ships. The earliest drawings of the Maori were made in this area, which lead in later years to the myth of the Lost Tribe of Fiordland.

Tragedy is also recorded. In the 1760s a ship also called *Endeavour* sank in the sound after being driven off-course on a Sydney-London voyage. One hundred and ninety survivors, including five women, built the first house in New Zealand while some men built a boat and sailed thousands of miles to Sydney for help. In a land that time forgot, their survival was no mean feat. Today the launch cruises capture magic without misery.

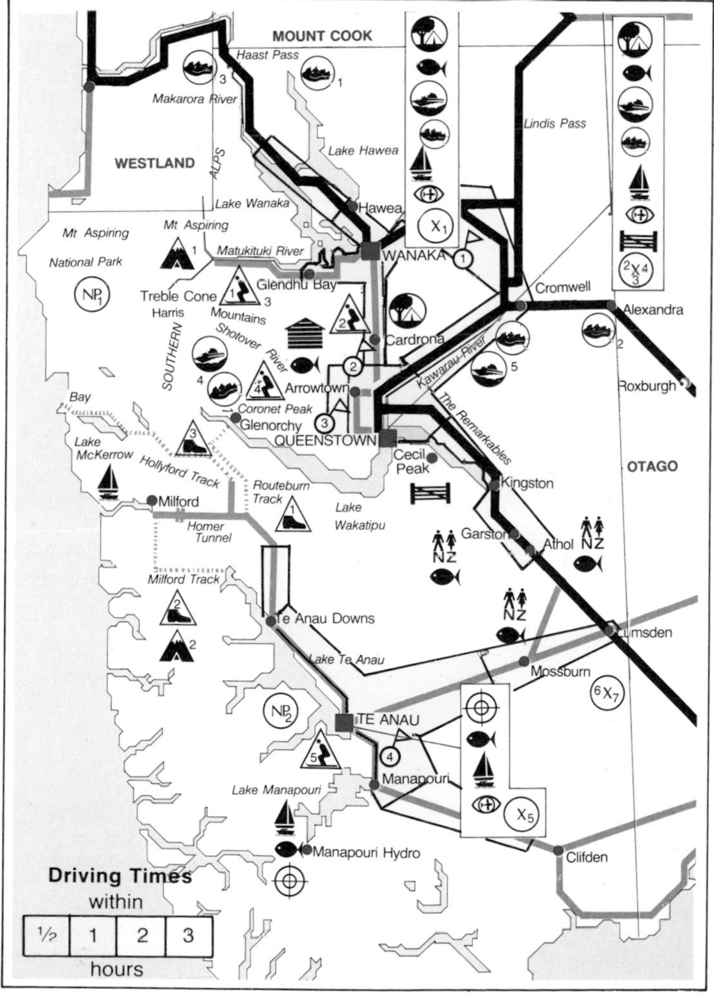

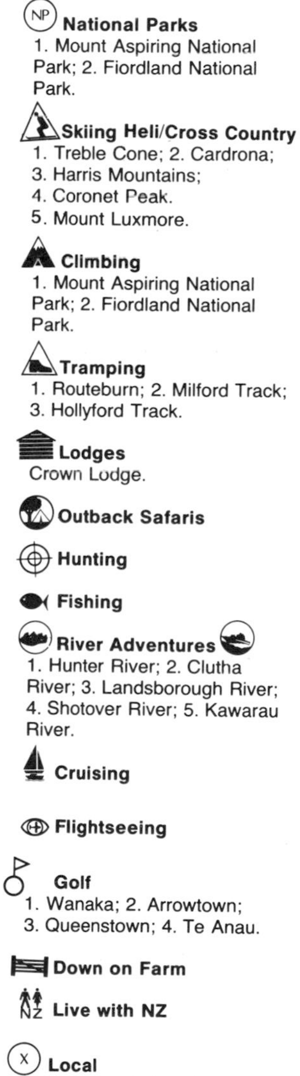

Te Anau

Abel Tasman Lakeside Lodge
32 Te Anau Terrace
Te Anau
Telephone: (0229) 7548
Hosts: Richard and Noelene Evans

Offers a high standard of accommodation in a quiet garden setting on the lakefront. Each suite provides spacious comfort with separate bedroom and lounge (sleeping extra persons). Facilities include electric blankets, colour television, kitchen, general laundry and putting green. A personal service assists you in arranging scenic or fishing requirements. From $45. Major credit cards accepted. Book direct or through Best Western chain (busy months November to April).

Amber Court Motel
68 Quintin Drive
Te Anau
Telephone: (0229) 7230
Host: Ann and Ray Falkiner

You are assured of a warm welcome at this small and peaceful motel, surrounded by lovely trees with five units (one- or two-bedroomed, accommodating up to eight persons). Units are well-equipped with separate kitchen facilities, full carpeting, heating, electric blankets, colour television plus continental breakfasts on request. Ann will be pleased to assist with your sightseeing arrangements. From $40 double. Off-season and children's rates available. Major credit cards accepted.

Black Diamond Motel
Quintin Drive
Te Anau
PO Box 65
Telephone: (0229) 7459
Telex: NZ5263
Owners: Allen and Margaret Merrilees

Centrally located and just 200 metres from Lake Te Anau. Twelve self contained units (one or two bedrooms) accommodating from two to seven people. Units have central heating, electric blankets and colour television. Additional facilities include putting green, car wash, childrens play area, continental breakfasts and babysitting service by request. From $44. Off-season rates available. Major Credit cards accepted. Book through Best Western, travel agent or direct.

Fiordland Motor Lodge
Main Road
Te Anau
PO Box 167
Telephone: (0229) 7511
Telex: NZ 4350 LODGES

One hundred and twenty-seven units, set among gardens, all with beautiful views of Lake Te Anau and surrounding mountains, central heating and tea/coffee making facilities (some with cooking facilities). Licensed restaurant and house bar, indoor swimming pool, sauna and spa pools provided for your enjoyment in addition to an 18-hole miniature golf course and giant draught board! Conference facilities available. From $50 double. Winter discounts. Credit cards accepted.

Luxmore Motor Lodge
PO Box 167
Te Anau
Telephone: (0229) 7526
Telex: NZ 4350 LODGES

Here, in the heart of Te Anau, the traveller is offered a home away from home. Sixty-eight rooms offer television/video and tea/coffee facilities. Additional features include Bailey's Family Restaurant, spa pool, Vista Room Restaurant and intimate Ranch House bar with open fire. Conference room seats 50. Courtesy car to off-site facilities (sauna and heated indoor pool). From $50 double. Winter discounts. Credit cards accepted.

Te Anau Motor Park
Te Anau-Manapouri Highway
PO Box 81
Te Anau
Telephone: (0229) 7457
Hosts: Jill and Clint Tauri

One kilometre (half a mile) from Te Anau Village is this beautifully situated motor park, with panoramic views over the lake and surrounding mountains. Offers spacious camping sites, cabins, cottages, bunkhouses and budget hostels, all supplied with electricity. Facilities include store, laundry, tennis courts and sauna. Local activities may be arranged from office. From $3 (sites), $13 (budget), $20 (cabins), $25 (cottages). Off-season rates June-September. Deposit required with booking.

Closest hotel/motel to Milford Sound. Departure point for the famous Milford Track walk. Serviced motel and self-contained units. Television/video, spa pool, fully licensed restaurant, children's playground, petrol station. Set on the edge of Lake Te Anau, 30 kilometres (18½ miles) closer to Milford Sound in Fiordland National Park. Economy units from $32 (2 persons), standard units from $42 (2 persons). All major credit cards accepted.

Te Anau Downs Motor Lodge
Te Anau – Milford Sound Highway
PO Box 19
Te Anau
Telephone: (0229) 7753
Telex: NZ 5263 ATTN TA DOWNS

This 96-room resort hotel is situated on the shoreline of beautiful Lake Te Anau. Comfortable, well-appointed rooms offer a lake view, with bath and showers, in addition to telephones and colour television. A spa pool is available for your use. Features include the New Zealand cuisine of the Blue Stone Room restaurant, and private bar overlooking the water. From $68 single. Major credit cards accepted.

Vacation Inn
Te Anau Terrace
Te Anau
Telephone: (0229) 7421
Telex: NZ 4379

This lakeside hotel offers a choice of two restaurants.
The Grill Room has a great selection, including a salad bar at reasonable prices in an informal setting. (Hours: 6.00 p.m. – 8.30 p.m., reservations not required).
In the Blue Stone Room enjoy a selection of local specialities such as venison, whitebait and crayfish. Formal dining with good service. (Hours: 7.00 p.m. – 9.30 p.m. Reservations essential).
(Open 5.00 p.m. – 11.00 p.m. Happy Hour at 5.30 p.m.)

Vacation Inn
Te Anau Terrace
Te Anau
Telephone: (0229) 7421
Telex: NZ 4379

You will find these purveyors of perfection in fine foods situated on the lakefront in both Te Anau and Manapouri. Pop In offers a wide range of home cooking from traditional confectionery to traditional and hearty New Zealand breakfasts as well as light lunches and snacks. Open daily from 7.00 a.m. until 6.00 p.m. Spacious, modern and clean with great views and rest rooms next door.

Pop In Catering
Lakefront, Te Anau or Manapouri
PO Box 19
Te Anau
Telephone: (0229) 7807 or Manapouri 670

With spectacular views of mountains and Lakes Te Anau and Manapouri, this fully licensed restaurant is most unusually and beautifully designed and built of native timbers. Relax to a background of soft music in the sunken conversation pit around a huge fire, while the sunset provides a vista unsurpassed. Traditional New Zealand fare served, with set menu, with barbecues in summer. Hours: 12 noon to 2.00 p.m. and 7.00 p.m. to 8.30 p.m., daily. Transport available.

Rainbow Downs Gamepark and Restaurant
RD1
Te Anau
6 kilometres, 3½ miles, on the Te Anau – Manapouri Highway
Telephone: (0229) 7567
Host: John Barker

Planning to walk the Milford Track? This specialist shop stocks all your clothing requirements. In addition to a wide range of fashion and outdoors hand-knit garments at reasonable prices, this is the place to find the world-famous Milford Trekker Walk socks and pure wool shirts. Don't get cold – here you'll find everything you require. Open normal trading hours, weekdays and weekends.

Fiordland House Wool Apparel
Cnr Milford Road and Te Anau Terrace
Te Anau

See this excellent 20-minute presentation of the 'finest walk in the world' and beautiful Milford Sound – before you go, after you've been, or in case you haven't the time to experience this wonderland! There is also a range of calendars, slides, photographs and paintings available for purchase at the audio-visual theatre. Book by telephone. From $2.50, adults; $1, children. Group discounts by arrangement.

The Milford Track Audiovisual Film
C/- Glenn Minshall Photography
PO Box 205
Te Anau
Telephone: (0229) 7648

Much rolling farmland between Te Anau and Mossburn is owned by the luck of the draw. Here several large sheep stations or tracts of marginal land have been divided and developed by the Lands and Survey Department, fenced, stocked and balloted off to aspiring farmers as a going concern.

Mavora Station (50,000 hectares or 123,500 acres), once owned by one family, is now farmed by 44 farmers, who drew the right marbles out of a barrel.

On the road to Mossburn, about 15 kilometres (10 miles) from Te Anau, look out for the Wilderness Reserve and appreciate the difference between the original vegetation and the farmland. Established to protect an area of bog pine *(Dacrydium bidwilli)* growing on dry shingle (an anomaly considering its usual wet subalpine habitat), it is of considerable scientific importance.

Matuku Engine Museum and Bee Bazaar
York Street
PO Box 36
Mossburn
Telephone: Mossburn 109D
Owners: Russell and Janet Cloake

Engine Museum: A fascinating collection of old American, English and New Zealand agricultural engines/equipment, many still working. Engines range from ½ to 57 horsepower and include efficient petrol engines like the 1929 Anderson 2½ hp, designed and built in Christchurch; the Ideal petrol engine – an overhead camshaft engine designed in 1895 (the only known one remaining); a huge 1925 Aveling/Porter 5 hp coal-fired steam roller, one of the few remaining working models in the world. See the original Richardson Winnowing Machine used at Chewing's Glenelg Estate, old American petrol cases plus collections of old tobacco tins and New Zealand magazines. An amazing display.

The Bee Bazaar: Janet spins and weaves natural wool into rugs and other articles. Examples of her weaving are for sale. Try New Zealand honey – 15 different varieties – and see the working hive on display. Open seven days, 9.30 a.m. to 5.00 p.m., except May to August when open weekdays only.

12 Southern Lakes

On the Milford Track, Southland. *(National Publicity Studios)*

Scenery ranges from dramatic to picturesque through this region.

Inland, great dry valleys barely support even the hardy tussock grasses that cling tenuously to life, seeking meagre moisture in areas ravaged by climate, by moa-hunters long ago and by rabbits introduced last century. Here there are hot, dry summers and bitter winters, an inhospitable, harsh landscape with its own distinctive beauty.

There are also broad green rolling hills and long plains thick with sheep and dairy cows, a landscape of soft bucolic charm. In gentle river valleys the willow-edged streams and rivers wind their way through meadows, anglers seek monster brown trout in quiet pools and, in spring, the green gives way to the fresh pinks and white of spring blossom in apricot, apple, peach and cherry orchards.

Old stone fences edge fields. Old cottages or farm buildings made of stone or sod, some derelict, some restored, stand by the roadside. In the back-country hills run holders built great stone homesteads in times of prosperity.

Travel into the heart of Otago, to the old goldfields in the barren hills. Take the road known as the Pigroot from Palmerston near the coast and travel past old stone buildings – inns and stables that served miners, sheep-station homesteads and farm buildings.

Throughout this southern region stone and brick dominate the small towns and villages that grew up alongside rivers and railway. Many communities began as gold towns in the 1860s and then prospered after the gold rush as farming centres or used river waters for the development of paper mills, oat mills, wheat-flour mills, woollen mills.

Naseby, in the northwest of the region, is one of the prettiest former gold towns, filled with trees in an otherwise treeless, dun-coloured landscape. Holiday cottages surround the village, nearby there are relics of gold-mining days in the stark Kyeburn Diggings, and horsetrails lead over old miners' routes. In winter tiny Naseby becomes a centre for outdoor ice skating and the Scottish ice sport of curling.

The Scots influence in the region is readily apparent in place names such as Dunedin, Duntroon, Mosgiel, Bannockburn, Balclutha, Invercargill, Lochiel, Balfour. The cities of Dunedin and Invercargill began as essentially Scottish settlements, their early prosperity based on gold, wool, wheat and meat. Predictably perhaps, this is the only New Zealand region to have ever grown significant crops of oats; and in the Hokonui Hills behind Gore early highland settlers manufactured a heart-warming reminder of home – illicit whisky. This activity continued up until World War II, with the distillers making elaborate attempts to conceal their still from the customs men. (One of the illicit stills can be seen in Invercargill's Southland Museum.) Today whisky is made, legally, at a distillery in Mosgiel.

The Southland Museum in Invercargill is a gem. There are relics of sealing and whaling days around the coast, curiosities from early shipwrecks and a tuatarium containing two live tuataras, reptiles that are close relatives of dinosaurs that lived 200 million years ago. At the door of the museum is a section of fossilised forest 160 million years old.

Settler homestead, Otago Peninsula. *(National Publicity Studios)*

Otago – Southland

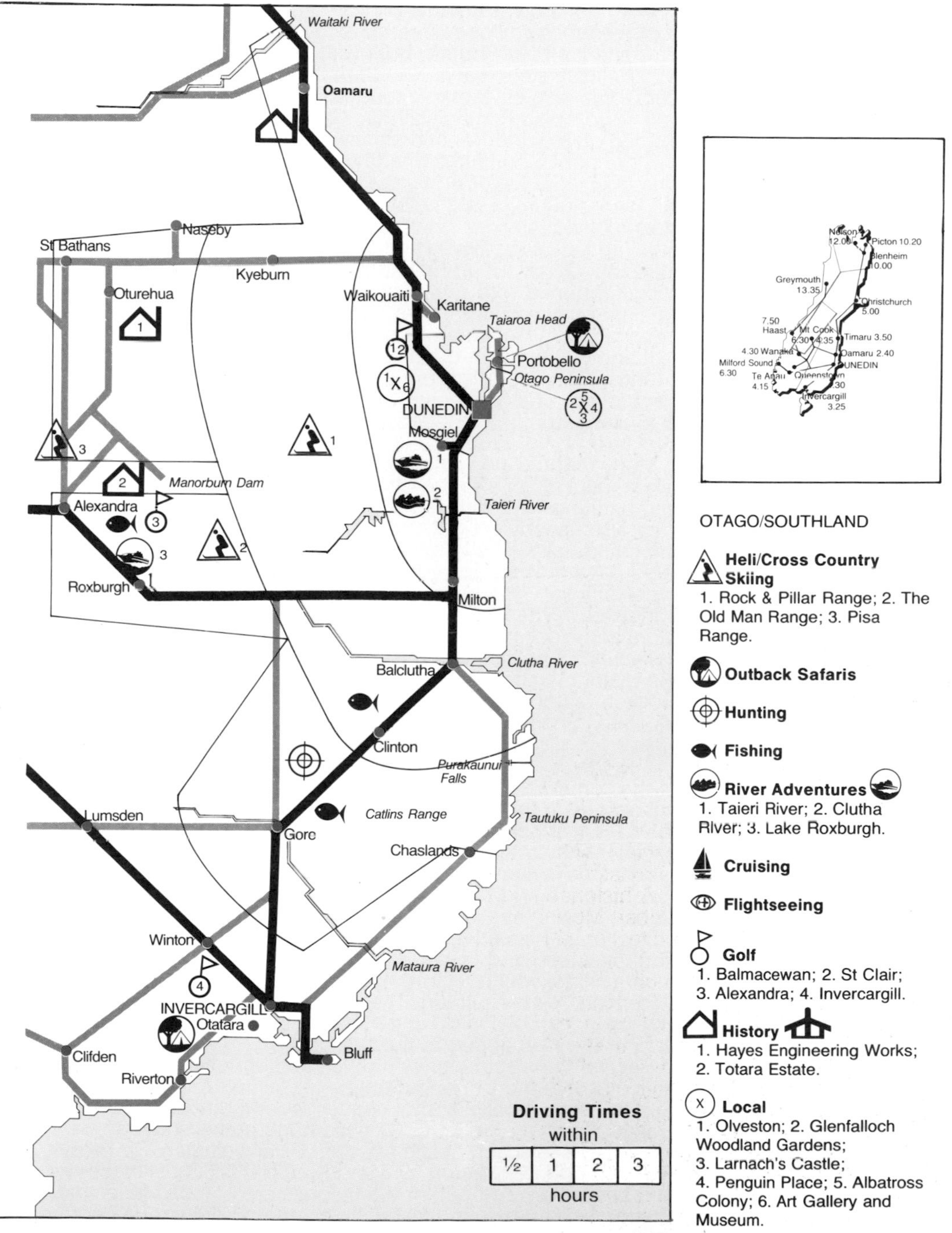

Dunedin

A city of turrets, spires, gables and gargoyles, Dunedin is rich in decorative Victorian and Edwardian stone buildings built by wealthy merchants when the city was the country's most prosperous. The times of prodigious growth and great wealth have gone, but the legacy is a city of splendid, elaborate architecture.

isit the railway station, even though you may have no intention of catching a train – the building is a marvellous construction in bluestone, emblazoned with heraldic lions. Inside there are ornate stone scrolls, stained-glass windows, gleaming brass fittings, elaborate plastered ceilings and intricately contrived mosaic floors. See the three main churches: the Presbyterian First Church, built with creamy Oamaru stone with delicate stone carving in the interior; St Paul's Anglican Cathedral, also of Oamaru stone with huge vaulted ceiling; and St Joseph's Roman Catholic Cathedral with beautiful stained-glass windows and stonework.

Other public buildings to admire include the Municipal Chambers, the Law Courts, the brick Victorian police station, old bank buildings, old hotels, the Otago Museum, the slate-roofed bluestone university buildings and the bluestone buildings of Otago Boys High School. There's a grand mansion, Olveston, an Edwardian house built in Jacobean style, crammed with European antiques and art collected by its wealthy businessman owner. Many of the materials were imported from Britain, even the joinery, and the banqueting hall and gallery were modelled on those at Chequers, the country estate of British prime ministers. More modest houses remain from the nineteenth century – terraced brick cottages displaying iron fretwork decorations uncommon in New Zealand.

Many of the early settlers were people with a background of liberal education; into their trunks they crammed their classics and paintings. As well as keeping in touch with European arts, they also eagerly sought to document, understand and collect the culture of the fledgling colony. Some were rich, some had vision; many were generous, and evidence of Dunedin's early prosperity survives in the art gallery and museum, richly endowed by these culturally aware patrons. Dr Thomas Moreland Hocken gave the Dunedin public an extensive collection of books, maps, paintings and manuscripts. One of the major resources for research into New Zealand history, the Hocken Library is housed in the arts block of the University. It has been greatly enlarged by further bequests including the Charles Brasch contemporary painting collection.

The Otago Museum profited from the turn-of-century wealth of the community, and today possesses one of the best collections in this part of the world of art and sculpture from the Classical periods in Greece and Rome. There are also excellent Maori artifacts from the Otago region, including greenstone ornaments and weapons.

A historian and Member of Parliament of great foresight, Robert McNab avidly collected books, and his extensive collection is housed in the Dunedin Public Library. There, also find the Alfred and Isabel Reed collection of early bibles and manuscripts, which feature handwritten works of the the great American, Walt Whitman. The vast and valuable Reed collection can be found on the third floor of the new library in the Octagon.

Several benefactors have swelled and enriched the collections of the Dunedin Public Art Gallery. Archdeacon Smythe gave a collection of eighteenth and nineteenth-century watercolours, a number of Gainsborough portraits and an impressive selection of Old Masters. Peter Smeaton, Sir Percy Sargood and Dr Norcroft also endowed the gallery with gifts and bequests. Look out for the magnificent Claude Monet and Claude Lorrain paintings recently given by Edmund de Beer.

Otago – Southland

Leave the city and head for the Otago Peninsula for an extraordinary variety of special sights. You can whizz round the peninsula on a 64-kilometre (40-mile) round trip, but it's possible to spend several days exploring all that it has to offer at a leisurely pace.

At the very tip of the peninsula is Taiaroa Head, a special reserve that includes a rare mainland nesting site of royal albatrosses, among the world's largest birds with a wing span over 3 metres (10 feet). Visits to the colony are under careful control and occasionally prohibited at critical times. From a look-out the birds may be seen taking off on the wind or returning to feed their chicks with regurgitated fish and squid. Nearby is a penguin nesting place, where yellow-eyed penguins rush ashore on the tide to waddle home through coastal grasses. On the rocks a few metres off shore seals may be seen basking.

A formal driveway and shaped trees lead to Larnach's Castle, the dream house of a Dunedin businessman and politician, created in 1871. There's very little that's 'New Zealand' about the house. It was designed in Scotland (with turrets and battlements), built by workmen brought especially from Europe for the task, using materials sought world wide, such as cedar, mahogany, ebony, oak, ceramic tiles from France, glass and marble from Italy, including massive Italian marble fireplaces.

At Glenfalloch is a garden idyll, with trees and shrubs from all over the world planted over a hundred years. Trim lawns and paths lead through the gardens and the original 1871 homestead, peacocks roam the lawns and doves flutter in the trees.

The peninsula is indented with bays, with many good picnic places. Above the bays the hills, criss-crossed with old dry stone walls, offer constantly changing views, and at Lovers' Leap and The Chasm, cliffs drop 200 metres (650 feet) and 130 metres (426 feet) sheer to the rocky shore.

Entertainment. – The pubs in Dunedin and throughout the region offer convivial fun. Visit local A & P Shows and horse racing, highland pipe bands and concerts and theatre in Dunedin.

Robert Burns statue and St Paul's Cathedral, Dunedin. ***(National Publicity Studios)***

Dunedin

The Otago Peninsula

Newton's Sightseeing Tours
Government Tourist Bureau
Princes Street
Dunedin
Telephone: (024) 52-199

This company introduces with comfort and convenience the many fascinating attractions of Dunedin.

Tour 1: Incorporates historical city sights, a visit through a unique old home – Olveston; the historic romance of Larnach's Castle and the peaceful and beautiful Glenfalloch Woodland Gardens. Departs daily at 1.30 p.m.

Tour 2: Essential for nature lovers, this leisurely adventure takes you the length of the Otago Peninsula, past magnificent seascapes and tiny townships to Taiaroa Heads to visit the unique royal albatross, seal and penguin sanctuaries, with a refreshment stop at Glenfalloch on the way home. Departs Monday, Wednesday and Saturday, December to April. Twin-tour discounts are available. Tours depart from the Government Tourist Bureau in Princes Street. Bookings may be made through any major hotel or the bureau.

Royal Albatross Colony
Taiaroa Heads
Otago Peninsula
Bookings: Government Tourist Bureau
Telephone: (024) 740-344 (after hours: (024) 775-020)

Internationally famous as the only place in the world where these giant birds (wing span of up to 3.3 metres (10 feet) breed on a mainland. The first egg was discovered in 1920, and by 1938 the first Taiaroa-hatched chick had flown. This most spectacular and legendary seabird mates for life and rears young only every second year. The colony is heavily protected; viewing is permitted from a specially constructed lookout, and may be closed to the public between May and October. Admission by ticket only, from $5 per person (towards upkeep). Transport: private car, Newton's Sightseeing Tour Bus or public bus to Portobello and a 9.6-kilometre(6-mile) walk.

Penguin Place
McGrouther's Farm
Otago Peninsula
Telephone: (024) 780-286/ 480-478
Host: Mr McGrouther

Penguin Place is at the farthest end of the Otago Peninsula, sign-posted from Taiaroa Heads. From the carpark, enjoy a short walk to this sanctuary to see marine life at Penguin Bay and Seal Island. Seals bask on a rocky islet close to the shore, and the yellow-eyed penguins emerge from the surf and climb to their nests. These penguins are unique to New Zealand, and are distinguished by their yellow head. The birds are shy and as is often the case with rare species, threatened with extinction. This haven has been created to save these birds. Best viewing time is 5.00 p.m., when they are returning to their nests from fishing. Nesting begins in September. Open all year round, camping facilities available upon request. Transport: Newtons Sightseeing Coach, private car, or bus to Portobello and a 9.6-kilometre (6-mile) walk.

Larnach's Castle
Highcliff Road
Otago Peninsula
Telephone: (024) 761-302
Owners: Mr and Mrs Barry Barker

Overlooking the Otago Peninsula, 14 hectares (35 acres) of grounds, stables and out-houses, stands this historic and romantic castle, where the declaration giving New Zealand women the right to vote, was signed in 1893 (a precedent in the western world). The neo-Gothic Victorian mansion was constructed by 200 workmen and internal furbishing completed much later by European masters. An enterprising banker and politician, Larnach was judged an extravagant 'playboy' by the struggling colonial town for marrying three times! Each wife jettisoned her predecessor's decor, creating domestic and financial havoc. Larnach shot himself at Parliament when his third wife ran away with his son. Twenty-seven of the 42 rooms have now been restored to former elegance. Admission from $2.50 adults, .50c children. Accommodation, conference and dining facilities available (reservations essential). Transport by private car or Newton's Sightseeing Tour Bus.

Glenfalloch Woodland Gardens
Portobello Road
Otago Peninsula
Telephone: (024) 761-006
Hosts: June and Kevin Mills

Owned by the Otago Peninsula Trust, Glenfalloch is the site of an original kauri homestead built in 1860, now rebuilt and refurbished. It is surrounded by an idyllic woodland garden of some 10 hectares (27 acres), ideal for a peaceful wander through native bush and English oaks, with showpiece flowers such as rhododendrons, azaleas and roses. The gardens are in full bloom September through October, but picturesque the year round. The quiet is only disturbed by the calls of roaming peacocks. Watch local potters and see various exhibitions, held regularly to assist with maintenance costs. Swiss-style chalet offers relaxed dining – morning and afternoon teas (try the scones) and lunches. Bookings taken for evening dining. Open daily 10.00 a.m. to 5.00 p.m. Admission charge from $1.50 for adults and .30c for children (refreshments included). Transport by Newton's sightseeing coach, private car, or catch the Portobello bus from town.

Olveston
42 Royal Terrace
Dunedin
Telephone: (024) 773-320

A unique, original home, built circa 1905. Standing among stately trees, this Jacobean-styled building of brick and stone mirrors the life and times of the Theomin family, for whom it was built. Olveston created a stir among the locals of Dunedin when it was built, and captivates visitors today. It has been retained exactly as it was in the 1920s – complete with modern conveniences like heated towel racks, interphone systems and central heating. Thirty-five rooms reflect a scale of entertaining belonging to elegant times. View art treasures from around the world, including a collection of paintings by New Zealand artists. Reservations essential for guided tours. Open daily (apart from some statutory holidays). Sunday tour times vary. From $4 (minors accompanied please). Tour Olveston with Newton's Sightseeing Tours.

Larnach's Castle, Otago Peninsula. *(National Publicity Studios)*

Wilderness Shop
101 Stuart Street
Dunedin
PO Box 5175
Telephone: (024) 773-679

Outdoor outfitters and adventure activity specialists, the Wilderness Shop has an extensive range of tramping, mountaineering, ski-touring, Nordic skiing and alpine skiing equipment, backed with sound advice from a staff with a reputation for being actively involved. This company stocks leading brands in high-technology equipment and clothing and can outfit you from head to toe for anything from valley walking to an Antarctic expedition. An equipment hire service is available for packs, parkas, ice-axes, crampons, pieps etc; plus alpine and Nordic hire and a full ski workshop. Wilderness Shop is also a booking agent for all types of outdoor experiences – tramping, mountaineering, skiing, Nordic skiing, ski mountaineering, heli-skiing, rafting, kayaking, jet boating, fishing – right through to ballooning! Discuss your requirements with these experts and take the hassle of organising out of your voyage of adventure.

Aggies Restaurant
Pacific Park Motor Inn
21-24 Wallace Street
Dunedin
PO Box 391
Telephone: (024) 773-374
Telex: NZ 5645

For locals and visitors alike, this restaurant means excellence. Set in native bush and gardens and offering panoramic views of Otago harbour, the atmosphere is more than matched by the cuisine. Seafood, game and classic French dishes are prepared to world-class standards. Classic vintage wines are available from an extensive cellar. Relax before dining in Polynesian-style Aggies Cocktail Bar. Open daily, breakfasts from 7.30 a.m., evening dining from 6.00 p.m. (reservations essential).

Pacific Park Motor Inn
21-24 Wallace Street
PO Box 391
Dunedin
Telephone: (024) 773-374
Telex: NZ 5645

Set in native bush and gardens overlooking Otago harbour, Pacific Park is just two minutes from Dunedin's city centre. Full five-star accommodation is complemented by tennis courts, mini-golf, barbeque area, laundry service, daily courtesy coach and 24-hour room service. Full conference facilities, the Polynesian-style Aggies Cocktail Bar and superb cuisine of Aggies Restaurant, offer a superb accommodation package. From $51 double.

Larnach's Castle
PO Box 1350
Dunedin
Telephone: (024) 761-302
Hosts: Mr and Mrs Barry Barker

Stay at the castle lodge overlooking the Otago Peninsula and harbour, and set in beautiful gardens and grounds beside the castle. Your choice of share or private, well-appointed facilities. Bunkroom accommodation is also available in a historic coach house. The castle tearooms provide lunches and teas, continental breakfasts and dinner are available. From $28 to $45 (bunkroom from $15). Book direct or through RHC reservations (03) 799-126/7.

Travel around Otago and Southland by rental car from Dunedin or Invercargill. Explore the back country with a self-drive rental four-wheel-drive from Dunedin or Invercargill. Flight-seeing from Dunedin, Invercargill, Mosgiel, Winton. Travel by train through Invercargill and Dunedin along the east coast. N.Z.R. Road Service buses run throughout the region.

Food. – Dunedin is a university city and has a good range of low-key, inexpensive restaurants and take-away food. Pub eating can also be good value. In up-market restaurants, look for fresh crayfish, Bluff oysters (in season March to August), blue cod, venison, lamb, salmon, pheasant. A local speciality mutton bird, probably won't appeal but adventurous palates might try it. Mutton birds are the young of the sooty shearwater, pulled from burrow nests on clifftops and stuffed with salty fish. The oily, fishy flesh is an acquired taste. Throughout the region old hotels are likely to serve traditional roasts of mutton or beef. Morning and afternoon teas remain substantial.

Accommodation. – Ranges from hunting and fishing lodges in the countryside down to camping grounds by coast or river; in Dunedin there are hotels, motor inns, motels, old hotels, private hotels, guesthouses; youth hostels at Oamaru, Palmerston, Waikouaiti Beach, Dunedin and Invercargill.

Otago – Southland

North to Waikouaiti and Oamaru

A jagged spectacular natural pa site, the peninsula walls rise sheer from the sea, providing resistance in the past against warring Maori tribes. Huriwawa peninsula has three foaming blowholes and offers fine coastline views.

Leave Dunedin on State Highway 1 to reach Waikouaiti, one of the South Island's oldest European settlements. A few kilometres from Waikouaiti are the old Matanaka farm buildings. Well kept and sturdy after 136 years, the granary, barn and stables are a memorial to their builder, Johnny Jones. In exchange for a boat, a cask of tobacco, and ten dozen red shirts, Johnny Jones took control of 40,000 hectares (100,000 acres) from the Maori From his vast agricultural estate, which fed the fledgling Otago colony and southern whaling stations, several other buildings survive. The

Fishing boats mooring in the estuary of thc charming seaside village of Karitane are sheltered by the Huriwawa peninsula.

South to Invercargill via the Catlins

The transition from virgin bush through to well-cultivated tidy farms in the space of a few kilometers is startling. Although the timber trade is long past its heyday, milling is still depleting forests.

A perfect crescent of curving golden sand leads to the Tautuku Peninsula, a magical place of lush grassy slopes and tiny secluded coves, which sheltered the earliest inhabitants during their moa and fish feasts, the whalers resting from voyages, and, more recently, holiday-makers and bach owners.

Just south, another glorious beach may be reached through a bush track; at the northern end of Waipati beach are the grand Cathedral Caves, eleven lofty caverns and echoing tunnels carved by the sea. Discover at low tide a second set of caves around the point.

The road weaves on to Invercargill through the Chaslands coast, famous for many shipwrecks and loss of life.

The coast road from Balclutha to Invercargill climbs over hills of lush grass, which encroach on the primeval Catlins Hills, dressed in beech forest, crimson rata, kahikatea and rimu.

Southland Progress League Inc.,
Oreti House,
120 Esk Street,
Invercargill,
P.O. Box 311.
Telephone: (021) 84538

Invercargill

This restaurant has a most interesting Edwardian/colonial decor, inside a building 105 years old. In a warm and friendly atmosphere of small, intimate dining areas, surrounded by tasteful museum pieces from the Southland of yesteryear, enjoy a varied menu including traditional local dishes and fresh seafood. Licensed as a B.Y.O., it is open for dining daily from 6.00 p.m. to 9.30 p.m. unless by arrangement.

Strathern Inn Restaurant
200 Elles Road
Invercargill
PO Box 7023
Telephone: (021) 89-100
Host: Barry Chilton

Set back from the main road into Invercargill, this quiet and well-appointed motel offers a heated spa pool, sauna, conversation lounge and pool table. Twenty-three heated units offer varying facilities from full cooking to bed-sitters, depending on your requirements. Close by are restaurants, general stores and a sports complex. Mrs Duncan prepares cooked or continental breakfasts upon request. From $32 single and $38 double.

Monarch Motel
633 Tay Street
Invercargill
Telephone: (021) 76-114
Hosts: Alan and Ezilda Duncan

This four-star-plus motel is situated in quiet surroundings close to town. As well as general facilities, it offers video, spa pool, waterbeds and honeymoon suites. Each well-appointed unit is provided with individual heating and a fully equipped kitchen. Continental breakfasts are prepared for you upon request. Units can accommodate up to five persons. From $36 (single), $42 (double).

Townsman Motel
195 Tay Street
Invercargill
Telephone: (021) 88-027
Hosts: Gwen and Ian Dore

'Heart of Gold'
Alexandra Business and Development Association and Borough Council
Citizens Advice Bureau
Centennial Avenue
Alexandra
Telephone: (0294) 7771

In Alexandra, a walk over the Shakey Bridge (sign-posted from Tarbert Street) can lead to the Graveyard Gully Memorial and up the hill for a closer inspection of the largest illuminated clock in the world. Note the thyme thriving amongst the rocks, another inheritance from gold-mining days. A stroll about the streets of Clyde will evoke something of the atmosphere of its hustling mining-town past. West of Clyde is the Clyde Dam, the country's largest concrete dam under construction. Take a jet-boat trip to explore the gold diggings and settlement below Alexandra, on the shores of Lake Roxburgh.

ICE SKATING

Summer tranquillity at the Manorburn far is shattered in the winter, June to August, when the lake behind the dam freezes (becoming the largest natural ice skating rink in the Southern Hemisphere). Ice skaters and curlers revel in the freedom of 28.3 hectares (70 acres) of singing ice. Skates can be hired.

FOR SPORTSPEOPLE

At Alexandra enjoy squash, bowls, stadium facilities, tennis courts and heated swimming complex. Golf courses at Alexandra (which has a resident professional) and at Clyde. Nearby irrigation dams offer good fishing.

GOLD

Drive to the gold dredge tailings at the end of McPherson Road, off Earnscleugh Road, just a few minutes from Alexandra or Clyde. Although the last gold dredge stopped in 1964, there were 27 dredges working within 8 kilometres (5 miles) of Alexandra in 1900. The often dramatic scars can still be seen, though softened by time and vegetation. For longer day trips to historic spots such as St Bathans and Oturehua, consult information on the Goldfields Park, available from the Lands and Survey Department. Museums in both towns display memorabilia of this colourful past.

FESTIVALS

Alexandra's Blossom Festival (held fourth weekend in September). Thousands throng to this festival (recognised nationally as the major spring festival in the Otago-Southland area), which is highlighted by the colourful and artistic procession of floats.

Easter Arts Festival displays work created by the many local professional and amateur craftspeople in the region, including potters, spinners, weavers and painters.

LOCAL PRODUCE

The area is famed for its golden apricots, peaches and nectarines, its luscious cherries and apples, from December till March/April, all available from roadside stalls. The hot, dry summers offer ideal conditions for the growing of flowers (and wild flowers) for drying. Some of the best fine wool in the world is produced on the surrounding hills. Deer farming is another growth industry.

ACCOMMODATION AND TRAVEL

Variety available from youth hostel camping and caravan parks to motels, hotels and guest houses. There are daily buses and air services to and from the 'Heart of Gold'. Rental car agencies operate here as well as a taxi service. On arrival, pick up a local brochure which contains all the necessary details.

Oliver's Courtyard and Restaurant
PO Box 38
(opposite Dunstan Hotel)
Clyde
Telephone: (029442) 860
Hosts: Fleur Sullivan and John Braine

This historic property has been redeveloped, and you are guaranteed a most wonderful range of experiences, from varied dining to a selection of delightful shops. The estate comprises a beautiful old stone home, buildings and gardens, enclosed in high stone walls and iron gates. It evolved from a general store for miners in 1863, re-opened by this enterprising twosome in 1977 as Oliver's Restaurant. The huge old stone barn (fully licensed) caters for lunches, barbecues or banquets, with patisserie attached (selling breads/quiches/confections). Wander through the courtyard among stables and coach houses, now offering a variety of local produce. Eat smoked eel from the original smokehouse, or take home delights such as local perfume, herbal tea, local sun-dried fruits, wild elderberry jam, smoked cheeses, thyme honey, and natural hand-made soaps. Products are beautifully packaged and all recipes have been taken from old books found in the cellar. 'Stable' shops include hair salon, antiques and exclusive leather clothing. The garden is filled with resident birds such as peacocks and Chinese Silky Hens. Select lunch, enjoy it here or hire a bicycle and ride to the river for a picnic! Oliver's Restaurant offers elegant evening dining in a superb atmosphere, with open fireplaces and a cuisine of international standard. The extensive wine cellar enhances dishes like Beef and Olive Broth (rich and chunky soup seasoned with cumin and saffron) and Braised Apple Steak (rib-eye steak grilled and braised with apple, raisins and brandy). Browse through the old store day books, dated from 1864! Steeped in colourful history, Clyde remains little changed from 100 years ago. Stay and absorb this wonderful past. Inexpensive accommodation available in two beautiful old stone hotels opposite (complete with real brass beds).

Lombardy poplars line an irrigation canal near Cromwell, Central Otago. *(National Publicity Studios).*

SEE ALSO:

Fishing: Fishing Paradise Safaris (Clinton).
Hunting: NZ Trophy Safaris (Fish) (Gore).
Outback Safaris: Otatara Riding Centre.
NZ Historic Places: Hayes Engineering Works (Oturehua), Totara Estate (Oamaru).
Outback Safaris: Hereweka Pony Treks (Portobello).
Water Adventures: Silverpeaks Tours (Flightseeing/Outback Safari/Down on Farm/Hunting/Fishing) (Mosgiel).

A fisherman on Cook's Arm with the granite peaks of Gog and Magog in the background. ***(Courtesy Stewart Island Pictorial Promotions)***

Imagine an island covering 1,680 square kilometres (648 square miles), twice the size of Singapore, with an indented coastline of 755 kilometres (470 miles), only 20 kilometres (12 miles) of road, 220 kilometres (124 miles) of walking tracks and a permanent population of less than 500.

For those who love wilderness, seclusion, unique dense forests and exciting birdlife, who enjoy the experience of living totally removed from the modern world, Stewart Island offers extraordinary opportunities.

Even in Oban, the island's only village, in Halfmoon Bay, the pace of life isn't exactly speedy – action centres on the island's one hotel, the southernmost hotel in the world, and on the Oban wharf, where ferry and fishing boats berth. Near the shore there's a tiny museum and a shop selling ferns propagated from the island's wild ferns. Small though the museum may be, it is well worth a visit, with seafaring relics from shipwrecks and the island's days as a sealing and whaling base. There's an emphasis on the rich plant, bird and marine life too, although stuffed birds mightn't be as cheering as the real thing.

To find out more about the island, visit the Forest Service headquarters. This is of interest to day visitors, and essential for anyone planning to take off into the remote parts of the island. The Forest Service administers much of the island, maintains tracks and huts (accommodation free) and will provide all the information needed.

Stewart Island becomes an adventure the moment you leave the mainland by boat (two or three times a week) from Bluff, or by air (several times daily) from Invercargill. You can make the journey for a day's outing, see Halfmoon Bay where houses hide in the enveloping bush, explore some of the island on a brief mini-bus tour – with only 20 kilometres (12 miles) of road there are obvious limitations – or perhaps take a launch trip to out-of-the-way bays.

Stay for a day or two, or more, in Oban and make the same excursions or venture on foot to points within easy reach – to hilltops with views over forests, coasts and rocky islands, along coastal paths that lead to sandy bays or rugged promontories. Take off for days on end into that wilderness of virgin rainforest, golden beaches, steep hills and cliffs that rise starkly from the sea – tramping, bird watching, fishing, boating, beachcombing, deer hunting, diving.

For such 'backwoods' expeditions, participants naturally need to be well equipped and experienced – it is not territory for the novice, nor anyone who objects to an encounter with mud.

Although so far south, the climate is surprisingly mild, never very hot or cold, with frost a rare winter occurrence. But it is damp – frequent light rain is a fact of Stewart Island life. The result, however, is forest thick with vines and ferns, with tiny native orchids hiding in the lush jungle-like growth under a canopy of totara, southern rata, miro, rimu. Another result of the rain is some very muddy moments.

At times the forest fills with birdsong – a rewarding sound for those interested in New Zealand's unique birdlife. The forest and scrub are home to tuis, bellbirds, wood pigeons, fantails, kakas, wekas, kiwis, parakeets, brown creepers, moreporks, welcome swallows and fernbirds. It is also the last-known natural home of the kakapo, the flightless night parrot, although visitors are unlikely to stumble upon this rare bird in the wild. On the shore birds include blue penguins,

yellow-eyed penguins, mollymawks, sooty shearwaters, gannets, skuas, shags, white-faced herons, oystercatchers, New Zealand dotterels and terns.

The young of the sooty shearwater are the 'muttonbirds', taken from the cliff-top burrows on the nearby Titi islands. The perilous occupation of muttonbirding is the traditional right of local Maori tribes.

Accommodation. – One hotel, camping ground with cabins, sometimes cottages available in Half Moon Bay. Forest service huts strategically placed through northern part of island – the rest is even more wild, no tracks, no huts.

Food. – Apart from mutton birds, fresh fish is available, especially blue cod and crayfish caught by the fishing fleet based at Oban. Country-style cooking can be sampled at the South Seas Hotel; Robinson Crusoe types live off land and sea, catching fish, gathering paua and mussels, hunting deer. Food supplies can be bought at Oban, but it makes better sense to stock up before crossing to the island.

Entertainment. – Where else but at the world's southernmost hotel. Find a kind of international set in the huts – trampers from many parts of the world seek out the special qualities of trekking on Stewart Island.

Less than 20 minutes by air from Invercargill, Stewart Island awaits your discovery – accessed by at least three return flights daily in twin-engined 'Islander' aircraft. Southern Air arranges package tours, incorporating accommodation, fishing trips and sightseeing. The Scenic Excursion includes a coach tour of the island, a photographers' delight. The Luncheon Excursion included coach tour and hotel Luncheon, with time to explore, take a launch trip, go fishing, walk through bird-filled native bush, or just browse in the unique museum. Don't miss meeting this historic and timeless island and its friendly people.

Southern Air Limited
(Invercargill Airport)
PO Box 860
Invercargill
Telephone: (021) 82-168/ 89-120
or Half Moon Bay 69
Manager: Max Paulin

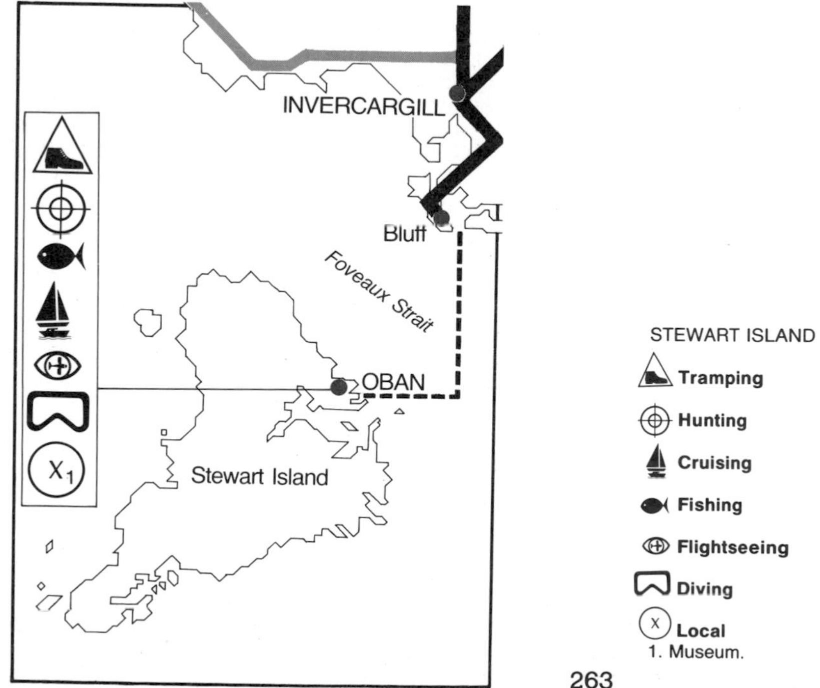

Travel Notes for Overseas Visitors

Passports

Passports are required by all visitors to New Zealand with two exceptions: children under the age of 16, who are included in the passport of the accompanying parent; and Australian citizens, who do, however, require a passport to re-enter their own country. Passports must be valid for at least six months beyond the intended departure date from New Zealand.

Visas

Visa requirements differ according to nationality, purpose and length of stay. Generally, citizens of the countries listed below do not require a visa or entry permit before embarking for vacation or business visits to this country.
Unrestricted entry for six months:
Australia, United Kingdom, Republic of Ireland, Canada, Belgium, Denmark, France, Luxembourg, The Netherlands, Norway, Sweden, Switzerland.

Unrestricted entry for three months: Federal Republic of Germany, Finland.

Unrestricted entry for thirty days: United States of America, Japan, Tahiti, New Caledonia.

Visa or prior entry authority are required for citizens of the above countries who wish to extend the maximum visit, work, obtain medical treatment or settle in the country. Applications for visas or entry permits are granted on various criteria, including proof of pre-booked and pre-paid onward travel, and the funds to maintain self-sufficiency while in New Zealand.

Entry Procedures

New Zealand maintains three levels of control at all points of entry: immigration, customs and agriculture. Forms are issued to all arriving air travellers prior to landing, and upon arrival passengers will be required to wait while agriculture officers spray the aircraft cabins to ensure that no insects are carried into New Zealand. These sprays are not harmful, but travellers may care to cover their noses with a cloth. Agricultural restrictions are very important to an economy so dependent upon agriculture and horticulture. New Zealand is free from most major plant and animal diseases – it really is one of the last unspoiled lands. To keep it this way, travellers are asked not to bring into the country without declaration: foodstuffs, plants, and plant and animal materials. Please co-operate — it only takes a little of your time to preserve our natural heritage. Goods brought into New Zealand by travellers will not be subject to customs duty or sales tax, provided they are for personal use (your own property) and are taken from the country on departure.

Vaccination Certificates are not required. However, should a traveller fall ill within three weeks of arrival, promptly consult with and advise a doctor of previous countries visited.

Health and Emergency Services

Health insurance is advisable. Most hotels and motels can advise on calling a doctor if required. In emergencies, an ambulance may be called by dialling 111 on the telephone. This number also applies to police and fire services. Chemists (drug stores) are open from 9.00 a.m. to 5.30 p.m. Most cities have 'Urgent Dispensaries', which are open between these hours and throughout weekends (consult the front section of local telephone directory under Hospitals). Should you fall ill, New Zealand is known internationally for its high standard of public and private health facilities. New Zealand specialists have led the world in heart surgery and many aspects of infant care.